LOUIS RIEL

William Barker VC

Major William George Barker describing an attack to American pilot Lieutenant Walter Carl Simon, DFC, with 139 Squadron in Italy, 1918.

WILLIAM BARKER VC

THE LIFE, DEATH & LEGEND OF CANADA'S
MOST DECORATED WAR HERO

 WAYNE RALPH

© 1997, 2007

John Wiley & Sons Canada, Ltd.

National Library of Canada Cataloguing in Publication Data
Ralph, Wayne, 1946-
    William Barker VC : the life, death and legend of Canada's most decorated
war hero / Wayne Ralph.

First ed. published 1997 under title: Barker, VC.
Includes bibliographical references and index.
ISBN 978-0-470-83967-6

    1. Barker, William, 1894-1930. 2. Great Britain. Royal Flying Corps—Biography.
3. Fighter pilots—Canada—Biography. 4. World War, 1914-1918—Aerial operations,
British. 5. World War, 1914-1918—Aerial operations, Canadian. 6. Canada. Royal
Canadian Air Force—Biography. I. Ralph, Wayne, 1946- Barker, VC. II. Title.

UG626.2.B384R34 2007   940.4'4941092   C2007-901301-5

Production Credits
Cover design: Mike Chan
Interior text design: Mike Chan
Maps: Andrea Andrew
Wiley Bicentennial Logo: Richard J. Pacifico
Front cover photo: A BE2 Corps Cooperation aircraft in flight during the First World War.
(Courtesy of Wing Commander Lee-Roy L. Brown, DFC, collection via The Canadian Museum of Flight, Langley, BC)
Back cover photo: William Barker in flight in a BE2 aircraft in November 1916.
(Courtesy of the David Mackenzie Collection)
Printer: Friesens

John Wiley & Sons Canada Ltd
6045 Freemont Blvd.
Mississauga, Ontario
L5R 4J3

Printed in Canada

1 2 3 4 5 FP 11 10 09 08 07

LOUIS RIEL

To my late wife, Patrice Shore, for her loving and patient support in all things.
She was a woman with a crystal spirit and a fighter pilot's heart.

Also to Stewart K. Taylor, historian and author,
for his invaluable knowledge, generosity and enthusiasm.

Curtiss JN4 in flight near training field in Ontario, 1917-18.

Contents

Time exposure of the interior of living quarters for 66 Squadron pilots in Italy, 1918.

ACKNOWLEDGEMENTS

This biography took six years to research and write and many generous people and organizations provided invaluable assistance and ongoing encouragement. A special thanks to four noted "aero historians": Stewart K. Taylor, Dutton, ON; the late Harry E. Creagan; the late Kenneth M. Molson; and the late Ronald V. Dodds. "Stew" Taylor became my mentor, was unfailingly generous and candid with his encyclopaedic knowledge, and made a huge contribution. A thankful salute to Carl Christie, formerly of Directorate of History (DHist), Department of National Defence (DND); and Timothy Dubé, Library and Archives Canada, Ottawa, and their many able colleagues.

My humble gratitude to four old warriors who served with Barker, and have now 'gone west': the late Lt Gerald A. Birks, MC and Bar, the late Air Vice-Marshal Kenneth M. Guthrie, CB, CBE, CD, the late Air Vice-Marshal Thomas A. Lawrence, CB, CD, US Legion of Merit, and the late Capt Thomas F. "Voss" Williams, MC. Their great respect and love for Barker, the man, as well as the hero, was my best incentive to tell his story.

The late Air Marshal C.R. "Larry" Dunlap, CBE, CD, US Silver Star, former Chief of Air Staff, RCAF, was unfailingly helpful and enthusiastic about this project. I am especially grateful to Larry, as well as the late J.D. "Jack" Hunter, and Sylvia Graham Rex for their eyewitness memories of Barker's final flight on March 12th, 1930.

I owe a huge debt to the Barker, Alguire, and Mackenzie families. William Barker's brother, the late Orval Barker, and Orval's wife, Marie, and his sister, the late Edna Barker Buchannon, of Dauphin, Manitoba, shared their memories, and warm hospitality, and trusted me with the reputation of their famous relative. The late William Alguire, who farmed west of Grandview, Manitoba and was named by his father, Howard Alguire, in memory of his famous relative, generously provided hospitality, documents, and photographs, as did Ellen Alguire Sainsbury, Barker's cousin, and her late husband Percy Sainsbury.

I am deeply indebted to Lt Colonel Barker's daughter, Jean A. Mackenzie, Vancouver, BC, for permission to release her father's RAF personnel files, to quote from his letters at Library and Archives Canada, and for interviews. My thanks also to her husband, Dr C.J.G. Mackenzie, MD, CM, DPH, FRCPC, and their youngest son, David W.G. Mackenzie, Victoria, BC, for interviews and many valuable insights, and also for reproductions from the photo album of William Barker, VC. I would like to acknowledge the gracious permission of Her Majesty Queen Elizabeth II to quote from the 1919 diary of King George the V.

The staff at the following institutions provided outstanding support to the author: Canada's Aviation Hall of Fame, Wetaskiwin, AB; Canadian War Museum, Ottawa; City of Winnipeg Archives; City of Toronto Archives; Commonwealth War Graves Commission, Maidenhead, UK; Ontario Tobacco Museum & Heritage Centre, Delhi, ON; Hagley Museum and Library, Delaware, MD, USA; Imperial War Museum, London, UK; Manuscript Division, The Library of Congress, Washington, DC, USA; Mount Pleasant Cemetery Crematorium and Mausoleum, Toronto; Personnel Records Centre, Ottawa; Provincial Archives of Manitoba, Winnipeg; Provincial Archives of Ontario, Toronto; Regimental Museum, Lord Strathcona's Horse (Royal Canadians), Calgary, AB; RAF Personnel Management Centre, MOD, Innsworth, UK; Riverside Cemetery, Dauphin, MB; The Royal Archives, Windsor Castle, Berkshire, UK; Toronto Harbour Commissioners, Toronto; War Pensions Directorate, Norcross, Blackpool, UK; Western Canada Aviation Museum, Winnipeg; and by no means least, the staff of public libraries in White Rock, South Surrey, Vancouver, Victoria, Edmonton, Dauphin, Russell, Winnipeg, and Ottawa.

All my friends provided encouragement to write this book, and that meant so much. Many others became friends in the writing process because they were connected to William Barker's family or life, or were experts in fields that I was not. My thanks to the following: Virginia B. Alexandor, Vancouver, BC, daughter of the late Lt Gerald Alfred Birks, and her husband Michael Alexandor; Joe Barker, Arcadia, MO, USA, Bill Barker, Palos Hills, IL, USA, the late Jim Barker (former RCAF and RCN fighter pilot), and Wayne Buchannon, Winnipeg, four nephews of William Barker; Sharon Golden, Winnipeg, and Shirley M. Wray, Arlington, TX, USA, cousins of Barker. In addition, Margaret Hilborn Sawyer, Burnaby, BC, niece of the late Capt William Carrall Hilborn; Diana Pasmore, Victoria, BC, wife of the late Lt Hubert Martyn Pasmore; the late Mary McKee Selby, sister of the late Lt George Sears McKee; Lorraine Branton and Carl McTaggart, daughter and friend of the late Mabel Buchannon Disney; Alec Mackenzie, eldest grandson of William Barker, and his wife Marlene Mackenzie.

My gratitude to the following people who added to my knowledge in various ways: Surgeon Commander John Blatherwick, CM, CD, MD, New Westminster, BC, author and expert on medals; Keith Hawkins, St. Catharines, ON, historian;

Stephen Heinemann, St. Catharines, ON, historian and antiquarian bookseller; Mary H. Hull, Saskatoon, SK; Vic Johnson, Ottawa, ON, editor, *Airforce*; Dr Barbara S. Kraft, PhD, Washington, DC, USA, researcher; the late Philip Markham, historian and author; the late Helen Marsh, editor, *Dauphin Herald*; Frank McGuire, Victoria, BC, historian and author; Curly Medina, Redding, CA, USA, owner of a Fairchild KR-21 biplane; W. Ross Richardson, Pointe Claire, PQ, historian and author; Ron Robinson, CBC Radio broadcaster, Winnipeg; Susanne Shaw, Port Alice, BC, graphologist; Bruce Tascona, Winnipeg, MB, historian and author.

Many people read various drafts of the manuscript, and their suggestions were always appreciated and sometimes even followed. The remaining faults are entirely my own, and I take full responsibility for my interpretation of William Barker's life, career, and character. Readers are welcome to contact the author to discuss the book at *wayneralph@telus.net*.

My wife, Patrice Shore, who died on March 8th, 2006 at age 52, was an integral part of this biography from the very beginning. She was unfailingly supportive and generous; she was a woman with a crystal spirit and a fighter pilot's heart.

T.O.M. Sopwith, aircraft designer wearing a bowler hat, looks on as Edward, the Prince of Wales, and Lt Colonel William Barker, VC, get ready to fly in his Sopwith Dove at Hounslow aerodrome, England, spring of 1919.

Library and Archives Canada

PREFACE TO THE 10TH ANNIVERSARY EDITION

They are all gone now—they "flew west" as the Great War flyers used to say. It was their habit in the Mess to raise a glass, just before dinner, in memory of dead pals. Some knew that they were on the dawn patrol the next morning, and perhaps a similar death awaited them. Their squadron mates would, in turn, raise a glass to them. A great and sad tradition was born in that first air war. The generation that followed them, their sons and daughters who fought the next inevitable war, are also dying away. Soon there will be no one to interview about that past, no one with even indirect memories of that time. It has become history—no longer a living memory —rather like, for example, the Battles of Agincourt, Waterloo, or Gettysburg.

Many aspects of Canadian society have changed since that spring day in 1991 when I viewed for the first time the crypt of William Barker, VC. Noticeably different is our national attitude towards the profession of soldiering and our Canadian Armed Forces. I was occasionally asked in those years why I wanted to write a book about an obscure flyer, someone they had never heard of. The answer, in part, was so that we might, as a country, think differently about war heroes. My wish has come true and more quickly than I ever expected. A generation has grown to maturity in the past ten years that has no recollection of the 1960s, of any anti-war movement, and for whom Vietnam is just a nation in Southeast Asia. If the phrase "the war" gets used, it often means The Gulf Conflict of the 1990s, or Bosnia, or current conflicts in Iraq or Afghanistan.

I believe that Canadians have adopted an American sensibility about our military. For example, as a nation we now adhere to the American custom of bringing home our dead soldiers, with pomp and ceremony. Each death is a national, public event,

symbolic, albeit in an ill-defined and undebated fashion, of the national will. The Boer War, Great War, and Second World War tradition of burial near the battlefield in far-flung lands is neither acceptable nor romantic.

Due to these significant changes in the national psyche, the story of William Barker, the nation's most decorated war hero in our entire history, has been well received. He is now better known because of the enthusiastic interest of a new generation. His resurrection from obscurity was helped by the efforts of many. In the years following the publication of this book, steps were taken by Inky Mark, the Member of Parliament for Dauphin-Swan River-Marquette, to have Barker formally recognized by the federal government. His Private Member's Bill in the House, and persistence with Heritage Canada, led to an historical marker being authorized. While that was underway, the municipal airport at Dauphin, Manitoba, was renamed as W.G. "Billy" Barker Airport. Most recently, in July 2006, a statue was unveiled in the city of Dauphin.

Two television documentaries, firstly on Discovery Channel in 1999, and then in 2003 on History Television, provided Canadians with the first video profiles of the nation's most decorated war hero. Some day, some way, I believe that Barker's dramatic arc of a life will be told as a feature-length movie—it is simply too compelling to ignore, especially as we will soon be marking the 100th anniversary of the 1914–1919 conflict.

Wayne Ralph
Lower Jenkins Cove, Durrell,
South Twillingate Island, Newfoundland;
and White Rock, British Columbia
Summer of 2006

Billy Bishop, VC, in suit, and William Barker, VC, in uniform, by Fokker D.VII in Toronto in the summer of 1919.

PREFACE TO THE 1997 FIRST EDITION

Captain Thomas F. Williams, MC, former World War One ace, persisted in talking more about Lieutenant Colonel William Barker than himself when I interviewed him back in 1981. Because of his high regard for Barker, I was left with a vivid impression of a Canadian hero about whom I knew little. Shortly after, I saw The National Film Board production, *The Kid Who Couldn't Miss*. This revisionist history that questioned Lieutenant Colonel Billy Bishop's war career was still being debated 10 years later, when I lived in Ottawa. In search of the story behind the story, I visited the Directorate of History (DHist), Department of National Defence.

One of the questions I asked was: "Who is Canada's most decorated war hero?" To my surprise there was no ready answer. However, if by most decorated one means the most medals for gallantry before the enemy (as in the US military tradition), Canada's most decorated war hero is William Barker. Indeed, he is the most decorated hero not just of the First World War, but all of our wars. His medals include the Victoria Cross; the Distinguished Service Order and Bar; the Military Cross and Two Bars; the French Croix-de-Guerre; two Italian Silver Medals for Valour; and also three Mentions-in-Despatches.

At the end of the First World War thousands had known that Lt Colonel Barker was Canada's most decorated soldier. *The Canadian Daily Record* of the Overseas Military Forces of Canada wrote that Barker, "... the third Canadian airman to win the V.C., comes from Dauphin, Manitoba, and holds the record among Canadians for fighting decorations won during the war." In fact, he was not only the country's most decorated soldier, but had tied for first place with another British officer as the British Empire's most decorated.

With this unique gallantry record, Barker should have remained a household name in Canada. That has not happened. I wanted to know how Barker had achieved fame, and why that fame had faded so quickly after his death, leaving behind scarcely a trace in the national memory? How had Canada's most decorated war hero become virtually the Unknown Soldier? From these apparently simple questions grew this biography.

Wayne Ralph
White Rock, British Columbia
April 1997

Curtiss JN4 trainer in Ontario in the First World War.

The Canadian Museum of Flight collection, Langley, BC

xiii

Future fighter ace Lieutenant Gerald Alfred Birks, MC and Bar, with a JN4 during his 1917 instructional duties in Canada.

THE WAR HERO IN THE CRYPT

The door to the crypt is bronze. A stained-glass memorial window of an angel in white and purple garments casts a dim glow inside the narrow chamber. The five coffins within are stacked from floor to ceiling against the right-hand wall, sealed behind white marble facades. Peering through the large viewing grate of the locked door, I could not quite read the names of the dead engraved into the marble.

Mount Pleasant Cemetery in Toronto is the final resting place of more than 170,000, including such luminaries as Mackenzie King, Timothy Eaton, Frederick Banting, and Glenn Gould. But I had come there on a cool spring day in 1991 to see the grave of only one man. I wanted to see the final resting place of Canada's most decorated war hero, Lt Colonel William Barker. I had expected to stand on a patch of grass under the open sky and read a faded headstone. However, my guide, Keith Hawkins, led me up the steps of an impressive grey granite building, past two large pillars, and inside the west entrance of the Mount Pleasant Mausoleum.

Immediately inside the entrance is a large chapel, but we turned towards the hallway on the right of the chapel, and walked to the centre hall in the south wing. It was pristine and well lighted, with a high ceiling, and a leaded-glass window at the far end. I read the engraved names to the left and right of me as I walked towards the window. We stopped at the last door on the left-hand wall.

The name I was looking for was "Barker," but the inscription on the door of Room B was "Smith." The promotional literature for Mount Pleasant Cemetery assured me that Barker lay beyond this door. The literature provides biographical notes on some of the Cemetery's famous deceased. Barker is listed just behind Ziltcho Demitro, World King of the Gypsies, but ahead of Glenn Gould, pianist and composer.

I had travelled a long way just to peer through the bars of the grate. One of the Mausoleum's service counsellors generously unlocked the door.

I had never been in a crypt. Cold though it was in the hallway outside, it was colder inside. Daylight glanced across the inscription:

LIEUT-COLONEL WILLIAM GEORGE
BARKER, VC, DSO, MC.
BELOVED HUSBAND OF JEAN KILBOURN SMITH.
NOVEMBER 3 1894 — MARCH 12 1930.
IN MEMORIAM.

Just below is an engraved pair of Royal Flying Corps pilot's wings, and a Latin motto - PER ARDUA AD ASTRA: "Through adversity to the stars," the motto of the RAF, and also the RCAF.

In March 1930, the newspapers had written that William Barker's state funeral was the largest in the history of Toronto. The cortege was two miles long, with 2,000 uniformed men from all the local garrisoned regiments. An estimated 50,000 spectators had lined up along St Clair Avenue West and Yonge Street to pay their respects. Thousands of boys, out of school on a Saturday afternoon, swarmed through Mount Pleasant Cemetery, breaking through the cordon, ignoring the shouts of policemen on horseback. The boys were running ahead of the black caisson, which was being towed, at 60-paces-to-the-minute, along the winding dirt path.

As Barker's flag-draped oak coffin was lifted from the gun carriage before the Mausoleum, six biplanes flew low overhead and the pilots sprinkled rose petals. An honour guard fired three volleys, and trumpeters played "The Last Post." Eight pallbearers, the coffin digging into their shoulders, cautiously moved up the steps into the building.

Nowadays, few recall Barker, and those who do can be forgiven for confusing him with a more familiar name, Billy Bishop. Many mistakenly link Barker to the death of a German flying ace nicknamed the "Red Baron." The marble crypt is seldom visited. Once in a very long while someone asks

1

Major Barker, VC, stands next to the remains of his Snipe E8102 in London in April 1919; it was on display with the Beaverbrook Canadian War Art Exhibition.

to see the grave of William Barker, and is directed to Room B in the south wing. Slightly nauseous, I backed out of the small enclosure, and the heavy bronze door was locked.

If Barker had been an American, he would almost certainly be interred at Arlington National Cemetery, perhaps near the Tomb of the Unknown Soldier, as is America's most decorated soldier, Audie Murphy. But there is no military cemetery on the scale of Arlington in Canada, and, until a few years ago, no Canadian Unknown Soldier had an honoured, public shrine in Canada. Our most decorated soldier's final resting place, without a public marker at Mount Pleasant Cemetery[1], has conferred upon him anonymity only a little less complete than the unknown man at the base of the National War Memorial in Ottawa.

Why was this hero in a crypt with the name "Smith" on the door? How did a Prairie farmer's son, worthy of a national state funeral, end up in a private tomb? The literature for Mount Pleasant Cemetery provided no answers. The others entombed with Barker—of the Smith, Kilbourn, and Greene families—are not mentioned in the cemetery brochures

or illustrated guide. Barker had received a state funeral full of pomp and circumstance, including the flourish of trumpets, the crack of rifle volleys, even rose petals falling from the sky. But his broken body was entombed in 1930 in a crypt with another man's name on the door.

When I walked away from Mount Pleasant Mausoleum I knew I wanted to learn more about Barker's life and death. I wanted to free him, at least metaphorically, from the crypt. This book is that attempt.

Photo taken by the author Wayne Ralph in 1991

Bronze door of the Smith family crypt, Mount Pleasant Cemetery Mausoleum, Toronto.

---

1 The Mackenzie family, including the three grandsons of Barker, Alec, Ian, David, decided in 2006 that their famous relative deserves an historic marker at the Smith family crypt to mark his resting place, and his place in Canadian society. So, some 77 years after his death, William Barker's remains will be acknowledged in a visible way at the Mausoleum.

Lieutenant Colonel William George Barker, The Victoria Cross, The Distinguished Service Order. (artist Raymond Lintott)

⇒ VICTORIA CROSS CITATION ⇒

Air Ministry, 30th November, 1918.

His Majesty the KING has been graciously pleased to confer the Victoria Cross on the undermentioned officer of the Royal Air Force, in recognition of bravery of the highest possible order:-

Captain (Acting Major) William George Barker, D.S.O., M.C., No. 201 Squadron, Royal Air Force

On the morning of the 27th October, 1918, this officer observed an enemy two-seater over the Forêt de Mormal. He attacked this machine and after a short burst it broke up in the air. At the same time a Fokker biplane attacked him and he was wounded in the right thigh, but managed despite this, to shoot down the enemy aeroplane in flames.

He then found himself in the middle of a large formation of Fokkers, who attacked him from all directions, and was again wounded in the left thigh, but succeeded in driving down two of the enemy in a spin.

He lost consciousness after this and his machine fell out of control. On recovery he found himself being again attacked heavily by a large formation, and singling out one machine he deliberately charged and drove it down in flames.

During this fight his left elbow was shattered and he again fainted, and on regaining consciousness he found himself still being attacked, but, notwithstanding that he was now severely wounded, in both legs and his left arm shattered, he dived on the nearest machine and shot it down in flames.

Being greatly exhausted, he dived out of the fight to regain our lines, but was met by another formation, which attacked and endeavoured to cut him off, but after a hard fight he succeeded in breaking up this formation and reached our lines, where he crashed on landing.

This combat, in which Major Barker destroyed four enemy machines (three of them in flames) brought his total successes up to fifty enemy planes destroyed, and is a notable example of the exceptional bravery and disregard of danger which this very gallant officer has always displayed throughout his distinguished career.

Major Barker was awarded the Military Cross on 10th January, 1917, first Bar on 18th July, 1917, Distinguished Service Order on 18th February, 1918, second Bar to Military Cross on 16th September, 1918, and Bar to Distinguished Service Order on 2nd November, 1918.

G.170, 581

William Barker in fur flying uniform by B6313, 1917.

CHAPTER ONE

A MAN OF PIONEER STOCK

"Willie never asked himself if it was possible to do something, he simply did it."
HOWARD ALGUIRE, WILLIAM BARKER'S UNCLE

Droglandt aerodrome was blanketed by fog. The canvas hangars and Nissen huts were grey and ghostlike in the soft drizzle. For the RFC pilots at the aerodrome, it was a "dud" morning for flying, a chance to sleep in, a chance to breathe easier. But not for Captain William Barker, commander of C Flight, 28 Squadron.

It was Friday, 26 October 1917. Barker had planned a low-level attack on a German airfield, 30 miles to the east, and had gone over his commanding officer's head to Wing Headquarters for permission to lead a formation of volunteers. Lt Colonel Vesey Holt had authorised the patrol, and bad weather was not going to stop Barker. He knew this sector of Flanders like the back of his hand. With such a low ceiling, he reasoned that the German Air Force would not be expecting hostile visitors. Not even the leader of Jagdgeschwader 1, Freiherr Manfred von Richthofen—the "Red Baron"—based at Marckebeke aerodrome.

Barker was one of the most experienced flyers in the RFC, twice-decorated for bravery, but not as a fighter pilot. He had been flying Camel scout machines only a month. It had taken him more than a week after the squadron's arrival in France to score his first official victory, too long in his own estimation. He was impatient to make his mark. What better way than to machine-gun the home of the Richthofen Flying Circus?

He had ordered four Camels of C Flight rolled out of their hangar, and prepared for flight. While the fitters squirted petrol into each of the nine cylinders of each rotary engine, priming them for start-up, Barker briefly reviewed the mission with his wingmen, 2nd Lieutenants Malik, Jones, and Fenton. They asked few questions. They felt a hollowness in the stomach, and the dampness penetrated despite the layers of silk, wool, and leather clothing. They could just pick out the far end of the field through the fog.

These young men of C Flight had not known Barker very long, but his confidence, the enthusiasm of his voice, the intensity of his delivery were compelling and seductive. Just the day before, right after he had outlined his mission, they had volunteered. They didn't have to. This was not an offensive patrol laid on by Major Hugh Glanville, the squadron commander. No one would have thought less of them for staying on the ground, and enjoying a leisurely breakfast.

Settling himself into the cane seat of B6313, Barker checked his rudder pedals and control column for proper and full movement, and confirmed that his Verey flare pistol, .32-calibre automatic, and cockpit fire extinguisher were secure. His engine fitter, standing by the cockpit, held his leather flying helmet and gloves, while Barker snugged down the lap belt. A second fitter at the front of the machine waited patiently to make the calls: "Switch off, petrol on, suck in ... contact."

Barker grabbed the plunger of the hand pump to pressurize the fuel tank up to 3 psi. After his fitter yelled "contact," Barker switched on the alternator and repeated "contact." The engine caught on the first hard downward pull on the propeller, and a mist of castor oil blew towards the cockpit, coating Barker's goggles, and carrying a burnt-almond stink that he loved because it smelled of action.

Easing back on the throttle, he turned on the engine-driven air pump, and adjusted the fuel/air mixture, smoothing out the engine idle. After a brief run-up to full power, the aircraft tail held down by the weight of air mechanics, Barker lifted his left hand straight over his head, a signal to the mechanics on each wingtip to pull away the wheel chocks. Droglandt aerodrome was cinder-covered, but on this day it was a sea of mud.

Barker glanced back to the men in the aircraft behind him to see they were ready. Holding the stick well back, he advanced the throttle, moving away from the hangars, and towards the west end of the narrow field. There was little wind. Malik, Jones, and Fenton lined up in loose echelon right formation, staggered behind Barker's right wing.

The takeoff was easy for Barker, a pilot with over 500 flying hours in combat, but sweaty for his wingmen, who had done few formation takeoffs, and none in such low visibility. Had the ceiling been higher they would have joined formation at 1,000 feet, an easier task. In cloud at less than 500 feet above the ground, Barker nudged the left rudder to pick up a compass heading of 110 degrees, set his throttle to maintain a climbing speed of 80 mph, centred his controls, and glued his eyes to the glass inclinometer—his only useful instrument to maintain his wings level while flying blind.

Jones, in number 3 position, and Fenton, in number 4 position, soon lost sight of their leader in the grey dense clouds. But Malik, who was number 2 and the closest to Barker, never once looked away from his leader's right wingtip, and the ghost-like outline of his Camel.

The only Sikh pilot in the RFC, Hardit Singh Malik flew with a specially crafted leather helmet over his turban. He was an honours history graduate at Oxford, who, nevertheless, had to fight hard to gain a commission in the RFC. Having fought his way in, he had something to prove—that he was as good as any other pilot, with or without a turban. Barker liked having Malik in C Flight, calling him the "Indian Prince."

The sun, after several minutes in cloud, was painfully bright. The upper wing of the Camel blocked Barker's vision above and to the east. Trying to get his visual bearings, still maintaining 110 degrees, he

climbed with Malik about a wing-span out on his right side. He looked behind, but could no longer see Jones and Fenton. Nevertheless, he still pressed on into the deadliest hunting ground on the Western Front. To the leader of an enemy formation at higher altitude, invisible to Barker against the mid-morning sun, the two olive-drab Camels were brilliantly silhouetted against white clouds. Just like Barker, the German flight leader figured nobody would fly on such a day.

The German signalled his wingmen and they followed him down in a steep dive. Barker and Malik were now facing the fight of their lives. Instinct and experience saved Barker. He snapped into a fierce right-hand turn, turning towards his attackers. But he forgot about his wingman, who could not follow such an abrupt steep turn. Malik fell well back and below B6313. No longer an effective team, the two men were heavily outnumbered, and easy prey for experienced German scout pilots.

Malik dived back to the west, engaged in a running battle in which he managed to drive one enemy aircraft down out of control. He was searching desperately for a familiar landmark through the broken cloud cover. But his Camel, B5406, was better at turning than running—and the four German pilots chasing him knew that. Their shooting was far more accurate than his own, and two of the many bullets that riddled his machine punctured the fuel tank under the seat, and ripped through Malik's leg.

In pain, blood pooling inside his flying boot, unable to outdistance his enemies, unable to manoeuvre because of damage to his fuel system, and burning up the few precious gallons left in the gravity-feed tank in the upper wing, the Sikh pilot figured he was a goner. He was certain Barker was done for; the last he had seen of him, he was in the middle of a multi-coloured circle of German machines.

Hedgehopping a few feet above the ground, Malik finally spotted a familiar shape, Zillebeke Lake in the Ypres Salient, and crash-landed near the shore. His pursuers had broken off the attack, perhaps out of ammunition, more likely reluctant to stay long on the Allied side of the lines. Malik passed out, but was pulled from his machine and carried by motor tender back to the aerodrome, where he made a report, and was then taken to hospital.

Barker was not dead, as Malik had reported, but was certainly humiliated and angry. Brilliant evasion had saved him from harm—none of the German pilots scored even a single hit. But his mission to attack Marckebeke was aborted. He had lost his wingmen; he had no idea where they were, or where *he* was. He had come within a hair of dying, after two long years in action. He must salvage something out of this morning. Alone, he continued searching the enemy skies, all the while climbing for altitude.

East of Roulers he sighted 15 enemy aircraft, and singled out and attacked an Albatros D.V with a red-painted nose. He fought a tight-turning, descending battle against its German pilot, who was no novice. For 15 minutes Barker struggled to gain a shooting advantage until, finally, at only 1,000 feet above the ground, and just 20 yards' distance, he fired a burst of 30 rounds, and the aircraft ignited in flames and crashed. His victim may have been a Jasta 18 veteran named Leutnant (2nd Lieut) Otto Schober.

Attacked by another Albatros D.V, Barker banked into a steep right-hand turn, diving down to skim the tree-tops between Thielt and Roulers. This heart-pounding fight at very low altitude lasted for 10 minutes, until Barker fired 40 rounds into the enemy machine at 100 feet above the ground. The pilot, Offizierstellvertreter [Under officer] Johannes Klein, also with Jasta 18, lost control of his machine. It burst into flames on impact, but Klein managed to get out of the cockpit of the Albatros and crawl away.

Barker's ambition and relentless will to fight had paid off. He had redeemed himself in his own eyes, achieving his second and third victories. But his wingmen were alone over enemy lines, and he was pretty sure that Malik was dead or a prisoner of war.

Fenton, after falling out of the formation, had descended below clouds, sighted a convoy on the Staden-Roulers road, and fired 100 rounds that set two Lorries on fire. But he was wounded during his attack by ground fire, and recovered to Droglandt at 11:35 a.m., where he made a short report, and was then transported to hospital. Jones flew around for over an hour, but had no engagements, returning to Droglandt at 11:50 a.m.

After the confusing dogfight with Klein, Barker had no idea where he was. Low on fuel, he descended through cloud and landed near Arras, more than 40 miles south of his aerodrome. By the time he scrounged fuel for his machine and took off for home, it was mid-afternoon. In the meantime, Malik had filed a report stating that Barker was, when last seen, fighting like hell against great odds, but undoubtedly a victim. As soon as Barker got out of B6313 back at Droglandt, he started to relate a similar story about Malik to the squadron's Recording Officer. He was quickly told, to his great relief, that Malik, Fenton, and Jones had all made it back.

It had been one costly mission for C Flight. This was the only mission flown by the squadron on that Friday. It had resulted in two victories, but two wounded pilots. The 22 (Army) Wing HQ authorised two "destroyed" credits for Barker, although there were no RFC witnesses to the actions, and disallowed Malik's "driven-down-out-of-control" claim. Malik later labelled the whole mission "a most foolhardy operation," but, like many others, was proud to say he had been one of Barker's pilots.

Barker agreed that the mission had been "a balls-up" and vowed that, in future, he would take better care of his wingmen—a promise he kept over the next 11 months in action. But that Friday marked Barker's true baptism as a fighter pilot, from that day forward he trained himself relentlessly not only to lead effectively on offensive patrols and close with the enemy, but also bring his wingmen home safely.

He quickly transformed into the fighter pilot's fighter pilot, and the kind of hero that other heroes admire. Lt Colonel Billy Bishop, Canada's most famous scout ace, contributed to Barker's legendary reputation by calling him the "deadliest air fighter that ever lived," capable, Bishop said, of killing Richthofen had the opportunity ever come his way. Barker's 50-plus opponents, many of whom were killed, might well have agreed with Bishop's assessment.

Twelve months after his abortive mission against Marckebeke, on 27 October 1918, Barker became the third Canadian flyer in World War One to receive the

Victoria Cross, the British Empire's highest award for military gallantry. The aerial battle that resulted in the VC was labelled by some historians as "the greatest one-sided air fight of the Great War," because Barker had fought alone against at least 10 or 15. The newspapers in London emphatically declared "60 enemy pilots" and, due to journalistic hyperbole, that number became the imperishable truth, officially endorsed, though Barker himself made no such claim.

By 1918, however, the Canadian ace was already a legend among those who flew or served with him. It came as no surprise at all to fellow scout pilots that he could survive a long-odds combat.

* * *

William George Barker was born 24 years earlier in the tiny log cabin on the Barker homestead. He was Jane Victoria Alguire's first baby, and her husband, George Barker, Junior, paced outside the cabin, looking anxiously out across a field of frozen stubble. The wheat had been harvested, and a raw wind, with a whiff of snow, was blowing out of the northwest.

George had first met Jane when her father's wagon was stuck in the spring gumbo. William Riley Alguire and his family had left Stormont County in eastern Ontario, to stake a claim in the Dauphin Valley. Alguire had six children in the wagon, and his wife, Melissa Adelaide, was expecting their seventh. Jane hated the ugly, mosquito-infested frontier that lay around her, and cried bitterly at the loss of her dear home at Finch, north of the lovely St. Lawrence River.

George, and his brother-in-law, Bob Ferguson, managed to break the Alguire wagon free of the gumbo, but all the way home George remembered the teary-eyed 15-year-old. He vowed that he would marry her immediately, before such a good-looking lady was spoken for by some other fellow. The Alguires were of so-called Pennsylvania Dutch lineage (i.e., German). Their United Empire Loyalist forerunners had come to Canada from the US, following the Revolutionary War.

The Alguires were scandalized by George's request, but he was undeterred by their opposition. On Jane's 18th birthday, 12 December 1892, the two were married in the newly built St. Paul's Anglican Church.

William George Barker, born 3 November 1894.

Provincial Archives of Manitoba

George would always say in later years that he had met his wife in a mud hole. Jane gave birth to nine more children between 1896 and 1919: Percival, Cecil, Ilda, Lloyd, Edna, Roy, Leslie, Orval, and Ross.

* * *

The Dauphin Valley in the early 1890s had trails rather than roads. There was no railroad, and travel was mainly by oxen or horse-drawn wagons and, in winter, dog teams. A veteran of the Riel Rebellion, Captain David McIntosh, had established the first general store and post office 10 miles west of Dauphin Lake in 1886. A stopping-off place for Plains Cree and Métis trappers, the store was surrounded by fur-laden sleds and dog teams during winter. From McIntosh's store had grown the Dauphin village, informally called "Dog Town." A competing village, Gartmore, grew up around the Hudson's Bay Company trading post four miles south.

The Dauphin Valley was sheltered by the Duck Mountains to the north and Riding Mountain to the south. It was not as hot and dry as the land along the

William Alguire collection

Barker family circa 1898: William Barker, mother, Jane Victoria Alguire, father, George William John Barker, infant in arms, Percy Barker.

North Dakota–Montana border, and it was said that the district had fewer blizzards in the winter. A reputation for a kinder climate and rich soil guaranteed Dauphin a year-after-year influx of newcomers from eastern Canada, Europe and the United States, as well as drought-stricken areas of Manitoba and Saskatchewan. The "Garden of Eden" reputation of Dauphin Valley was the attraction for the Barkers, who were Britishers that had immigrated to Ontario.

William Barker's great grandfather, also called William Barker, was born in England in 1807. He arrived in Canada in the 1830s, and married Frances Johnson in 1837. He was a cobbler by trade, first in Galt, and then Stratford. In Canada's confederation year of 1867, Barker owned a boot and shoemaking business on Huron Street in Stratford, and he and his wife had eight children, ranging in age from seven to 28. One son, Henry, followed his father's trade, and was still running a large general store on Huron Street more than 50 years later.

George William Barker, Senior, the third-born son, became a plough maker and blacksmith near his father's boot shop. He and his wife, Mary Jane Parrish, an east-end Londoner, had three daughters in Stratford district, and one son, George William John Barker, Junior, born in 1871. Finding Stratford claustrophobic, George Barker, Senior, went west with his family to homestead at Minnedosa, Manitoba, later moving north in 1888 to Dauphin, where he built one of the first blacksmith shops. He founded several small businesses, was well respected for his common sense, and became the bailiff of the village. After the incorporation of Dauphin in 1898, he was elected the village's first mayor.

Jane Barker grew to like Dauphin, but it took time. She regaled her children with stories of a sod hut, her first home on the frontier, with the snakes slithering through a hole in the roof. She was not much more than a child herself when she married George Barker, Junior. Because his wife looked so youthful, George was sometimes mistaken for her father.

George was of medium build, with strong, beefy hands. His stolid face was dominated by a bushy moustache, close-set, piercing blue eyes, and a prominent nose. He liked to play a game of cards at the kitchen table in the evenings, Euchre or King Pedro, which was frowned upon by the Alguires, being strict Methodists. George was a temperate man. At the age of 17, he and his pals had got drunk on a barrel of beer. The aftermath was painful, and he never drank again until his 70th birthday.

He was a gifted handler of any animal, especially horses, but also had an inventive streak for machinery and engines. Hardworking, but not very lucky, he always preferred the uncertainty of self-employment over the predictability of a steady pay cheque. In addition to farming and blacksmithing, he owned, at various times, a sawmill, a livery stable, and a bakery. He shifted his family from Dauphin to countless other Manitoba towns and villages during and after the Great War, always in search of a new deal and a better future.

His ambition to be rich led to high-risk speculation. George invested his crop profits in wheat futures on the Winnipeg Grain Exchange. Any farmer could

William Alguire collection

Percy Barker in uniform of a highland regiment in Canada.

the barn on the James Attwood farm near Russell, a visitor from Inglis, Harriet "Essie" Berrington, watched 13-year-old Will climb up the ladder, and walk barefoot along the ridge pole of the barn from one end to the other, 30 feet above the barn floor. Essie met Will only once, after he descended from the rooftop, grinning from ear to ear, but she was not surprised to read of his flying exploits in the war.

Will had come into the world less than 10 years after the Riel Rebellion, less than 20 years after the Battle of the Little Big Horn, and the history of the Great Plains was much more for him than simply a story in a school book. When Barker went out on horseback, the landscape looked much as it had for the explorers of an earlier time. But the frontier he knew so well was transformed to relative civilization between 1893 and 1914. By age 12 he had seen the arrival of trains, automobiles, electricity, and telephones, and by age 16 was gazing open-mouthed at aeroplanes looping the loop.

The train was the main catalyst for Dauphin's rapid growth, and a section of the tracks were laid down on land that Grandfather Barker owned. As the steel rails advanced from Gladstone in the summer and fall of 1896, the locals speculated on the precise route the tracks would take. William Mackenzie's and Donald Mann's Lake Manitoba Railway and Canal Company ran the tracks, not directly through "Dog Town" or Gartmore, but rather on a southeast-to-northwest line between the two villages.

Grandfather Barker sold his quarter section between the two villages for $9,000 to Mackenzie and Mann, shortly after the wheat had been harvested in October. The surveyors then moved in to lay out a commercial and residential grid for a new village. The citizens put their homes, stores, churches, and banks on wheels and moved them to the new lots adjacent to the railway tracks. By Christmas Day, 70 buildings had been transplanted to the new Dauphin, and train service was introduced to Portage là Prairie.

George Barker, Junior, welcomed the railroad, and was a man in love with the internal combustion engine. The traditional methods of clearing, planting and harvesting the land were not enough for George.

buy 500 or 1000 bushels of wheat on margin for $1.00, hoping to sell out when the price per bushel went from $1.00 to $1.50, or even to $2.25. Few could resist the temptation to buy additional blocks as the price kept rising. When the price swiftly headed downward, many farmers lost money. Obsessed by dreams of wealth that never came true, George Barker's last thoughts on his deathbed in 1950 were characteristically about work: "Is everything all right at the mill?" he whispered to Jane.

The oldest sons, William and Percy, grew up to be much bigger than their father, taking after the Alguire men. Percy was over six feet tall, with his father's blue eyes. William was just a little under six feet, and had prominent medium-brown eyes and brown hair just like his mother, and when he smiled he looked the "dead spit" of the Alguires.

He almost invariably was called "Will" or "Willie" by family and friends, who believed that his daring as a pilot was foreshadowed by a precocious flair for the dramatic. When his father helped build

He was the first homesteader in the Dauphin Valley to use steam engines to break and clear land, and for threshing. The Barker boys learned to fire the engine and run the separator, and even construct new parts in the blacksmith shop when, as often happened, the steam-driven machines broke down.

As the first-born son in the family, much was expected of "Willie." His father took him out of school, sometimes for weeks at a time, to help cut logs at his sawmill in the Riding Mountain. He had to stand on a wooden box to reach the controls for the planing saw. Barker also hunted game to feed the workers in his father's camp, with his mother being the camp cook. His favourite hunting rifle was the classic Great Plains weapon, a lever-action Winchester, which he modified with a peep sight of his own design.

Even by the high standards of the frontier, Barker was a deadly shot. He was very good on a target range, but exceptional on the move. He mastered the ability to point unerringly and rapidly at a fleeting target. His snap-shooting ability was so outstanding that Barker could likely have made a living as a trick shooter in a circus. One day while riding on horseback next to the family wagon, he spied a prairie chicken in the brush by the side of the road. Without slowing down, he fired his Winchester from the hip and hit the bird on the fly, all in one graceful motion. Because of this talent, Joseph "Bird" Winters, Dora Alguire's husband, always took his young nephew to the local turkey shoots, where he invariably beat the adults.

After retiring from local politics, Grandfather Barker owned a shooting gallery and bowling alley in downtown Dauphin. He always bet on his grandson against the shooting "sharks" who travelled the rural circuit. Old man Barker managed to lose a round or two to the visiting hustlers, before calling the kid over. The kid never let him down.

It was Will Barker's character more than his shooting prowess that left the most indelible impression. The good and bad traits of Barkers and Alguires seemed to merge in him, producing a remarkable mixture of leadership, intelligence, tenacity, and recklessness. Barkers tended to have an argumenta-

tive streak, a fierce stubbornness coupled to a quick temper. Full of pride, a Barker was more likely to lead than to follow, sometimes striking out on an independent path, and taking on the world for a point of principle. In contrast, the Alguires were gregarious, easy-going, and devil-may-care.

He was an emotional, intense boy with his heart on his sleeve, wanting very much to be liked. In his desire for approval, he reined in his emotions, and grew up with a sense of pride, dignity, and responsibility to others. Impatient and impetuous, he often reacted too quickly and jumped to conclusions. He recognized this flaw and practised any skill until it was second nature.

Full of energy, he loved being on the move, and he excelled at thinking on his feet. The greater the chaos, the clearer his mind worked. Howard Alguire always marvelled at Will's exceptional poise in unfamiliar situations, and believed it to be a kind of genius. He said of his nephew: "Willie never asked himself if it was possible to do something, he simply did it."

Despite a natural physical poise, Will was not an exceptional athlete. When the Church of England minister taught Percy and Will to box, it was Percy who excelled because of his phenomenal reflexes.

William Alguire collection

William Barker's maternal grandparents: Melissa Adelaide and William Riley Alguire.

13

Wayne Buchannon collection

William and Percy Barker after duck hunting, with the family dog.

Percy and Will attended the same schools, hunted together, and usually got into trouble together. A large black mutt served as duck retriever and sidekick.

Practical jokes were planned with fiendish glee by the two, sometimes in cahoots with Uncle Howard. One of their favourites was to dismantle a farm wagon in the middle of the night, carry it piece by piece to the peak of the barn and reassemble it. The following morning the farmer would walk outside to see his wagon silhouetted against the sky, looking for all the world, as sister Edna exclaimed: "... like it had been born there."

Will's mentor was Howard George Alguire. Although six years older, Howard was more than simply his uncle; he was a role model and his best friend. He was also a great tease, quick to deflate the pompous, and easily able to get under his nephew's skin. He tagged Will with the nickname, "The Dog," a play on Will's last name, and also "Squaw," because of the infatuation of a young Cree Indian girl who followed him everywhere. After the Barkers left Dauphin to homestead further west, it was Howard to whom Will wrote most frequently.

In 1902, George and Jane Barker had moved their family 50 miles west to the James Attwood

farm, about 10 miles north of Russell. The Barkers lived for 10 years in the farmhouse, or in the town. In addition to managing the Attwood farm, George continued to run his sawmill on the western edge of Riding Mountain.

Will's and Percy's high jinks sometimes interfered with the orderly flow of education in the one-room Londonderry School. One teacher, Gordon Kippan, once grabbed the two by the scruff of the neck and threw them out of the door of the school house. Despite the stunts, Will was a student who attained high marks, seemingly without effort. But his frequent absences because of the work on the farm and sawmill extended his education. By age 19 he still had not completed his final year of high school, which in those days in Manitoba was Grade 11.

At Londonderry, and then Russell High School, the Barker children received an education that reinforced family values devoted to honesty, integrity, and the Protestant work ethic. The Manitoba School Board believed in the Dominion as an obedient citizen of the British Empire. The world map on the classroom wall showed many countries in red, all pledging allegiance to a British monarch, and children of British stock understood they were both Canadian and British.

The Canadian government encouraged a larger military in the first decade of the century, mainly in volunteer reserve forces across Canada. Youth organizations with a military flavour such as the Boy Scouts were also founded. Will and Percy joined the first Boy Scout troop in Russell. When the Department of Militia and Defence established a cavalry unit in 1912 at Roblin, Will, Howard, and their friend, Duncan Leigh, enlisted as troopers in the Non-Permanent Active Militia (NPAM), in the 32nd Light Horse (soon renamed the 32nd Manitoba Horse). The three attended two-week summer camps and occasional parades during spring and fall.

In 1913, the Barkers moved back to Dauphin, by then the largest community in north-western Manitoba, with 4,000 people, four banks, four hotels, and a large red brick train station. Will attended classes on the third floor of the Mackenzie High School,

William Alguire collection

Howard Alguire (left) and Duncan Leigh (2nd from left) with companions in the summer of 1913 while serving with the 32nd Light Horse.

that particular floor being called Dauphin Collegiate Institute. The village had become a major town since Grandfather Barker was mayor.

Edna Barker Buchannon fondly remembers William as a doting big brother who believed in the importance of education for everybody. He walked hand-in-hand with Edna on her first day of school and met her after class. From that moment on, Willie was the finest big brother any girl could have. Edna enjoyed riding in the family wagon, sitting between Willie and his high school sweetheart, Mabel Buchannon, and jumping down to open the farm gates.

Around the dinner table the Barkers argued fiercely about almost anything, each brother and sister attempting to outdo the other. The merits of 20th-century technology—electric lights, indoor toilets, horseless carriages—were all enthusiastically debated by the Barkers, but Will's heart was captivated by flying machines, the first of which arrived in Manitoba in 1910.

A pilot from San Francisco, Eugene Ely, showed off a Curtiss biplane powered by a 30-hp engine at the Winnipeg Industrial Exhibition in July of that year. Finding that the Exhibition grounds were too small for the aircraft's limited power, Ely made three flights from a field on the west end of town. On his third flight he crashed, but was not seriously hurt. Barker, standing at the edge of the field, was spellbound as he watched Ely dive and soar, banking effortlessly like a prairie hawk.

The next summer Frank Coffyn demonstrated a Wright Flyer at the Exhibition. To attract crowds, the Exhibition's organizers featured a race between Coffyn's biplane, an automobile, and a motorcycle. The oval race track at the Exhibition grounds was used for annual motorcycle races. A newspaper notice asked: "Auto or Aeroplane—Can the automobile hold its own with the aeroplane?" A motorcycle racer riding a 50-hp Indian was pitted against the Wright Flyer. The race included 20 circuits of the half-mile-long oval dirt track, with Coffyn's aeroplane circling above, and the Indian running flat out in the dust below.

Barker had pushed his way through the crowds to the front railing before the race. The Winnipeg newspaper said that the keen-eyed pilot was favoured by the locals to win, and had become a popular personality with the Winnipeg business community:

The crowd around the railings during the race broke all records. The whole oval of the fence was a double, and in places a triple, rank of watching faces. Behind the crowd groups sat in automobiles; and Coffyn waved his hand gaily to a trio of girls as he sped over the fence in his arrowy angle to the upper air ... Seldom if ever has such a spectacle been on the boards at any fair, and the enthusiasm and excitement of the crowd was aroused to the highest pitch ... doubtless Coffyn was prime favourite. He has won the hearts of all Winnipeg, and the cheers that welcomed him after his victory were the loudest and longest ever heard on the fair grounds. Baribeau, on his motor cycle, was second.

Barker managed to retrieve a small piece of fabric or wood from a flying machine that had crashed during an exhibition. This fragment became his most treasured possession; a talisman for a teenager who had seen the future and wanted to be part of it. It may have been from the Ely aeroplane, or Sam

William Alguire collection

Farewell dinner in Dauphin in 1914 for the recruits of the 1st Canadian Mounted Rifles; most became casualties of war by the summer of 1916.

Tickell's Curtiss-type pusher, or Georges Mestach's Morane monoplane, all of which had accidents during demonstration flights. By July 1914, when he watched Lincoln Beachey demonstrate his loops at the Canadian Industrial Exhibition in Winnipeg, he knew he wanted to fly. He just didn't know how he was ever going to save up $400 to pay for lessons at the Wright School in Dayton, Ohio.

However, when war was declared less than a month later, on 3 August, Will gave little thought to flying with the military, because Canada had no air force to speak of. He had training as a mounted rifleman, and wanted to go to war on horseback. The 32nd Manitoba Horse provided volunteers to the 6th Western Canada Overseas Battalion. But Barker was not a member of this early draft, and did not enlist in the first contingent of the Canadian Expeditionary Force (CEF).

On a hot August evening in the small kitchen of the Barker home, Will told his family that he wanted to join up with the first volunteers. Standing erect

by the kitchen door, one arm behind his back, he argued that every man had an obligation to serve, to do his part. His father pleaded with him to finish his last year of school before enlisting. George wanted his son to apprentice at a local law firm, which was reserving a position for him upon his graduation. Respecting his father's wishes Will went back to complete Grade 11. But his heart was not in it.

About 65 percent of the first and second contingents of soldiers sent by Canada to fight for the Empire had been born in the United Kingdom. But the Canadian-born sons of British pioneers also enlisted by the thousands, and native-born Manitobans were over represented as a percentage of the national population.

All the families in the Dauphin district to which Will Barker was related by blood or marriage provided sons: the Alguires; the Winters; the Hicks; the Fergusons; and the Leighs. Bob and Mary Ferguson's son, Herbert, who, at 20, had already received a Bachelor of Arts degree from the University of

Manitoba, enlisted as a private just to get overseas faster. Duncan Leigh was as keen as Will to enlist. George and Clara Leigh, of Bristol, England, had raised Duncan, Marie, and Enid while homesteading in the Dauphin Valley. Enid had married Germaine Alguire, Barker's uncle, in 1910. As long-standing friends it seemed only natural that Duncan and Will should enlist together, reinforced in their determination by Uncle Howard.

On a cold November day, they volunteered for service with the second contingent of the CEF, enlisting in a newly authorized unit, the 1st Regiment, Canadian Mounted Rifles. Many other men had already enlisted in the infantry, but Barker wanted no part of marching if he could ride. After a couple of weeks of training in the Dauphin area, all the volunteers for the Canadian Mounted Rifles left town on 1 December for Brandon. The local newspaper described the farewells at the Canadian Northern Railway station:

Dauphin has probably given as many of her sons to the service of the Empire in this present world-wide struggle as any other town of similar size in the province ... During their couple of weeks of training in Dauphin since they enlisted, the boys have shown remarkable aptness in getting into military discipline and reflected credit upon their instructors, Sgt Major Goodall and Sgt Trooper Highfield ...

Occasions such as these are fortunately few in our Dominion, for although there were only expressions of best wishes, loyalty, and jolly farewells, one could easily detect a sadness beneath the surface on the departure of loved ones, some of whom doubtless will not return to Dauphin. It is hoped, however, that the war will soon be ended, and that few, if any, of our homes will be saddened by the loss in battle of our boys ...

That hope of 1914 was not to be. Eighty-three from Dauphin and 76 from Russell were killed in action, or died in military service, their names engraved on many town and village war memorials. Duncan Leigh was blown to pieces in the Battle of Mount Sorrel, and Herbert Ferguson became one of the missing-in-action at Passchendaele. The Leighs and Fergusons never got past the grief that their sons had no known grave.

The CMR recruits did not yet have uniforms and posed for a photograph in the snow by the train station, still in their "civvies." Will was well dressed in a shirt and tie, a dark overcoat, grey, soft-peaked cap, and leather gloves. He was keen to serve, but as the oldest boy he felt guilty for ignoring his father's wishes. George Barker would never see his son become a lawyer, or take over a family business, and after the war—well, everything was different.

William Alguire collection

The 1st Canadian Mounted Rifles recruits lined up near the Dauphin train station enroute to Brandon; Barker is 6th from right in front row, with Howard Alguire on his right side.

Last photo taken of the Barker family prior to Will's departure overseas; Will Barker (right rear) in CMR uniform, with Edna to his left in front, and infant Orval on lap of Jane Barker.

CHAPTER TWO

MACHINE GUNNER IN THE CANADIAN MOUNTED RIFLES

"Believe me this year in the army has seemed like about four to me. I have seen quite a lot of the world alright ... But now we are down to the 'hard stuff.' Of course it is all the game over here and we like it fine. But I can imagine plenty of occupations better than life & trench warfare in winter in Flanders. It rains nearly all the time here now and it sure is muddy especially in the trenches."

TROOPER WILL BARKER, YPRES SALIENT, 1915

William Barker's post-war Canadian Armed Forces record of service is preserved on microfilm, but there are a small number of 1914 paper documents that have survived. One of these is Barker's Attestation Paper filled out when he enlisted in the CEF. It has his Canadian Mounted Rifles serial number, 106074, scribbled in the upper right hand corner.

Barker's original medical examination has also survived, providing a physical description of the 20-year-old that went to war. On Christmas Eve, an Army Medical Corps doctor entered the following statistics: "height 5 ft., 10 and ½ ins.; girth 37 and ½ in. and 34 and ½ in.; range of expansion, 3 ins.; complexion, fair; eyes, grey; hair, light brown; religious denomination, Wesleyan." The one-page medical summary included this signed declaration: "I have examined the above-named Recruit and find that he does not present any of the causes of rejection specified in the Regulations for Army Medical Services. He can see at the required distance with either eye; his heart and lungs are healthy; he has the free use of his joints and limbs, and he declares that he is not subject to fits of any description."

Will had joined the mounted rifles, infantry on horseback armed with carbines. While they did not have quite the glamour of cavalry, mounted riflemen were a notch above infantry. Moreover, they reflected a Canadian tradition stretching back to the 1870s. It had been

Prime Minister John A. Macdonald who had changed the name "North West Mounted Rifles" to "North West Mounted Police." Two regiments of Canadian mounted riflemen had served in the South African War.

At the end of the 1914 summer camp in Manitoba, the largest concentration of cavalry and mounted riflemen in Canadian history—about 5,400 officers and men, and 3,400 horses—was reviewed on parade at Camp Sewell by Colonel Sam Hughes, Minister of Militia and Defence. Hughes did not include mounted riflemen in the first contingent of the CEF. But authority was granted by the British War Office for them in the second contingent, and the first three of 13 Canadian Mounted Rifle regiments were mobilized in western Canada, with the headquarters of the 1st CMR Brigade located in Winnipeg.

However, these three regiments trained in their home provinces through the winter of 1914-15, and were not assembled on parade in one location until June 1915. Manitobans formed the majority of the 1st CMR Regiment, but there were also volunteers from Saskatchewan, from the 29th Light Horse at Saskatoon and the 16th Light Horse at Yorkton.

On the west coast, the 2nd CMR Regiment was raised from the 30th Regiment, British Columbia Horse, in the Okanogan, and from the Victoria Independent Squadron of Horse, on Vancouver Island. They trained

William Alguire collection

Trooper Duncan Blake Leigh in 1915 in 1st CMR uniform.

at the Willows Exhibition Grounds in Victoria. The 3rd CMR Regiment was raised in Alberta from the 21st Alberta Hussars and the 15th Light Horse, and trained in Medicine Hat.

The quality of military-issue clothing and equipment was mediocre, and many did not get a uniform for months. The recruits slept on straw-filled paillasse mattresses on armoury floors, with only CEF-issue long underwear and blankets for warmth. Like thousands of others, Barker had been issued poorly manufactured boots that quickly wore out. On 10 March 1915, he scribbled on YMCA stationery: "The government shoes are rotten. I have just bought a new pair and spent two dollars on my issued ones. Howard has done the same."

Barker had all the hallmarks of a natural soldier. He could shoot and ride well, he was observant and

quick-witted, and he was naive and enthusiastic. In army slang, he was "full of piss and vinegar." As a hard-riding trooper, he suffered his share of upsets. He was hospitalized on 19 March with injuries after his horse stumbled. He wrote:

> I have at last found plenty of time to write as I am laid up for a few days (Not Serious). I got hurt this morning out on the hills east of the city. We were taking up a position on a hill & had to gallop nearly a mile & when about half way [as] Howard and I were enjoying the run my horse fell and rolled over me which knocked me out for a few minutes. However, I count myself lucky as I was able to ride back to camp and I feel pretty good now except that I am sore in general & [have] a sprained ankle ...

The 1st CMR Brigade sailed to the United Kingdom in June 1915 as a mounted formation, but its days as cavalry was short-lived. The CMRs never got to Egypt, as had been originally predicted. The need to replace the combat losses in Belgium, and the decision to form a 3rd Canadian Division meant the end of the Mounted Rifles on horseback. The enlarged, dismounted infantry battalions fought under the name "Mounted Rifles." They were never considered fashionable regiments, despite many medals, including four Victoria Crosses. They were promptly disbanded at war's end, their battle honours and medals assigned to other regiments.

Will Barker jumped at the chance to change occupations at Brandon. The machine gun was a more exciting and unfamiliar weapon than the carbine, and he competed to get into the Machine Gun Section. A letter written to his parents, and published in the *Dauphin Press* on 11 March, claimed he was the Section's youngest "No 1" - i.e., the man on the trigger:

> Just a few lines tonight as it is late. Well, I have some great news for you—I have been promoted to gunner on one of our four machine guns. I have worked hard for it and have won. There are eight men to each machine gun.

On Number One Gun I am gunner and in command under the sergeant, and am entirely responsible for the gun when it is in action or out. The gunner sits on a seat with push buttons and levers at his fingertips. A slight pressure of a button and a touch of a lever starts the gun at the rate of 600 rounds per minute … Howard Alguire is Number Two and feeds the gun with ammunition which is fixed in belts, so we are together. Duncan Leigh is Number Three and brings up the ammunition, so we are all on one gun.

The 1st CMR was equipped with four machine guns, the .30-calibre Colt-Browning. Colt Firearms was the US manufacturer of John Moses Browning's 1895-model gas-operated design. The Colts that equipped the CEF in Belgium generated no more affection than the infamous Ross rifles. The heavy, complex gun tended to overheat and "cook-off" rounds, it did not like mud, it jammed easily, and the actuating lever often broke. None of this was evident to Trooper Barker back in Manitoba, who crowed about his new status:

Well, mother, I am a mighty pleased boy with a position of gunner on a machine gun. Ask Lloyd how he would like to be in my shoes and get a bead on some Germans ha! ha! I don't think it would please him much more than myself though … I am studying my gun up pretty well as we are going out on the hills to do some shooting shortly. Sixty shots will be fired by each gun at a range of five hundred yards. The targets are steel plates set up on the ground resembling heads in a trench. We are to fire these 60 shots in 12 seconds so I hope that I am lucky …

With the spring thaw, the 1st CMR Regiment was transferred from Brandon to Camp Sewell, 22 miles southeast of Brandon on the Canadian Pacific Railway line. Sewell was a depressing landscape of sand hills, brown grass, a few struggling poplars, scrub oaks, and ground cedars.

The camp lay south of the railway tracks, with rows of white tents already set up by the first arriving infantry battalions. The CMRs spent only three weeks there before boarding the train for eastern Canada, but Barker was at home for embarkation leave. His mother and father knew they might never see him again, and arranged for a family photograph. The photographer clustered the nine children around their parents, and snapped what was to be the last picture of the entire Barker family.

Fear about the future was underscored by a violent act during Will's leave; a dark event that was whispered about in the family for years, but never acknowledged to others. One morning soon after getting home, Will decided to take a stroll through Dauphin in his uniform. As he walked by one of the livery stables, a group of tough guys made some disparaging remark. He responded with a comment or two of his own about civilian slackers. This precipitated a brawl. The livery stable gang "put the boots" to Barker, beating him unconscious.

At first it seemed that his internal injuries might end his military career. While his brother was recovering, Percy relentlessly tracked down each man who had participated. He took them, in turn, into a locked barn, and beat them up. He was not going to allow an act of mean-spirited violence against his brother to go unavenged.

When William was fit enough to travel, the Barkers and Alguires went with him to the Canadian Northern Railway station to see him off—but not seven-year-old Edna. She was bewildered that her favourite brother was going across the Atlantic Ocean. When she asked her teacher how big it was, she was told that it was deeper and wider than a thousand Dauphin Lakes. Edna was heart-broken, and could not be consoled. She hid under the horsehair couch in the front room. Her parents tried to cajole her into coming, but she was overwhelmed by the loss of her dear "Willie." He finally asked his parents to "leave her be."

When the time came to transport the 1st CMR Brigade to Montreal for the voyage to the United Kingdom, the 2nd Regiment in Victoria was the first to pack. The unit filed aboard a CPR ship on

Machine Gun Section of the 1st CMR; William Barker on left kneeling by Colt-Browning, Howard Alguire standing directly behind, and Duncan Leigh to Howard's left.

Friday, 4 June. The same train that left Vancouver carrying the 2nd stopped to load the troopers of the 3rd Regiment in Medicine Hat, and stopped again at Camp Sewell to pick up the troopers of the 1st. When Barker climbed aboard at Camp Sewell on a bright Tuesday morning, many of the coaches were festooned with enthusiastic banners: "Berlin or Bust" and "Here Comes the 2nd CMR."

With the 2nd was Lance Corporal George Randolph Pearkes, a 27-year-old British-born former Mounted Policeman, and future Victoria Cross recipient. Pearkes was an enlisted man who, like Barker, would be commissioned in 1916. He finished the war as a battalion commander, was a major general in the Second World War, became Minister of

National Defence in the Diefenbaker government of the 1960s, and concluded his career as the Lieutenant Governor of British Columbia.

The 1st CMR Brigade, with 92 officers and 1,853 other ranks, had the good luck to be assigned one of the larger vessels in Montreal, the *Megantic*. It was a ship of the White Star Line, the same company that had owned the *Titanic*. The *Megantic* had sailed the Liverpool-to-Montreal route from 1909 to 1914, carrying more than 1,100 paying passengers. She went back to peacetime crossings until she was sold off for scrap in the 1930s, her iron and steel melted down and recycled to build the first of Japan's warships that saw action in the Second World War.

2nd Lieut Billy Bishop of the 7th CMR Regiment was also crossing the Atlantic at the same time as Barker. Bishop had been commissioned in the 9th Mississauga Horse, a cavalry unit in Toronto, shortly after the war broke out. He had later been transferred to the 7th at London, Ontario. Like Barker, he had been attracted to the machine gun and, for a period of time, was officer-in-charge of the Machine Gun Section. Although they trained at the same UK camps in the summer of 1915, Bishop and Barker did not meet then, and their paths never crossed in the Royal Flying Corps.

It had taken Bishop's ship, the *Caledonia*, 14 days to reach England, where it docked at Devonport on 23 June. The ship was not as seaworthy as the *Megantic*,

and many of the soldiers were sick, and quite a few of the horses in the ship's hold died. Barker's passage was comparatively pleasant. Leaving Montreal on the 12th, *Megantic* passed *Caledonia* somewhere in mid-Atlantic, and arrived at Devonport four days ahead. Pearkes remembered the crossing as uneventful: "We did a certain amount of PT [physical training]. We were packed in pretty tight and it wasn't very comfortable but who cared—we were going overseas at last … we kept a look-out armed with rifles in case any submarine came … Machine guns were mounted on the upper deck … many of the men were seasick but it was not a rough crossing."

The English landscape was both foreign and familiar. For many who grew up in Canada reading the books of Charles Dickens and Rudyard Kipling, the country was enchanting. One man in particular, Private Lester Bowles Pearson, a Medical Corps orderly, was thrilled when his ship, the *Corinthian*, finally docked at Plymouth, partly because he had been sick during the crossing. Pearson, a future Canadian prime minister, soaked up the scenes in the sunshine-drenched harbour, previously just a name in a history book.

The 1st CMR Brigade travelled by train from Devonport on 19 June to Caesar's Camp South, a "tent city," with the soldiers living in groups of eight in bell tents. Caesar's Camp South and Caesar's Camp North were not far from the English Channel, and the town of Folkestone. The green soldiers of this second Canadian contingent were viewed with some regard by British citizens because of the 1st Canadian Division's stand in the gas warfare attacks the previous April.

The training provided for the Canadians in the UK in no way prepared them for trench warfare in Belgium. The shortcomings were described in the diary of Private Donald Fraser of the 31st (Alberta) Battalion:

> After four months' training in Kent ... we were considered fit and skilled in the art of warfare, ready to meet the hated Hun ... our training was decidedly amateurish and impractical. It consisted mainly of route marches and alignment movements. Our musketry course amounted to nothing; we had only half an idea about the handling of bombs. We were perfectly ignorant regarding rifle grenades.

For the troopers of the CMRs, it was often a case of hurry up and wait, sometimes no horses and plenty of saddles, sometimes the reverse. The 2nd CMR did the same route marches as the infantry while waiting for mounts.

Will, Howard, and Duncan received additional training in machine-gun operations at Hythe, and Will received a first class machine gunner's certificate. He expressed no gripes about his training, writing his father that the Hythe course was "about as good as a term at

college." By the end of the war, the CEF had efficiently integrated automatic weapons into their platoon-level trench raids, but this evolution was a long way in the future during Barker's time on the Colt. His education on the mobility and flexibility of automatic weapons came with his transfer to the RFC.

The 1st CMR Brigade received embarkation orders for the Ypres Salient in Flanders in September. Barker's regiment had, by this time, been honed down to war strength of 577 all ranks, with only 89 horses. Barker knew that he was going across the Channel because he had been given new identity discs. A few days before the crossing, each trooper of the Brigade had been issued with two metal dog tags. The original fibre dog tags dissolved quickly in the mud of Flanders, and were hard to remove from corpses. Capt Bennett of the 4th CMR Regiment recalled that:

> Probably nothing was so significant in all these young soldiers' preparation as receiving their identification discs. Not even the field dressing or the rifle and its bayonet had the same sobering effect or was so indicative of the seriousness of the conflict in which they were about to participate as the reception of these little metal discs.

On Monday, 20 September 1915, Will boarded train X-507, along with the 77 other ranks and four officers of the Machine Gun Section. The train pulled out in darkness for Southampton, arriving at the seaport in the early hours of the morning. The troopers waited around all day, boarding the ship to Le Havre at 10:30 pm. Will scribbled on a postcard:

> Dear Ilda—We are on our way at last and I am writing this from the train. I have no stamps and don't know whether this will reach you or not but hope it will. Howard, Duncan, and I are all well and looking forward to seeing France in a few hours.

The rest of the regiment sailed from Folkestone harbour aboard the La Marguerite, arriving

THE YPRES SALIENT IN THE WINTER OF 1915-16

The British Expeditionary Forces was concentrated at two sectors of the more than 400 miles of trenches stretching through Belgium and France—the Ypres Salient in Flanders, and the Somme front in Picardy. The triangular Salient, named for the town, was only about nine miles wide at the base of the triangle, and intruded only about four miles inside the enemy lines. The Salient was held throughout the war, but at an enormous cost in lives and human misery.

The Canadian Corps, part of the British Second Army commanded by General Sir Herbert Plumer, occupied a sector of trenches that zigzagged about six miles northwest from Ploegsteert Wood to the Vierstraat-Wytschaete road. The 1st CMR Brigade was assigned trenches on the left of that front line, running approximately east-west through the Vierstraat-Wyschaete road. Opposite the CMRs were Bavarian regiments of the German Sixth Army.

The CMR Brigade entered the front lines during a relatively quiet period. There would be no major engagements for it, or the Canadian Corps, until the Battle of the St Eloi Craters and the Battle of Mount Sorrel the following spring. The Canadian Corps between September and December 1915 suffered 688 fatalities and just over 2,000 other casualties, but the 1st CMR Regiment was hardly touched over the winter.

From September 1915 to March 1916, 14 members of Barker's unit were killed in action, two soldiers died of their wounds, and about 20 more were wounded. Will never carried his Colt-Browning into a major action that winter, but he lived in "a troglodyte world" that quickly dampened his enthusiasm for the Army. This sector of the front had seen bloody fighting in 1914, and Private Fraser, who entered the lines just five days before Barker, less than a mile away, wrote:

> ... the trenches are old and evil smelling, in some places the stench being almost unbearable. This is usually caused by shells bringing refuse or dead bodies to the surface. Anyway chloride of lime or creosol is issued as a ration and sanitary police attend to its distribution. Every company has its sanitary policeman whose duty it is to see to sanitation wherever the company may be placed ...

Inside the small triangle of the Ypres Salient were many thousands of soldiers, who moved only at night from hole to hole. Since the positions held by the British projected into German-held territory, the enemy had the advantage of being able to lob artillery and mortar shells from three sides. The Somme may be the more evocative battlefield of the Great War, but soldiers who knew both battlefields especially dreaded Ypres. It was unquestionably hell in a very small place. Bennett of the 4th CMR wrote:

> Everyone lived a rodent life; in the daytime, nothing stirred but at night the Salient was a hive of moving troops and transports ... The night was made more unreal by the flares and Verey lights which seemed to surround the mysterious darkness.

in Boulogne by 9:10 pm. Six days later the regiment marched into Ploegsteert, Belgium. The headquarters of the 1st CMR Regiment was set up at the Convent of St. Paul-de-Croix.

* * *

A large number of Barker's letters and cards were saved by his mother. When a letter arrived the whole family would gather around the kitchen table in the house on 4th Avenue NE in Dauphin, and Jane Barker would read, and Willie's brothers and sisters would listen, silent and wide-eyed.

Barker's great desire to be a source of pride for his family clearly shines through all his youthful banter. His political and religious opinions, at least as he expressed them in letters home, were the conventional ones of a Methodist-raised son of the British Empire. He was occasionally boastful, embellishing

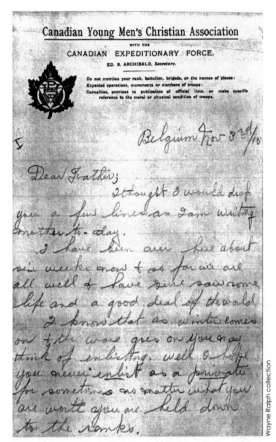

Reproduction of Barker's letter to his father offering advice about enlisting in the army.

If you go do not enlist to fill up an old regiment for then a recruit is put in the "Base detail" and gets the bad end of everything ... get in a new Battalion really before it is formed, and take nothing whatever except the machine gun section ...

It also pays to work for stripes. I should have been a corporal now but another fellow a middle aged Scotsman got around the officer and got ahead of me. However, I am still on the gun so am pretty lucky ...

Will never did get his corporal's stripes. Thinking of his career after the war, he decided to send almost all his soldier's pay home to his mother. He knew that his family could use the extra money, but he hoped that something could be put aside. He fretted about the details of his pay allotments:

Now mother, I am going to try and make plain to you some money matters. I am going to send home practically all my money at least $25 a month. If you can put this in the bank for me do so, but if you can't—do the best for me, for I want to have some little capital if I ever get back. Up to now I have saved practically nothing but am determined to save now ...

After a few weeks in Flanders, Will had seen enough of regimental operations in a war zone to take the edge off:

I have had two spells in the front line and one in support and find the trenches pretty muddy & cold, but knowing it will be worse this winter we try to make light of it.

We will be in the trenches for Xmas and any parcel of eats or anything you can send will go good, to be sure, especially a little honey ...

I believe my writing is getting worse every day. But perhaps the shells have something to do with it. The ground here tonight is shaking from the fire of heavy guns.

stories that put him in a favourable light, but he also liked to tell a joke at his own expense. He worried about his family, and was not entirely confident of his father's ability to provide. George Barker had thought of enlisting in the CEF, and his eldest son complained about his own stalled career, offering the following earnest advice:

Say, father, Howard said something about a recruiting sergeant wanting you to enlist. Well, here are my views, I have been in the army for a year next month & I advise you not to go. There are many reasons but I guess you know them ...

On his 21st birthday, 3 November, Barker was in a reserve line dugout. He scribbled glum insights with a blue pencil, his only light being a single wax candle. The YMCA letterhead on which he wrote cautioned him against mentioning his rank, battalion, brigade, any place names, any casualties, or anything to do with the moral or physical condition of troops:

I know that as winter comes on & the war goes on you may think of enlisting. Well, I hope you never enlist as a private for sometimes no matter what you are worth you are held down to the ranks.

But if you should want to go I think the best thing to do would be to apply for a commission as Lieutenant & then things are easy. A Machine Gun officer has the only job for he is independent of all superior officers ... I think it only right you should get [a commission] when two sons are serving in the ranks ... Well, dad, I hope I have not appeared too imperative in any of my words as I thought it only right to tell you a few things I have learned out here.

In a separate letter to his mother on the same birthday Will's spirits were so low that he told her:

Believe me, this year in the army has seemed like about four to me. I have seen quite a lot of the world alright & had a fairly good time while in England. But now we are down to the "hard stuff."

Of course it is all the game over here and we like it fine. but I can imagine plenty of occupations better than life & trench warfare in winter in Flanders. It rains nearly all the time here now and it sure is muddy especially in the trenches ...

During his field service with the CMRs, it was Barker's mother, and the other women in the Dauphin Valley who comforted him, and sent him treats:

Say, mother, will you please send me a dozen Gillette safety razor blades as soon as possible ... Howard & I always shave with it so he goes half on the price ...

I recieved [sic] a lovely parcel from Eva [Ferguson] of a dozen packages of spearmint gum. Wasn't that kind of her? ...

I divided up [the cake] & recieved [sic] no end of compliments ... please do not send any more chocolate (as I can get it here), but the homemade toffee is great ... The socks are always needed & they were fine ... we are all anxiously awaiting our leave as it would seem like Heaven to have dry feet for even a few hours again.

Barker was lucky enough to be in the support trenches for Christmas. The contrast between the Ypres Salient and the Dauphin Valley was keenly felt:

This is Xmas Day & we are enjoying it fine under the circumstances. But oh! what a difference from a Christmas at home ... we had a splendid dinner ... goose, dressing, apple sauce, plum pudding and beer. We also had cigars and cigarettes. I have not recieved [sic] any letters or parcels lately. There must be a holdup someplace. We hear rumours of large quantities of mail being burned up ...

Soldiers in Flanders looked for diversions when in rear-echelon camps. They hated the monotony and inadequacy of army food, and bought extras—usually eggs and chips, or a home-cooked meal. Belgian families in the rear areas sold necessities from their houses, and cooked meals for a small charge. It was here that Will managed to recapture some of the warmth of home:

I am writing this from a Belgian farm house as we are sleeping in a very cold place. Howard, Duncan, & I had supper here last night and also breakfast this morning & as the people seem so kind, the place so homelike, we are having them roast a chicken & prepare a good

27

supper for us to-night. Of course all this costs some little money but it is not wasted …Well, Mother, I think I will close for now as some of the kids are shaking the table & jabbering away in Flemish enough to drive one crazy.

* * *

Memories of peaceful summer fairs, and loops by Curtiss and Wright biplanes, were renewed by the aerial warfare in the sky above. Seeing flying machines spin down in flames, and the remains of a particularly gruesome crash, caused Barker to think twice before transferring to the RFC.

By January 1916, however, he had submitted an application for transfer to the head of the Machine Gun Section, Lieut Conrad W. Laubach, asking to join the RFC. Laubach, from Yorkton, Saskatchewan, willingly endorsed it, and had the satisfaction of visiting Barker, VC, in a London hospital four years later—both men devoutly grateful to have survived.

Will waited anxiously for his transfer to come through, confident that his skills as a machine gunner would serve him well. He was sure that in the RFC he would receive an officer's commission, and bypass his miserable prospects for advancement in the CEF.

Commanding officers did not like to release their experienced men for service in the RFC and, as the war dragged on, obstacles were erected to discourage young men from seeking an escape. Only a tiny percentage of the CEF's veterans in France and Belgium ever made it into the RFC. Despite the cliché about mud below and blue sky above, most World War One "grunts" had no desire to fly.

Will Barker wanted out of the trenches in the worst way, before something, or someone, delayed or blocked his transfer, or a sniper's bullet put an end to any future. He was interviewed by Brig General Victor Williams, commander of the 8th Infantry Brigade, on 20 January. Barker wrote that the general treated him kindly and promised to recommend him.

By 1 February, the Machine Gun Section was back in the front lines and Will was anxiously awaiting word of leave. He had drawn a low leave number, 4,

better than Howard's 8, and Duncan's 9. The casualties in the Machine Gun Section, and the battalion, were very light, but still not reassuring: "One of our Corporals got shot through the head this morning at eight by a German sniper. They sure seem able to hit a fellow's bean sometimes." A few days later he described his life in more detail:

Our artillery shells Fritz unceasingly by day & night and of course he always retaliates by tearing up our line. I have done a considerable amount of firing since I came in one day. Guns tore up Fritzes [*sic*] front line and I trained my gun so as to catch the German working parties when they as usual started to repair the damage done. I spent a lively night & fired two belts, five hundred shots, at this work during the night. Sometimes we almost sleep on our feet. I am now in charge of two gun and am up till twelve at night, sleep if possible to four, then up again as then "stand to" every man at his post [*sic*] … Believe me it pays to play the soldier all the time.

Will did not hesitate to enlist his mother's help to buy and ship illegal bullets. Being a machine gunner, he carried no rifle, but could not get so-called "dum-dum" cartridges for his side arm, so a request had gone back to Dauphin. When they arrived, he wrote a warrior's acknowledgement:

Well, Mother, I got the parcel last night with the soft point shells in it. Thanks very much. You know I do not have to carry rifle or bayonet so I carry the 32 automatic and two Mills bombs with me. I often go out in No Man's Land even up to Fritzes barbed wire so as to pick out objects for effect we fire & these weapons are the only thing if surprised and I do not intend to be captured easily. I think my turn for leave will come about in three weeks time as 1 has gone …

Howard & I went sniping yesterday morning we saw plainly two Germans in grey about 650 yds away. I took a strange rifle as

No 1s have none of their own. I fired carefully
at one but missed him, however, he flopped so
I had some satisfaction. Better luck next time.
I just got down from the parapet when smash,
a sniper had spotted me & cut the very bag
I was leaning on a second before. However, a
miss is as good as a mile, but it makes a fellow
think for a moment. They sure are dead shots
& seldom miss.

A few days after this close call an RFC form
arrived at the 1st CMR Battalion, requesting information on Barker's weight, height, mechanical
experience, and military qualifications. When his
coveted orders finally came, he quickly packed up his
meagre personal belongings, shook hands with Lieut
Laubach, and swallowed hard as he said goodbye to
Uncle Howard and Duncan. They had been together
so long, so inseparable at home, that the farewell was
hard to get through.

Howard was confident his nephew would excel
at flying, just like everything else. Willie was never
coming back to the Machine Gun Section. Barker
travelled by road about 70 miles south to an aerodrome near Amiens, to 9 Squadron for training as a
gunner/observer. But he was on probation with the
RFC for only one month and, if he failed to measure
up, would be returned to that pocket of hell called
the Ypres Salient.

Howard Alguire (right) with Trooper Lee, MIA at Battle of
Mount Sorrel.

William Barker in 1916 as observer in flying uniform with map, just prior to operational flight.

CHAPTER THREE
CORPS COOPERATION DUTIES ON THE SOMME

"I was flying with my flight commander during this last great push & I must admit that it was almost a case of bullets or medals. However, we both have been decorated with the M.C. for our work ... I will be some nut now with my decoration up, Eh? ... I am awfully glad that I am going back to the home establishment for a while ..."
2ND LIEUT WILL BARKER, No. 15 SQN, RFC, DECEMBER 1916

Joining the RFC saved Will Barker from an infantry soldier's squalid existence, and the transfer almost certainly saved his life. His confidence, independence, and versatility made him ideally suited to this new kind of warfare, and by entering the RFC at this time, he became a witness to the dramatic growth of air power. The odds were also working in his favour, because the RFC was regaining temporary air superiority over the Imperial German Air Service, the Luftstreitkräfte, a superiority which see-sawed back and forth between the air forces throughout the war. Will's chances of survival while learning to be an observer were significantly better in the spring and summer of 1916 than they would have been a year later.

When Barker joined 9 Squadron, he may have been reassured to learn that his commanding officer was a Canadian, Major Frederick Wanklyn, of Montreal. A 1909 graduate of the Royal Military College at Kingston, Wanklyn was a colonial who had been commissioned in the Royal Artillery of the British Army. He learned how to fly in 1912, one of only nine Canadians to qualify as a pilot prior to the war. Wanklyn was the first Canadian to join the RFC, being seconded to the newly created service in November 1912, and also the first Canadian aviator to see combat in France.

Will had a few days of hangar instruction prior to getting airborne on his first flight. His gunnery skills were well developed, but he knew nothing about wireless telegraphy. He had a small pocket camera for taking personal photos (in violation of regulations), but he had no training on the large "C" model aerial camera, the type that used 4-inch by 5-inch glass-plate negatives.

He flew for the first time on Monday, 6 March. His pilot, on what was just a 20-minute test flight, was Captain H.E. van Goethem, an experienced officer who took Will airborne several times during March. The early flights concentrated on airborne gunnery—practice shooting at a wooden mock-up of a Fokker monoplane parked on the ground. He wrote his parents:

> Believe me it is not an easy matter to hit a target like this especially when the weather is rough. To get at this target I had to stand right up on the seat and lean over, all this is done in a hurricane just behind the propeller while at a speed of 80-90 miles per hour ...

The amount of training provided in England for pilots at this stage of the war was modest—some arrived on squadron with less than 20 hours of flying experience. But observers selected, as Barker was, from the trenches were expected to learn on the job. In the early days of the war, there was no training at a school in England on the craft of observing.

Canadian Airmen and the First World War, the RCAF official history, described the changes that gave Barker his chance to fly:

A I R - T O - G R O U N D
C O M M U N I C A T I O N S ,   1 9 1 6

In 1914-15, the quality of artillery cooperation by aeroplane crews was not very good, in part because there was no reliable means of communication. Flares, electric lamps, smoke grenades, even talcum powder were used to send signals to the ground. If that did not work, a pilot could land his flying machine near a battalion headquarters, or artillery battery, and he and his observer could discuss the situation with the commanding officer.

A relatively light-weight wireless transmitter had been installed in Corps Cooperation machines by late 1915. The 20-pound set was manufactured by the Sterling Telephone Company, hence the name Sterling wireless. It could transmit signals to the ground, but could not receive any. Except for occasional experiments, this was the situation throughout the war.

The ground station or artillery battery had to rely on a visual means of reply or instruction to the aeroplane. The simplest were white cloth strips about a foot wide and 12-feet long. The strips were laid on the ground to transmit a specific instruction. For example, "L" meant ready to engage the target, "L IV" meant ready to engage target number four. A triangle meant battery receiving signals but not ready to fire. Two bars under the triangle meant that the battery would be ready to fire in 20 minutes. With variations like this, gunners communicated to their eyes in the sky.

The panneau signaller was an alternative means of communication for artillery batteries. It looked like a venetian blind, but it was placed flat on the ground. By manipulating a rope, the sections of the blind which were black would be opened to reveal a white background. Long and short flashes of white became the dashes and dots similar to that of wireless.

In order to build up the level of strength Haig's [Field Marshal Sir Douglas Haig] plans demanded, Trenchard [Major General Hugh. M. Trenchard] had to dilute his squadrons with many airmen who had little or no combat experience … In the spring, Trenchard had increased the establishment of observers in two-seater squadrons from seven to twelve, most of the new intake coming from army units already in France, including the CEF. A new observer got little formal training. Beyond what was imparted at the squadron, he might, if it were thought necessary, be sent for a short period to an artillery battery or to a front-line infantry unit to develop an appreciation of the needs of the ground forces with which he must work. All observers had to learn Morse code and how to operate a wireless set and camera. They had to acquire, as rapidly as possible, a detailed familiarity with their squadron's "beat" at the front; they had to master the handling of machine guns. They picked up what they could by word of mouth, but there was no substitute for practical experience.

Barker was on trial with the RFC to become what was called a Corps Cooperation airman, one of those unsung flyers who supported the troops on the ground. Nine Squadron was responsible for the *ab initio* training of probationary observers. Equipped with 18 BE2c two-seater machines, the unit was based at an aerodrome near the village of Bertangles, about five miles north of Amiens, on the west side of the road that led to Doullens.

The pilots and observers of the Corps Cooperation squadrons flew as a team, doing photographic and visual reconnaissance; artillery spotting (called by its participants, "a shoot"); contact patrols at low altitude in support of infantry, bombing, general liaison and communication, and even spy drops behind enemy lines. The personal qualities needed for this multi-role occupation were different from Army scout operations (i.e., aircraft fighting mainly against other aircraft). As *Canadian Airmen and the First World War* noted: "Grit, constant watchfulness, and, above all, patience were the hallmarks of good corps squadron airmen."

After 16 months with the 1st CMR, Will was greatly impressed with the RFC, and was positive he wanted to stay with it. He was thrilled with flying, and admired the skill of the pilots on the squadron. He was inclined to boast somewhat to his family, and did a bit of "line-shooting" about his accomplishments, magnifying his role in certain dramatic events at his squadron. As his war-weariness grew, these exaggerations diminished, but he never lost his facility for spinning a good yarn.

After a couple of months of operational experience as an observer, Barker stopped being so complimentary about his pilots, but in March he was still a wide-eyed enthusiast:

I have done a lot of flying during the last three weeks and always over the lines where we were shelled. I always flew with a young Captain who sure can take a fellow's breath [away] in the air. One day we were coming home up about 9,000 feet well up above the white clouds in nice sunshine. It was so odd—above us was sky & sun, below all we could see was fields of clouds, but of course we know the earth was 6 or 7 thousand feet below them. We were flying along at about 90 miles per hour when suddenly with the engine full open the pilot turned the plane nose down. There was a terrific rush-down dashed [sic] through the clouds and the earth seemed to fly up at us. Slowly he righted her & I felt more at ease. You can imagine what a nose dive is (not a plane down), but a dive with engine full open straight down, some sensation, believe me. You know it is a terrific speed & the wires, wire rigging, etc. etc., sing & scream through the air [sic]. Also some noise, ha! ha!

The Captain & I were out on patrol over the lines today. Although it is Sunday we know no difference for if anything there is more flying. We were up for two hours & I got one of my ears frozen for we flew high watching for German planes.

The young captain was probably P.C. Maltby, flight commander of C Flight. In addition to training, Will flew about nine operational patrols in March, to prove to the RFC that he could apply in action over the front lines what he had been taught on the aerodrome.

Apart from operational losses, squadrons in the field suffered injuries and deaths in flying accidents, and pilots damaged many flying machines, usually on landing or takeoff. Barker witnessed a mid-air collision soon after his arrival at 9 Squadron. A Bristol Scout and a BE2c, both types belonging to 9, collided on 12 March near 4 Squadron's aerodrome at Baizieux. Remarkably, there were no deaths in this collision. The pilot of the BE2c, Lieut F.W. Lerwill, was seriously injured, and the Bristol pilot, Capt R. Egerton, broke his arm and suffered a severe concussion. Will may have embellished his role in the incident:

I am enclosing some souvenirs of a wreck we had here. The reason I am sending them is that I used to fly in the plane that these splinters are from. I am not allowed to tell you all particulars but sufficient to say that two planes crashed together in mid-air up about 3,000 & dived to the earth. I was first on the spot and helped pull the crushed men out from amongst the wires and twisted debris. I certainly never want to see such a mess again ...

Will quickly demonstrated talent as an observer. He had excellent eyesight, was one of the best machine gunners in 9 Squadron, easily mastered the clumsy cameras used to take aerial photographs, and had no difficulty transmitting wireless messages in flight. If he survived long enough to become combat seasoned, a big if, he would be a great asset to the RFC, and the British ground forces in the Somme sector.

But he really wanted to be a pilot—flying the BE2c rather than taking photographs from the front seat. Better yet, he wanted to become a scout pilot, fighting against the German pilots in their Fokker monoplanes. In the First World War most pilots considered themselves fighting pilots, and the modern term "fighter pilot" had not even been coined.

Barker's letter to his parents on commissioning in the RFC, 12 April 1916.

Wayne Ralph collection

The pilots of single-seater aeroplanes who escorted two-seaters, or hunted on the enemy side, were called "scout pilots."

In the RFC, the scout pilots in their single-seater machines formed squadrons that ostensibly supported the Army formation on the ground, hence grouped into an Army Wing, partners alongside the Corps Cooperation Wings. One Army and one Corps Wing, along with a Balloon Wing or Company, was the operational heart of every RFC Brigade. (In this biography, the term "scout pilot" and "scout machine" is retained, although the modern equivalent of "fighter pilot" and "fighter" may occasionally be used.)

With less than a month in the RFC, and still on probation, Barker wrote home predicting that, any day now, he was going to be retrained as a pilot:

I was recommended by my O.C. yesterday & this morning I went before the Wing Commander & after asking me many questions he recommended me for a Commission in the Royal Flying Corps. So now it is only a matter of days. I am told that I go to a civil aviation school in England & will be in civilian clothes for about two months until I have learned to fly & obtained a pilot's certificate.

This was just wishful thinking, and the RFC had different plans for this cocky Canadian trooper. Passing his probation at 9 Squadron, he was commissioned into the General List, and Royal Flying Corps, as a temporary 2nd Lieutenant, at the beginning of April. Shortly thereafter, he was sent back to England to be outfitted with his uniforms, and take his release from the CEF, to which he still officially belonged.

Trooper Barker was now 2nd Lieut Barker and a member of the Imperial Forces of Great Britain. He had received no formal training as an officer, and limited training as an observer, but was catapulted not only into a new branch of service, but also into a different social class. To a young man educated at the one-room Londonderry School, Russell High School, and Dauphin Collegiate, a commission was a great achievement. It was all a bit overwhelming: "Now, Father, one thing I want to make plain is that the R.F.C. is a class of (officers) Lords sons. Heirs & young men of rank & titles ..." Father was later advised to stop putting his son's regimental number, 106072, on the envelopes: "I forgot to tell you that officers do not have numbers ..."

Will's salary jumped from $1.00 per day to the equivalent of about $7.00. However, like other officers without a private income, he soon learned that a £50 uniform allowance and a pound-and-a-half *per diem* could not easily support him in the field. He fretted about his ability to make ends meet, even asking his father to return part of his pay assignment from the CMRs.

He complained to his family about the cost of hotels and meals while in London, the expense of his uniforms, and his monthly mess bills. As a virtual teetotaller, he did not like having to pay for liquor guzzled by his fellow officers at every dinner in the Officer's Mess. He stopped asking for money from home, but no longer sent monthly allotments to his mother, loftily advising: "The last two letters I got from you contained two dollars each. Thanks very much. But please do not send me any more as I do not need it. I am an officer now mother & my cheque is good anyplace." When his mother sent him cheques worth $70.00, he returned them uncashed.

As an escapee from the Ypres Salient, Will soaked up every sight and sound on his way to London. With a seven-day leave pass, he travelled to Boulogne, where he caught the night Channel boat. He stayed at the Hotel Cecil, a big step up from the 23-room Grandview Hotel back home in Dauphin:

Barker in officer's uniform with observer wing, 1916.

Provincial Archives of Manitoba

I would like to stay at a quieter place than the Hotel, but they make a speciality of officers from the front & also now I cannot stop [overnight] where I like. They put officers from the front up for $4 - $5 per day and it is pretty good too for the Cecil Hotel is the best in London & they say the best in Europe. Great dining Halls, Orchestra, Bands, Dancing halls, Restaurant, baths of all kinds. Everything known for comfort. I believe one banquet hall holds 2,000 guests alone ... I would give worlds if I could only spend this short leave of mine at home which beat all the European Hotels going. Best love to all your loving son, 2/Lieutenant Barker.

A photographer took studio shots of Will in his new uniform, which he had made into postcards for relatives and friends. He was not permitted as yet to wear an observer's badge. Unlike a pilot's wings, it was awarded only after operational service.

He visited the tourist attractions: the Tower of London, Westminster Abbey, St. Paul's Cathedral, and his favourite, Madame Tussaud's Waxworks Museum. The latter was "wonderful beyond description ... [The figures] were so life-like that I was fooled once. A man in evening dress, gloves in hand, etc., really life like stood in my way & I waited for him to move on. But 'nix' I was stung ..."

His mother wrote that Percy had been promoted to corporal. Percy had enlisted in the Cameron Highlanders of Canada not long after Will left for overseas. He razzed his younger brother about his own leap in rank:

I am awfully glad to hear that Percy is getting on so well. Corporal, Eh! You know, mother,

I have accomplished quite a thing. I jumped from the rank of gunner to Lieutenant & have not been to an officer's training school at all. You can imagine I went into the Cecil Hotel in my trench clothes & when I came out in full uniform on the Strand I had to acknowledge & return the salutes of hundreds of Australians, New Zealanders, Canadians, Imperials, etc. Some change. However, you know I am very conceited & that I believe carried me through ...

* * *

Barker was posted to one of the oldest of the RFC squadrons, number 4. He worried about fitting in with the other officers at the squadron, and felt uncertain about his social standing with people he believed were young men of "rank and titles."

The unit had 13 BE2c machines (increased to 18 by June), and was stationed at Baizieux, an aerodrome quite close to the front lines, only six miles

Photo by William Barker; Mabel Buchannon and Carl McTaggart collection

Barker's BE2 on an advanced landing field during the Battle of the Somme campaign.

from the town of Albert. On 23 April, Will scribbled a short letter:

My dear Mother: Just a few lines tonight to let you know I am still well & o.k. I am writing this up in my room & the shelling is so violent up at the line that it shakes everything. Incidently [sic], we are within shell range if they cared to shell us. I done [sic] 3 hours up to day—we were directing artillery fire & were successful ... we got into a very dense cloud & dived down so as to get our bearings & found ourselves only 2,000 feet over the Hun lines ... we come home with three bullet holes through our plane ... It sure was fine sport & they stand a small chance of hitting us.

On one of his early missions Will survived a crash that shook him badly, making him doubt if he had picked the right occupation:

... the engine began to chug & miss & suddenly stopped ... My pilot did the only thing possible which was a vertical nose dive. I never will forget that dash as long as I live ... in another 10 seconds we would have crashed into the German lines but the pilot brought the nose up & shot over to our lines, and tried to make a landing somewhere but failed ... we crashed into some low trees a mass of wreckage [sic]. The impact dazed me for a moment but I was not hurt except that a branch ran through my coat & scratched my side a little. Some scotties [sic] were close by & helped to get the pilot out from under the crumpled tail. But he was not so lucky as I for he had an arm, a leg & his collar bone broken. It took my nerve completely.

As a newcomer to flying, he described to his family the many sights, sounds, and physical demands of life in the air:

I was up on special patrol for 3 hours & 35 minutes this morning. We flew one which failed through engine trouble & had to land. we got back alright by a long plane & landed well. Not thank goodness ... like the crash I had four weeks ago. We immediately got another machine & went up. We got up to 11,500 feet this time & hovered around for over 3 hours. I nearly froze to death & besides this dizzy height seems to affect one's lungs. I found I had to breathe faster, etc. I can't explain it clearly. We came back to our aerodrome at 9,000 & did a spiral to 1,000. Trouble again—a sudden drop of 8,000 ft. leaves you absolutely deaf. The cure for this is simple—just hold the nose & try to blow. Funny isn't it?

Oxygen starvation (anoxia) due to high altitude was still a novelty for Barker, as was the painful pressure on his eardrums caused by a rapid descent. Oxygen was not available to RFC aircrews in 1916. Experiments conducted by RFC medical officers showed that supplemental oxygen was beneficial above 10,000 feet, and flyers performed better and for a longer period. However, only limited use was made of it by the end of the war.

Barker's aeroplane could not get much higher than 10,000 feet, but flyers of the Great War did without oxygen even above 20,000 feet, but not without serious physical deterioration. Deep-seated fatigue and lassitude were normal post-flight side effects, along with headaches. Men varied in their susceptibility to anoxia, and it was recognized even at the time that good health and fitness improved one's tolerance. The habit of eating only a light breakfast of bread and jam, with tea, or skipping breakfast altogether, actually aggravated the anoxia, and led to hypoglycaemia. Repetitive exposure over many missions forced squadron medical officers to ground flyers that had developed cardiovascular problems.

There was no uniformity of medical opinion as to why flying caused physical deterioration, and why some men eventually had to be grounded, while others seemed immune. However, by the end of the war, the phrases "altitude sickness" or "aviators' disease" had been coined by military doctors, themselves

37

newly labelled as "flight surgeons." Going "stale," the polite word for nervous breakdown also entered the military language.

This peculiar assault on mind and body was something new in warfare. Flying in unheated, open cockpits exposed men to buffeting airstreams, petrol fumes and, in some machines, burnt castor oil that could infect the eyes. Frostbite was a constant risk in minus 40 degree temperatures, and whale oil, fur face masks, and layers of silk, wool, and leather were never sufficient protection. Numbed feet and hands were a constant, and pins-and-needles pain was typical after three-hour missions. Ear infections also went with the job, and men learned that flying with a head cold could cause severe pain, as well as injury to sinuses and ear drums. The noise of the engine and machine guns eventually damaged a man's hearing.

Barker learned quickly, and was already a veteran after only three months. In the ten-day period from 15 to 25 May, he flew about 29 hours, which, according to Will, established a record in the squadron. As he racked up missions, often flying two or three times a day when the weather was good, he became a better judge of the flying ability of his pilots. After only six weeks with 4 Squadron, he was edgy enough to grumble about them. Given the inadequate standard of pilot training in England, this was always a worry among experienced observers who had to coach their pilots on where to go and what to do:

> I am booked for a 5:30 to 8 morning patrol tomorrow. I am a little uneasy for the pilot is a brand new man just out & know[s] very little about flying & less about the country. I tell you I will be mighty glad when my term of observing is up & I learn to pilot myself. I certainly begrudge trusting my neck to some of the bloaks [*sic*] just over.

His mother was wild with anxiety after reading these comments. Realizing that his letters had upset her, Will gave a reassurance worthy of the most muscular Christian of the British Empire:

> Say, mother, you must not worry yourself so much about the war & Percy & I ... It certainly does a fellow good & moreover what else could a young man do now. You don't want to think that he is going, try & think that you are sending him & also that you have sent me to do a Britisher's duty. Isn't that much better ...

Despite the surface jingoism in this letter, Will's intelligence sometimes struggled for supremacy over his patriotism, and it was usually his intelligence that won out. He feared that his brothers might not survive the war on the Western Front. His own duty was clear, but the Barkers had given one soldier for King and Country, and as far as Will was concerned, one was enough. By July 1916, he held few illusions about glory on a modern battlefield, and wrote his mother that Percy must not volunteer for overseas service:

> I think Percy is very foolish if he insists on coming over. It is a terrible grim business & I would like to see him out of it for awhile yet. I was very anxious myself to see the front but I can tell you truthfully I have had enough as far as my curiosity is concerned. But of course am here to see it through to the end ...

Men who served with Barker remembered his unflagging enthusiasm. He appeared to be, and was, a robust, natural warrior. After 10 months of Corps Cooperation, however, Barker's letters home were much darker in tone. In private correspondence he reveals himself as a cautious patriot who did not want his brothers slaughtered on the Western Front. In December 1916 he endorsed his brother's decision to stay in Canada, and continue as an instructor on machine guns:

> You see, Percy, it is like this. I am in it proper now & have settled down to it. Also I have done quite well ... I think you have done the proper thing ... I also want you to keep Cecil where he is. I know exactly what it is like, so exert every influence you can ... I am hardened to it. It is just like going to school—all

BATTLE OF MOUNT SORREL

It was the German assault in the Ypres Salient on Friday, 2 June 1916, that permanently dampened Barker's youthful optimism about war. The troopers of his regiment received the full brunt of a well-planned attack by the 13th Württemberg Corps. The intensity of the opening barrage blew corpses and body parts up into the branches of trees. Hours later, few trees were standing.

After the artillery barrage lifted, four mines were exploded under the CMRs' trenches, and then Bavarian soldiers marched in a slow, deliberate, line-abreast formation, wave on wave across the Ridge. Some carried an evil new weapon of war, the flame thrower. The 1st Battalion, Canadian Mounted Rifles, was wiped out as a fighting unit in its futile attempt to hold a patch of ground called Observatory Ridge.

Only 135 of its 692 officers and men survived the battle. Of the regiment's 21 officers, five were killed, including the commanding officer, five were wounded, and 10 were taken prisoner-of-war. Barker's childhood friend, Duncan Leigh, was blown to pieces that day. Duncan's mother, Clara, never got over the horror that her only son had no known grave.

The commander of the 3rd Canadian Division, Major General Malcolm S. Mercer, was killed that morning, and the head of the 8th Infantry Brigade, Victor Williams, was wounded and captured. It may have been the only occasion when two Canadian generals were casualties on the same day, in the same action. Both generals had been paying a visit to the 8th Brigade when the German artillery opened up with unparalleled intensity at 6:00 a.m.

If he had stayed with the CMR, Will likely would have been killed in the opening barrage, like Duncan, or taken prisoner-of-war. More than 500 Canadians were captured that day. "The Battle of Mount Sorrel," as it was later called, does not evoke, as does Vimy Ridge, any national pride or even a spark of recognition in Canada. It was a bloody rout for the CEF, but only a few historians and the families of the dead even remember it. No romantic painting of the actions of the CMRs on 2 June was ever commissioned.

Recapturing the lost terrain was the first assignment for the new commander of the Canadian Corps, Lieutenant General Sir Julian Byng. By the end of the 12-day battle to regain what was lost, the Canadian Corps had suffered more than 8,000 casualties, and more than 11,000 by the end of June. It was the worst month for the Canadians since the beginning of the Great War.

I do is to study how to kill the most Huns in the quickest way & believe me I have scored enough for one family …

* * *

Fortunately for the Alguire family, Howard was on his first leave in London. The night before the assault, he attended a concert at The Palladium, organized by Arnold Bennett in aid of the Wounded Allies Relief Committee. The following day, while his friends were fighting and dying, he cheerfully bought a ticket for "The Super Cinema," at The Pavilion, Marble Arch, where he watched movie serials featuring Pearl White and Lionel Barrymore, and laughed at Charlie Chaplin's newest comedy.

While Howard was enjoying his well-earned leave, his nephew was in hospital after falling off his horse. Will was abashed at occupying a bed there, as wounded officers from the Battle of Mount Sorrel were brought onto the ward:

Just a few lines to let you know that I am improving rapidly except my back and neck is pretty sore. … I am going to get up for a while to-day & will, I hope, soon be able to go down to the sea. I have not heard from Howard or Duncan yet but expect a letter any day now …

I see where my Regiment C.M.R.s have almost been wiped out. I always knew they would fight like tigers. I see where Colonel Shaw, who recommended me [for the RFC], gathered a company around him & fought to the end. When he was killed a junior officer took his place & died fighting. I do not know how Howard or Duncan are & only got the casuality [sic] list of officers. I only wish I could have been with them on my old machine gun with the Huns in sight ...

Fighting in the air did not seem quite so hazardous after this, and Will was back to flying duties on the eve of the Battle of the Somme. He was a good observer who also asserted himself with confidence. For a junior officer, he was remarkably candid with men who outranked him, a trait that did not enhance his career progression. He believed that accurate information was essential for an army commander, and this could be provided only by aggressive crews flying at low altitude, and prepared to land near units in the field for face-to-face briefings. Some of his pilots did not like Will's taste for low flying. But he was determined to provide the best possible report. If that meant putting himself and his pilot in harm's way, so be it.

His patrols with 4 Squadron in July were filled with action. In the first week, he flew a very long four-and-one-half-hour mission with Lt C.W. Thomas. Although they made it back to the aerodrome, a "missing-in-action, believed killed" message had already been sent to the RFC HQ:

... we got terribly busy & I was straffing [sic] a Hun Battery with a 6 in. How. [howitzer] & time went quickly. At 11:00, two hours later, we were at 8,000 feet & I saw what I thought was a Fokker over on the Hun side. I signalled back & pointed to the supposed Fokker. Lieut Thomas is a very bold & dashing pilot so turned and went for him. I got my two m. guns & over we went ... we dived 2,000 feet at him & only then did I realize that we made a mistake & that it was a Morane monoplane exactly like a Fokker ... Well, on our way back the Huns had about 3 miles of

"Archies" for us to go through, as soon as we turned they started. Crash! Crash! All around us & they soon got so close to us that we had to do something. So down went the nose & we dived for 3,000 feet. Now here was the trouble, some artillery officer saw us dive & I guess never waited to see whether we hit the ground or not but rushed to a phone, called up our major & said —one of your machines hit by shell crashed in flames on German side. The major knew that Thomas & I were the only ones up & as we were then one hour overdue he sent in the report of our fate to H.Q. ... all the officers came out to where we landed & began shaking hands with us ...

I have told you this so that if you hear the report you will know it is wrong. I know you won't worry and you can, but I will look out for No. 1 when possible. Four and a half hours is a long time to be in the air but we had such an exciting time that were only warned when the engine began to miss for want of petrol ... With Love for all. Son. William B.

William B. soon learned that he was not invulnerable when a machine gun bullet went through his leg during a fierce fight. His mother received a cablegram from the War Office stating that he had been hospitalized:

They shouldn't have made such a fuss over my injuries as they did. My left ankle is still very weak but I do more flying than walking so can get along o.k.

I am nearly dizzy from flying & work for we are awfully busy. Yesterday when over the lines at 9,000 feet I saw a Fokker coming over & straightway ... attacked him in the rear. He gave fight & the duel lasted about 5 minutes. we circled round & round & once I was within 80 yards of him. All the time I worked my m. gun like a demon, remedying jams & putting on new drums. Suddenly he turned and planed away to his lines with a dead engine which I must have hit. Our plane was hit in many places & I had

DEVELOPMENT OF THE BE2c MODEL

The biplane Barker flew in was showing its limitations by mid-1916. It was a somewhat more powerful version of a design by Frederick Green and Geoffrey de Havilland that had first flown in 1911. It had been the first aeroplane of the RFC to land in France after the outbreak of war.

According to Cooper, more than 700 BE2c aeroplanes were manufactured just in 1915. This was over 40 percent of England's total aeroplane production for that year. By July 1916, there were about 185 of the BE2 family serving in five RFC Wings in France. There were a total of only 421 aeroplanes distributed in 27 squadrons with the RFC in France on 1 July, and the BE2 was definitely the backbone of Corps Cooperation.

The "c" model had a 90-horsepower, Royal Aircraft Factory (RAF) engine, 20-hp more than the "b" model's Renault. This gave it a cruising speed of about 70 miles per hour. The machine (as aeroplanes were usually called within the RFC) had an empty weight of about 1,370 pounds and, depending on the day and the payload, might take between 45 minutes to one hour to reach 10,000 feet, the service ceiling. The machine's greatest asset was docility. Cecil Lewis described it as a maid of all work, "... a general purpose hack, which could be used for reconnaissance, artillery observation, photography, spy dropping or any other job that turned up ... It was steady, reliable, easy to handle and though, from a pilot's point of view, it left lots to be desired, it was the best thing going at the time."

The BE2c had several improvements, including ailerons on the wings for turning. The BE2a and BE2b employed wing-warping to manoeuvre laterally, just like the Wright Flyer of 1903. A Canadian pilot, Lieut Donald Brophy, liked the "c" model, and wrote in his diary: "The joy of riding in a 2c can't be imagined. One couldn't be more comfortable in an easy chair and it just sails along and doesn't take any notice of bumps ... I let go all the controls and let it fly itself while I surveyed the scenery. Truly a joyous machine ..."

The standard armament was a single Lewis machine gun, using detachable canisters, known as drums, loaded with 47 rounds of .303-calibre ammunition. The Lewis could empty a drum in about five seconds, requiring the observer to detach the empty, and then lock a full drum in place, before re-engaging the target. A larger 97-round drum was developed for exclusive use on the Lewis guns in aircraft.

The stability of the BE2 made it a good photographic platform. The observer sat in the front cockpit and the pilot in the rear. Later designs, the RE8 and F2B, reversed this, and observer in the rear cockpit became the standard. The front cockpit of the BE2 was a miserable place from which to fight, with the observer virtually inside a cage of struts and wires. Due to the limited field of fire, and the risk of shooting the propeller to pieces, the BE2 pilot was forced to manoeuvre crab-like to fight another aircraft.

Any flying machine that cruises at only 70 mph will be much affected by winds. Throughout the war, RFC pilots had to contend with the prevailing westerly winds which pushed their aircraft into enemy-held territory, and made the return journey to the home aerodrome sometimes excruciatingly long. Barker's experience was typical:

It has been terribly windy lately. This morning I went up on artillery patrol and we had a hard time getting back. At 6,000 feet we had our engine running out at 1,600 revolutions per minute & we were not moving. So we dived down to 1,200 feet & came home. we had to land against the wind with the engine on. Men were ready for us & we no more than touched the ground when they clinched the wings to hold it down. It sure was rough business but we got down o.k. Our engine ran perfect & believe me I was glad, for engine failure here would have meant a forced landing in Germany.

the armpit of my leather coat shot away but was not touched. It was a fight I will never forget but am sorry to say that I could [not] bring him down in flames or meet [*sic*] him out some such fate. However, better luck next time.

There is no mention in the RFC communiqué for 11 July 1916 of Barker's aerial fight. Impressive though it was to his mother, it probably left the Intelligence Officer (IO) unmoved. Without corroboration, the IO perhaps decided against the claim in the squadron's daily action report. One of his jobs was to separate the facts from the conjecture, and disallow exaggerated claims before Wing HQ looked at them. Neither Barker nor his pilot received a "driven down" credit for their fight with the Fokker monoplane.

Will drove off German aircraft quite a few times while serving as an observer. However, none of these actions would have qualified as formal claims of victory, unless,

a. the aircraft was destroyed in the air; or
b. crash landed or force landed; or
c. was captured; or
d. driven down out of control (DDOOC).

These were the four categories recognized by the RFC by 1916, although in the early days of the war, claims had been approved for simply driving down an enemy machine. Barker's surviving letters (with one exception) mention no victories, and the records from 4 and 15 Squadrons do not confirm any.

However, some historians have credited him with at least two before becoming a pilot—a Roland machine on 20 July over Miraumont, and a second Roland on 15 August near Achiet le Grand. A communiqué on 23 March 1917 may also have credited Barker, by then a pilot, with a crashed Fokker near Cambrai.

Typical of the air fights between German scout and BE2 is a 15 Squadron combat report for 16 September 1916 signed by Lieutenant G.R. Travis. He and Barker encountered a hostile aircraft over Miraumont at 4,500 feet:

Biplane FOKKER. Tractor. Rotary Engine. Very fast.

While dropping Bombs on Miraumont we were attacked by [Fokker] machine from above.

H.A. fired about 50 rounds, we turned round sharply and gave him one drum from rear Lewis Gun. Tracers seen to hit H.A.'s engine.

He immediately turned and made off in direction of Bapaume.

*   *   *

By the end of the war, Barker's victory record was 50 hostile machines and kite balloons, but this total does not include any of his actions as a Corps Cooperation observer and pilot. Nevertheless, he sometimes is credited with 52, presumably for the unconfirmed claims while with 15 Squadron.

The Corps Cooperation squadrons during the Battle of the Somme suffered increasing casualties. Will witnessed several losses due to enemy action. On 16 July, he saw Capt A.J. Evans and Lieut H.O. Long of 3 Squadron shot down early in the morning. Both men survived their crash landing, but were taken prisoners-of-war.

He lost two of his best friends in an enemy attack over Contalmaison on 20 July. 2nd Lieut G.V. Randall, the pilot, was killed by a bullet in the head, and 2nd Lieut G.M. Angier, the observer, was pulled from the wreckage by British troops, suffering from shock. The following day Will attended the funeral of two more officers whose machine had been hit by a British artillery shell in flight.

Sometime during the third week of July, Barker was transferred from 4 to 15 Squadron, both units being part of III (Corps) Wing. As part of the expansion phase leading to the Battle of the Somme, the RFC had formed into four Brigades consisting of an Army and a Corps wing, plus supporting units. III (Corps) Wing, with four squadrons (3, 4, 9, and 15), was teamed with 14 (Army) Wing. The Corps flyers were frequently protected from German scout attacks by the Army scouts of 22 and 24 Squadrons, the latter commanded by Major Lanoe Hawker, VC, DSO. III and 14 Wings reported to IV Brigade, RFC, and were attached to the Fourth Army commanded by General Sir Henry Rawlinson.

Fifteen Squadron was to be Barker's operational home for more than a year, until August 1917, and he became one of the squadron's most accomplished and famous airmen. It was stationed at Marieux, about 10 miles northwest of Baizieux, on the road between Albert and Doullens, and was commanded by Major H. le M. Brock. Barker served in C Flight under Capt W.G. Pender.

From late July through to December, Barker saw his unit lose more than 20 of its pilots and observers—killed, wounded, or taken prisoners-of-war. This was not exceptional, and other squadrons suffered worse, often exceeding 100 percent turnover in two or three months. According to Jones there were more than 400 RFC aircrews lost in the four-and-a-half-month Somme campaign: 308 pilots and 109 observers killed, wounded or missing. There were almost twice as many flying machines lost: 190 went missing, and 592 were written off in various ways. Wise places the total RFC casualties between June and December at 583, most of these on the Somme.

Crashes during operations were frequent. Barker himself was involved in at least three or four as an observer or pilot. Due to the slow landing speed of the BE2, men survived with only cuts and bruises, but not always. The paramount fear among all First World War flyers was death by fire. It horrified even the most war-like. Barker saw dozens of men burned to death during the war, and never became hardened to it.

Like all combatants he was haunted by death. He even photographed the bodies of dead soldiers lying on the battlefield at Beaumont Hamel, and sent the pictures to his family. One photo that has survived shows a Highland soldier with a letter, presumably from his family, next to his body. But Barker never sent home pictures of burnt flyers:

... we have also suffered casualities [sic], 3 officers killed, 2 missing, & two burned to death. This was a very sad accident. They left the ground & when about 200 feet up their engine failed & in trying to get back to the aerodrome they side slipped & nose dived to earth. The plane then caught fire & although they were alive we could not save them. Forty gals. of Gasoline makes some fire. I have seen some awful things happen but I think this is the worst. One, Lieut Laird had just mailed a letter to his mother saying that he would be home on leave in a few days & he was dead within a few minutes. It will be a shock to her. I always seem to get the weird & sad job of writing to relatives killed here & am going to stop. A person doesn't know what it is like until they have tried it several times ...

2nd Lieut Andrew C. Laird was an observer like Barker, aged 22, while the pilot, 2nd Lieut Philip Haarer, was 20.

Despite his private misgivings about the war, Barker boasted to his family that the Battle of the Somme was a major success for the BEF:

We are doing wonderful over here. The Huns haven't a look in. We are absolutely supreme in the air, our artillery is much better & our infantry never fail to take their objectives so all goes well here. During a great battle to-day [26 Sept] in which was captured miles of Hun positions & several villages our aircraft done splendid [sic] ...

But by late 1916 he had made a pessimistic forecast to his mother that the war might not end till the spring of 1918.

Exhaustion gradually wore down even the most robust characters on a flying squadron. Some men found themselves on the Channel boat back to England only weeks after joining their unit, their nerves and self-esteem shattered. Others were amazingly resilient, but everyone had a limit. Barker's nerves were becoming a little frayed by late summer, but his experience was invaluable, and he was given more responsibility in the squadron.

His convivial nature and organizational skills made him a good choice for duties other than that of flight commander, a position to which only pilots could be appointed. He became 15 Squadron's

ARTILLERY COOPERATION

More than half of Will's operational flying was in support of artillery. As an observer, he was the eyes of the artillery batteries on the ground, helping them range in accurately on enemy targets. He had to see where artillery shells fell in relation to a target, and then transmit by wireless the impact point so that gun batteries could make adjustments for errors. The biggest obstacle to any successful "shoot" was communicating correct information quickly. To efficiently destroy targets, flyers and artillery gunners had to have a common language.

RFC officers developed large-scale maps of France and Belgium organized in rectangular grids. They also designed a circular, celluloid disc inscribed with range circles and clock positions that could be placed on top of a position on the map. The inner range circle inscribed on the transparent disc was designated by the letter "Y," and represented 10 yards from the centre of the circle. The next circle was "Z," representing 25 yards from the centre, and in succession were circles "A," representing 50 yards; "B"-100 yards; "C"-200 yards; "D"-300 yards; "E"-400 yards, and "F" -500 yards.

The 12 o'clock position marked on the transparent disc represented magnetic North, with 3 o'clock being East, 6 o'clock being South, and 9 o'clock being West. The combination of eight concentric circles for range, and 12 lines for the cardinal points of a clock, provided an accurate overlay for pinpointing. The maps of France and Belgium used by aviators and artillery batteries were numbered in sequence, and each rectangular map represented a piece of land 22,000 by 36,000 yards. This map was itself divided into 24 squares designated from A to Z, each square representing a 5,000-by-6,000-yard chunk of terrain. Each of these chunks was further divided into 36 squares, and then further sub-divided into four squares with the letter a, b, c, or d attached. The smallest of these squares was finely segmented into a grid numbered vertically and horizontally from 0 at the bottom left, or southwest corner, to 9 at the northwest or southeast corners.

This grid-system was essential, providing the gunners and the airmen with a common map-reference system. With practice, pinpointing a location was not too difficult. A sequence of numbers and letters, tapped out with a wireless key in the cockpit, described the specific square or rectangle within each map segment, right down to a patch of ground a few yards square. This method of pinpointing or "registering," as it was then called, worked surprisingly well.

If a Corps Cooperation crew saw a column of troops marching east along a road, the observer might send the following message to the closest artillery battery: "500-fan-e-28-M-27-d-6-7." This translated to: "500 infantry going east on Sheet 28; Square M; Sub-square 27; Quarter-sheet d; at a pinpoint 300 yards southeast of the zero reference mark, and 420 yards north."

Most airmen had little difficulty in learning the basic principles, but applying them in the air was still a challenge. Much practice was needed to observe accurately from a moving aeroplane, map read carefully to determine precise location, and then transmit quickly using a wireless key. Moreover, all this observation and calculation had to be done within the range of anti-aircraft guns, in windy, bumpy conditions, often in restricted visibility, and with an eye peeled for hostile aircraft. Performing consistently in such conditions was not only exhausting, but also hard on the nerves.

This particular work was rated so important within the BEF that, by mid-1916, the Corps Cooperation squadrons of the RFC were devoting about two thirds of their resources to "shoots." Barker later remembered his aerial assistance to the artillery of the BEF with pride. Ten years after the war, he remarked that nothing compared with the sheer god-like power of directing artillery fire onto an enemy gun emplacement, or column of infantry.

Barker's letters during the Somme campaign sometimes closed with a comment like: "I have some important work & important positions to study. We are all awfully busy ..." By September he was an old hand at artillery coopera-tion: "The days are getting shorter now & we seldom fly before 6 a.m. This morning at 6:15 I was ranging two of our heaviest Hows [howitzers] on a redoubt. Early bird Eh?"

Contrary to movie legend, pilots and observers did not spend every evening eating, drinking, and flirting with pretty French women in cafes. When possible, observers visited or telephoned the battery commander to discuss the next day's operation. What were the objectives for the shoot? Did the commander want to register the target or destroy it? What kind of shell was the battery using? What was the allotment of shells, and what was the time of flight of those shells? If more than one target was being engaged, in what order did the commander want them engaged, and what interval did he want between corrections and the next order to fire? To be any good at artillery cooperation, evening study before a pre-dawn flight was essential.

Artillery shoots were flown at relatively low altitudes, typically 3,000 to 6,000 feet above ground. Over the target area, the observer unwound the communication antenna from the drum. It was a 100-foot length of copper wire with a lead weight on the end, rather like the weight on a fishing line, trailing below and behind the tail of the aircraft. This antenna had to be rewound if under aerial attack and, of course, prior to landing (although crews did sometimes forget). The observer identified himself to the battery by code (Barker's call sign at the time was R32). The battery signalled when ready to proceed.

Many factors could limit the success of a shoot: equipment failures; lack of proficiency; mistaken identification of targets; anti-aircraft fire; attacks by hostile aircraft; and so on. Barker lectured at the RAF Staff College in 1925 about these limitations. He believed that the suppression of enemy anti-aircraft artillery was crucial:

> I am convinced that in the future if army co-operation machines are to carry out their duties efficiently, some provision of this kind must be made in order to reduce anti-aircraft fire ... It is no secret that during the war, many shoots, owing to interference of anti-aircraft fire, were not as successful as they should have been. At one period many shoots were done from our side of the lines, which of course cannot result in the same success as if done from over the target.

To protect his machine while on a shoot, Barker got into the habit of asking for suppressing fire from the artillery batteries with which he worked:

> In 1916 and the spring of 1917, enemy anti-aircraft guns became quite numerous and very accurate. They were furnished with excellent targets, for our machines were very slow and were compelled by the nature of their duties to remain over the lines at a height which provided perfect range.
>
> I recommended a plan whereby every machine on Artillery Observation would also observe for a section of 60 pounders against active anti-aircraft guns. For some reason or other this was frowned upon. However, I was able to make arrangements with one of these 60 pounder batteries to always have a section stand by during my flights.

In addition to artillery support, the first close coordination between the RFC and the British Army formations on the ground was during the Battle of the Somme. These missions were called contact patrols. Troops worked with aircraft, passing along status reports so commanders knew what was happening in the front lines. The information provided to ground commanders was meant to dispel some of the fog of war, but it was not always accurate, and was not always acted upon. Barker was enthusiastic about contact work, but it was difficult to do well, as he later recalled:

> ... no sure method has been devised which will enable pilots to distinguish enemy from friend ... during the war the flare, which gave the most promise, proved absolutely unsatisfactory and at times very misleading; for instance, I have had them ignited in our reserve and support lines, and on two occasions by the enemy... as a rule our troops would not show them [flares] because it meant giving their position away, with the natural result that they would be promptly shelled ... white oil-cloth sheets, etc., which in theory were to be displayed by the infantry, were a failure. If once displayed, these were usually left behind, causing confusion ... tin sheets attached to the troops' packs could not be seen ...

45

Intelligence Officer in August, a challenging secondary duty: "I have to know everything of our army & supposed to know a lot about the Hun army regiments before us, etc. also make out all reports as to enemy movements, etc. & send them in. It sure is a busy job."

On 27 August he was given permission to wear the single-wing observer's badge above his left pocket. He already had six months of field service as an observer, so the wing with the "O" (nicknamed by RFC flyers as "the flying asshole") conferred no special status. Even so, Barker had his picture taken, and sent a photo postcard home for publication in the local Dauphin newspaper.

He was devastated only two days later to see a good friend killed in action, while powerless to do anything:

A pretty sad thing has just happened. An officer, Lieut Burleigh that I generally fly with was killed yesterday. Lieut Harry a new observer went up with him as I was busy breaking in a new pilot. I was in the air at the time & saw the fight. 4 Fokkers attacked him by surprise & killed him instantly. I immediately dived & shot one down but too late for I saw him crash to earth on our front line vertically with the engine on from 5,000 feet. It made me sick to see it. My Hun planed back to his lines & also crashed.

The infantry pulled them into the trenches but they were dead. Their engine alone went 4 feet into the ground. I went up last night to the trenches & got all his valuables from his pockets & am sending them home. You know I had agreed only a few days back that if anything was to happen I would write his mother. This I am doing ...

It would seem that the shock of seeing Burleigh's crushed body drove Will to claim that he had avenged his death, which was not true. Will may have fired at the Fokker scout with his Lewis gun, but he did not shoot it down.

The hostile machine that had shot down Burleigh was attacked by a DH2 scout of 24 Squadron.

2nd Lieut A.E. Glew was credited with driving the German pilot down out of control. All four Fokker D.I and D.II scouts were part of a newly formed German unit, Jasta 1. Its records show no losses that day, but one of its pilots, Oberleutnant (1st Lieutenant) Hans Bethge, claimed the BE2c as a victory, the second for this new German fighting squadron.

Robert Burleigh, formerly of the Royal Engineers, was one of four sons of a war correspondent, the late Bennet Burleigh. Robert's brother, also named Bennet, had died of wounds received at Gallipoli. The two other brothers were serving in the Army. In Will's letter to Robert's mother, he wrote:

Robert and I flew together until a few days ago when he was given a different observer. I have done many hours in the air with him. Day after day we carried on our work, and I never saw him anything but cheerful. One day not long ago he fought single-handed six Huns when over on photography, and although his plane was badly hit, he landed perfectly. Robert was a true Britisher through and through. He accomplished feats in the air which Huns cannot understand possible; deeds which have given us command of the air. I have seen his grave, and when on leave I will give you one of my maps with the position marked.

* * *

The month of September was frenzied for the RFC flyers, and Friday, 15 September, has been credited by historians as the busiest day in the history of the Corps, to that point in the war. The day was also marked by the assault at Flers-Courcelette, the first use of tanks in the war, and the first action of the CMR Battalions on the Somme front. Barker watched his former CEF battalion advance to take Mouquet Farm, and saw other Canadian units capture Courcelette.

Sunday, 17 September, marked a turning point in air superiority over the Somme. The RFC lost several machines to a brilliant German tactician, Hauptmann (Captain) Oswald Boelcke, leading his new scout squadron from their aerodrome at Lagnicourt.

BE2 flying by the mill at Franvillers, 25 August 1916.

Ronald V. Dodds collection

On the previous day they had received their first six new Albatros D.I aircraft, a well-armed, sleek-looking machine powered by a 160-hp Mercedes engine.

Boelcke was an outstanding teacher for his fellow-pilots, which included a newcomer that he had personally selected, Manfred von Richthofen. Richthofen scored his first of 80 victories on that Sunday, killing the crew of an FE2b from 11 Squadron, 2nd Lieut L.B. Morris and Lieut T. Rees. Fortunately for the RFC, Boelcke was killed in a mid-air collision in October. But his tactical doctrine laid the groundwork for a new kind of German fighting pilot, one who was professional, prudent, and dangerous.

Will must have wondered if he was going to survive his first operational tour, between the new German Albatros scouts, and vicious anti-aircraft guns:

I have had awful luck lately but have been very lucky. Yesterday [20 October] I was up doing a shoot with a 12. in. Batty [battery] and when returning our engine failed & we crashed into a bank. Our machine was absolutely smashed to pieces. I was badly bruised but was able to fly to-day & have just had if anything a worse time. We were coming about 5 miles over when two shells burst right on us one on our tail & one just over us. Putting in all 36 holes through us, stopping the engine, punctured the tank I sit on & shot away our lateral controls & the plane almost got out of control. However, we done pretty good but could not land so turned over in a field. I have had just about enough of it now & am soon going to apply for a sick leave if I don't soon go back to England.

A shrewd squadron commander could extend the operational usefulness of a pilot or observer by granting a long weekend, an overnight ferry flight, or a seven-day pass. Six months was considered the limit for most, qualifying one for a tour as an instructor, or easier flying with a home-defence squadron.

For those waiting to be sent home—the short-timers—the strain was excruciating. By November, Barker was the senior observer of commissioned rank on squadron. He needed a rest, and told his parents

that he envied Uncle Howard, who had a "blighty"—a wound not life threatening, but bad enough to spend time in hospital: "So you have heard that Howard was wounded. However, you need not worry for he is not seriously wounded & as you say he will be away from this awful strife for awhile. Personally, I think he is lucky. I know if I ever can get it not too hard I will not grouse."

Barker was called in to Major Brock's office on 8 November, and told he was being recommended for pilot training. He was being sent back to England, to "Home Establishment," as it was called, by Christmas:

He told me this after an unusually successful day for me. I was only out of the air for 2 hours that day & that was just for lunch & a little rest from the strain. During my days flying I ranged 7 siege [sic] batteries on Hun trenches & batteries & had one fight with the latest & fastest little machine I ever saw. He punched us full of holes but I got one good burst on him which apparently put him out of control & I last saw him diving vertically & disappear below the clouds.

Contrary to the prevalent belief at the time, bad nerves were not confined to only the high-strung people of poor breeding. In fact, many of the most accomplished flyers suffered all the more because of the demands put on them to set an example. Heroes like Lanoe Hawker, James T.B. McCudden, Edward "Mick" Mannock, and Albert Ball all wrote candidly to their families about their frayed nerves. The knowledge that weaker souls were being sent home short of six months service gave rise to outbursts, if only in letters and diaries. This is how Lieut Donald Brophy expressed himself:

Another youth is being put in for "special leave" ahead of Watkins and me as his nerves are reported 2nd class type. He has only been out four months and has not done nearly so much work as either of us. We are considering the advisability of returning, after a trip over the lines, trembling in every limb and weeping copiously and mayhap, I say mayhap, we'll get some leave *aussi* ...

After Burleigh's death in August, Barker had flown many of his missions in September and October with his flight commander, Capt W.G. Pender. He saved his life during a mission in early November, after Pender lost consciousness in the air. They were on a low-level reconnaissance to check out enemy barbed wire and trench conditions:

I flew low & got the required information & also got 62 m. gun holes through our plane. However, I am as lucky as ever & was not touched but we were not to get away untouched for just as we were leaving several m.g.s started & I felt the plane give a sudden lurch. Instinctively, I took the controls & upon looking around saw the pilot was mighty pale. He signalled that he was hit but seemed all right at the time. However, a few minutes later he fainted so I took control and landed the plane on the aerodrome without crashing. In the meantime I had called for a doctor by wireless & we soon had medical aid. My plane is fitted with dual controls & I can fly fine.

* * *

Barker had received unofficial flying lessons, probably from a Canadian pilot, Lieut A.V. "Paddy" Acland. Other observers in the RFC had saved the aircraft after their pilot was incapacitated or killed, and occasionally medals were awarded. It was not very easy for observers to win gallantry medals, but Will greatly coveted the Military Cross. He had received verbal praise for work done, and that was fine, but he wanted the white and purple ribbon of the MC on his chest. In the last gasps of the Somme campaign, during particularly fierce ground fighting, Barker got his chance.

David Mackenzie collection

A page from Barker's personal photo album showing a corpse photographed by Barker on the Beaumont Hamel battlefield; an airman's grave in Italy, perhaps that of Major A.M. Vaucour; and a photo of Robert Burleigh's brother, Jimmy, killed on 01 July 1916.

One of the BEF goals, before winter set in, was to take the fortified village of Beaumont Hamel, which had previously been unsuccessfully attacked on 1 July, with horrific losses, in particular to the Newfoundland Regiment. The village had more symbolic than tactical value. It may have been attacked simply to provide a modest success for Haig, in an otherwise grim campaign which had so little to show for 420,000 British Empire casualties. Taking the village provided a token success for the forthcoming Paris Conference of Allied leaders.

Will sat in his hut, writing a letter to his mother, on the night before the offensive, wondering if this might be one mission too many:

> A mighty battle is coming off to-morrow. The enormous guns are now cannonading & preparing the way for our infantry. I have a rather serious job on. My job is to fly at 500 ft. to 1,000 feet & keep the Generals of the divisions informed of enemy movements, counter attacks, etc. also to let them know where our own infantry are so our barrage can conform. It is mighty serious work to go up there & send down reports which mean so much. Consequently I fly so low that I almost touch the ground for no report that I send in is any other than what I see with my own eyes.

It was this contact patrol that elevated Barker from competent to heroic. He was to win many more gallantry awards for grace under fire, but none would have the feel of this first medal. After the mission was a memory, and he was safe on the ground, he boasted:

> I was flying with my flight commander during this last great push & I must admit that it was almost a case of bullets or medals. However, we both have been decorated with the M.C. for our work ... I will be some nut now with my decoration up. Eh?
>
> Well at all costs I am awfully glad that I am going back to the home establishment for

awhile. I have been receiving congratulations from every side all day, so am pleased with life in general.

The *London Gazette* published the citation for Barker's first of nine medals on 10 January 1917:

> His Majesty the King has been graciously pleased to confer the Military Cross on the undermentioned officer in recognition of his gallantry and devotion to duty in the Field:-
>
> Temporary 2nd Lieutenant William George Barker, General List and R.F.C.
>
> For conspicuous gallantry in action. He flew at a height of 500 feet over the enemy's lines, and brought back most valuable information. On another occasion after driving off two hostile machines, he carried out an excellent photographic reconnaissance.

Major Brock did not assign Barker any further operational missions after his recommendation for the MC. Brock himself was due for promotion, and left 15 Squadron a couple of weeks after Barker. As promised, he recommended him for pilot training, and Will was posted on 9 December to 8 Reserve Squadron. Greatly relieved to be getting leave, his first in 14 months, Will wrote Percy from the British Officer's Club in Boulogne, enroute to England: "I am going to learn to fly a very fast (130 m.p.h.) little fighter single seater scout & will then come out again to create what havoc I can." But the RFC had no intention of losing his talents as a Corps Cooperation airman. He would not get to create havoc on scouts for quite a while. In the meantime, he had the rest of December off in London, and was welcomed into the home of the Burleigh family at 19 Glyn Mansions, Avonmoor Road.

Barker had left Manitoba hoping to make a name for himself, as well as serve his country. This he had done. His home town newspaper learned of his decoration, and ran the following story:

DAUPHIN BOY DECORATED

Word has been received that our townsman, Lieut Wm. G. Barker, M.C., of the Royal Flying Corps, has been decorated with the Military Cross which is only given to those who distinguish themselves in action. The work for which the Lieutenant received the coveted decoration was performed during the battle preceding the capture of Beaumont Hamel. During that engagement Lieut Barker was engaged in contact work between the infantry and the generals commanding. The danger lies in whether one flies high or low, and he flew on that day in the execution of his duty at the dangerously low altitude of between 300 and 200 feet. Lieut Barker is at present in England and he expects to obtain a pilot's certificate before returning to France or elsewhere. Will has a host of friends in Dauphin, where he has lived all his life, and his schoolmates, with whom he was a great favourite, and others, will be delighted to hear of his getting the coveted decoration. But—well, Will was always plucky.

Barker in the back seat of BE2 in November 1916.

David Mackenzie collection

Barker sitting in the rear cockpit of a BE2 Corps Cooperation aircraft; a post card sent to his high school sweetheart Mabel Buchannon.

CHAPTER FOUR

A PILOT AT LAST

"I expect to go to France next week as a full blown pilot. I have turned out ... a stunt pilot or at least they tell me so. I fly a very sensitive fast biplane here & when I go up everybody turns out to see the fun ... I do all kinds of stunts on it. I looped 7 times this afternoon then some tail slides & ended up with a very steep spiral."

LIEUT. W.G. BARKER, MC, BEVERLEY, YORKSHIRE, FEBRUARY 1917

Barker wanted to go home to Canada to see his family, and requested leave from RFC Headquarters in London. To cross the Atlantic by ship, travel by train 2,000 miles, and return he needed at least five or six weeks, but was granted only two. Canadian flyers in the RFC normally did not get leave to go home unless there was a death in the family, or if they were recovering from serious wounds. Will's consolation was Christmas with the Burleigh family:

Mrs. Burleigh … was bound that I would stay here & I am only too glad to. I pay the ordinary lodging fee & in most cases have luncheon & dinner out down town. I like these people fine. They are a real good old English family … [Mrs. Burleigh] has had awful bad luck. Lost her husband & two sons in this war so far. The youngest Lt. Burleigh has just arrived home from Salonica & Egypt & we have a great time together … as he knows the place well we get on fine. He is also going in for a pilot's certificate.

Will welcomed a fellow soldier with whom to see the sights because the streets of London were a little disorienting after months of action. The proximity of the front lines to England, family, and safety was hard to comprehend, and the scant distance between home and hell seemed absurd. An aviator on patrol at dawn, might, that same night, eat a meal in a London restaurant.

Flying east towards the German front lines at 15,000 feet he could, on a clear day, see the British coast on his left, and had only to turn his head to take in the Swiss Alps on the far horizon.

Proximity to home only increased the loneliness. Diaries, letters, literature, and poetry, all spoke to or about the vast gulf between civilians and warriors. As Fussell has articulated, the experience of war also generated a feeling of irony in fighting men that was more intensely felt at home than at the front. Talking about the experience to relatives and friends was difficult, and most never even tried. The patriotic fervour of civilians was usually unsettling to soldiers and airmen who knew the reality of France and Belgium.

The aviator not only felt the alienation that other fighting men experienced, but also had to adjust to the adulation accorded that rare individual who did his fighting in the skies above, rather than in the mud below. As Cecil Lewis recalled: "… to belong to the R.F.C. in those days was to be singled out among the rest of the khaki-clad world by reason of the striking double-breasted tunic, the Wings, the little forage cap set over one ear, but more than this by the glamour surrounding the 'birdmen.' "

Will liked the attention as he walked around London, and very soon had the ribbon of his MC sewed on his tunic, and photographs taken for his family. It was fun being a tourist in the big city, but, having waited so long, he was impatient to start pilot training. While waiting, he spent some time in the Members Gallery of the House of Commons during a post-election address by the Prime Minister. He liked what he saw and heard of Lloyd George: "I can tell you frankly that I believe he will save this nation & I believe if he remains in power & we put all our effort forward until 1918 'spring' we will beat them. I for one will be terribly disappointed if they patch up a peace. I know we can win if we only stay with it to the end."

Barker was ordered to report to Netheravon aerodrome on Salisbury Plain on Friday, 12 January, and he drove the 100 miles from London on a motorcycle borrowed from a friend. He wrote his mother that the trip had taken him four hours and 20 minutes, including his stop for lunch.

Before many days had passed he was the talk of the school because of his rapid progress. The name of his instructor is not known, but Will's dual training took place on the S11 Farman "Shorthorn," serial numbers A2472 and/or A2522. He is believed to have soloed after only two dual trips, one of 50 minutes, and one of five minutes.

Barker was a phenomenon, that exceptional student who could surpass in ability even the most experienced instructors. By the time he finished his training he had been nicknamed "Slippery Bill," because of his natural ability in aerobatics. He wrapped up his entire course in only six weeks, less than half the usual time. His flying talent seems even to have surprised himself, and he was pleased to gain the notice for which he had often hungered as a CMR trooper:

I did 4 flights today & 7 landings in the neighbouring fields. my first landing was rather poor & I broke two wires but made such progress that I am counted a star & will not be here long ... This [is] a rotten place. I am in an old tin hut & our mess is also rotten & very dear. I will soon be going for higher instruction somewhere else & hope to strike a better place ... Remember me to everybody for I am too busy to write.

By 18 January he had already completed his *ab initio* training, and was boasting to his family:

Well I have good news for you. I succeeded in taking my ticket to-day & instead of my observer's wing I now wear the [double] wings for I am now a pilot. I made 16 flights to-day all alone without mishap. My first landing was a bit bumpy but I am doing well now. I climbed up to 3000 feet & did some pretty lively stunts & then came down in a spiral. I am through with this place now & go to some aerodrome ... to fly faster machines.

It was likely the Royal Aero Club certificate which Barker received at this time. His service records indicate he was graded as a "Flying Officer" on 14 February, not 18 January.

Flying instruction was at the time divided in two phases and organizations: elementary training squadrons and higher training squadrons—both called Reserve Squadrons. Barker passed through 8, 37, and 36 Reserve Squadrons, as well as the School of Military Aeronautics at the University of Oxford.

In the days before lesson plans and structured syllabus, a typical dual instructional flight rarely exceeded 50 minutes, and many flights were 20 minutes or less. Learning was more by osmosis or intuition, than through explanation, demonstration, imitation, and correction.

Many flying instructors in the RFC viewed their job as tedious, nerve-wracking, and hazardous. Often they were posted to training units to settle their nerves after combat. Understandably, it seldom had the desired effect. Since few had any background in teaching, the calibre of instruction varied from reasonable to awful. Instructors sometimes refused to let their students handle the controls, or constantly overrode them in their faltering attempts to learn. It was common for the students to study together after hours to overcome the deficiencies of their short-tempered teachers.

Talented men like Barker suffered less from poor instruction, but more sensitive students were badly served, often learning to fly in spite of, rather than because of their instructor. A belief held by many instructors was that a couple of accidents were a positive learning experience, and a good measure of the

Flying Training
Aircraft in the RFC

Elementary training squadrons used the Farman "Longhorn" and "Shorthorn," a so-called pusher design of the three Farman brothers, Henri, Maurice, and Dick. The Farman trainers had been invented and manufactured in France, but were also built under licence in England. The biplanes looked a bit strange, even by the diverse aerodynamic standards of the day.

The S7 "Longhorn" was delicate, stately, and docile, with a speed range of only 15-20 mph between stalling and maximum velocity. By 1917 it was being phased out in favour of the slightly more advanced and conventional S11 "Shorthorn," and this is what Barker first learned to fly. Its elevator controls were attached to a single tailplane, and the "longhorn" skids, so conspicuous on the S7, were cut back to short stumps. The Renault eight-cylinder engine behind the cockpit turned a propeller at about 1,200 rpm.

Fitted with a camera and machine gun, the "Shorthorn" had served as a reconnaissance aircraft in France, as late as 1916. By 1918 the "Shorthorn" had largely been replaced by the Avro 504, which was Will's second training aircraft. Earlier in the war, the 504 had flown on operations, with the RNAS at Dunkirk. It had a rotary engine, in front of the pilot, making the Avro a so-called tractor design as opposed to the pusher configuration of the Farman, with its engine and propeller behind the cockpit.

The 504 was docile enough for a student pilot to master, but capable of performing many of the same aerobatics as a front-line scout. It made a very good transition aircraft to operational machines because of its rotary engine. The 504's propeller was attached to the crankcase of the engine, and the crankshaft to the aircraft frame, and the entire engine and propeller rotated as a unit, just as in the Sopwith Pup, Camel, and Triplane. In Canada, the RFC students were trained exclusively on the Curtiss JN4 with an in-line engine, and had no opportunity to fly rotary-engined machines, requiring a transition course after arriving in the UK.

stoutness of the student's nerves. The testing standard was not that rigorous, and passing the ground school examinations at Oxford was not considered a great challenge by most.

Accidents were frequent, and the attrition from ground school through to combat could be high. John M. Grider, an American from San Souci, Arkansas, was in a class of 210 US pilots. He was immortalized after the war by Elliott Springs in *War Birds—Diary of an Unknown Aviator*.

According to Springs, 21 Americans in the class of 210 died in training accidents; 25 were killed in operations; 14 were wounded; 14 became prisoners of war; and 16 were injured in crashes. In addition, 20 were assessed mentally unfit for flying before finishing their training, making 110 of the 210 casualties or wash-outs in just over a year. Grider's contempt for those who washed out of training (at least as Springs portrayed it in *War Birds*) was typical

of young men of his generation: "About ten of the boys have given it up and just quit flying. No nerve. They never should have enlisted if they didn't intend to see it thru after they found out it was dangerous. Jeff Dwyer gets them jobs at Headquarters or puts them in charge of mechanics. But yellow is yellow whether you call it nerves or not. I'm just as scared sometimes as any of them."

After a few hours building up time on the 504, Will was posted to 37 Reserve Squadron on 1 February for advanced training. The unit was equipped with the BE2c, and its single-seater version, the BE12, divided into two flights, each with nine aircraft and five flying instructors. According to his service records, he logged time not only in the BE2c, but also several other types, including an hour or two in a Morane; the FE2b; de Havilland DH2 and DH4; Bristol Scout; Armstrong Whitworth; Sopwith Pup; and Nieuport.

In an amazing demonstration of his talent, intelligence, and focus, Will wrapped up not only his advanced flight training, but also his ground school training at Christ Church College, Oxford, in just three weeks. The normal duration of ground school alone at the School of Military Aeronautics was six weeks, but Barker successfully passed every examination in less than a week. He boasted to his mother:

I am afraid you will be worrying about me. It has been impossible for me to write as I have been on the move. I went to Oxford & in 4 days I passed & graduated in all the written exams which as a rule take 2 months. 600 officers are down there now on this course. But some hard work on my part & my flying experience put me through ... I am now in a Zeppelin straffing [sic] squadron & if I ever get a chance you will hear of me. I have had several practice night flights so know my job ... I am well & in much better health than when I left France.

There were no German bombing raids in February by Zeppelin airships anywhere in the vicinity of 37 Reserve Squadron. But because most of the raids took place at night, all the Home Defence pilots practised night flying. They relied on the rudimentary cockpit instruments and lighting in the BE2c, and flares to light the aerodrome landing area. Even Barker found this training nerve-wracking:

I have broken all records in flying. It has only taken me 3 weeks to get my pilot's certificate. I am going to do night flying to-morrow night. It is very difficult taking a machine off the ground flying them & then the most difficult manoeuvre is to make A landing by aid of flares for misjudgement in landing is rather dangerous ... A very sad accident happened here to day. A fellow who was trying for his pilot's certificate got into a spinning nose dive & crashed from 500 feet. On crashing the petrol caught on fire & he was burned to death. I have seen about 9 go like this since I started flying in England.

He told his mother that flying was going to be his life after the war. He reminded her of Lincoln Beachey's stunts at the Winnipeg Exhibition:

Well, I am now a fully qualified pilot & today I was flying an American machine, a Curtiss, & I thought as I flew of how I used to watch Beachy [sic]. For he flew the same machine. I also did some of his stunts & can now do them all, with a good many more that fighting has taught us so this will be my career when peace comes ... I have made up my mind that if I can get a plane after the war, with my knowledge, I would make fortunes throughout Canada & the States so am going to work towards that end. It is the easiest & best way of making money I have ever heard of.

Smooth, graceful aircraft handling was not Barker's forté. He quickly gained a reputation with his fellow-pilots and observers as a rough pilot, one who could get the most out of his machine by pushing it right to the edge. He was assigned instructional duties for a couple of weeks, but had no patience for teaching others. However, his aggressive handling served him very well in combat, where smoothness and predictability simply provides the enemy with an easier target to shoot at:

Just a few lines to let you know that I am still in England. I expect to go to France next week as a full blown pilot. I have turned out ... a stunt pilot or at least they tell me so. I fly a very sensitive fast biplane here & when I go up everybody turns out to see the fun. It is new & has never been crashed so I do all kinds of stunts on it. I looped 7 times this afternoon then some tail slides & ended up with a very steep spiral. I also met one of our airships up in the air & made him feel very uneasy for I practised all sorts of attacks on him. I have been instructing pupils to fly & I don't like the job a little bit in fact I would rather be in France.

* * *

Barker's RE8 after a crash in 1917 at 15 Squadron, just one of several he experienced as an observer and pilot in Corps Cooperation duties.

By 23 February Barker was back in France. He returned to the same sector, the Somme, and to the same aerodrome he had left in December. Fifteen Squadron now belonged to 15 (Corps) Wing, in the RFC V Brigade. It supported the V Corps of the BEF Fifth Army, commanded by General Sir Hubert Gough.

By going back to his old squadron, Barker's transition was rather easy. He knew the sector over which he was going to fly like the back of his hand. He had all the skill and knowledge of an experienced observer, plus natural flying ability. While he had been away, a decision had been made to transfer the wireless signalling duties to the pilot from the observer in all Corps Cooperation squadrons, leaving the observer to concentrate on defensive gunnery against hostile aircraft. This was already the practice in the Corps Cooperation squadrons attached to the Fourth Army.

Clairfaye Farm at Lealvillers was the home of 15 Squadron, but the site was considerably improved from the muddy field it had been the previous fall. Airmen were no longer living in tents, but in metal

Nissen huts, with a surrounding buffer of sandbags. The unit had changed commanders twice while Barker was in England, Major H.S. Walker taking over from Major Carmichael, who had replaced Brock for only two months. Barker was sent to C Flight, which was commanded by Capt A.S. Redfern.

On 25 February Will flew his first operational mission, with 2nd Lieut C.S. Goodfellow. Skimming as low as 50 feet above the trenches on a contact patrol and trench reconnaissance, and never getting much above 500 feet, the two men obtained valuable information on German positions. Barker and Goodfellow were many times mentioned in RFC communiqués (communiqués 79, 82, 85, 86 are typical examples) especially for their aggressive work in contact patrols, bringing back information on German troop positions. They were also very good at transmitting "zone calls" to British gun batteries, asking them to strike targets of opportunity that they had uncovered.

In an emergency, or where the enemy was vulnerable, Corps Cooperation airmen could command

BLOODY APRIL AND THE RFC CULT OF THE OFFENSIVE

April 1917 marked a milestone both in the air and on the ground. In Canada it was celebrated for the Battle of Vimy Ridge, a major success for the four divisions of the Canadian Corps, and the British 5th Division. The taking of Vimy Ridge stood out in contrast to the many other disappointments during the Battle of Arras.

For the RFC it was one of the darkest months in the war, going down in history as "Bloody April." Inexperienced airmen became easy targets for German Jagdstaffels, fighter squadrons of aggressive pilots flying superior aircraft. The victory-to-loss ratio exceeded 8-to-1 in favour of the Germans, even though the Luftstreitkräfte was significantly outnumbered. Richthofen alone would shoot down 21 aircraft, raising his victory total to 52.

According to the RCAF official history, the Luftstreitkräfte lost about 30 aircraft in action from 31 March to 11 May, while the RFC lost about 122. The Germans lost 33 aviators killed, 16 missing, and 19 wounded in those six weeks, but the RFC suffered, between 1 and 27 April, 238 killed or missing, and 105 wounded. Jones claimed one RFC flyer was killed or declared missing-in-action for every 92 hours flown.

The majority of the RFC losses in April were in Barker's speciality, Corps Cooperation. The slow two-seaters were required to fly many of their missions without protective escort, while the scout pilots were ordered to fly into German-held skies by Major General Hugh "Boom" Trenchard, the head of the RFC, thereby carrying the war to the enemy well behind the lines.

Losses in the scout squadrons, although high because of these so-called Distant Operational Patrols (DOPs), were not even close to those of the Corps Cooperation units. Around Vimy Ridge, in the First Army sector, 38 aircraft went missing-in-action, crashed on return to their aerodromes, or landed with wounded men. Only three of those 38 were scout machines. The Corps Cooperation aircraft were simply unable to run away. They turned towards their attackers, and sometimes inflicted losses, but not without a cost.

The temporary air superiority held by the RFC over the German Air Force in the summer of 1916 had reinforced Trenchard's belief that the aeroplane was best as an offensive weapon. Pilots and observers had a duty to pursue hostile machines well behind enemy lines, taking the war to the enemy, no matter what the cost.

Historian Timothy Travers has argued that the British Army in the Edwardian period, in particular its officer corps, had developed "... an unofficial doctrine or cult of the offensive, and the associated concept of the psychological battlefield ..." This doctrine asserted that human qualities could overcome firepower; that on a battlefield, the psychological counted for more than the technological. Soldiers must close with the enemy, no matter how intense the firepower opposing them.

Trenchard, as a product of the Edwardian Army, simply applied the principles of social Darwinism to aerial warfare. The quality of the aircraft and weapons mattered, but not as much as the character of the pilots and observers who used them. By and large, character was seen to be a matter of breeding and education.

Reinforcing this faith in the supremacy of character over firepower was the time-honoured British attitude towards war as simply an athletic event with a higher penalty for losing. This sporting mentality was evident in all RFC squadrons. A fight-hard, play-hard philosophy was considered essential to being a good officer.

an artillery barrage, by transmitting a standard code, LL, demanding fire from all local gun batteries. In Barker's words: "... the L.L. call is an aerial S.O.S. call, and is only used in emergencies. When this call is sent down by a machine and a target given, every battery in that area must, no matter what it is doing, train guns and fire, taking corrections from the airman till the signal N.F. is sent down, which means target dispersed or destroyed."

The next couple of months were just about the most hazardous for an RFC flyer in the entire war. March saw a sharp rise in casualties after a cold winter. Although hours flown were only up about 20 percent from February, to 14,500 from 12,000, casualties more than doubled to 143 killed or missing in action. This represented one aviator eliminated for every 101 flying hours, the worst losses since the war began—until April.

Barker's emotional nature and ambition made it easy for him to accept the RFC's offensive philosophy. But he also had an independent streak, enormous pride, and the courage of his own convictions. He was not, in any sense, subservient. Often, in the heat of combat, his emotions ruled his head and, if the choice was between following orders and attacking the enemy, he attacked the enemy. He was so aggressive in his work at 15 Squadron, and so effective, that his colleagues viewed him with awe. At reunions decades after the war, his former pals still remembered him as a god-like, larger-than-life warrior.

He and his observers were mentioned in RFC daily communiqués at least twice in March. On the 14th, Goodfellow and Barker were commended for a contact patrol, and on the 30th they returned with useful information for the 7th Division of the Fifth Army, a mission they repeated a couple of days later. They were mentioned twice in April, and six times in May.

During those two months, 15 Squadron's patrol area was around Bullecourt in support of Australian and British units, flying from an advanced landing ground at Courcelles-le-Comte, just a few miles northeast of Lealvillers. The task of the 4th Australian and 62nd British Divisions was to break through the Hindenburg Line, and take the village of Bullecourt. Between 11 April and 16 May an intense struggle cost the Australian Imperial Force about 7,000 casualties, in what became known as the Second Battle of Bullecourt. On 16 May, the Germans withdrew from the Bullecourt area, and the Australians, like the Canadians at Vimy, had a victory, in an Allied spring offensive that had many setbacks.

15 Squadron's record book shows that Barker flew at least 17 flights in a two-week period, 13-28

April, but not all of these were operational missions. Two were solo flights, and a couple involved so-called "travelling flights" to visit other aerodromes, or ferry an aircraft to or from the RFC Aircraft Park at St Omer. Now that Barker was a pilot with his own machine, he could visit Howard Alguire, still with the 1st Battalion, CMR, and take his uncle flying. According to Howard's son, Bill Alguire, if the CMR soldiers were playing cards in the reserve lines, Barker enjoyed flying just over their heads, scattering the cards off the table with a blast of power from his engine.

Goodfellow flew with Barker on eight of his operational missions, more than any other observer. One of their most successful was on 25 April, and was summarized in the squadron's daily report:

… about 1,000 infantry in a trench were reported by zone call by 2/Lts Barker and Goodfellow, and were successfully engaged by artillery of the 5th Army. They reported several other parties of infantry and two hostile batteries, and in most cases the shooting was successful. This pilot and observer also obtained valuable information and took valuable photographs. The work was all carried out at a very low altitude, under rifle and machine gun fire.

Barker was determined to provide the most accurate information to ground commanders, and displayed pit-bull tenacity. He almost always landed his machine, and made a verbal report, if he was unhappy with the response to his airborne intelligence. A characteristic example of his persistence occurred during this period, and was later cited by Barker in a post-war speech:

In the spring of 1917, the Australians just south of Bullecourt were suddenly attacked by the Prussian Guard. They had been driven from a portion of their lines. I sent the L.L. call with fair effect, but it was only upon landing and explaining the full situation that sufficient artillery fire was concentrated on

Barker in flight, probably in the cockpit of an RE8.

that point to defeat the enemy ... Again, just north of Bullecourt our troops were supposed to be holding a certain line. Quite by accident, for I was only going down to cheer up the troops, I found this position strongly held by the enemy. The L.L. call did not produce any fire. I then landed at the nearest Divisional Headquarters where I was told that our own troops held this position in strength. However, I was sure of what I had seen; my machine carried ample evidence, and the artillery was turned on ... On another occasion when we had captured Bullecourt for about the fifth time, I found our troops who were in the town, being heavily shelled by our artillery. A hurried landing at the nearest Division put a stop to this confusion.

Will was always prepared to go to the top if artillery commanders were unresponsive and he telephoned Brig General Charles Longcroft who commanded the Corps squadrons of RFC V Brigade, insisting that his eyesight was good and his report accurate. Longcroft knew Barker by reputation and ordered the local commander to follow this pilot's advice. It was this moral and physical courage that so impressed the commanding officer of 15 Squadron, and led him to recommend Barker for a second gallantry award, a Bar to his MC.

Formally gazetted on 18 July, but given for his actions in April–May, the citation read: "For conspicuous gallantry and devotion to duty. He had [sic] done continuous good work in co-operation with the artillery, and has carried out successful reconnaissances under most difficult and dangerous conditions."

After only two and a half months as a pilot, Barker was promoted to temporary captain and given his own flight. On 9 May he took command of C Flight from Redfern. RFC squadrons normally had three flights. It was the flight commanders, usually holding the rank of captain, who were the senior operational leaders in the air. Squadron commanders might occasionally lead their squadron in the air, but they were officially discouraged from crossing the front lines, after 1916, due to the scarcity of experienced senior officers. The squadron commander was usually regarded as the fatherly, and sometimes eccentric administrator who assigned the next day's patrols, sent the exhausted and incompetent home, defended his men against HQ, and kept track of the paper work. Often he was little older than his own men.

Barker was pleased to be promoted, but thought it was overdue. He was also happy to relinquish his irritating secondary duties in the squadron:

> In addition to all my flying I am Mess president & have to buy all the mess supplies & run the mess. You can imagine what the work is when I tell you that I spend over 4,500 francs per month. A franc is 20 cents so it is no small job ... I think I deserved this promotion for I have done 13 months flying & nearly 500 hours in the air out here so it is high time I was getting something.

* * *

Will's decorations and promotions were all the talk back in Dauphin. He was becoming the best-known of the local boys who had marched away to war. He promoted his own growing reputation by sending home photographs and fighting accounts which the *Dauphin Press* and the *Manitoba Free Press* were only too happy to publish.

All through the war, however, the Barker family were working harder and harder to maintain their standard of living. Jane Barker had a bakery shop in town, but it had not been a success. Will had bought a toy aeroplane from a wounded soldier in Belgium, and told his mother to display it in the shop window, so as to attract attention. George wanted to cash in on the high prices for wheat, and decided to rent a bigger farm. But windfall profits due to war demand were not without long-term costs, and many farmers achieved little in the way of long-term stability because, as Thompson observed:

> The war's high price brought temporary prosperity to Prairie agriculture, but the scramble

for short-term profits led to increased levels of debt, costly damage to the land, and continued over-dependence on wheat to the detriment of a more balanced agricultural development ... The three Prairie Provinces grew enough wheat to feed the British Isles, but they did not grow enough potatoes to feed their own populations.

Will was emotionally drifting away from his family. This was inevitable after two years overseas, and more than a year of combat. Nevertheless, he still worried about their financial security. He believed that civil aviation, if he survived, would be a profitable business and he, the eldest son, would secure real prosperity in the Barker name:

So you may go out to Russell on a big farm. Do you know mother I agree with you that I think it would be much better all around. At least it sounds good to me but I am not much of a judge out here. We could never live with that little business & besides a farm is much better all around.

To tell you the truth mother, if I can raise enough money to buy an aeroplane after the war I could make a fortune, enough for all. I could probably get one for about $6,000 & I certainly will have one if possible for I would like to do stunt flying after the war. I am trying to save money from my pay but cannot. Very few officers live on their pay for they cannot do it & so draw on private means.

* * *

With his promotion to flight commander, and a Bar to his MC, Barker had proved to others that he was an outstanding military fighting man. This official recognition reinforced his natural confidence. He was coming into his own in the RFC, and was maturing, but still found it hard to control his emotions, especially in action.

David Mackenzie collection

Barker gathers all the mechanics at 15 Squadron around his aircraft for a group photo before leaving for England, August 1917.

INTRODUCTION OF THE RE8 "HARRY TATE"

The tired BE2 was being replaced in 1917 by Royal Aircraft Factory RE8s. Fifteen Squadron was re-equipping with the new machines, and five were with the unit by the end of May. The squadron continued to operate the BE2e until the summer. Several units already had the RE8, but the "Harry Tate," as the RE8 was nicknamed, had not inspired instant loyalty. The nickname was that of a music hall performer, popular at the time, who was known to do some very funny tricks, but at the most unexpected moment.

Crashes during the development of the Corps Cooperation two-seater revealed that it burned easily because of the location of the fuel tank, directly behind the engine. The tilt of the fuselage relative to the wing chord led pilots to overshoot on landing. The poor reputation that the RE8 soon acquired aggravated the senior command of the RFC, at a time when the Corps' offensive operations and high casualties were being criticized in the House of Commons.

Moreover, as a new type of aeroplane, the RE8 was unfamiliar to Allied artillery batteries and scout pilots. It was sometimes attacked by friendly forces, particularly in the Ypres Salient. A Canadian pilot with 15 Squadron, T.C. Creaghan, was wounded by Raymond Collishaw, the RNAS scout ace, because of Collishaw's mistaken identification of the RE8.

The first squadron to receive the RE8, 52, had two fiery crashes in January, and this resulted in the unit exchanging the machines for the old BE2e for about six weeks, until greater confidence was gained. It had not helped the RE8's reputation that, during the Battle of Arras, six were lost by 59 Squadron in one mission. Ten of the 12 pilots and observers were killed near Douai by pilots of Richthofen's Jasta 11, on Friday, 13 April. Four RE8s provided the protective escort for the two photographic RE8s, on a mission to bring back images of the counter-battery area around Etaing, due east of Arras. They were not in any way able to protect the photo aircraft, and the outcome was tragic.

In the air, Barker was not a cool-headed introvert who liked stalking and killing for its own sake, but rather was an energetic extrovert who fought brilliantly, but emotionally, in the chaos around him. As later Second World War studies showed, for men like Barker, pitched battle had the intensity of sexual orgasm.

For a man who was so aggressive in the air, he was surprisingly amiable on the ground. He was quiet-spoken in conversation, but definitely had a presence, even in a crowded room. He never abandoned his Methodist upbringing, and throughout the war drank little alcohol. At a time when almost everyone smoked, he never did. His deportment in uniform was impeccable, and would have met with approval in the best of regiments, which cannot be said for many RFC flyers.

Physically, he had piercing brown eyes that missed little, a high forehead, and dark hair combed straight back and oiled down with brilliantine. He used his hands when he talked—but even more so than the average pilot—and was parodied in the newsletter of 66 Squadron for gesturing like a French chef.

He radiated boyish high spirits. Men who flew with Barker remembered him as tireless and likeable, but sometimes unpredictable, and sometimes truculent. An aviation historian, the late Harry Creagan, met an Australian pilot who flew with Barker during the war. When asked to describe his memories of Barker, the elderly pilot's whole demeanour softened. After a pause, he drawled a brief, but telling summary: "Barker—he was a going boy."

Mixed with Will's emotional intensity was an insatiable intellect. He was a student of tactics, and wanted to know the how and why of aeronautics. He had a retentive mind that soaked up details like a sponge, while still able to grasp the broader principles that governed aerial warfare. He had an admiration for the professional soldier, yet, paradoxically, was not an obedient soldier himself.

63

His drive to experiment and improve was aggravating to the fitters and riggers taking care of his flying machine. He liked to modify and test and he had the mechanical knowledge to invent alternatives that usually worked. His boyhood skills in his grandfather's blacksmith shop had not gone to waste. He was always tweaking up his machines to gain maximum performance, and this generated a strong rapport with and respect for the mechanics who maintained them—a respect that they reciprocated. Having worked so hard with his own hands on the farm and in his father's sawmills, Will had none of the commissioned officer's traditional disdain for those in the military who did the manual labour.

Of all the high-scoring scout aces of the Great War, he may have been the keenest shutterbug. He had a camera with him most of the time, and his personal album, which he assembled and annotated after the war, contains more than 250 photographs taken by him. They include enemy aircraft that were shot down, crashed RFC machines, tourist sights in France and Italy, as well as the typical candid snaps of life and horseplay in the squadron.

Despite the concern about the RE8, Barker offered no criticism of this new machine in his letters, and was happy to have a fixed Vickers machine gun synchronized to fire through the propeller arc, in addition to the flexible Lewis gun for the observer. It was far from being a nimble scout, but Will adopted the symbol of the skull and crossbones, having it painted on the tip of the nose, directly behind the large, four-bladed propeller. He had at least one crash with the RE8 (serial number A3598—see photo of A3598 on page 57), following an aerial fight, but was not seriously injured.

Fellow Canadian Billy Bishop, however, was getting to fly the kind of aircraft that Barker coveted, from an aerodrome just a few miles away. Bishop had managed to escape from Corps Cooperation, after a stint as an observer, into Army scout operations. He joined 60 Squadron a few weeks after Barker returned to 15. He flew his first offensive patrol in his Nieuport 17 on 22 March, and by the end of April had 14 victories. By this stage of the war pitched aerial fights over the lines were common, but there was still scope for

individuality—for the scout pilot as a solitary hunter, something at which Bishop excelled.

Since the days of Immelmann and Hawker, scout squadrons had multiplied, and in all the air forces there was competition to be the high scorer. On 7 May, the RFC lost its highest-scoring pilot, 20-year-old Albert Ball, of 56 Squadron, with 44 victories. He was the prototype of the aggressive solo hunter, and his record became the benchmark against which the next generation of aces was judged. Ball was an inspiration to everyone in the RFC, and was posthumously awarded the Victoria Cross. He had earlier been awarded the MC, and the Distinguished Service Order (DSO) with two Bars. His scoring record was now the one to beat.

Barker longed to be on scout aircraft and lobbied every chance he found for a transfer, but his contributions to Corps Cooperation were simply too worthwhile. On 1 and 2 May, he and Goodfellow worked with the 93rd Siege Battery to take out five German machine-gun emplacements. On 4 May the two flew low and fired 500 rounds into a German bombing party east of Bullecourt. Four days later, Barker and Lieut Strudwick transmitted zone calls that brought down an artillery barrage on German infantry, following which they made a strafing run with their BE2e. The two repeated this type of mission on 21 and 25 May, receiving another mention in the RFC daily communiqué (number 89).

On 12 May, Barker and his observer, 2nd Lieut F.V. Hoskins, were attacked while patrolling over Bullecourt in a BE2e (serial number A1860—see photo of A1860 on page 36). Six German Halberstadts, also on patrol at 6:00 a.m., spied Barker's machine below them at 1,700 feet. One of the German scouts attacked, firing a mixture of high explosive and tracer rounds. Barker turned into the attack and "... tracers seen to go close but apparently he was not hit. The Hostile machine then made off. This Hostile machine was covered with Black and White stripes along planes, fuselage and tail which made the black cross very difficult to see."

Sometime towards the end of May, his nerves a bit frazzled, Will was sent on leave. While he was away, his squadron received orders to shift to a new aerodrome. On 6 June, the pilots of 15 Squadron flew their BE2s and RE8s north to Courcelles-le-Comte, for attached duty with the 12 (Corps) Wing of III RFC Brigade. This put the squadron closer to the Messines Ridge.

The ignition of 19 underground mines, 465 tons of explosive, early on 7 June, part of the British assault on Messines Ridge, shook windows in southern England, and woke many people in their beds. Barker was sleeping at Brighton that morning: "... am at the sea-side enjoying the fresh sea air. Go swimming about twice daily. Am feeling in good shape for another go at the Huns. Return to France tomorrow."

After about a month working with III Brigade, 15 Squadron was removed from front-line operations. There was no particular reason, other than to give the squadron's personnel a rest. They were not the hardest pressed, or suffering the highest casualties. The crews ferried their RE8s to La Gorgue aerodrome, there to report to I Brigade, part of General Headquarters Reserve in the First Army area.

However, Barker's C Flight was given a different assignment from the rest of the squadron, being sent on attached duty to 27 Squadron, a Martinsyde G100 bomber unit. Barker's men worked with V RFC Brigade and the VIII Corps on experiments in signalling between troops on the ground and aeroplane observers, from Clairmarais aerodrome just north of St Omer. These contact patrol experiments were low-risk, undemanding missions, that left plenty of time for swimming, horseback riding, and dinners in the town.

The summer and fall of 1917 was one of the wettest in Belgian history. The weather that turned the Ypres Salient into a horrific sea of glutinous muck, also made operational flying hazardous. On the opening day of the Passchendaele campaign, 31 July, it pelted down rain, and the low ceilings and restricted visibilities made it extremely difficult for the RFC to support the ground forces.

Unable to do artillery shoots, the RFC was directed to offensive patrols and ground strafing runs, which, according to official histories, provided little

useful intelligence about the movements of German units in the rear areas. The failure of the RFC to clarify the typical confusion of war highlighted the ongoing deficiencies in air-ground communications. The July experiments of C Flight, on loan to 27 Squadron, were aimed at developing new solutions. But it was a frustrating exercise that, in Barker's opinion, accomplished little.

After five-and-a-half-months of field service, Will was due for a new job in England. July had been relatively easy for him, but the next month he was wounded for at least the third time in his flying career. He almost lost his eye, and came within a whisker of having his head blown off. On 7 August, during an artillery shoot for a 9.2-inch howitzer, his machine was riddled by anti-aircraft fire. A steel splinter struck him in the face, and cut him above the left eyebrow. He recovered the aircraft, and kept flying missions with a bandage over the wound.

Believing that Will was due for a longer rest, Major Walker arranged for his transfer back to England. Almost six months to the day after arriving back in France, on 18 August, Barker was transferred to Home Establishment. In his only surviving log book he summarized all his flying in Corps Cooperation, both as observer and pilot—570 hours on the BE2c, 2e, and RE8, between 2 March 1916 and 20 August 1917.

If correct, and the exact total cannot be confirmed since no personal log book prior to September 1917 exists, it is arguably one of the highest by any RFC aviator. At this point, Barker could have honourably withdrawn from war operations for good, and spent the rest of his time in England as a training or staff officer. He wanted no part of such a dull career—it was scout machines, or nothing.

But higher authority had dictated that he be sent to 53 Training Squadron, Narborough, Norfolk, to instruct *ab initio* pilots. The legendary chapters of his war career were still to come, but first he had to tolerate a spell as a flying instructor, something he was unwilling to do.

William Barker in the rear cockpit of an AVRO 504 trainer, Hounslow aerodrome, April 1919; from a glass plate negative that was cracked, hence the fracture marks seen here on the positive image.

CHAPTER FIVE

FLIGHT COMMANDER IN A SCOUT SQUADRON

"I expect to get a good many Huns & will send you a piece of the first Hun I get down on this side. Mother, don't worry about me because I am a past master at flying & a good shot & although I intend getting a lot of Huns I will take care of myself so don't worry ..."

CAPT. W.G. BARKER, C FLIGHT, 28 SQN, OCTOBER 1917

Barker had no intention of serving quietly in England, and missing out on the action across the Channel. He decided to be the worst instructor the RFC had ever seen. His reckless insubordination would have put most military pilots behind bars. However, some RFC senior officers decided that a court martial was not in anyone's interest, and Will was back in France by October.

One who claimed to be a witness to Will's craftiness was an artillery officer named Lieut Conn Smythe, of Toronto, later the owner/manager of the Toronto Maple Leafs hockey team. Smythe had transferred from the CEF artillery to become an RFC Corps Cooperation pilot, because of a disagreement with his battery commander. Barker was never Smythe's instructor at 53 Training Squadron, Narborough, but he left an indelible impression:

I was posted to England for training. Soon after, I first met Billy Barker who later was president of the Toronto Maple Leafs and to me the greatest Canadian flyer of the time, which is saying something ... Before I got my wings, Barker showed up as an instructor. He took one of our fellows up. When the man came back, his hair practically had turned white. "Nobody go up with that guy ever again!" he advised. From then on, nobody would go up with Barker. He got sore. One day when there was an inspection he took a plane up and flew it right through one of the hangars, in one end and out the other, buzzing some senior officers so that they had to flatten out right on the ground.

When he came down he was told, "You're under arrest."

"All I want to do is go to France," he said. "You say you want volunteers, send me ..."

Smythe's version makes a good yarn, perhaps because he was recalling the story over 60 years later. He also made the unlikely claim that he saw Barker land his squadron on his aerodrome on the Western Front. However, Lt Colonel George Drew and Lt Colonel Billy Bishop also confirmed the gist of Smythe's story in their magazine articles and books.

After Will asked to be transferred to a scout squadron, and was turned down, he did whatever he felt like in an aircraft. While training at Robert Smith-Barry's School of Special Flying at Gosport, Barker beat up villages and towns, terrorized boaters, and stunted over Piccadilly Circus and RFC Headquarters. Capt Harold H. Balfour (later Lord Balfour) had loaned his personal machine, with the following result:

Each flight commander was allotted a Sopwith Pup as his private perquisite ... We were naturally reluctant to trust these precious possessions to those on the course, but, for Barker, although at this time he had not gained the fame which he later enjoyed, I made an exception ...

Smith-Barry ... was walking across Piccadilly Circus when he heard a roar overhead. He looked up, and to his horror recognized the bright colouring of the Sopwith Pup of my flight low over the Circus, just scraping the chimney pots. The Pup then proceeded to loop the loop at about 200 ft, and after a final display of aerobatics which held up completely the life and traffic of Piccadilly Circus disappeared towards the Hounslow direction. Smith-Barry said he could not bear to look any longer but dived into the Underground Station before the inevitable crash could occur. On his return he sent for me ... there was no schoolboy pride about me and I at once gave away who was the culprit. Barker had, however, left for France that morning so nothing happened except that I received a postcard from him thanking me for the loan of the Pup.

Yet another version of this legendary story, retold by Barker's former wing commander, was that Will had flown to London just to beat up the War Office. The residents of the War Office were apparently irritated, but actually secretly amused by the cheek of this anonymous pilot.

* * *

Barker flew less than 60 hours in England. Between 4 and 23 September, he logged about 32 hours in the AVRO 504A, 59 trips in all, about two thirds of which were with students. He instructed 16 different students, and the most flights with a single individual were nine with a Lieut Robinson. A student named Middleton, who later served in Barker's squadron, remembered him as a rough and impatient instructor.

Barker had arrived at Gosport, where Smith-Barry was revolutionizing the method of RFC flying instruction, on 23 September and left about a week later. If he performed aerobatics over Piccadilly Circus, it was probably in that week. Therefore, the War Office had time to catch up with the Canadian, since he did not leave for France till 10 October. Perhaps somebody at high level, or perhaps an admiring

Smith-Barry, decided that Will's offensive spirit should not be dampened by a court martial.

Barker was transferred to 28 Squadron, located at Yatesbury, which was then re-equipping with the Sopwith Camel. He flew this demanding machine for the first time on 30 September, and spent the first nine days of October at Yatesbury familiarizing himself with it, and his duties as a flight commander.

The Barker legend that he picked the scout machine he wanted to fly—i.e., the Camel rather than the SE5a—is not true. It has been suggested that he turned down SE5s at 56 Squadron. He definitely liked the Sopwith's knife-edge character, but there is no evidence that he ever flew the Royal Aircraft Factory SE5.

Both machines had entered service in 1917, and both were formidable weapons in the right hands. The SE5 and the improved SE5a were faster, more robust (the 5a was more than 400 pounds heavier at takeoff than the Camel), flew better at high altitude, and were more stable gun platforms. They were easier to fly, and a pilot's chances of survival in combat were better.

However, the SE5a could not touch the Camel at lower altitudes in any turning fight, it didn't climb much faster, and it didn't have the concentrated firepower of the Camel's two synchronized Vickers guns. The Sopwith was more multi-role, having the versatility to be a ground-attack machine armed with bombs; a shipboard naval fighter; and a night fighter. The Camel's rotary engine did not need the warm-up period of an inline engine and, therefore, a Camel could immediately scramble into the air on a cold night.

Had Barker joined the famous 56 in which Albert Ball had served, he would have flown alongside several high-scoring British aces including James McCudden, Geoffrey Bowman, and the Canadian, Reginald Hoidge. "Slippery Bill" knew that he would have plenty of competition in 56 in any scoring contests. He was unlikely to get command of a flight in an élite unit. His career would have taken a different direction, and a less fortunate one, since along with its outstanding record of more than 400 victories over enemy aircraft, the unit also had about 90 casualties.

Wayne Ralph collection

Painting by British artist James Leech of B6313 in the markings of 28 Squadron.

The squadron that Barker was offered had been established at Fort Grange, Gosport, as a training unit in November 1915, and for 22 months flew only in England. It was operating a mixture of de Havilland DH5s, Bristol Scouts, Sopwith Pups and Avro 504s in the summer of 1917, but was the first RFC squadron (65 being the second) to re-equip with the Camel prior to being sent to France. The commanding officer of 28 Squadron was Major Hugh Fanshawe Glanville, and only two of his pilots had flown before in France—Spain and Barker. Barker became the commander of C Flight, Capt P.C. Campbell, the head of B Flight, and Capt G.A.R. Spain, the head of A Flight.

Spain and Campbell lasted less than two weeks in France. Spain was sent home on 21 October, Campbell two days later, the latter experiencing difficulty with his vision. Campbell's successor, Capt J.G. Smith-Grant, lasted only until December. Ironically, RFC Headquarters had not originally intended for Barker to be a flight commander. He told his family

that he got the job because of a fatal accident within days of his arrival: "... the former flight commander Capt White was killed while stunting so I have modified my flying somewhat."

Capt L.S. White was delivering a new Camel, B6343, to the squadron from 7 Aircraft Acceptance Park (AAP) at Kenley, when he spun into the ground near Wantage on 28 September. Because of this unfortunate accident, Barker set an unusual precedent among RFC scout pilots. He was never led on an offensive patrol by any other pilot, and never flew in a formation as No 2. His first and all subsequent patrols were as a leader.

Personality conflict is not uncommon among aggressive pilots, and Barker's promotion ruffled the feathers of an experienced flyer, Lieut James Hart Mitchell, who had several months in 28, and was already a deputy flight commander. Mitchell soon got his own flight, taking over from Spain. But he held a grudge against Barker for beating him to the command of C Flight.

The former Royal Artillery officer from Yorkshire wrote an unflattering profile of Barker in the 1930s in *Popular Flying*, rating him as no great shakes as a flight leader. Mitchell's opinion was a notable exception to that of others who flew with the Canadian. He flew several offensive patrols as Barker's deputy before being promoted, and became a decorated ace, credited with 11 victories.

The rivalry between these two young men was nothing more than flyer's ego. But there was also animosity in 28 Squadron between the British pilots and those from the Dominions. There was tension between Barker and his commanding officer from the moment the two met, and Barker usually worked around rather than through Glanville for operational planning.

The morale in and personality of a squadron is complex. While most flying stories of the Great War emphasize how closely knit squadrons were, units varied in their happiness and effectiveness. Conflict could blossom quickly—due to jealousy, the competition for higher victory scores, and the robust egos of young men. Many scout squadrons had a synergy, but some did not. Certainly, 28 Squadron was effective in combat, but it was not a harmonious unit on the ground. Nevertheless, Will was overjoyed to be there:

I have at last got what I wanted. I have a flight in a scout squadron. It is a splendid little machine & I hope to do well on it.

I didn't expect to go out so soon but we go in two days time so will have been in France 2 weeks when you get this ... We are in good shape & my boys are keen. This is entirely different work than I used to do. Now I line up my flight of six or eight machines & away we go in formation. It is my duty to lead them to our objectives & back again so as a flight commander now I will be able to do something. No more artillery observation no more wireless & contact patrol just fighting Huns. Well mother I must close I am very keen on my new work & hope to be able to send you news of victims soon.

It was Barker, not Glanville, who led 28 Squadron across the Channel. Log books and Barker's own letter contradict each other as to the date of this flight. It was either Tuesday or Wednesday, 9 or 10 October. According to the log book for Barker's machine, the squadron took off from Yatesbury at 9:00 a.m. on the 10th in three flights totalling 15 Camels. The non-stop leg to Lympne in Kent took 90 minutes, and by noon the squadron was back

Barker's C Flight, 28 Squadron, 1917.

in the air for the 40-minute leg to St Omer, France, where the unit remained overnight.

The following morning the squadron arrived at Droglandt, just on the French side of the French-Belgian border. This aerodrome was about seven miles west of a town well known to Barker and thousands of others in the Ypres Salient—Poperinghe. Twenty-eight joined another Camel unit, 70 Squadron, belonging to the 22 (Army) Wing of the V RFC Brigade.

Some historians have claimed that Barker shot down a German Albatros on 8 October during his first (unauthorized) patrol. Judging by Barker's letter to his mother, this patrol was actually flown on the evening of 9 October. His own log book has two entries (for 10-11 October) where the phrase "offensive patrol" is crossed out, and replaced by "practice patrol."

According to Mitchell's recollection, two senior officers who knew Barker, Brig General Charles Longcroft and Lt Colonel F. Vesey Holt, met 28 Squadron's pilots when they first landed in France. Longcroft commanded V RFC Brigade, and Holt commanded 22 (Army) Wing. They gave Barker permission to lead the other flight commanders to the Ypres Salient front lines, but no further.

Mitchell was with Barker when he reportedly led this formation into an attack against "... a circus of 22 gaudily painted machines about 2,000 feet below us. As they passed underneath us, Barker did a half roll and dived with engine full on at the formation below." At about 100 yards, Barker fired on a "tail-end Charlie" which instantly broke up in the air. He then led his three novices home at full speed.

There is no combat report to confirm this story, perhaps because Barker knew better than to file a victory claim when he had been ordered to stay on the Allied side of the lines. In his first letter home after arriving in France, Barker wrote: "I am the senior flight commander here & last night I took up six to show them the lines & we had a good look around. We ran into the 'Circus' but they were three times our number. However I dived on one & [it] then went down in a spin. It is a different life on scouts & I think I will do well on them."

Will embellished his performance, if only to his family, for the first few weeks of his third tour in France. He was desperately keen to succeed, and exaggerated his accomplishments on patrols. In a letter to his mother, and a postcard to his brother, Lloyd, written on 21 October, Will falsely claimed to have shot down an aircraft actually credited to another pilot in the squadron. He also turned an indecisive fight on 18 October into a more dramatic story of flaming wreckage.

Blessed with all the skills to become an exceptional scout pilot, Will wanted to prove that he wasn't just another Corps Cooperation "retread," and made sure his family recognized the difference:

I am flying what I have longed for, a fast single seater scout which does 130 m.p.h. & has two m.g. firing through the propellor [sic]. I like it very much & yesterday I did a dive of 4000 ft. at 250 m.p.h. so it is strong. I expect to get a good many Huns & will send you a piece of the first Hun I get down on this side.

Mother, don't worry about me because I am a past master at flying & a good shot & although I intend getting a lot of Huns I will take care of myself so don't worry.

* * *

There were about 19 pilots in 28 Squadron, with Barker's flight having six pilots including Mitchell. Of the others, two were British, two were Canadian, and one was a Sikh from the Punjab region of northern India. Due to transfers, accidents, enemy action, sickness, and bad nerves, a scout flight could change personnel rapidly. C Flight certainly did, with five casualties between 10 and 28 October, Three men of Barker's flight were wounded, one was wounded and taken prisoner-of-war, and one died of injuries from a crash on the aerodrome.

When Barker joined 28 there were four other Canadians: J.N. Blacklock; H.B. Hudson; G.S. McKee; and L.P. Watt. Two others arrived at the squadron in the last week of October: J.P. Ironside and C.M. McEwen. These six men were like many others who joined the RFC to fly—full of hope, anxious about their performance, and varied in ability.

THE SOPWITH CAMEL

Barker became one with his Sopwith Camel, serial number B6313, and the aircraft shared in his fame. Although there were dozens of scout designs in the First World War, somehow the Camel has managed to live on as the archetype of all Great War fighters. The machine was about as challenging to fly as an aircraft can be and still do a useful job. No other aircraft prepared a pilot for the Camel.

Pilots enjoyed the reputation of having mastered it, in an age that had many demanding machines. The phrase of the time—Once a Camel pilot, always a Camel pilot—certainly applied to Barker. Some pilots liked to boast that they had never crashed one on landing or takeoff—the best evidence of talented hands and feet.

The Camel is the fighter in the RFC and RNAS credited it with the greatest number of destroyed enemy aircraft. Estimates in various books range between 1,294 and 1,543. A less known fact is that 690 Camels were lost on the other side of the front lines in France, Belgium, and Italy, due to enemy action. The more docile SE5 and SE5a had only 321 losses.

All the weight of the engine, guns, and pilot was concentrated in the first seven feet of a short 18-foot fuselage. The various models of rotary engine fitted to the Camel, from a 110-hp Le Rhone, to a 130-hp Clerget, to a 150-hp Bentley, had the propeller attached to the engine crankcase and the crankshaft to the aircraft so that the propeller and engine revolved together at more than 1250 rpm. This heavy whirling engine was lubricated continually by castor oil which was not recycled, but rather was burned in the combustion process and vented overboard, soaking the aircraft, the pilot's flying suit, helmet and goggles.

The gyroscopic forces that were generated varied in intensity based on a complex interaction of engine rpm, aircraft speed, and control input. The Scout had a different character turning left or right, as did all the rotary-engined aeroplanes, but the Camel to an extreme degree. It was sluggish in left turns and the nose always pitched up, while right turns were very quick, with the nose dropping sharply. Without plenty of top (i.e., left) rudder to correct the pitch down, it would spin.

A Camel pilot had to apply left rudder turning left or right, the amount varying with aircraft speed and engine rpm. Since the engine rotation countered the input of left stick and rudder, some pilots made all turns to the right because the aircraft was quicker through 270 degrees, than 90 degrees to the left. The Camel's elevator was powerful and sensitive, while the rudder was too small and relatively ineffective.

Coordinated turns demanded a fine touch. Correcting sideslip, the tendency of the aeroplane to slide to the inside of a banked turn, by applying opposite rudder, caused the Camel to tighten up in the turn. In steep turns over 45 degrees of bank, the aircraft tended to pitch up its nose, and tighten up its bank angle as speed reduced, requiring continual adjustments in the amount of forward pressure on the stick with engine rpm changes. In the words of test pilot W/C Paul A. Hartman, RCAF, the Camel has no "dynamic longitudinal stability" in steep turns.

Accelerating the aircraft caused the nose to climb, and swing to the left. At 110 miles per hour, there was about 15 to 20 pounds of back force on the control column, which could not be trimmed out because the aircraft had no pilot-adjustable, moveable horizontal stabilizer. Therefore, Camel pilots had to fly two-to-three hour missions, continually applying forward pressure just to maintain level flight. Letting go resulted in the aircraft pitching up, and rolling inverted to the right. Moving the stick forward to enter a dive caused the Camel to yaw left because of gyroscopic force, and correcting this yaw with right rudder caused the nose to pitch down sharply. By today's standards the Camel was completely unacceptable, and yet many pilots of 1917-18, most with fewer than 100 hours of flying time used it as a lethal weapon.

Barker flew one particular Camel, B6313, almost exclusively for 12 months. It was rare for RFC pilots to keep the same aircraft for extended periods in the field. For example, Billy Bishop's 72 credited victories were accumulated in six different airframes of two types, 29 of which were while flying one Nieuport 17, serial number B1566, perhaps the most successful Nieuport in RFC war service. James McCudden had his personal SE5a modified to wring the maximum performance out of the airframe—he is credited with 34 of his 57 victories flying this one machine, serial number B4891, making it the most successful SE5a of the war. In comparison, Donald MacLaren was credited with 54 victories in only eight months, flying in at least five Camels.

But Barker's record stands alone. Although he flew 10 different Camels, virtually all his patrols, and all but four of his 50 victories were in B6313. No other scout machine in the RFC or RAF served as long in combat with one pilot. British authors have declared B6313 "the single most successful fighter aircraft in the history of the RAF." Moreover, 44 of Barker's 50 hostile machines and balloons were claimed as destroyed: "the highest such ratio of the war for an RFC, RNAS or RAF pilot."

Barker's machine was built by the Sopwith Aviation Company Ltd at Kingston-on-Thames, the 313th Camel manufactured, under contract number AS6175. At least nine companies manufactured the Camel, and less than 10 percent were actually built by the designer. B6313 was shipped by road to 7 Aircraft Acceptance Park (AAP) at Kenley; when it arrived there on 11 September, it was already fitted with a 130-hp Clerget, manufacturer's number R1601, and a Sopwith "airscrew," number L-16052, as well as the following cockpit instruments: watch; aneroid barometer (i.e., altimeter); revolution indicator; and airspeed indicator.

At 7 AAP, B6313 was rigged, inspected, and fitted with additional cockpit equipment prior to being test-flown and transferred to a squadron. A compass and a clinometer (a curved glass tube containing liquid) were installed, and a Pyrene fire extinguisher was fixed to the cockpit floor. The .303-calibre Vickers machine guns (serial numbers C3441 and C4488) were mounted on the fuselage, then timed and harmonized on a range. The guns had the standard Sopwith-Kauper interrupter gear, and there was a ring-and-bead sight fitted to the right-hand gun.

B6313 was finished in standard RFC paint scheme. The linen fabric of the fuselage, wings and tail had the standard brownish olive finish. Wing and tailplane undersurfaces were painted with clear dope and clear varnish in a creamy yellow. The plywood panels on either side of the cockpit cowling were varnished, and the unanodized aluminum cowling surrounding the nose and engine was left unfinished.

Barker customized his own aircraft, and it was redecorated to his taste at least three times. At 28 Squadron the aluminum cowling was polished, not painted. The squadron marking, a white square, was painted on either side of the fuselage and on the top wing, along with a large number "1," and the letter "c." Barker's machine was assigned to him, but he was not its only pilot. Eleven flights or offensive patrols were flown in B6313 by other men. Amazingly, Barker had no successful fights in any other Camel, and no pilot other than Barker had a successful fight in B6313.

Some pilots used the Aldis collimating sight without exception, while others did not like them. Barker had no use for the Aldis gunsight (fellow-countryman Donald MacLaren felt the same), and it was removed from B6313. The Aldis was a sealed metal tube, 32 inches long, two inches in diameter, mounted between the Camel's two Vickers guns. Internal lenses provided a 1:1 image—looking through the sight, aircraft were neither magnified nor reduced. Two concentric rings engraved on glass provided an estimate of distance to the target, with the inner 100-yard ring being a guide for opening fire.

Barker also had the armourers cut off the ring-and-bead foresight, replacing it with a single horizontal band welded between the muzzles of the guns. A similar band cut with a "V" groove was welded across the breeches. This primitive gunsight was entirely in keeping with Will's instinctive shooting technique, and he had no problem hitting targets, at short or long range.

Clifford "Black Mike" McEwen.

DND DHist Biographical Files

George Sears McKee.

Mary McKee Selby collection

Second Lieutenant George Sears McKee, an 18-year-old high school student, son of a doctor living in Vancouver, flew with B Flight until December when he was invalided due to sickness and bad nerves back to England. He was later reassigned to a training squadron in Egypt, and survived the war, only to die at the controls of a Western Canada Airways Fokker Super Universal in September 1929.

Second Lieutenant Leslie Perry Watt, of Montreal, served with C Flight until mid-January 1918. Unable to master the Camel, he was sent home after his third accident, a collision with another Camel on takeoff from an icy aerodrome.

Second Lieutenant Joseph Neilson Blacklock, of Elora, Ontario, flew three missions with 28, had a traumatic aerial fight and, shortly thereafter, started to have eye problems. Invalided back to England

at the end of October, his left arm unaccountably became paralyzed and he was subsequently released from the service. He later qualified as a dentist, one of his patients being Billy Bishop.

Harold Byrne Hudson and Clifford McKay McEwen thrived under Barker's leadership, becoming aces, but Ironside never got the chance. Second Lieutenant James Paul Ironside, aged 28, had been a Mounted Policeman, and a private detective before the war. On his first flight in France he stalled in a turn just after takeoff and crashed in B6315. He was taken to 64 Casualty Clearing Station (CCS), but died the following day due to head injuries.

In aerial warfare the difference between success and failure can hinge on seemingly inconsequential acts. A faulty engine, a lucky shot, a moment of inattention, and a man's career or life was over. Barker

Harold Bryne Hudson.

Stanley Stanger.

was experienced, but still had hard lessons to learn about aerial fighting and leadership. He was dangerously close to failing at both in his first month: "... by the way I came very nearly being sent to England for stunting too much. It happened over the general's house & I sure got into trouble—Never again."

Will's promise of "never again" was never kept. He invariably performed aerobatics in the most public way, where there was no difficulty in catching him. He also launched occasional unsanctioned offensive patrols, usually with one or two keen volunteers. This spontaneity, sometimes, but not always winked at, did not improve his chances for promotion.

A comparison of his only surviving log book with B6313's maintenance log book reveals that, on the whole, Barker's written descriptions of major combats match closely the squadron reports that

credited him with victories. Pilots and observers were not required by their squadron, when on active service, to keep a log book, and some squadron commanders discouraged the habit.

Some men kept a methodical record, and quite a few kept an illegal diary, while others made only casual entries, as it suited them. Barker was offhand about his entries. In a few cases he recorded his flights days afterwards, resulting in some errors. He did not record the time that he went airborne, and only occasionally wrote down the names of his wingmen.

From 10 to 31 October, Barker logged 25 to 30 flights, and 35 flying hours from Droglandt. He claimed in his own log book three hostile aircraft destroyed, one driven down in a spin, one driven down out of control. He attacked a Gotha bomber, and claimed to have driven it down damaged. However, his credits, as approved by Wing HQ, were three hostile machines destroyed.

Barker scored his first victory during a well-co-ordinated mission on the morning of 20 October laid on by 22 (Army) Wing. Twenty-three, 28, and 70 Squadrons attacked the German aerodrome at Rumbeke. Seventy Squadron was assigned to bomb and strafe the field at 400 feet. Twenty-three Squadron (a unit with French SPAD SVIIs) and 28 Squadron provided high cover protection against attack. Twenty-two bombs were dropped, causing major damage on the aerodrome, and strafing attacks were also carried out against ground targets in the area, including a train. In pitched air fighting at least seven victories were achieved, four by 70's pilots.

Barker fought against and defeated a German pilot in a green Albatros. He later wrote in his log book: "offensive patrol 12 Huns encountered, one engaged & shot down. wings came off." The official report recorded:

> 12:15 p.m. – Height – 10,000 ft – Locality – South of Roulers aerodrome – Albatross [*sic*] Scout – While returning from Thielt we met about 10 Albatross Scouts and dived to the attack. After a very close engagement. the E.A. [enemy aircraft] (painted green with small black crosses) went down with both wings off. I saw another machine also going down with wings off.*

He has sometimes been credited with shooting down Gotha bombers, but the closest he came to doing this was on 24 October, when he attacked one in the vicinity of Ypres. This was probably his only fight with this large aircraft, which weighed almost 8,000 pounds and carried more than 600 pounds of bombs. The bomber had a front and rear observer, and cruised, according to Barker's combat report, at about the same speed as a Camel:

> While patrolling over lines at 7,000 ft a formation of 18 Gothas approached from east, crossed lines. I climbed to 10,000 ft and engaged

one from the rear and just under the tail. At about 200 yds, fired about 150 rounds and then closed to about 100 yds range and fired about another 100. Both guns then stopped and I could not remedy them. By this time the Gotha was at 7,000 with right-hand engine stopped and the rear observer ceased to shoot. I followed him over the lines which he crossed at 5,000 but gliding steeply down.

It was two days after this exchange, that Barker's scout career nearly came unglued. The abortive attack against Marckebeke aerodrome, and the wounding of two men in his flight, was salvaged only by his dual victories (see Chapter One).

Fenton and Malik spent some weeks in hospital. Fenton never came back to 28 Squadron, and Malik was convalescent until January 1918, when he returned for a brief period to 28 Squadron in Italy, but then transferred back to France on Bristol F2B Fighters. Malik survived the war, and had a long and distinguished civil service career. In 1947, he was the first High Commissioner to Canada from the newly independent nation of India, and some years later returned to his old flying grounds, as India's ambassador to France.

* * *

Barker's last three offensive patrols on the Western Front in 1917 were on Saturday and Sunday, 27-28 October. A catastrophic breakthrough that week by the enemy in northern Italy changed his fighting career. The combined forces of the Central Powers, the Austro-Hungarian Empire and Germany, launched the 12th Battle of the Isonzo. German General Otto von Below opened his campaign with a major bombardment by 300 artillery batteries. The first assault at 8:00 a.m. on 24 October by the German 14th Army, in rain, sleet and high winds, was a great shock to the Italian 2nd Army. At Caporetto, the Italian front lines, held by the 19th Division, were broken by soldiers of the Austrian 50th and German 12th divisions, who penetrated over 15 miles into Italian-held territory.

---

* The pilot in the German fighter may have been Leutnant (2nd Lieutenant) Walter Lange of Jasta Boelcke, but Barker never knew who he had killed. He was both exhilarated and relieved that he had his first victory. Even by the high standards of top aces Barker was deadly, and Lange became the first of more than 40 to have his aircraft destroyed by Will's guns. Since most of his victories were so decisive—the target broke up or burst into flames, or was identified at the crash site—it is somewhat easier for aviation buffs and historians to make an informed guess about the fate of Barker's victims. In this biography, the names of victims are primarily from Shores/Franks/Guest, *Above The Trenches.*

For a few days it looked as though there would be a complete rout, and that Italy would be taken out of the war. The Italian Army fell back from the River Isonzo and finally came to a halt nearly 90 miles southwest at the River Piave, a wide, shallow, but fast-flowing river which easily overflows its banks during the autumn rains. It was this autumn flooding that helped stall the offensive of the Central Powers.

General Luigi Cadorna requested British and French assistance. There were already British and French artillery batteries attached to the Italian Army. Lloyd George ordered the Chief of the General Staff to send two divisions, and Premier Painleve provided four divisions, at the request of General Foch, who was, as it happens, in Italy at the time.

The XIV British Corps, with the 23rd and 41st Divisions, was commanded by Lieut General, the Earl of Cavan, and was joined within a couple of weeks by the XI Corps. The two Corps were under the overall command of General Sir Herbert Plumer. Ultimately, five RFC squadrons were transferred to Italy in support of these ground forces: 28, 34, 42, 45, and 66. Since 28 was newly arrived in France and still learning the ropes, it was considered the most expendable to the side-show in Italy. Barker preferred to believe otherwise:

> I know you will be surprised for I am myself. I am on my way to Italy. Our squadron has been chosen & we are on our way now. You know we broke all records for a new squadron. Our losses were heavy but we did the work. Up to date I have destroyed 4 & driven down 3 out of control ... We will probably have plenty of fighting to do but I don't think they will be as good as the real Huns we get here.

Will's derogatory opinion of Austro-Hungarian flyers was widely held. All the flyers of the RFC in France believed they were in the hottest war zone, fighting the most talented of the German Air Service. The general view in the RFC that the Austro-Hungarians were second-rate opponents resulted in

Barker (centre) with C Flight members: left to right, Waltho, Cooper, Hudson, Davis holding the 28 Squadron mascot, Italy, 1917.

David Mackenzie collection

victory scores gained in Italy being discounted in value when compared with the Western Front.

Surprisingly, the RFC squadrons did not fly south to Italy as might be expected for a front in crisis. The Camels were dismantled and crated for shipping at 2 Aircraft Depot at Candas. The pilots, fitters, and riggers left by train on the evening of 6 November, travelling south through the Rhone valley and along the Riviera on a four-day journey with many stopovers. Women and old men, young boys and girls, lined the tracks to wave at the soldiers and airmen heading south to assist the Italian Army. Ceremonies of various kinds took along the route, and there was something of a mood of liberation.

The Italian people, on the whole, were happy to see the arriving forces from France, but by the time those forces were in a position to assist the battle in any major way, the Italian Army, under its new commander, General Armando Diaz, had turned around a dire situation. The advance of the enemy had been halted at the River Piave on 9 November.

By this stage of the war, Barker had accumulated over 600 hours of war flying, a remarkable figure in the RFC where 250 hours in the field was very good. He was appointed the acting commanding officer of 28 Squadron for the train trip. When the unit arrived in Milan there was no transportation officer assigned to take care of them. According to author George Drew:

... to make matters worse, no one on the train could speak Italian, nor could they find anyone at the station who could speak English. His first step, therefore, was to find an interpreter. Walking along one of the main streets he saw the sign of a well-known American shoe company, and going inside was met by a clerk who had been born in the United States but had been living in Milan for some time. As soon as he heard of Barker's difficulty, he volunteered his services and became interpreter for the squadron.

Barker (right) with James Mitchell (centre), Italy, in billets.

Having reported their situation by telegram to Headquarters, the officers of the squadron decided they might as well enjoy themselves; so they went to the Metropole Hotel and spent a few joyous days while waiting for orders.

Barker apparently met the head of the Caproni factory, Gianni Caproni, who offered his facilities to the RFC so that their machines could be reassembled more quickly. While waiting for serviceable aeroplanes, however, the pilots of 28, 34, and 66 Squadrons lived the good life at the Metropole and the Cavour, two first-class hotels in Milan.

Barker's B6313 was ready to fly on 15 November, and he put on an impromptu aerobatic show for pedestrians in Milan: "Flying around the cathedral & putting the wind up people in the square—all traffic stopped." He kept a post card of the Cathedral of Milan, with an "X" marking the two spires through which he had threaded B6313. The second-largest medieval cathedral in Europe served as a navigation marker for all flyers, its dominant spire visible at long distance.

The 51 (Corps) Wing HQ, commanded by Lt Colonel R.P. Mills had arrived in Milan on 12 November, and moved five days later to Montichiari, southeast of Brescia. While waiting to move to an operational airfield, Barker took B6313 on 14 relatively brief flights, taking photographs, and testing his guns at high altitude. On 28 November, 51 Wing was relocated at Villalta, east of Verona, and 28 and 34 Squadrons settled in at Grossa aerodrome, four miles north of Camisano.

Barker's enthusiasm for the new and unfamiliar was recharged in Italy, where he explored like a peacetime tourist on holidays: "Just a line. Am still roaming about. I find [sic] the most beautiful old city, wonderful old historic places. Romeo & Juiliete [sic] died here [Vincenza] ..."

Ernest Hemingway referred to wartime northern Italy in A Farewell to Arms as "the picturesque front." It was a strikingly beautiful region, but hazardous to flyers. The geography and climate were a dramatic contrast to the gently rolling terrain of northern France and Belgium, and the RFC flyers had to make many adjustments. Grossa was a small aerodrome, challenging to get into and out of because of surrounding dikes and trees.

From the field, the Italian front lines formed a semicircle from southeast to northwest starting at the Gulf of Venice, following the Piave northwest past Vidor, then turning west to Mount Grappa, Asiago, and Rovereto. Flying north from Grossa in a Camel, the front lines could be reached in 15 minutes, or 20 minutes east to the Piave.

The horizon was lined with the snow-capped mountains of the Italian Dolomite Alps, south of which lay the broad Venetian Plain, and the Gulf of Venice. Peaks rose to over 5,000 feet only a few miles distant from an alluvial plain practically at sea level. In 1918, it was an agricultural district, divided into fields bordered by willow trees, and watered by agricultural drainage ditches. The rivers flowing to the sea, particularly the River Piave, often flooded the lowlands, and the lumpy surface was hazardous to aeroplanes in a forced landing.

The weather could be very cold and clear over the mountains, but sudden snowstorms were frequent. In low visibility there was little to distinguish a snow-covered mountaintop from stratus clouds. Moist air over the Gulf of Venice mixed with winds blowing off the mountains, and the result was fog. As Wing Commander Norman Macmillan of 45 Squadron remembered it:

Weather changes were sudden. At bewildering speed, sunshine might vanish into damp fog, a shallow fog, perhaps no deeper than two hundred feet, but sometimes five hundred, yet always thick enough to enshroud the ground from the view of the pilot flying over it and the aircraft and all else from that of the man on the ground.

Lacking any modern navigation aids, a pilot could be trapped above a fog layer with fuel running low. Limping back with a damaged aircraft, he could then be obliged to penetrate a fog bank with forward visibility reduced to a few yards. Some pilots ended upside down in a farmer's muddy field, and even Barker had his only crash in B6313 attempting to land (after an engine failure) in a ground fog at Asolo.

Fast-moving fog banks were most common in the spring and fall, and flights departing on missions might find their aerodrome reduced to zero visibility shortly after takeoff. This happened to a Canadian flight commander with 66, Capt Hilliard Brooke Bell:

> I saw a heavy bank of fog away to the south apparently approaching our aerodrome. I went on with the patrol, however, and realized too late that we could not get back before the fog rolled over the aerodrome. We raced the fog to another aerodrome at Istrana and just got there in time. A number of pilots were caught and none of them got down without crashing. I was mighty glad to get my flight down with no casualties.

* * *

RFC aerodromes on the Western Front usually had a gypsy atmosphere, as though any day now everyone would be moving. The standard hangar had a wood frame, but canvas roof and walls, for easy dismantling. Farm buildings were used, if available, but otherwise everything was built so as to be quickly transported. In Italy it was little different. There were few facilities in place, and the aerodromes were built in farmers' fields.

The personnel stationed at Grossa were housed in the ubiquitous metal-clad Nissen huts. The Officer's Mess was a huge barn. The squadron office was the standard wood-planked hut with a tar-paper roof nailed down with strips of wood. Light streamed in through four shuttered windows down each side of the hut, and two windows on either side of the narrow entrance. The flying machines were hangared in the standard canvas tents.

After nearly a month of rest and recreation, the pilots and observers of the RFC Italy detachment went back to war. The first offensive patrol was flown on Thursday, 29 November, by 28 and 34 Squadrons, with Barker leading a four-plane formation as pro-

tective escort for two RE8s. The two "Harry Tates" were flown by Capt Thomson and Lieut Luxton; Lieut Banting and Lieut Fitton. The observers had to photograph the area around the Montello near the River Piave. Barker's formation took off at 11:20 a.m., climbed to 11,000 feet, and set course to the east to join up with the RE8s, which had left about 30 minutes earlier.

The four Camels crossed the Piave and Will shortly thereafter spotted a formation of Albatros scouts. The enemy pilots were real professionals. They ignored the Camels and attacked the RE8s. Thomson successfully exposed 14 photographic glass plates from 10,000 feet, but Lieut Banting's camera jammed. The repeated attacks, in two or three formations of four or five machines, forced Luxton and Fitton to run for home.

Barker attempted to engage four German scouts separately, but they would not fight. The enemy were able to use their superior speed to disengage at will. Nevertheless, the Camels were able to protect the two RE8s long enough for them to make it back to friendly territory. But one German pilot did fight against Barker—Leutnant d. R. Hans Hartl of Jasta 1. After a lengthy struggle, each seeking an advantage, Barker wounded Hartl, and scored the first victory in Italy for the RFC. His combat report stated:

> ... we fought for about 20 mins. and the H.A. were reinforced. I dived on one & fired about 50 rounds and he went down in a vertical dive. I followed and as he flattened out at 5,000 feet I got a burst of about 80 rounds at close range. His right top wing folded back to the fuselage and later the lower wing came off. I also saw one E.A. going down out of control below 5,000 feet. Altogether about 12 E.A. were encountered.
>
> Notes:-
> During all the above fighting we were outclassed in speed and climb. The average engine revolutions at 10,000 feet were only 1050 R.P.M. At 5,000 feet the R.P.M. increased and the Camel was a match for the D.4. [*sic*].

A few days later, Barker achieved his fifth victory, becoming in the recently created jargon, an "ace." This five-victory milestone was not universally recognized—the Germans considered 10 victories a minimum—and "ace" was not an official designation in the British flying services. The RFC senior command did not encourage scoring lists or keep official tallies, and the cult of personality that underlay such scores was just not in keeping with the goal of a collective national effort.

Barker was not the only flyer to keep score of his victories, but he did it in a way that has since become standard in squadrons around the world—he marked each victory on his aircraft. The left and right outboard front struts of B6313 were painted with a small horizontal white stripe for each hostile machine or balloon. As his score rose, the white marks progressed down each strut, so that by the summer of 1918, both struts were a solid white.

Barker's style was relentless aggression at all times in the air and, like Victoria Cross recipient Lanoe Hawker, the first RFC ace, believed in the adage "Attack Everything." He set up his attacks from a favourable position, but rarely stalked hostile aircraft. He was always willing to engage in a turning fight at which the Camel excelled, and usually fired at ranges well under 50 yards. As a result, many of his targets broke up in the air. His fifth victory on 3 December 1917 epitomized Hawker's *dictum*:

After finishing escorting R.E.8's, Lt. Cooper, Lt. Waltho & I crossed the river Piave at a low altitude and attacked a hostile balloon N.E. of Conegliano. I fired about 40 rounds into it at a height of 1,000 feet and it began to descend. I then observed an Albatros Scout about to attack Lt. Waltho. I immediately engaged the E.A., drove him down to 300 feet, and then succeeded in getting a burst of fire into him. He dived vertically, crashed, and the wreckage burst into flames. I then re-attacked the balloon, and after firing at very close range, saw it in flames on the ground. I broke up a party of enemy who were at the balloon winch. A large covered car proceeding E. from Conegliano turned over into a ditch when I attacked it. Later I attacked small parties of enemy and dispersed them.

The scout, an Albatros D.III, was piloted by an experienced German pilot with three victories in Italy, Leutnant Franz von Kerssenbrock, of Jasta 39. In his log book, Will wrote that "... he crashed vertically at a colossal speed & the wreckage burnt up."

* * *

By 1918 the glamour of the scout pilot for civilians had transformed a few of them into household names, particularly in Germany and France. Like film stars,

McEwen with his Camel in Italy after the Armistice in November 1918.

DND DHist Biographical Files

81

their photos, in autographed postcard size, were collected and swapped. The word "ace" has entered the language as a pilot with five or more victories in combat, and it all started in the Great War. The best aces then were inclined to be a little older, but still in their twenties. But a great many scout pilots, and

some aces, were teenagers, frequently dead before their 20th birthday. A man over 30 was considered ancient, and the oldest pilots on squadron commonly had nicknames such as "Granny."

The belief that flying was a young man's game got its foundation in this war, but there is no doubt

AUSTRO-HUNGARIAN FLYERS AND AIRCRAFT

The enemy flyers of the Habsburg Empire, also known as the Dual Monarchy, were outnumbered and outgunned, especially after their German Air Force allies left the Italian Front in 1918. At the peak of the fighting, the Austro-Hungarian Army and Navy had a combined fleet on three fronts (the Italian, Balkan, and Russian) of only 550 aircraft. The "kaiserliche und königliche Luftfahrtruppen" translated literally as "the Imperial and Royal Aviation Troops," but was usually abbreviated as "K.u.K. LFT." It had started out as a balloon corps in 1893.

The countries under the Dual Monarchy had an active flying community prior to the war, and Austria-Hungary held 18 world flying records in 1912, second only to France. Few now recall the Hapsburg Empire as being an ally of Germany, and their flyers, if remembered at all, are usually lumped together as "Austrians." In reality, the nationality of Dual Monarchy flyers included not only Austrians, but also Hungarians, Czechoslovakians, Serbians, Croatians, Poles, and Russians.

Despite these ethnic complexities, and the small size of the K.u.K. LFT, its pilots and observers were well trained and battle-experienced, most having served in the other combat arms prior to joining the K.u.K. LFT. Many pilots had extensive previous flying as observers.

The Austro-Hungarian industrial complex could not produce aircraft on the scale of its German ally, or its enemies. The Habsburg Empire was obliged to buy military aircraft from Germany, and invite German companies to establish branch plants, which Albatros and Aviatik did in Vienna, and Deutsche Flugzeug Werke (DFW) did outside Budapest. Through the first three years of the war, the K.u.K. LFT flew license-built and imported models of German two-seaters, but by 1918 the UFAG and Phönix companies were manufacturing an indigenous two-seater design, the C.I.

There were four main types of Austro-Hungarian single-seater fighters. The Berg D.I was the design of Julius von Berg, a German engineer with Aviatik in Vienna. The RFC/RAF usually referred to it as simply "Berg scout" in combat reports. It was the first indigenous scout design for the Austro-Hungarian military. It had good handling characteristics, was manoeuvrable but also stable in flight, and had a spacious, comfortable cockpit. However, its Austro-Daimler engine was prone to overheating, and the synchronizing gear for the two Schwarzlose 8.0 mm machine guns was not particularly robust. When these guns jammed in the air, they could only be cleared back on the ground.

The Phönix D.I and Phönix D.II scouts were designs of the Phönix Flugzeugwerke AG company. The earliest in the D.I series suffered occasional wing failures. With a beefed up wing structure, and redesigned tail, the D.II and Phönix D.IIa models started joining Austro-Hungarian squadrons by May 1918. The machine was competitive in performance with other types, but had the same troublesome twin Schwarzlose machine guns.

Most of the leading Austro-Hungarian aces liked the Oeffag-built version of the German Albatros D.III better than the Berg or the Phönix D.I or D.II. The Oeffag company took the German Albatros and installed a 225-hp Daimler engine, and made other improvements. The resulting D.III (Oef) was arguably the best of all Albatros scouts, superior to the D.III and D.V flying on the Western Front.

Barker taking off in B6313, 28 Squadron, 1917–18.

at all that the experience of combat hardened and aged even the most youthful flyers. Brooke Bell commented on this at the end of his life:

> Soon after [my episode with the fog bank], I got my first "flamer." He was a lone Albatross [*sic*] D.III painted in spiral stripes like a barber pole. We were well over the line and cut him off trying to get home. It is a wonderful and terrible sight to see a machine go down burning like a torch. At the time, I cheered as though I had won a game of something, but afterwards started to think of the fellow who was killed and of his family. This viewpoint fortunately wears off as one gets hardened to the idea.

Barker was a remarkably versatile scout pilot, with none of the typical Camel pilot's reluctance for air-to-ground missions. He appears to have liked strafing and bombing, and he always attacked kite balloons, despite the risk of being shot down by anti-aircraft batteries. He stood apart from many of the other high-scoring aces in his eagerness for all types of combat. He was not satisfied simply with aerial victories, or the stalking of easy targets.

The only squeamishness Barker ever expressed about ground attack duties had to do with horses. He did not like strafing them. After the war he commented: "Horse lines present an ideal target and it should be borne in mind that trained horses are very valuable and cannot be quickly replaced ... the destruction of tethered horses is a most unpleasant task, but of course is a military necessity."

The key to successful ground support missions, in Barker's opinion, was training and tactical planning combined with rapid execution. In contrast to the conventional wisdom of the time that pilots should remain at or above 500 feet, he believed in extremely low-level attack:

... every endeavour was made to keep out of sight, using all available cover such as river beds, trees, ravines, etc., but not clouds or sun ... too much stress cannot be laid on the necessity of controlling ammunition expenditure. We suffered considerable casualties during the war through keen pilots being caught without ammunition after a ground attack. ... Results are altogether dependent on training, and with this in view I trained my pilots in attacking and setting on fire a partly filled two gallon petrol tin. This was ideal training for ground attack and its effects were quickly visible.

* * *

In the first weeks of December, the RFC in Italy was expanded, and squadrons were shuttled back and forth as RFC HQ rearranged its forces in accordance with the location of the British divisions. On 3 December, the RE8s of 34 flew from Grossa to Istrana, an aerodrome about 15 miles behind the front lines, west of the Piave. This left room for a second Camel unit, 66, to join 28. Another Corps Cooperation unit, 42, moved back to Grossa to make way for the RFC's third scout squadron in Italy, 45, which arrived on 26 December. These three RFC scout squadrons had a total of 54 Camels; while the two Corps Cooperation units had 36 RE8s.

The British air forces in Italy were small compared to the Aeronautica del Regio Esercito, the Italian Army Air Service. During the Battle of Caporetto, the Italian Army Air Service had 15 scout squadrons, with more than 220 fighters of various types, and this expanded to 18 squadrons and 270 fighters by the end of the war. The Italian pilots were well able to hold their own against their opposition, their Hanriots and SPADs a match for the licence-built Albatros D.III, and the Austrian-Hungarian-designed Berg and Phönix scouts.

Barker flew 21 offensive patrols in December, and achieved his seventh victory on the morning of 29 December by destroying an enemy kite balloon. The pilots flying with him for this patrol were Waltho, McEwen, and Hudson. Despite their supporting gunfire to set the balloon on fire, 28

Squadron and 51 Wing credited the victory to Barker alone. The following afternoon, perhaps spurred on by Barker's victory, McEwen and Cooper destroyed an Albatros D.III in flames just northeast of Conegliano.

This was McEwen's first of 27 credited victories. Like Barker, he was an excellent gunner, with 23 out of the 27 victories credited to him representing aircraft destroyed in crashes or consumed by fire in the air. Clifford MacKay McEwen, born in Griswold, Manitoba, and educated in Moose Jaw and Saskatoon, Saskatchewan, was the son of a hardware store owner. He became particularly good friends with Malik, and enjoyed listening to the Oxford graduate quote passages of poet William Butler Yeats. The two men, strikingly different in background, were still keeping in touch many years later when Malik was a high-ranking diplomat for India, and McEwen was a high-ranking officer in the RCAF.

McEwen, nicknamed "Black Mike" by fellow-pilots because of his dark tan after a leave on the Riviera, ultimately had the most outstanding military record of any who served under Barker. In addition to his 27 victories, McEwen received the MC, the Distinguished Flying Cross (DFC) and Bar, and the Italian Bronze Medal for Military Valour.

Proud of his own record, and very competitive, "Black Mike" nevertheless considered Barker as the bravest man he had ever met. Air Vice-Marshal McEwen commanded 6 Bomber Group of the RCAF in the Second World War. He was a great believer in training, and more training in that war, something he had first learned from William Barker on the Italian Front.

The most dramatic offensive patrol flown by Barker in December was unauthorized. It became a legendary tale, often written about after the war in magazines and books, and revived by Ernest Hemingway in *Esquire* magazine in arguably his most famous short story, *The Snows of Kilimanjaro*. The patrol took place on Christmas Day, and a teenager named Hudson was Barker's sidekick.

Lieut Harold Byrne Hudson was typical of many British-Canadian transplants who had enlisted in the RFC. Born in 1898 in Cobham, Surrey, a son of the village's medical doctor, he was educated at home and at Epson College. Dr. A.B. Hudson immigrated with his family in 1912 to Victoria, British Columbia, and Harold attended the University School there, but left to work at the Bank of Montreal.

Round-faced, dark-complexioned, and boyish, he looked somewhat East Asian in appearance. Nicknames are inevitable on a squadron, and Hudson's pals promptly tagged him "Chink," although because of his features, he was also known as "Baby." Barker was Hudson's idol, and the boy cheerfully followed his flight leader into any kind of action. When Barker proposed to attack an enemy airfield on Christmas morning, Hudson immediately volunteered.

Apparently, no one else in C Flight stepped forward, perhaps because Major Glanville had not ordered the mission. Most importantly, however, it was Christmas Day, and low cloud and fog covered the Venetian Plain. It was a "dud" day for flying, actually bad enough to prevent 45 Squadron, the third Camel unit just arrived on the Italian Front, from

flying their machines the short distance of 25 miles from San Pelagio, near Padua, to Istrana.

Barker never recorded in his log book what airfield he selected, simply scribbling that he "attacked hostile aerodrome with good results. One hangar set on fire, etc. with Buckingham from very ... [illegible] ... low height. various other targets were attacked with success." The aerodrome was most likely San Fior, the home of a German squadron, Fliegerabteilung (A)204. This is predicated on a German 14 Army weekly report which stated that two Camels shot up the airfield at which 204 was based, damaging several hangars and four machines.

Squadron records show that Barker and Hudson took off at 7:35 am, and were gone for two hours. The brief report filed with the Recording Officer of 28 states: "San Felice Aerodrome attacked with MG fire and after 400 rounds one hangar burst into flames. Mechanics were also engaged with good effect. On the return flight a hostile battery of 4 guns with gunners standing by was attacked—the latter were scattered in all directions."

The pilots of 28 Squadron; Harold Hudson is 6th from left; Stanley Stanger 7th from left.

Stewart K. Taylor collection

Barker never shed any light on this low-level attack, and there are many variations on this legendary story. In one published version, Barker and Hudson are said to have strafed a staff car with a motorcycle escort, then some trenches, and a balloon section. Just before the aerodrome attack, Barker is reported to have tossed a hand-written placard out of the cockpit, on which was written: "To the Austrian Flying Corps from the English RFC—Wishing you a Merry Xmas."

In the Hemingway fictionalized account, Barker was said to have also strafed a train filled with officers going on leave, killing as many as 11 men. This may have occurred during an authorized 14 Wing ground attack mission, but probably not on 25 December 1917.

The sheer chutzpah of the raid apparently so irritated the Germans that they launched retaliatory bombing missions on Boxing Day. More than 30 aircraft attacked early in the morning, followed by a smaller formation around noon. Since many of the German flyers had been partying, some flew with a hangover, while a few were still drunk. One pilot, forced to land after running out of fuel, fell asleep in the cockpit, and was awakened by his British captors. The *ad hoc* nature of the mission, using different types of bombers, resulted in an uncoordinated attack, conducted in broad daylight, without protective escorts.

One author wrote that Barker and Hudson had landed after their patrol at Istrana, ostensibly to wish their pals a face-to-face Merry Christmas. The German bomber force attacked Istrana, not Grossa where 28 was stationed. The accuracy of their bombing was poor, and losses were high, particularly during the second raid around noon. As many as nine of the German bombers were shot down by Italian scout pilots at Istrana, with some claims being shared with the

RFC/RAF airfield in northern Italy in 1918.

Camel pilots of 28. The German bombing may not have been well planned, but was still accurate enough to kill one British and five Italian air mechanics on the aerodrome, and wound several others.

Understandably, the destruction and death caused by the German bombing generated antipathy towards the man who had decided to fight instead of eat and drink on Christmas Day. As a 1930s dime-paperback account put it: "By merely paying our squadron a friendly visit, Barker had us practically blown off the map. The chap was worse than a black cat." Hemingway's portrayal of Barker in *The Snows of Kilimanjaro* was more sinister still:

But he had never written a line of that, nor of that cold, bright Christmas day with the mountains showing across the plain that Barker had flown across the lines to bomb the Austrian officers' leave train, machine-gunning them as they scattered and ran. He remembered Barker afterwards coming into the mess and starting to tell about it. And how quiet it got and then somebody saying, "You bloody murderous bastard."

The Germans switched to night bombing after their losses on Boxing Day, and for seven nights bombed various Italian towns, such as Treviso, Mestre, Castelfranco, as well as the city of Padua. On 28 December, members of the British General Staff in Padua felt the impact of some bombs in a house next door, and several civilians were killed, and others wounded, outside the Storione Restaurant. All this horror may well have been precipitated by the actions of an unrepentant William Barker, who considered war a 365-day affair.

A New Year's Day bombing mission was launched by the RFC, sending ten RE8s from 42 Squadron, along with two flights of five Camels from 28 and 66 Squadrons for protection. The target was the 14 Army HQ at Vittorio. The bombing was successful, but 66 Squadron got the worst of the exchanges with 18 enemy scouts. Their leader, Capt R. Erskine was killed in action, and Lieut A.B. Reade had his ailerons shot away. Barker's flight—Hudson, McEwen, Cooper, and Wright—came through unscathed, with William Barker achieving his eighth victory:

Captain Barker dived at an E.A. which was firing at an R.E.8, and drove him down in a spin, but the E.A. subsequently flattened out. Capt Barker was then attacked by 2 E.A., one of which, after receiving a burst at close range, dived and fell out of control, finally crashing on a mountain side north west of Vittorio. The wreckage burst into flames and was seen rolling down in the valley. The other members of the patrol fought several indecisive combats.

The man in the flaming wreckage was Offstv Karl Lang of Jasta 1, who had been in Italy with his squadron since November, and had himself driven down an Italian two-seater in flames on 7 November. Barker was confident of his shooting, telling his mother that Lang was dead before he hit the mountainside:

Just a p.c. [post card] as I wrote you only 2 days ago … I have started the new year rather well. I brought down the first Hun for our arms in 1918 in Italy. I was leading 10 of our scouts & we met 15 Hostile scouts & in the fight I drove two down & crashed one out of control on the mountain side of the Alps where he burst into flames & rolled thousands of feet down the mountain. He was killed in the air. We are very busy & have little time for anything except flying.

Barker had now made his mark on the Italian Front. He was maturing as a flight leader, developing into a brilliant air power tactician. Nineteen-eighteen would be his year of glory and pain.

Barker standing by Italian SVA aircraft he flew on 20 June 1918 near Genoa.

CHAPTER SIX

AIR WAR OVER THE ITALIAN ALPS

*"He was a young man who hated inactivity, and ... his keen sense of fun was apt to get him into trouble ...
Having known him so well and liked him so much, I hope I shall be forgiven if I say that of all the fliers of
two world wars none was greater than Barker."*

AIR CHIEF MARSHAL SIR PHILIP JOUBERT DE LA FERTÉ, 1962

Barker's enthusiasm for impromptu missions only further strained his already tense relationship with Glanville. Despite this, his commanding officer recommended him for the DSO, even after Barker's unauthorized Christmas Day raid. The citation for the DSO, announced in the *London Gazette* on 18 February, said that he had destroyed enemy aeroplanes, although twice attacked by superior forces: "On each occasion the hostile machines were observed to crash to earth, the wreckage bursting into flames. His splendid example of fearlessness and magnificent leadership have been of inestimable value to his squadron."

As soon as the RFC in Italy was up to full strength with five squadrons, the commander of the RFC VII Brigade HQ, Brig General Thomas Webb-Bowen, laid down the general policy for daily flight operations. He called for a continuous daylight presence in Italian skies, and a relentless application of the offensive style of operation common on the Western Front.

By 15 January he had established the standard RFC Western Front brigade organization: a Balloon Wing; an Army Wing; and a Corps Cooperation Wing, numbered 4, 14, and 51, respectively, along with the usual Aircraft Park (7). The two Corps Cooperation squadrons, 34 and 42, reported to Lt Colonel Mills in 51 Wing, and the three Camel squadrons, 28, 45, and 66, reported to Lt Colonel Philip Joubert de la Ferté.

Two months later, the British had reduced its presence in Italy, and Webb-Bowen and his VII Brigade staff were back in France. They left behind a consolidated 14 Wing beefed up with a flight of Bristol F2B Fighters, sent directly from England, to offset the loss of 42 Squadron's RE8s. Joubert was appointed the head of the RFC Expeditionary Force in Italy, and held the position until the war ended.

Joubert was born in Calcutta, India. He joined the infant RFC in 1912, and is credited with the first wartime reconnaissance mission of the RFC in France, in August 1914. He retired from the RAF with a knighthood and the rank of Air Chief Marshal at the end of the Second World War. Joubert was a very *pukkah* officer who took an immediate liking to Will. He was typical of the pearl-voiced British upper middle classes, while Barker was typical of the Canadian flat vowelled, farm-raised working classes. In short, they had nothing in common.

At 75, Sir Philip wrote a fond recollection about the Canadian for *The Sunday Express* in the UK. An abridged version was reprinted in the *Weekend Magazine* in Canada:

Barker was a powerfully built fellow, 5 ft 10.5 in, and over 12 stone [180 pounds], almost burly in appearance. But his pallid complexion and prominent compelling eyes, coupled with a staccato, abrupt manner and a mood of nervous impatience, gave him an aura of intellectual introversion that contrasted oddly with his

Stewart K. Taylor collection

Barker visits 14 Wing Headquarters in 1918; Barker on right next to Lt Colonel Philip Joubert de la Ferté.

temperament and build. He was a young man who hated inactivity, and at such times his keen sense of fun was apt to get him into trouble.

Joubert may have liked Barker, but he was also quick to rebuke him for violations of flying regulation. In January 1918 he sent a telegram to 28 Squadron asking Major Glanville to explain what the hell Barker was doing attacking enemy balloons without permission:

Captain Barker's reasons in writing are required to explain why, contrary to orders, he attacked, in company with 2/Lieut Hudson, 2 enemy balloons and a ground target of transport vehicles?

The long-suffering Glanville forwarded Barker's feeble justification:

I have the honour to offer this my explanation for my attack on enemy observation balloons on the 24th inst.

2/Lieut Hudson & I were up engaged in practice fighting after which we proceeded to enemy's lines to test our guns. We were engaged in doing this when I noticed the two enemy balloons & column of enemy transport. I regret very much that for the moment I forgot the order against low flying. I have the honour to be Sir your obedient servant.

As far as we know, the rebuke ended with this letter. It may have been an unauthorized patrol, but Wing HQ still granted Barker and Hudson credit for two enemy kite balloons, the first and second victories for Hudson, but the ninth and tenth for Barker.

An eternal optimist, Will quickly forgot the rebuke, and went on being his spontaneous self. He embarrassed Joubert a few months later by scattering a formation of Italian aircraft performing a flypast at an awards ceremony presided over by the King of Italy, Victor Emanuel:

> The Italians tried hard to keep station, but the fly-past quickly degenerated into a skirmish, while the dignified ceremonial at the saluting base disintegrated as Barker finished his run a few feet over the heads of the king and his generals. Barker saw the episode as a wonderful prank, but the high command could not view it in that light. The Italians were our allies and a review was a review.

Despite all this aggravation, Joubert remembered Barker fondly: "Having known him so well and liked him so much, I hope I shall be forgiven if I say that of all the fliers of two world wars none was greater than Barker."

Replacements for casualties in 28 Squadron trickled in during December and January. Malik, recovered from his wounds, came back to the unit during this period, and two Canadian pilots arrived. They were Lieut G.D. McLeod, of Westmount, Quebec, and Lieut D.G. McLean, of Bridgeburg, Ontario. George Donald McLeod was the son of a McGill University professor, and a graduate from McGill's School of Architecture. Due to his educated middle-class Scottish origins, he was held in rather higher regard than some of the other Canadians by the British pilots at 28 Squadron. McLeod felt caught in the British versus Dominion crossfire within the unit—he was a Canadian, but in upbringing he had more in common with the British officers, than with Barker, McEwen, or Malik.

* * *

Barker flew only about 11 patrols in January and nine in February. He was on leave between 13 February and 7 March. Before leaving for Paris and London,

Will and his boys were credited with 12 victories in only three missions. On 2 February, he led McEwen, Hudson, and Waltho on a so-called "central sector patrol," during which he detected what he identified in his report as a low-flying formation of five two-seat Aviatiks, escorted by three Albatros D.V scouts, between Conegliano and Susegana.

Barker's keen eyesight picked out this formation looking down from 14,000 feet, more than two miles above the enemy machines. Signalling with his Verey flare pistol to his wingman to follow him down, he then dove at high speed on one of the scouts. The first enemy pilot that Will fired at lost control of his aircraft, and crashed and burned just southwest of Conegliano. This machine was not a D.V, but a Phönix D.I, just being introduced to service. The pilot was Feldwebel (Sergeant Major) Alphons Koritsky of Flik 28J.

Barker then shot down a two-seater which crashed near Gera. When a crowd gathered around the wreckage, he machine-gunned them and the downed aircraft, setting it ablaze. McEwen attacked two Aviatik reconnaissance aircraft in succession, and both crashed close together just north of Conegliano, his second and third victories. It was an impressive morning's work. Four Camels had attacked a superior force of eight, and achieved decisive victories over four enemy pilots, without damage or loss to themselves.

In the afternoon, Barker led his flight on another central sector patrol for over two hours, looking to repeat this success, but no hostile formations showed up. In a letter to his mother, Will boasted about his latest combat: "Have not yet got my leave but expect it soon ... I was leading 3 of my machines well over the lines when I met 9 of the enemy. I dived from 16,000 ft. to 1,000 ft. vertically & brought my first down in flames—attacked another damaging him. Then attacked & destroyed another—a 2 seater in flames & drove 2 more down. This makes 17 official victims for me [actually only 12]. It was sure some fight."

On the morning of 5 February, Barker and Hudson went hunting for an enemy two-seater that was on an artillery shoot near the front lines. The two Camels were cruising high, 17,000 feet, when they saw and attacked two Albatros D.Vs 1,000 feet below them,

Barker's photo of enemy kite balloon over the Alps.

David Mackenzie collection

"driven down." However, in his own log book, Barker did count this Aviatik C.I. as a victory. He also identified the scouts as D.IIIs in his log book, but they are referred to as D.Vs in the squadron combat report.

In February, the RFC fitted the Sopwith Camels in Italy with wooden bomb racks under the centre section of the fuselage, just behind the engine. This allowed the scout to supplement the RE8s, although the payload was modest—four 20-lb Cooper anti-personnel bombs. On 8 February, Barker took B6313 airborne with four bombs to see what altitude the machine could maintain.

Four days later, on his last mission for three weeks, he led Hudson on an afternoon patrol. The official purpose was to conduct a machine-gun test. There was thick ground mist over the River Piave, providing good concealment for machines hunting kite balloons. The two crossed the front lines and found five balloons at Fossamerlo. There were two large observation balloons, and three small (presumably unmanned) eight-foot-diameter balloons, all clustered together, and hovering only a few feet above the ground. Hudson and Barker ignited all five.

For less than five minutes work, the two pilots were credited with five shared victories—the most on a single mission for any RFC pilot in Italy, and the most by Barker in his career. It seems unlikely that the eight-footers were manned kite balloons, and it is rather surprising that these were considered worthy of a credit by 14 Wing.

Barker may have intentionally crossed the lines, yet again without authorization, just to win a contest in his squadron:

A period of bad weather set in and the pilots of 28 Squadron, bored with inactivity, bridge, poker, and letter-writing, were stirred by someone's suggestion to run a sweep-stake on the next enemy to be downed, the winner to be whoever drew the name of the victor ... Next day thick ground mist stopped most flying. But that afternoon Bill Barker and Steve [sic] Hudson went to the airfield and flew off into the mist ... They knew their purpose

driving them east towards their home aerodrome. Thirty minutes later, at noon, the two found an Aviatik two-seater with an escort of two D.Vs, just north of Oderzo. Barker closed to within a few yards of one of the escorts. A single burst of gunfire sheared off the Scout's left wing. The Albatros broke up completely, and Zgsf Josef Schantl of Flik 19D was killed.

Hudson was, at this time, fighting a descending battle with Feldwebel Karl Semelrock of Flik 51J. He pursued him all the way down from 17,000 feet to just 200 feet above ground in the vicinity of Portobuffole where Semelrock crashed. Barker relentlessly chased the remaining Aviatik, which entered a spin to evade, the pilot then recovering and managing to glide down to a safe landing. However, the pilot and observer were both injured when the two-seater tipped upside down.

This patrol added one victory each for Barker and Hudson, the Aviatik being rated simply as

...The two EKBs went down in flames ... then they destroyed the three sphericals ...

Re-entering the mess Barker quietly asked, "Do balloons count in the sweep?"

Everyone agreed that they did.

"Then whoever has drawn my name should get the money!" he said.

"How's that?" asked the CO, Major Glanville.

"Because I've been out with Steve and we got two KBs and three comic gas-bags."

Macmillan, who recounted this story in his book, *Offensive Patrol,* believed that Barker planned on winning the sweepstakes, just before going on leave. He did not think much of this kind of grandstanding: "Weather, a sweep-stake, and impending leave were the triple chance that decided the fate of five enemy balloons on 12 February 1918."

With Will on leave, McEwen had the time of his life leading C Flight. "Black Mike" adopted B6313 while his own machine, B5169, was in for repairs between 21 and 25 February. He logged about 10 hours, in five offensive patrols, but had no successful air battles. B5169 had had engine troubles on a noonday mission on the 18th, causing him to fall behind, but he had managed, while flying alone, to drive down an Albatros out of control. During this engagement, McEwen's goggles frosted over, and he could not see his target. Frost on goggles was a problem in open-cockpit biplanes, and whale oil was some times used as a preventative, but a common practice was to carry two sets of goggles.

Now able to bomb, as well as strafe, the Camel squadrons were sent on more low-level attack missions. Barker made it a practice that multiple flights were assigned different duties. The first flight dropped bombs, and strafed the anti-aircraft guns, helping protect the second and third flights inbound. The second flight, composed of the best air-fighting pilots in the squadron, dropped its bombs, but preserved all ammunition to fight hostile aircraft, climbing to about 500 feet to provide top cover for the third flight, which simply attacked the machines and hangars with machine guns.

One of the important roles of the formation leaders when flying to or from the target was to suppress any machine-gun crews that might be concealed along the route. The Austro-Hungarians had retaliated against low flying machines by installing machine-gun crews in the second-story windows of every house within five miles of the front lines. One Camel pilot, Lieut Arthur Cooper, recalled that "if you came over a hedge and saw a couple of men sunning themselves at a door of a cottage, you either killed them before they could get indoors or your patrol got chased with machine gun fire until it was out of sight. Therefore, as a leader one always flew with ... fingers on the gun triggers."

On one such attack, McEwen blew in two hangar doors with his bombs, setting the hangars on fire. He was then forced to limp home on the small gravity-feed tank in the upper wing, after his main fuel tank was punctured by ground fire. For this and other actions, he received the MC. February was a successful month, and he was happy that Barker was, so to speak, "out of town," allowing him more chances to achieve victories.

McEwen and Stanger credited some of Barker's victories to their important supporting role as his wingmen. Capt Stanley Stanger, of Montreal, was one of the most naturally gifted pilots on Camels in Italy. McEwen always claimed that "Stanger was the greatest smooth pilot, and Barker the greatest rough pilot I ever knew." Stanger implied, later in his life, that Barker was inclined to hog the enemy targets for himself: "For the most part my job was to protect the flight leader, and for that reason he was able to get credit for many machines. My leader was Barker until I took his place, and then I gave my escorts an opportunity to shoot down machines."

Stan later teamed up effectively with "Black Mike" at 28 Squadron. He was credited with 13 victories, and received the MC and DFC. Given the victories that other pilots had while flying on Barker's wing, Stanger's charge that Barker hogged the action was little more than fighter pilot's envy.

Winter has written in *The First of the Few* that "the fighter pilot's war was ... fought according to a basic rhythm as regular as a Benedictine monk." For those who survived the first few patrols and gained the necessary skills to be useful to their flight, life fell into a cycle of action and leisure. There were standard operating procedures in all the RFC units but variations caused by weather, casualties, leave, and the enemy meant no day was quite like another. Some of the best anecdotes about life on the Italian Front have been provided by Capt Thomas F. Williams:

> All the meals in the mess, from breakfast to dinner at night, were pretty much on a catch-as-catch-can, for some were always in the air if the weather was at all possible [*sic*]. We maintained a constant umbrella over our lines from dawn to dusk. Dinner was designed to return us from the savage to the civilized state, to erase both the glories and the sorrows that the day has brought. It would commence with the formality that gentlemen expect, but we were composed of compounds, volatile and unstable, and anything could happen.

Coping with frayed nerves after combat was critical to long-term survival, and pilots blew off steam through sports and parties:

> As soon as all the missions on the board were completed we were free to do anything we wished. A tennis court was a must; a sandbagged bathing pool another must, especially when one came down from two hours at altitudes from 12,000 to 18,000 feet in a Sidcot suit into 110 F in the shade; scatter-guns and clay pigeons; horses to ride to be found somewhere; billiard table; transport to Venice, Padua, Cittadella or Verona not too difficult to arrange for … Sports got much attention— Flights vs. Flights, officers and men teamed or competing without distinction. There was much talent in the Air Force. Shows were staged to which Italians and other Services were invited. The shows staged would do credit to any group. Every Mess had music anytime, or all the time.

Dining-in nights were used to celebrate decorations awarded, to entertain visiting VIPs, or bid farewell to friends posted out. The squadrons had menus printed for their more elaborate dinners, and stage shows or musical reviews required printed programs. Some units, notably 66, produced monthly newsletters.

All this diversion took a man's mind away from the war and tomorrow's patrols. Experienced flyers made friends with the "green" arrivals only after it seemed likely they would survive usefully with the squadron. This was less due to warrior insensitivity than emotional trauma. As flight surgeon Dr Douglas Bond wrote, it was the result of "having one's friends killed, one after another, and being left the only occupant in a formerly crowded hut. A sense of loneliness and despair is created, known only to those few who have survived long after their last close friend has died … The dead who lie between the 'old' men and the 'new' constitute a barrier that is not lightly broken."

Barker during a tennis game.

David Mackenzie collection

Within a few weeks a man had either learned the trade, and was useful in combat, or was sent back to England. Men anxious about dying or falling apart in combat often had physical problems that were the result of their underlying stress or neurosis. This included blurring of vision, sometimes blindness, a paralysis in one or more limbs, nightmares and sleeplessness, nausea and lassitude. Post-First World War medical reviews of attrition and failure in pilots, other than in combat itself, revealed that 80 percent were due to so-called nervous instability.

Scout pilots in the First World War were from a broad spectrum of society. Only a few were married, and many were still adolescent school boys. Most were patriots, but a few were soldiers-of-fortune. Two kinds of personality performed better: the man who could suspend his imagination, or lacked one, and therefore did not worry much, and the sociopath without feeling who loved the peak experience of hunting and killing other men. Barker unquestionably fit into the first category, but his love of action for its own sake certainly motivated him to hunt and kill. His post-war traumatic suffering, and his generally warm relationship with most of his wartime colleagues, is not consistent with a sociopathic personality.

How a man embraced or was traumatized by the peak experience of aerial combat depended on chance, his degree of exposure to specific trauma, and his initial success or failure in the air. Bond's WWII study of successful combat flyers revealed two common denominators: "... men who showed themselves outstanding seemed to have as their common bond both a strong love of flying and a still stronger delight in the expression of their aggression in the air."

If this aggression and love of flying were lacking, and a man was traumatized by a series of upsets, he formed a phobia for flight rather quickly. Some men continued flying despite great anxiety and eventually were killed in combat—others aborted missions repeatedly, or had to be grounded by the medical officer for various physical and/or nervous ailments. Flying provided a daily outlet for unconscious aggression, and mild-mannered men who quietly ate dinner in the Officer's Mess were often transformed in the cockpit of an aircraft.

As Bond described it: "The condoned release of aggression in war, like the enjoyment of flight, constitutes one of the strongest bulwarks against anxiety as well as one of the keynotes in success." For particularly outstanding flyers such as Barker, McEwen, and others: "... the satisfaction they obtained from combat stood as a bulwark against trauma and went hand in hand with a superior performance."

The RFC Italy detachment had a high percentage of outstanding flyers, many with hard-earned experience on the Western Front. The ability of the Camel pilots to fight their way out of a corner was highly respected by the Austro-Hungarians. Their eagerness to fight, even when outnumbered, came from the experience of the Western Front, as Capt Thomas Williams observed:

It was more of a gentleman's war in Italy ... the scout pilots we encountered in Italy didn't seem to have that same viciousness that we

Thomas Frederic "Voss" Williams.

95

met up on the Western Front. The Western Front was a blood for blood affair ... The Austrians, though, had some real good flyers, mostly seconded from the cavalry ... we had a superiority in experience [and] a lot of superiority so far as aircraft were concerned. There wasn't anything to match a Camel. A Camel could outmanoeuvre anything they had ... didn't need to worry about the numerical opposition ... If you became one with the Camel you had everything that you needed.

* * *

Well rested, but anxious not to be left behind, Barker dived back into flying immediately on his return from leave. But on his first offensive patrol, on 8 March, he survived an undignified crash in B6313, his first since becoming a scout pilot. After 90 minutes airborne his engine failed, and he could not get

it restarted. With ground fog in the area, Barker was forced to "dead-stick" his Camel down to a landing. He searched anxiously for a clear patch. He was near Asolo, in the vicinity of the 23rd French Division HQ, but all he could see below him was a grey soup. Inching his way down through the fog, with the wind whistling in the wires, he detected the faint contours of a hillside.

He tried to arrest his rate of descent as the stubble field came clearly into view, but his timing was slightly off, and there was no engine power to help him. On touchdown the machine flipped on its back. The wheels and the propeller broke off, and the machine settled onto its upper wing, and vertical tail fin. Embarrassed but unhurt, Barker released his harness and crawled out from underneath. Brushing the dirt and straw off, he started walking. He wanted to let his squadron know where he was. He probably made a call from the French HQ nearby. When the 28

Barker after a "dead-stick" landing near Asolo on 8 March 1918.

Squadron repair party arrived, he hitched a ride back to Grossa. He had some breakfast, ordered another Camel rolled out, and took it flying for 15 minutes.

The unit's riggers worked hard to repair B6313, taking a week to replace the upper and lower wings, the centre section, rudder, right-hand diagonal strut, undercarriage and wheels. In addition, they "trued up" the fuselage and put new linen over the wooden skeleton. Less than two weeks later, the original factory engine was removed, and a more powerful 140-hp Clerget installed by the fitters.

Barker flew Camel 4615 till 14 March, logging about 11 hours on offensive patrols, tests and fighting practice, but scoring no victories. As soon as B6313 came out of repair he took it for a test flight, and the following day for an uneventful eastern sector patrol. On 18 March he engaged seven Albatros scouts at 17,000 feet. Picking out the closest machine, Will fired a short burst of 50 rounds, at a distance of 40 yards, and the Albatros spun slowly to the ground. The impact near Villanova was confirmed by Lieut Arthur Cooper. Barker and his personal weapon were back in business.

The next day, he led Cooper, and an American, 2nd Lieut George Forder, against six hostile machines, engaging them in a descending fight from 17,000 feet, right down to 1,000 feet above ground:

Capt Barker engaged and forced 2 E.A. to spin, and then was attacked by 2. D.3s, one, after a short burst at close range stalled and went down out of control, result could not be observed as another E.A. was on his tail. Capt Barker then half rolled and after a burst, this E.A. spun, following the E.A. down and after several bursts on the way forced the E.A. to spin to 1,000 ft. of the river bed near Cismon. The E.A. then attempted to escape by "S" turning and flying north at about 800 ft. Capt Barker re-attacked and fired about 200 rounds at close range. The E.A. turned over and crashed just north of Cismon.

2/Lt. A.G. Cooper drove 1 E.A. down to 2,000 ft. but E.A. escaped owing to superiority in speed.

The confusion inherent in any fight is evident in this combat report, which is about average in bringing clarity to the whirling confusion.

Lieut Forder was the sole American serving in 28 Squadron at the time, although there were at least seven or eight others with the RFC in Italy. A native of Chicago, Forder was one of about 4,000 US citizens who had come north to enlist in the Canadian Expeditionary Force. He was wounded with the CEF, and wounded again in his final air fight on 11 May 1918. He was forced down and captured at Feltre aerodrome by a pilot nicknamed the "Falcon of Feltre," Oberleutnant Frank Linke-Crawford. After surviving in a prisoner-of-war camp, Forder was killed in a flying accident in February 1919.

Barker flew about 12 more patrols in March and early April, and a few test flights. But his two victories with Forder and Cooper were the last with 28 Squadron, raising his total to 22. The Austro-Hungarian squadrons were not very aggressive in March, and opportunities for fighting were rare. Barker had by now logged more than 180 hours of operational flying with 28, and had virtually completed his tour on scouts. He could have, had he wished, been posted to Home Establishment.

On 24 March, his second Bar to the Military Cross was announced, although it was not formally gazetted for seven months. Barker was the only Canadian flyer in the RFC in the First World War to receive two Bars to the MC. Two RNAS pilots from Canada, Joseph S. T. Fall and Theodore Hallam, equalled him with two Bars to their Distinguished Service Crosses. The *London Gazette* citation praised Barker:

For conspicuous gallantry and devotion to duty. When leading patrols he on one occasion attacked eight hostile machines, himself shooting down two, and on another occasion seven, one of which he shot down. In two months he himself destroyed four enemy machines and drove down one, and burned two balloons.

VICTORY CLAIMS OF PILOTS

Army scout squadrons stood apart from the Corps Cooperation and bomber squadrons because they had fewer personnel, and competition between flyers was keener. After a few offensive patrols the victims were separated from the survivors, and the competent from the brilliant. Ninety years after the Great War, it is not easy to separate the truth from the legends of the aces.

The quasi-official lists of victory scores have taken on a time-honoured quality that no amount of fresh information seems to alter. Almost every general book on this subject, for generations, has provided the same traditional multi-national ranking by score: von Richthofen, Fonck, Mannock, Bishop, Udet, Collishaw, McCudden, Guynemer, Beauchamp-Proctor, MacLaren, Loewenhardt, Barker, Voss, Little, and so on. Despite fresh research which shows that many victories cannot be verified, and a few of the major scores, and many of the minor ones, are probably inflated to one degree or another, the names on the list retain their time-honoured immortality.

The victory claims of most pilots of the Allied and Central Powers suffer from optimism and ambition. US historian Lee Kennett cites sources showing that the British, French, and American officially sanctioned victories totalled 11,760 from mid-1916 to war's end. But the German records reveal only 3,000 planes lost. The authors of *Canadian Airmen and the First World War* examined the "destroyed-in-the-air" claims for the Germans and British for 1918, and concluded that the figures should be reduced by at least one third, based on actual losses. At the same time, their analysis is qualified by the following statement: "the 'aces' of the air war—the Vosses, von Richthofens, Bishops, Barkers, and Collishaws—were anything but fakes."

The Aeronautica del Regio Esercito pilots had a jaundiced view of RFC/RAF victory claims. Italy's highest-scoring scout pilot, Major Francesco Baracca wrote: "British airmen are apparently shooting down enemy airplanes with the greatest ease, although we are able to verify that their opponents, rather than crashing, manage to fly away healthier than before." Barker and the other RFC/RAF pilots, in turn, did not think much of Italy's flying achievements.

There is no question that all air forces over claimed, and that the standards for confirming victories varied between air forces and especially between squadrons. There is little validity for historians and aviation buffs to closely compare scores among individual pilots in different air forces and different squadrons because of the dissimilarity of standards. Any list of scores of the aces is a meaningless document.

After the Great War, scores tended to be inflated even more for public relations purposes. For example, Barker's biography in *Canadian Who's Who* in the 1920s credited him with 50 "official" and 68 "unofficial" victories. The only value of such a claim was to place Barker second to Bishop in the unofficial British aces list. Barker was notably reticent about the whole subject, but did say in reply to a direct question from a journalist in 1919 that he had between 45 and 50 enemy machines downed.

The commander of 14 Wing had tightened the standards for victory claims by June 1918, insisting that all combat reports be signed as evidence that the actions described had been properly witnessed. Joubert also disallowed some of the more questionable claims. Despite this restrictive policy, there was still quite a bit of over claiming. Aerial victories claimed by the RAF in Italy included 386 enemy aircraft destroyed, 33 driven down out of control, and 27 kite balloons destroyed, for the loss of only 47 aircraft and three kite balloons. These numbers represent almost a 10-to-1 victory-to-loss ratio, which the Austro-Hungarian and German Air Service records do not confirm. In reality, the Central Powers on the Italian Front lost about 1.5 to 2 aircraft for every aircraft they shot down.

The Camel pilots believed that the 14 Wing discounting of their Italian-Front claims resulted in higher standards being applied also for the award of gallantry medals. Williams, who was credited with 13 victories (four in France, nine in Italy), maintained that inflated victory scores were often the result of lax authority at higher levels.

Capt Thomas F. Williams, a Canadian from Woodstock, Ontario, was the oldest pilot in 45 Squadron. He had been nicknamed "Voss" (after the German ace) because of his skillful evasion in an earlier aerial fight in France. Williams was never in Barker's squadron, but the two became friends when both were stationed for a time at the same aerodrome.

Williams shared his ideas for performance improvements, one or two of which Will adopted. He respected Barker, and to the end of his life remembered him with a feeling akin to reverence. He thought that he was an authentic hero who did not receive the public esteem, or attain the stature, he very richly deserved. With little prompting, "Voss" launched into stories about Will whenever he was interviewed about the war:

I regarded him very, very highly. Not only as a man but as a pilot and as a formation leader. I put him tops over some of the others, the others who got high scores ... I never knew him to drink and he didn't smoke. I remember that I had the mechanics make air intake scoops on the side of the fuselage to get a ram effect at high altitude. When Barker saw that he said, "That's an idea" and he had the same thing done to his Camel. In fact, he went one step farther. He had a hole cut in the carburettor box and another hole cut ... in front to get even more ram effect ... He was really tops as a flight commander ... his prime purpose when it came to air fighting was not to roll up credits for himself.

Williams had a high regard for Barker because he did not exaggerate his claims, but standards varied between units:

Joubert, who headed the 14 Wing ... insisted on a man putting his signature on the line that he actually saw the crash. Many others didn't insist on this. They couldn't have done or some of these people wouldn't have had all the high records they got ... As regards

"scores," however, there was obviously a great difference between various squadrons. Take Whittaker, for example—it seems astonishing that so many of his men on 66 Squadron got credit for so many E/A. There was one VC recorded there—and that's a laugh ... There were no "scalp hunters" on 45 Squadron ... I never knew any one in 45 who was not ready to give another man credit if there was any question about it. It was a good squadron. I can't say I was quite so happy in 28 Squadron.

Notwithstanding some optimistic claims by all combatants, the K.u.K. LFT unquestionably respected the British. The leading Austro-Hungarian scout ace, Hauptmann (Captain) Godwin Brumowski, commanding officer of Flik 41J, wrote to his colleague, Oberleutnant Frank Linke-Crawford, commanding officer of Flik 60J in February 1918:

I have stuck my nose in it just now—these wretched English have shot me down twice. You can see it isn't going any better for me than it is for you. The first time, alone against eight because my other gentlemen had no desire for the attack, I received 26 hits. Gasoline, bracing wires, motor kaput ... the second time the leading edge of the wing broke and the covering fabric of the entire left wing flew away.

Brumowski, a 29-year-old from Wadowice, Galicia, had visited and flown with Manfred von Richthofen's squadron in France in March 1917. When given command of the newly formed K.u.K. LFT scout squadron, Flik 41J, he applied many of the Red Baron's operational principles, including the deep-red colour scheme of the Prussian leader's machine.

Brumowski's background was not unlike Richthofen's. He was born into a military family, and graduated from the Technical Military Academy near Vienna. Commissioned as a lieutenant in the field artillery in 1910, he served on the Russian front after the outbreak of war, and was twice decorated. He transferred to Flik 1 as an observer in mid-1915, and became a pilot in that squadron a year later, achieving five victories by the beginning of 1917.

Brumowski's all-red aircraft was easily identified, having a large white skull against a black shroud painted on the top and sides of the fuselage. He was credited with 21 victories by August 1917, and eventually achieved between 35 (official) and 43 (unofficial) victories, the highest of any K.u.K. LFT pilot. He survived the war, much decorated, having flown a remarkable total of more than 400 missions.

In comparison, Barker flew more than 350 hours in one scout aircraft over 11 months, and completed 150 to 170 missions. His impressive record of 43 victories in Italy was achieved in only 26 air fights, a feat which may have prompted Billy Bishop, the ultimate in solo fighter pilots, to write: "In single combat, pilot against pilot, no enemy, German or Austrian—not Richthofen himself—could have

stood against the fierceness of a Barker attack and lived to boast a victory."

But Barker's influence as a flight leader is more impressive than his victory record, particularly when we look at how many of Barker's wingmen scored victories when being led by him. Quite a few pilots of 28 and 66 Squadrons improved their fighting ability, or became aces under his tutelage, and several others achieved this status by the end of the war in other squadrons. Moreover, no one died flying on Will Barker's wing, and no aircraft he escorted was shot down by enemy pilots. This is one of his greatest achievements as an air combat leader.

It was men like Barker, fighting in the first air war, who founded the doctrine for later air wars. The Great War aces established the basic principles: know your enemy's weaknesses; always turn towards your attacker; avoid decoys or traps; use the sun and clouds for concealment; always keep a good lookout; have an escape route to home. These practical survival rules

David Mackenzie collection

Swimming hole for the personnel of an RFC/RAF squadron in northern Italy, 1918.

developed by men like Boelcke, Hawker, Mannock, Barker and many others, have been rephrased over the years, but live on in today's world of air-combat-manoeuvring (ACM), and fighter weapons training. The Great War flyers created the tradition.

The biggest challenge in developing fighting skill is to survive long enough to make sense of what one sees. Inexperienced pilots see little or nothing on their first patrols, even if their flight actually engages the enemy. It is all a newcomer can do to just hang on his flight commander's wing, and not get separated. Unquestionably, the first step to survival is improving one's ability to see.

A modern phrase used by today's fighter pilots, "Situation Awareness" (SA), was called by RFC pilots in 1918, "knowing the score." SA is partly learned, partly intuitive. It includes having "an air picture," a mental three-dimensional map of the sky, and the position of every aircraft in it. Not really a quantifiable skill, being part science, part art, and part intuition, situation awareness can vary even with the same pilot on different days and in different battles. As author Mike Spick has pointed out, it is the most crucial variable separating the ace from a survivor, and the survivor from the dead.

Actually being able to see and anticipate, then manoeuvre into a firing position, and successfully engage a hostile machine is an exceptional ability that only a handful of pilots have at the outset. Few master the business of killing in the air, 5 percent on average, but those that do shoot down the great majority of enemy aircraft. Of the 5 percent of pilots who become aces, it is the ones with the outstanding gunnery skills who almost invariably have the highest scores. Barker seldom wrote about his experience in air fighting, but in a rare published essay about aircraft in war, he observed: "In aerial fighting possibly much more depends on individual skill and effort, than in any other branch of the service. Accurate shooting was the most important thing and next, skilful flying of the machine ... Aerial fighting was fraught with many dangers such as collisions, not only with hostile machines but with friendly ones."

There were no major battles on the ground in the winter of 1917-18 on the Italian Front. In February and March, British divisions were pulled out and moved back to the Western Front. On the enemy side, 11 German Air Service squadrons, with about 100 front-line aircraft, including three scout units (Jastas 1, 31, and 39), had left in February.

By March the RFC was being consolidated into one Wing, and Webb-Bowen relinquished command of the RFC in Italy to Joubert on 24 March. Forty-two Squadron was sent back to France, and to improve long-range reconnaissance, six Bristol F2B Fighters and six crews were shipped from England. After a brief period attached as a self-contained flight to 28 Squadron, they formed "Z" Flight at 34 Squadron.

The British XIV and French XII Corps were moved 30 miles west from the Montello area to replace and reinforce Italian forces on the Asiago plateau. To provide support in this middle sector of the front lines, three of the four RFC squadrons moved to new aerodromes—66 to San Pietro in Gu, then 45 to share the aerodrome at Grossa with 28, and 34 Squadron to Villaverla. The 14 Wing HQ relocated to Sarcedo to be near the British XIV Corps rear area.

This westward shift of the British sector presented greater flying challenges. The Asiago plateau where British soldiers were entrenched was over 3,000 feet above sea level. The RFC aerodromes were near sea level on the plain just to the south. Pilots had to climb to 5,000 feet just to clear the divisional rear area, and as high as 8,000 feet to clear the near vertically sloped peaks encircling most of the Austro-Hungarian aerodromes. These aerodromes and peaks were heavily "seeded" with anti-aircraft batteries that were deadly accurate due to their proximity to aircraft flying overhead.

* * *

On 19 March, Major Glanville was promoted and transferred back to England, being replaced by Major Claude A. Ridley, who had come from Home Establishment. Ridley had no operational experience on the Camel, although he had served in France with 60 Squadron in 1916. Barker was disappointed, and soon became truculent and surly. With two years of operational service, and nine months in the field as a flight commander, he wanted command of 28.

The Camel pilots from Canada serving in Italy felt strongly that he was eminently deserving. It did not help British/Dominion antipathies that, by the spring of 1918, the four squadrons of the RFC/RAF Italian Expeditionary Force had more than 40 percent Canadian aircrew, but no Canadian commanding officers. The appointment of yet another British commanding officer did not improve the morale. Harold Hudson was upset that Barker could be treated so shabbily by the RFC.

Barker could have swallowed his pride, but it was against his nature to do so. "Voss" Williams said that he left the squadron rather than serve under Ridley:

> ... he couldn't see sending a man who had a lesser amount of experience than he to take over the squadron and I think there was a little bit of jealousy there or something in connection with it which was the prime reason why Barker left 28 Squadron and went over to 66 Squadron. So far as Ridley was concerned I don't know whether I could say that he had differentiated between a man's nationality whether he was Canadian or not, but we Canadians felt that we didn't get too much credit compared with what we might have got.

Williams had just relocated at Grossa with 45 Squadron, and he was a witness to the personality conflict. Will stormed into Ridley's office and demanded a transfer back to France. When this request was denied, he insisted on being sent to another squadron. An exchange was worked out between Ridley at 28 and Major John Tudor Whittaker at 66.

A combat-fatigued flight commander at 66, with almost a year of operations behind him, was selected to replace Barker. But Capt John M. Warnock, from Nelson, New Zealand, never reported for duty at 28, being too exhausted to carry on. He was quietly transferred out to Home Establishment, and Stan Stanger went in his place.

Stan wanted an opportunity to out-fly and out-shoot any pilot in Italy, and was overjoyed to get his own flight. He had all the leadership qualities to excel in his new position. He had been leading patrols in B Flight since January, and had been deputy flight commander for some months.

Will did not feel good about leaving his pilots at C Flight, but knew they were well trained. He had made up his mind, and nothing was going to make him compromise. Moreover, he was taking his personal killing machine with him. At noon on 10 April, he started up the Clerget engine on B6313, and taxied out for takeoff at Grossa. Setting course to the north, he hedge-hopped for 15 minutes to another aerodrome, miles from anywhere, named San Pietro in Gu. He flew fast and low down the hangar line and pulled up in a steep chandelle, turning and looking over his shoulder, then sideslipping down to a landing. The fitters and riggers watched the landing, and a couple ran towards the machine to help Barker taxi in.

The airmen of 66 Squadron did not live on the aerodrome, being housed in Nissen huts a few miles further north at Casa Piazza. The three flight commanders shared one Nissen hut with the three most important non-flying officers on any squadron—the Gunnery Officer, the Executive Officer, and the Recording Officer. Major Whittaker had a comfortable farmhouse to himself, and the Officer's Mess was also a farmhouse.

Life was happier for Barker at 66 despite the fact he was joining the Camel squadron with the lowest number of victories, and highest casualties. It had lost eight killed-in-action or died in crashes, and another six shot down and taken prisoner-of-war over the previous four months. The most recent fatality had been 2nd Lieut H.B. Homan, who spun in on the aerodrome practising circuits. Whittaker got along better with Barker than had Glanville, and was not fazed by the Canadian's headstrong ways. He posted Will to the flight he always seemed to inherit in every squadron, C Flight.

For Will's part, he was now provided with a fresh opportunity. He built this C Flight into a highly efficient fighting unit, one of the best in Italy or France. In less time than at 28 Squadron, he shaped it into the most outstanding team that he would ever lead.

On the range with 66 Squadron pilots Reid (standing), Row, Stanger, and MacDonald, with machine-gun officer Edney at machine gun, March 1918.

Photo by Gerry Birks; Virginia and Michael Alexander collection

William Carrall Hilborn in his Camel, 45 Squadron, August 1918.

CHAPTER SEVEN

SPRING OPERATIONS AT 66 SQUADRON

"Franz Fritsch was the only name that I knew of. I was very sorry for him ... All the way down he knew that he had to crash. Italian solders ... told me that his plane burst into flames at about 1,000 feet and that he climbed out on a wing. They told me that he had jumped from about 300 feet, missing a large haystack by about one yard. They said that he lived for two or three hours. I have never seen a finer-looking or more handsome young man. Patzelt was more fortunate. Ten seconds after I opened fire on him, he was burned to a crisp."

LIEUT GERALD A. BIRKS, MC AND BAR, 66 SQN

In the many flying stories of the First World War, it is the Scout aces that receive the most attention. The pilots who flew with them and often protected them, their "wingmen," as they were called in the Second World War, are often just anonymous faces in faded photographs. One might conclude that the great aces always accomplished their heroics alone. Some did, and there were aces in the RFC who were solitary hunters, hating the responsibilities of leadership. But this was not typical. Most flight commanders and section leaders trained the new pilots to the best of their ability, and tried always to protect them until they learned the ropes.

Barker took his obligations to new pilots very seriously. Men who flew with him never forgot him, and his fighting reputation attracted to his flight many aggressive pilots who wanted to learn from his example. It was a mark of great distinction after the war to be able to boast: "I flew in Barker's squadron," or "I was led by Barker in aerial combat." In fact, it was such an accolade that many claimed to have flown with him who had never even met him!

The pilots at 28 had learned that he would never abandon them to hunt alone. Nevertheless, Capt Barker had shown himself to be a maverick with the Christmas Day raid, and with his balloon-hunting missions. Legend or not, he still had to prove himself in his new squadron, and the men of C Flight at 66 were sizing him up as soon as he climbed out of B6313.

Since Barker affected the lives of so many pilots, some of their biographies and achievements are included in these next two chapters. There were several pilots in 66 Squadron who responded positively to the compelling personality of their new flight commander. These men already were aware of his legendary achievements, but it was his energy and enthusiasm, coupled to a streak of devilment that made him such fun to serve with.

Barker's new admirers at 66 included Gordon Francis Mason Apps, aged 19, from Maidstone, Kent; Gerald Alfred Birks, 23, from Montreal; William Carrall Hilborn, 19, from the Cariboo district, British Columbia; and William Myron MacDonald, 29, from Vancouver. Hilborn joined 66 in November 1917; Apps arrived on squadron at the end of 1917, and Birks and MacDonald in March 1918.

Birks was one of seven children of Miriam Childs Gifford and William Massey Birks. Henry Birks was Gerald's grandfather. He was the founder of Henry Birks & Sons, a jewellery and silver business. A graduate of Lower Canada College, and an architectural student at McGill University, Gerry was a good athlete who won silver and bronze medals at the first intercollegiate ski competition held in North America.

He was commissioned in the 73rd Battalion of the Black Watch, the Royal Highlanders of Canada, and served in the Somme sector in 1916, until he was wounded by a sniper. After recovering from his wounds

Gerald Alfred Birks in April 1991 at home in Toronto.

Photo taken by author Wayne Ralph

in Montreal, he volunteered for the Royal Flying Corps in Canada. He trained on the Curtiss JN4 in Ontario, at Camp Mohawk and Camp Borden, and served a few months as a flying instructor.

When he left 54 Training Squadron in the UK to join 66 he had 138 hours, more time than many other RFC pilots going into combat in 1918. He shot down his first hostile aircraft on only his third offensive patrol. He was an exceptional gunner despite an astigmatism which he had managed to conceal at his RFC induction medical.

Sixty-six Squadron had good morale because it was an efficient combat unit where pilots generally got along. The unit was also happy because it was well rewarded with medals. It counted among its pilots quite a few MC recipients, some DSOs, as well as one recent Victoria Cross recipient, Lieut Alan Jerrard, taken prisoner-of-war on 30 March after being shot down by an Austro-Hungarian ace, Oberleutnant Benno Fiala Ritter von Fernbrugg.

Barker was keen to raise his score above 22 when he joined 66, but the weather through much of April was poor, with clouds and fog clinging to the Venetian Plain and blanketing the Alps. This curtailed the reconnaissance activities of 34 Squadron's Bristol Fighters, and also limited the chances for fighting. However, after a few uneventful patrols, Barker scored his 23rd victory on the morning of 23 April.

Clouds blanketed the mountaintops, and there was poor visibility in the eastern and western sectors, but he was able, through the murk, to pick up a formation of eight Austro-Hungarian D.IIIs. Over Feltre at 17,000 feet, Barker set up an attack against the leader of the large formation. But the enemy pilots were not caught by surprise. They split up into pairs, and two D.IIIs manoeuvred behind Barker.

Flying on Barker's wing that morning were Stanger and Hilborn. Stanger fired on one of the two D.IIIs and it immediately started to burn, and soon fell out of control. Hilborn watched the wreckage tumble down trailing greasy smoke. Barker then attacked another hostile aircraft head-on, and had not even fired on his enemy, when the machine suddenly spun out of control for about a thousand feet, at which point the right-hand pair of wings broke away. Hilborn then drove down two other scouts, but did not have the speed to catch them. The remainder of the K.u.K. LFT flight escaped to Godega and Mansue aerodromes.

After this heart-pounding fight, Barker's right-hand gun was seized up, and Stanger had a gun "stoppage." Will fired a white signal flare from his Verey pistol, indicating that it was time to go home. The three men excitedly relived the action on the ground. As always after such missions, everyone tried to sort out the confusion of battle as best they could for the Recording Officer. Barker signed the typed combat report, and the 14 Wing HQ credited the flight with two "destroyed," one each for Stanger and Barker.

Stanger left a week after this action for 28 Squadron, and Barker appointed MacDonald and Hilborn to act as his deputy flight commanders when he was not around. William Carrall Hilborn, affectionately known as "Willie" to his family, was a tall, rugged-looking kid with brown hair and brown eyes, and a "lady-killer" smile. He was rangy, and loped rather than walked, the result of growing up as a cowboy on a ranch at Kersley, BC. Getting into and out of the cramped cockpit of a Camel was challenging for such a big man.

He was from a family of eight children. His father, Stephen Lundy Hilborn, was a former Montana sheriff; his mother, Josephine Elizabeth Huot de St. Laurent, was the first non-native child born in the BC mining town of Barkerville. He and older brother Clarence had graduated as RFC pilots within weeks of each other. Willie was a quick learner, and was sent solo at Camp Mohawk by the famous professional dancer, Capt Vernon Castle.

Hilborn became a very good pilot, but seemed unlikely ace material, because he suffered terribly from airsickness. Even after training on scouts in England, he still could not shake the nausea that plagued him. At first he believed it would keep him out of combat, and in a training job. He told Clarence, serving on RE8s with 59 Squadron: "It looks to me as though I may get a chance to be an instructor. You see I get sick so much in the air that I am not very good to send to France. I am alright as long as I fly straight but as soon as I start to stunt I get sick."

Willie was able to control and/or conceal his airsickness, and he gradually improved through the winter, surviving his high-risk early missions. He was almost killed on his 11th offensive patrol: "I was badly shot up the other day with archy [*sic*]. My machine was hit all over. The engine was hit the worst. I have also several bullet-holes near me ... I was archied [*sic*] so bad my wheel was shot off. When I landed one wing went down and I turned over. The Major was pleased with me for staying with my formation when I was badly hit."

By late February Hilborn was leading B-Flight sections into combat, and hoping for command of his own flight. He had not yet been credited with any victories, missing one good opportunity due to jammed guns. He bragged to his brother about the amount of flying he was doing: "I have put more time in than any other officer since we came to Italy. I did six hours last week in one day. That was three patrols ... I have a great machine in my flight. About the best in the squadron. Two officers came near being Court-marshalled [*sic*] the other day for not following me. They won't get another chance."

Under Barker's tutelage, Hilborn's skill, and also his luck, had improved by May, when he achieved four victories. After Gerry Birks returned from leave,

William Carrall Hilborn in his Camel at 45 Squadron in August 1918.

Margaret Hilborn Sawyer collection

Margaret Hilborn Sawyer collection

Hilborn family during the First World War; Clarence standing on right, brother Willie standing on left.

he flew on Hilborn's wing on Wednesday morning, 1 May. He was able to confirm a victory for Hilborn, witnessing the death of an Austro-Hungarian pilot in an Albatros D.III that broke up in the air over Fonzaso.

The next day, Birks, and Lieut Norman S. Taylor, from Wandsworth, London, England, flew on the wing of section leader Lieut Robinson, an American from Detroit. Birks was that rare RFC pilot who kept a meticulous log book in a clear, legible hand. He sometimes transferred information from the squadron's daily record book and, because of this extra effort, many of his log entries are a model of clarity and abbreviated drama:

8 O. P. Patrol observed five D.IIIs over La-varone at 14000 ft. at 11:30 flying south (see

combat report). When over Levico at 11000 ft. at 11:45 am patrol observed one E.A. 2-seater. Type not distinguished at 10000 ft., with an escort of five D.IIIs. One D.III shot down by Lt. B. (see combat report). Lt. Taylor not yet returned. Last seen at 12 noon in the valley S.W. of Levico about 2000 ft. apparently al-right but loosing [*sic*] height. A.A. fire normal. Weather good but cloudy. Vis. Fair.

Charles Claude Robinson was a member of the first course of 18 United States citizens to graduate from the RFC training schools in Canada, after the US had declared war on Germany in April 1917. He had joined 66 in France in October and flew with the unit until early June 1918, when he was injured in a flying accident and repatriated back to England.

Barker had been in charge of C Flight for several weeks before he actually led Gerry Birks on a patrol. On 4 May Birks scored his fourth and fifth victories in a single fight. Hilborn did a smart job of protecting Birks, and also Parker and Apps. Crossing the front lines in the area of the Piave, he noticed a familiar two-seater flying towards them from the enemy front lines.

The Austro-Hungarian Air Service had captured a Bristol Fighter and was using it as a decoy. The lack of anti-aircraft fire around the British two-seater made Willie suspicious, and he refused to take the bait. But other enemy scouts were waiting to bounce the unaware:

Patrol over mountains abandoned owing to bad weather. Patrolled Piave front. When over Vidor at 9:45 at 14,500 ft. observed 12 E.A. scouts (mixed D.IIIs and D.Vs) at 16000 ft. coming towards them from over Conegliano. Patrol engaged E.A. Lt. Apps shot down one D.V in flames and one D.III down—DDOOC. Lt. B. [Birks shot one D.III down in flames. Lt. Parker shot one D.III down and Lt. Hilborn drove one D.III down out of control ... The D.III shot down by Lt. Apps was observed to crash by Lt. McLeod of 28 Squadron. E.A. pilot got out of crashed machine and Lt. McLeod shot him. Lt. Apps' machine was shot through engine, cowling, centre-section, L.H. bottom plane, elevators, and one flying wire shot away. A Bristol Fighter, with English national markings and apparently no sqdn. markings was observed to cross the enemy lines in the direction of Conegliano and return between 9:15-9:30. This machine was not engaged by enemy A.A. fire. Weather good. Vis. fair. A.A. fire above normal and very accurate.

After Hilborn signed a report for this successful mission, Birks wanted to find the Austrian scout that he had driven down, but had not actually seen crash. Major Whittaker offered Birks and Apps a vehicle to go searching the countryside. The two found more than they bargained for, in a macabre finale to what Birks later labelled, "the best scrap I was ever in."

Rather than burn to death, the K.u.K. LFT pilot had thrown himself from the cockpit without a parachute. He landed on the edge of a haystack, but was taken, still breathing, to a casualty clearing station. His name was Korporal Franz Fritsch, on his second offensive patrol. The other enemy that Birks had defeated was a veteran. He was Oberleutnant Karl Patzelt, the commanding officer of Flik 68J, a much decorated career soldier who had fought from the beginning of the war, and had five victories. At the end of a long day, Birks was an ace, having taken out an ace to achieve that distinction. He had not counted on viewing the broken body of one of his victims, and the haunting image did not fade with old age.

Sixty-three years later Birks met Patzelt's friend, Anton Boksay, at the 1981 Great War Aces reunion in Paris. The two men compared stories, shook hands, and went to the bar to have a drink. Gerry never got over the horror of that day in 1918:

Franz Fritsch was the only name that I knew of. I was very sorry for him. I shot his machine out of control at about 14,000 feet. All the way down he knew that he had to crash. Italian solders at the scene of his crash told me that his plane burst into flames at about 1,000 feet and that he climbed out on a wing. They told me that he had jumped from about 300 feet, missing a large haystack by about one yard. They said that he lived for two or three hours. I have never seen a finer-looking or more handsome young man. Patzelt was more fortunate. Ten seconds after I opened fire on him, he was burned to a crisp.

On a few occasions, RFC/RAF pilots, as well as the Italians and French, dropped wreaths over enemy aerodromes to mark the passing of some better known Austro-Hungarian airman. The Austro-Hungarians invariably approved of these gestures of respect, and placed the wreaths on the graves of the fallen.

The two men in C Flight with similar upbringing were Barker and Hilborn. Both young men had been raised on the frontier, grew up on horseback, and were efficient with a gun. However, Barker was closer to Gerry Birks, an affluent son of a dynastic family of entrepreneurs. By any of the usual measures, including physique, Birks was nothing like Barker.

Gerry was deceptively mild-mannered (on the ground), of average height and build, with a shy smile. He had none of Barker's flamboyance, yet the two men formed a mutual admiration society. Birks praised Barker to the author as "a magnificent leader, a very splendid fellow, easy to get along with, and full of energy ... he was never tired." When Barker wanted to go back to France, he asked Gerry to go with him. After the war he told a journalist that in a tough fight he would always want Gerry Birks and "Mac" MacDonald with him.

Birks appreciated that flying with Barker sharpened his edge, and was proud to have served with him, but in his own words: "Barker and I would race each other to get a Hun ... his Camel was always faster ... it was just blood lust." Birks was that rare scout pilot with an imagination. He knew if he was good, someone else was better, and eventually, if he flew long enough, he was going to be killed in action.

Personalities among scout pilots were not uniform and predictable, and introverts and extroverts, nice guys and sociopaths, served and fought side by side. By comparison with Barker and Birks, who liked to banter back and forth and were fiercely competitive in the air, Gordon "Mable" Apps was phlegmatic and withdrawn, looking much older than his 19 years because of his balding head. "Mac" MacDonald was a skilled card player who was driven to gamble, and was considered a hustler by the younger pilots at 66 Squadron. "Mac" was elderly at age 29, but Barker relied on his maturity. Will's other deputy, Hilborn, was, by comparison, just a kid, competent but not talented in air fighting, a survivor seeking neither medals nor glory.

Barker took this mixture of personalities and abilities and whipped it into a cohesive team. After a

few weeks, all the men of C Flight thought the world of him, and it showed in their fighting performance. His fearlessness made them fearless. Barker, Birks, and Apps alone accounted for 20 enemy aircraft in only seven weeks. MacDonald and Hilborn also scored victories, and all four men received gallantry awards for their actions in Italy. C Flight was one of the best fighting teams in the RAF in May and June 1918.

One of 66 Squadron's pilots who never flew with Barker, but admired him, Lieut H.N.E. "Daddy" Row, recollected Barker's many admirable qualities to historian Ronald Dodds:

> He was one of the finest Camel pilots I have ever seen. Apart from the usual stunts he seemed to have an uncanny sense of just how much his machine was capable of doing in an emergency. He was a dead shot & God help the E.A. which tangled with him on anything near equal terms. He was dedicated to his service & worked himself & his pilots assiduously to maintain fitness & efficiency over the line. New pilots to his Flight were lucky ... many of the survivors must owe their lives to his skill & care. He could have cut quite a few more notches for himself had it not been for his consideration for the other pilots of his patrols. In person he was unassuming & very likeable.

* * *

The month of May was the busiest for Barker in the entire war. He flew more than 65 hours in 27 days. Almost 29 hours were logged just in the week of 18-25 May. Birks also had a phenomenal month, flying 69 hours and 50 minutes.

The war in the air was heating up in May because the armies opposing each other were planning a spring offensive. The winter of 1917-18 had seen little fighting on the ground, after the front lines had stabilized following the Battle of Caporetto.

There were more than 50 Austro-Hungarian divisions divided into four armies on the Italian Front, but their soldiers were poorly clothed and armed, as

Virginia and Michael Alexander collection

Birks, Stanger, MacDonald, and Taylor at 66 Squadron.

well as being malnourished due to inadequate rations. Men had deserted by the thousands, and the divisions were much under strength compared to their Italian counterparts. Despite these problems, Field Marshal Boroevic's staff planned a 15-division assault across the Piave.

The codename was "Operation Albrecht," in honour of Archduke Albrecht's defeat of the Italian Army in 1866. The troops with grim trench humour tagged it "The Hunger Offensive." Launched early on 15 June, it was repelled over a 10-day period by the Italian Army at a cost of more than 85,000 Italian casualties (many of these losses being prisoners-of-war), almost 15,000 more than the Austro-Hungarian Army.

The Hapsburg Empire was handicapped by the disparity in size between its K.u.K. Luftfahrtruppen and the Entente air forces. By June 1918 there were more than 520 Italian, French, and British aircraft arrayed against 280 Austro-Hungarian aircraft, with not all of the 280 being serviceable, front-line machines. The K.u.K. LFT could offer only limited support to the tired troops on the ground, and were always on the defensive in air fighting.

While the Austro-Hungarian general staff was preparing for Operation Albrecht, the war in the air intensified. The K.u.K. LFT flew many more reconnaissance and photographic missions, and even dropped propaganda leaflets. The LFT observers were attempting to get new aerial photographs of the front lines near the Piave, as well as the high ground to the west. The Piave west bank was held by the Italian Third and Eighth Armies. The Asiago plateau behind it was held by the Italian Fourth and Sixth Armies, and the French XII and British XIV Corps.

Pilots of 66 Squadron in Verona café in May 1918; Barker 2nd from right, looking over his shoulder.

Photo by Gerry Birks; Virginia and Michael Alexander collection

The Italian and British scout squadrons had to force the Austro-Hungarian two-seaters to abort their photographic runs, or shoot them down before they made it back home with pictures. The reconnaissance crews on both sides had their work cut out for them because of the formidable geography. Most military positions in northern Italy were difficult to photograph from the air, and relatively easy to camouflage. The many deep ravines were shaded by mountains, and only during brief periods of the morning was there enough light for aerial cameras to pick up details. As Barker described it:

The most trying reconnaissance was that carried out over the Alps. The Austrians were good gunners and in addition their batteries were often placed on mountains of 8000 feet and above. The route was of necessity always the same and was along the Brenta Valley. The time of this reconnaissance could not be varied greatly, owing to the presence of shadow in the deep valleys.

The intensity of RAF scout operations in May and June exhausted the pilots—a typical offensive patrol was two and a half hours, and this could stretch to three. The many handling difficulties of the Camel, its unheated and cramped cockpit, the high cruising altitudes maintained without supplemental oxygen, the noise and vibration of the rotary engine, and the drizzle of castor oil, all combined to drain even the most robust flyer.

After a patrol, a man sometimes had to be assisted out of the cockpit. He danced about, shaking his frost-bitten hands and stamping his feet to regain feeling. The pins-and-needles pain was excruciating as his blood warmed and recirculated to numb fingers and toes.

Capt "Voss" Williams had to be sent home to England by early August on the recommendation of the RAF medical officer because of heart problems caused by his many months of high-altitude flying. Any Camel veteran on the Italian front with more than two months of operations suffered permanent damage to the inner and middle ear. Gerry Birks,

like many Camel pilots, was completely deaf in the last years of his life.

Almost every day, and often two or three times a day, the pilots of C Flight would take to the air. Usually they were led by Barker, sometimes by Hilborn or MacDonald. Barker had additional responsibilities during May when he became the acting squadron commander while Major Whittaker went on leave. When Hilborn got his leave at the end of May, Mac-Donald became the deputy commander of the flight.

Birks flew 22 of his 30 offensive patrols in May on Barker's wing. On 8 May they flew twice together during the day, bombing Motta aerodrome on their second patrol. Then Barker led a third evening patrol with Hilborn and Parker that resulted in a running battle with two LVG two-seaters over Cessalto. Barker and Hilborn both fired bursts of .303 into one of the enemy aircraft, the pilot diving away and attempting to outrun the Camels. Barker pursued the enemy aircraft down from 16,000 to 4,000 feet. At that altitude the wings of the LVG separated from the fuselage, and the aircraft spiralled down, crashing in a heap near Annone. Since anti-aircraft fire was deadly accurate in that sector, Barker led his formation home at low altitude, which also avoided the strong westerly winds aloft.

Crossing the lines over Zenson di Piave Lieut Parker was wounded in the shoulder by a rifle bullet fired from the trenches below. His Camel, B7358, which had been Stan Stanger's old machine, was not damaged. Parker was a new pilot from England, in 66 Squadron less than a month. He continued to fly in formation with Barker and Hilborn and landed safely back at the aerodrome. However, this stray bullet grounded the young pilot, and he did not fly again in C Flight.

The next day Barker took Birks and Hilborn back to Motta for a second bombing run. The flight's bombing efforts were not successful. But the day was not over, and Barker led a second patrol at 16,000 feet, with Hilborn, Birks, and Vincent. The latter pilot crashed on takeoff, but was not seriously injured, and the veterans carried on. The afternoon weather was no better than in the morning east of the River Piave, and so the formation headed northwest, dropping 20-lb anti-personnel bombs, but with little result, on an Austrian aerodrome located north of Grigno.

On Saturday morning, 11 May, C Flight had a more successful mission despite poor visibility over the mountains. Hilborn and Birks climbed with Barker across the southern Piave. Gordon Apps was climbing in formation with them when his engine coughed and sputtered. After a few attempts to smooth the Clerget out, "Mable" turned back towards San Pietro in Gu.

Barker sighted enemy aircraft over Torre di Mosto, and led his flight out over the Gulf of Venice, circling around to attack from behind. The three Camels were not sighted, and the five Austro-Hungarian scouts were caught at 15,000 feet: "Lt. Birks attacked the D.III, painted black and after firing a short burst E.A. [it] started to burn along the side of the fuselage, then the wings fell off and E.A. went down enveloped in flames. This was seen by Capt Barker and Lt. Hilborn."

Not to be outdone, Barker attacked another D.III but was then engaged in retaliation by a black D.V.

... who dived steeply to the left, and [Barker] followed E.A. down to 8,000 ft. when E.A. fell out of control. E.A. crashed south of S.Stino and burst into flames on the ground. This was seen by Lt. Birks. The pilot of the D.V handled his machine very skilfully. Lt. Hilborn attacked another D.III and after firing a short burst E.A. went down out of control and crashed west of S.Stino. This was observed by Capt Barker. The remaining two E.A. escaped.

Barker received his next gallantry award, in a ceremony on 19 May, for assisting the French Expeditionary Force. The citation for the Croix-de-Guerre stated that he escorted French aeroplanes. One historian (Drew) credits Barker with single-handedly driving off several hostile scouts that were attacking a formation of French Salmsons on their return from a reconnaissance of the Brenta Valley. One of the scouts reportedly fell in flames from a burst of gunfire at less than 100 yards.

There is no combat report of this action, and Barker did not fly alone at this period, unless separated inadvertently from his flight. He did escort the Salmsons from time to time, as did other Camel pilots, and it may be that his name was put forward by the British as a candidate for a French decoration, to recognize his outstanding day-to-day leadership.

Barker was taken aback at being kissed on both cheeks by some French *général* who had not shaved recently. But he now had his first foreign decoration, its green ribbon with vertical red stripes and small gold star contrasting with the muted shades of maroon and blue of the DSO, and the purple and white of the MC. The gold star on the ribbon indicated a mention-in-despatches by a Division of the French Army.

The Camel pilots were, in modern terms, both air superiority and attack specialists. They strafed anything that moved on the enemy side, and were often sent to bomb Austro-Hungarian aerodromes. The 14 Wing HQ once in a while assigned Camels against industrial targets, such as the hydroelectric power station at Trentino, north of Lake Garda. But the 20-lb bombs were ineffective against anything "hardened," and the modest damage inflicted was not worth the risks. When efforts were well coordinated and all three squadrons participated, the Camels could wreak havoc with softer targets.

One well-executed attack mission took place on 30 May. On that day 66 Squadron contributed 12 Camels out of a total force of 35 scout machines. The massed formation was divided into flights of about four or five aircraft, all of which were airborne before 7:00 a.m. They flew at less than 500 feet above ground in line astern at 100-yard intervals. The Austro-Hungarian positions were in a river valley, the Val D'Assa, 30 miles northwest of the British aerodromes. The targets included Ghertele, Osteria del Termine, Vezena, Lucerna, and Mandrielle.

Carpenter, commander of A Flight at 66 Squadron, led his formation to Vezena where 13 bombs were dropped, then another eight on so-called "hutments" near Lucerna, destroying four of them. The formation then strafed soldiers and machine gunners on the ground, reportedly killing or wounding as many as 60 or 70 men.

Barker led C Flight, including Birks, Apps, and MacDonald, against Mandrielle, dropping 24 bombs, destroying at least five hutments, and then turning his attention to other targets of opportunity. The 66 combat report concluded: "Capt Barker attacked a column of motor lorries near Mandrielle and one ran into a ditch. Then a column of infantry ... was attacked and dispersed, and several apparently killed. Mobile gun crew engaged and silenced. A big gun pit was engaged at 36.C.2022." In all, about a ton of bombs were dropped, and more than 9,000 rounds of .303 were expended.

* * *

The experience gained by the RAF pilots in ground-attack missions proved beneficial a couple of weeks later when the Austro-Hungarians launched their major offensive across the Piave. They were comfortable with low-level operations, and surprisingly accurate, considering that the Camel had no bombsight at all.

The week of 12-19 May was frustrating for all the members of C Flight, but particularly Birks. He flew nine patrols, but had repeated engine problems with B6424, twice returning to the aerodrome, and a third time having to make a forced landing at Castello di Godega because of a broken engine inlet valve spring.

There were no successful engagements by C Flight until the 19th. Barker himself had engine troubles with B6313 that Sunday, but landed safely, had his fitter fix the problem, and rejoined the formation. Barker's Camel was invariably the fastest in any squadron because Will modified the machine to wring out more performance, using the squadron's best fitter and rigger.

While Will had been sitting impatiently on the ground in his machine, his protégés, MacDonald, Birks, and Apps, accompanied by 2nd Lieut R.G. "Joe" Reid, a Newfoundlander, and 2nd Lieut Lingard, an Englishman, were attacking two Berg scouts at 13,000 feet over Borgno. Birks took out both aircraft quickly, raising his victories to eight. A few minutes later Barker tried to overtake a two-seat Rumpler, but the enemy aircraft was able to climb faster than B6313, and Lingard's and MacDonald's

Camels fell behind, unable to hang in formation with Barker's faster machine.

Spurred on by Gerry's latest victories, Barker was determined to do more. On Monday morning, Will, "Mac," and "Mable," took off at 6:15 a.m. for a western sector offensive patrol. After a lengthy 45-minute climbing pursuit over Frassilonga, Will engaged two Albatros scouts at the remarkably high altitude of 20,200 feet, sending one down out of control, the second in flames, all within five minutes. The latter crashed in the area of Levico, and "Mac" and "Mable" confirmed Barker's victories.

Around noon that same day, Barker, Apps, Hilborn, and Birks had another successful western patrol, engaging seven Berg scouts at 16,500 feet north of Cismon. Willie Hilborn achieved the first victory, relentlessly pursuing his target down to 7,000 feet, and watching it crash in a field. Birks attacked another hostile, firing at it from below as it climbed. The enemy pilot then rolled twice, with Birks firing a long, lethal burst as he came out of the second roll. Gerry now had nine victories after only two months in the field, and 38 offensive patrols.

The fighting continued, with "Mable" Apps driving off a scout that was on Willie Hilborn's tail. Barker was sitting below this action, climbing quickly, but not quickly enough. He pulled B6313 up into a stall in an attempt to shoot upward into the belly of the enemy aircraft. The Berg received some hits, but the pilot spun down, probably under control, to avoid Barker's fire. Apps and Barker then chased the remaining Berg scouts beyond Sacile.

There was no let up for the rest of the week. On Tuesday, Barker, and his wingmen, Birks and Apps, attacked a solitary reconnaissance aircraft, a converted Berg two-seater with 25-lb bags of ballast in lieu of an observer. Without a protective escort the Austro-Hungarian pilot was an easy target. After Barker fired a burst under his tail, the pilot held up his hand, signifying his wish to surrender. Barker pulled up alongside, whereupon the pilot made a bid to escape to the northeast.

Will fired another burst and the aeroplane spiralled down at high speed. Following it down, he attempted to force the enemy pilot to land at Treviso, but he high-tailed it towards his own lines. Eventually, the reconnaissance machine (identified in the combat report as a Lloyd) touched down in a field, and turned over. Barker was credited with a "destroyed" target, but the two-seater was also captured, having crashed on the Allied side at Colmello. The frequently reproduced photograph of Barker standing by, or sitting on, an Austro-Hungarian machine, surrounded by Italian soldiers and civilians, is probably this victory of 21 May (see photos, pages 120–21).

Friday, 24 May, was a memorable day for a lot of RAF pilots in Italy, with many offensive patrols and successful combats by Camel pilots from all three squadrons. According to the reports for C Flight, 66 Squadron, at least five victories were achieved, four in one mission, and one by MacDonald, his first, during an evening patrol.

* * *

The intense pace of the May flying was stressful on men and machines. Camels were logging a lot of air time, including frequent dogfights, where the repetitive "G" forces weakened the wooden airframes. By the end of May, B6313 had accumulated 275 flying hours since new. Will's machine was put in a canvas hangar, and completely overhauled with new parts, including wings, tail fin and rudder, and new linen for the fuselage. On 2 June Barker flight-tested the overhauled machine, and the next day he was back in action leading Apps and Birks.

"GERRY BIRKS KILLS JOZSEF KISS, FRIDAY 24 MAY 1918"

Aerial combat reports are rarely conclusive documents; indeed, they are often imaginative reconstructions of events lacking any apparent cohesiveness. In reading them, one should remember that their contents are based almost entirely on the heated recollections of several very stressed-out pilots, and the typing skills of one overworked Recording Officer. Nevertheless, World War One aviation historians and enthusiasts have used combat reports as the basis for determining who killed whom on a particular day and, thereby, who achieved the victories.

Even in the best of circumstances, combat reports are only a guide—with log books, squadron record books, and enemy records (if available) a reasonably full story can be deciphered, but not always the full truth. Unfortunately, documents get destroyed in subsequent wars or disappear. Since the Great War, many of the aerial combat reports for 66 Squadron in 1918 have gone missing from the UK Public Records Office files, making the historian's job all the more challenging. The gaps in documentation, and the variables in the composition, detail, and quality of the reports that have survived, understandably gives rise to different interpretations of specific aerial combats.

Undoubtedly, the most famous and controversial aerial combat of the war was that of Manfred von Richthofen, Roy Brown, and "Wop" May on 21 April 1918 in France. A less well-known controversy from the Italian Front involves Jozsef Kiss, Gerry Birks, and Will Barker, on 24 May 1918, when Gerry Birks fought a short action against Offizierstellvertreter Kiss (pronounced Kish), the top-scoring Hungarian-born scout pilot.

Barker, Birks and Apps had spotted three enemy scouts at 17,000 feet over Grigno at about 10:40 a.m. They engaged near Mount Coppolo, and the air fight was over in only 15 minutes. Will drove down one aircraft out of the formation, and Gerry, after a brief engagement, fired a burst of .303 which caused the wings of another scout (identified in the combat report as a Berg) to break off. On this day, Kiss was actually flying a mottled olive brown Phönix D.IIa, marked with a white stripe around the rear fuselage.

A second formation of three D.V Albatros scouts was spotted by Barker descending from the south towards Birks and Apps, who were fighting at lower altitude in the valley below. Barker manoeuvred unseen behind one of the D.Vs, and fired 40 rounds. The scout went down out of control and burst into flames after striking some hutments on the ground. An aircraft on Birks' tail was engaged by Apps, who was able to fire a long burst into the hostile machine as it executed a climbing turn. The enemy pilot lost control and crashed.

Barker spotted a solitary Berg C.I two-seater at 16,000 feet over Feltre. Acting as a decoy, he descended to about 14,500 feet, while the rest of the formation stayed level with the fleeing C.I. This allowed him to use B6313's better speed to overtake the reconnaissance aircraft, while its pilot was distracted by Birks and Apps. Will was able to close undetected to within 50 yards of the Berg C.I, and fire 100 rounds into the belly of the machine. The enemy pilot responded by rolling into an abrupt descending left turn. Will then chased the enemy machine and fired another 80 rounds. Diving through 5,000 feet, his guns jammed, and he was forced to break off, but Birks shortly after spotted parts of the hostile machine strewn on the ground near Fiume.

After several days of uneventful flying, Barker and two of his favourite pilots achieved three victories on the morning of 9 June. Engaging seven hostile machines with MacDonald and Birks, Barker fired 100 rounds at a Berg scout, which then fell out of control, and shortly after broke up. He then attacked a second Berg scout nose-to-nose. The enemy pilot dived, Will rolled in pursuit, and a few moments later the Berg was wreckage on the ground. Birks attacked the two-seater in the formation, but broke it off when attacked in turn by a D.V Albatros. Manoeuvring onto the tail of the D.V, Gerry fired into the scout until it started to smoke, and then burn fiercely at 6,000 feet. The remains of all three aircraft fell just east of Levico.

The 66 Squadron pilots continued fighting the remaining machines. One enemy, his fighter marked with a series of black and white stripes, manoeuvred skilfully for some time to avoid Birks and Apps. Eventually, Barker was able to hit him, and the striped machine fell out of control, striking the ground close to the earlier machine downed by Barker. In total, four enemy machines were claimed destroyed in the combat report filed with 66's Recording Officer, Lieut W. Topham. The report was forwarded up to the Wing HQ, and they accepted the narrative and authorized the victory credits.

There has been speculation among aviation historians in the years since as to who were the enemy pilots engaged in battle that day, and who triumphed over whom. Some have suggested that Barker was the victor over Kiss, while others have credited Birks, and others the Italian Air Force. The first formation engaged was most likely that of Deputy Officer Kiss, Sergeant Alexander Kasza, and Sergeant Major Stefan Kirjack, all of Flik 55J, based at Pergine. The remaining formation engaged shortly afterwards may have been from Frank Linke-Crawford's Flik 60J at Feltre.

There are no Austro-Hungarian records that confirm the deaths of any of their scout pilots on 24 May, at that hour, other than Jozsef Kiss. His machine was found in a stand of trees on a hillside near Lamon, a few miles west of Feltre, and his crushed body was identified by decorations on his tunic. He was the K.u.K. LFT's fifth-highest-scoring scout ace of the Great War, and probably died facing the guns of Gerry Birks.

The death of Kiss was a great blow to the flyers of the Dual Monarchy. His funeral was attended by most of the pilots and observers of the K.u.K. LFT on the Italian Front. In an unprecedented act, the Austro-Hungarian high command arranged that this Hungarian NCO be promoted to reserve 2nd lieutenant—the only posthumous commissioning of a "lower-class" flyer during the entire war.

He had been shot down, and seriously wounded, the previous January possibly by a pilot of 45 Squadron, Capt Matthew "Bunty" Frew. After surgery to save his life, during which a portion of his bowel was removed, Kiss had too-brief a convalescence, and returned to Flik 55J. His nerves shattered and his body ailing, he continued to lead formations, but could not add to his score of 19 victories. Ambitious to be promoted, vain enough to wear his medals on his tunic when flying, senior NCO Kiss wanted above all else to be an officer. He received posthumously the lowest rung of commissioned rank, and the distinction of an officer's funeral.

According to Dr Martin O'Connor, Enrica Bonecker, Kiss's lover while he was stationed at Pergine, visited his grave every day for 52 years. She never married. In a final postscript, Kiss's bones were removed from the abandoned military cemetery in 1970 and placed in the large war memorial ossuary at Rovereto, Italy. Found among the bones was Kiss's watch, the hands still readable as 11:00 a.m., the time of his death.

Birks' Camel B6424 during engine overhaul in hangar; according to Birks one of the mechanics is named Ramsbottom.

Photo by Gerry Birks; Virginia and Michael Alexander collection

Early the following morning, "Mac" Mac-Donald flew a dawn patrol in which he scored two victories in 15 minutes, raising his total to four. MacDonald eventually had eight victories, and was awarded the DFC for his work in Italy. A newcomer to C Flight, 2nd Lieut Harry King Goode, from Nuneaton, Warwickshire, showed great promise flying on the Barker team. He had one credited victory before Barker left 66 and another 14 by the end of the war, receiving the DSO and DFC.

Everyone knew something big was likely to break soon on the Italian Front. From 10 June, the 14 Wing HQ, in anticipation, had ordered so-called "barrage patrols" between Forni and Gallio on the western portion of the front lines, on the Asiago plateau. Between Casotto and Cismon east-west patrols were flown, parallel to, and ten miles beyond the front lines. The intent of these special missions was to block reconnaissance of rear areas.

Early on the 15th, at 3:00 a.m., the night sky lit up like a Christmas tree, signalling the opening salvo of the Battle of the Piave. The entire front came under attack, shells raining down on the Italian forces of the III, IV, and VIII Armies on the west bank of the Piave; the French 23rd and 24th Divisions on Mount Grappa; and the Italian and British Divisions (the 12th, 48th, and 23rd) on the Asiago plateau. At the time it was pouring rain, and there was widespread fog.

Due to low visibility, none of the early morning activity on the ground was seen from the air, although there were several dawn patrols. Barker led Birks and Goode on a 5:15 a.m. mission to the area of Feltre at 14,000 feet, and later dropped six 20-pounders in the Val D'Assa, about 20 miles west of Feltre. They saw nothing unusual. However, by 11:45 a.m., a general alarm had been issued and Barker was back in the air with Goode, MacDonald, Birks, and Symondson, bombing pontoon bridges, and soldiers on the banks of the Piave. "Voss" Williams' recollections to historians about that day provide an excellent picture of tactical air support, First-World-War style:

Birks' Camel B6424 being loaded into a truck.

I can well remember the masses of troops up on the east side of the Montello, shooting into the Austrians making the crossing. We were down low enough to see the expressions on their faces. ... We were going from dawn to dusk, dropping bombs and strafing. ... We bombed so low that the blast of the bombs just lifted our aeroplanes. ... The enemy suffered very heavy losses, and they admitted these. ... Eventually there was a flood—which did the job better than we had been able to. This flood caught a lot of the Austrians and then the Italians could boast of a big success. As regards the actual stopping of the enemy. ... I think you'd have to give the air force credit for a lot of it.

Certainly, the combined efforts of the Italian and British air forces made a major contribution to the defeat of the Austro-Hungarians, and the Battle of the Piave is a little-publicized episode in the Great War, one of those actions where tactical

air support was effective. As *Canadian Airmen and the First World War* stated: "Rarely did aircraft play so significant a part in a major military operation during the First World War ..." William Barker was actually quoted by Jones in *The War in the Air*, in the volume describing the Italian campaign. He credited the Camels with stemming the assault:

They had succeeded in crossing the Piave opposite the Montello. The Montello, owing to its height, dominated the Venetian plain and under its cover they had thrown two pontoon bridges across the river. The leader selected the bridge farthest upstream and individual bombing commenced from about 50 ft. This bridge was quickly broken in two places and the pontoons, caught by the fast current, were immediately dashed against the lower bridge, carrying it away also. When this attack commenced these bridges were crowded with troops which were attacked with machine-gun

Barker standing by the wreckage of one of his victims, likely in May 1918.

David Mackenzie collection

fire. Many were seen to be in the water. This done, troops on small islands and in rowboats were machine-gunned.

On the second day, Barker flew at least two missions against the troops crossing the Piave. He was accompanied by Birks, MacDonald, Symondson and Goode in the morning, and on the afternoon patrol by Birks, MacDonald, and May. Sixty-four 20-pounders were dropped on the pontoon bridges and troops, and every Camel exhausted its supply of 500 rounds of .303. By the next day, however, the weather was so wretched that it was impossible to launch formations, and 66 Squadron did not fly.

In total, the RAF flew about 44 ground attack missions between 15 and 18 June. Three Camel pilots were casualties, all from 28, and all from Williams' flight. One was wounded in the leg, one died of wounds from ground fire, and the third was believed to have died of a heart attack on the way home from

an evening mission. The bad luck continued on 19 June when a fourth pilot from this flight inadvertently flew in the wrong direction and was taken prisoner-of-war. In addition, three Bristol Fighter crews with 34 Squadron crashed, force landed, or were badly damaged by ground fire, and one RE8 observer was wounded. In 1925, Barker summarized his own opinion of the operation:

Owing to the high ground of the Montello the machines had difficulty in closing with the target. It was only possible to operate from the enemy's side. These bridges were rebuilt at night and destroyed during the day until at last some 30,000 Austrians surrendered ... Had these bridges escaped discovery or had we failed in their destruction, I feel sure that we would have experienced a second Caporetto. The Italians were getting out of the way with all speed. The British and French were with great difficulty holding their own

Barker sitting on enemy aircraft, likely in May 1918.

David Mackenzie collection

and undoubtedly these attacks saved the situation. The Italians bombed these bridges day and night but always from great heights. They failed to damage the bridges on any occasion ... the Italians did not carry out artillery observation to any degree, and as the Austrians had gained the Montello it was impossible for the Italian gunners to observe these bridges.

Barker's rather disparaging opinion of the Italian military was unfair, but also typical of the views held by most British officers who served in Italy. He overstates the significance of taking the bridges out with bombs, while making no mention of the torrential flooding due to heavy rain. The deluge on the Piave overwhelmed the Austro-Hungarian efforts to gain the west bank in strength, by washing away all the pontoon bridges more completely than any bombing.

Field Marshal Boroevic at first wanted to redouble his efforts to cross, and then realized it was best to withdraw. The commander-in-chief of the

Austro-Hungarian armies, Kaiser Karl, would not permit or even consider a withdrawal on 17 June. When it did get under way on 22 June it cost many casualties, including thousands on the west bank taken prisoner-of-war. For the remaining months, the Habsburg Empire fought an entirely defensive battle, and there was no further consideration of another Caporetto. The Battle of the Piave turned out to be the Dual Monarchy's last hurrah.

The battle marked a turning point for Gerry Birks. Combat fatigue due to the pace of daily operations had taken a psychological and physical toll. He had logged more than 100 hours since the beginning of May, and wanted a rest. In turning down Barker's offer to transfer to France, Gerry told him: "... there is quite enough action for me here." Explaining his decision to the author 70 years later, Gerry said, "If I had gone to France with him, I would have been with him when he fought 45 or 50, and I wouldn't have come through ... he was a remarkable fellow to get out of that scrap..."

The helmet, mitts, goggles, and DFC of Willie Hilborn; also log book of his brother Clarence.

Photo by the author Wayne Ralph; Margaret Hilborn Sawyer collection

Between 17 and 24 June Gerry flew his last seven patrols, all with Barker, but the weather was not great and the enemy squadrons were not aggressive. On his second last patrol, a fatiguing three hours airborne with Barker and Apps, Birks achieved his final victory. He had flown 39 missions on Barker's wing, more than half of his total in the war, and more than any other pilot that served with Barker.

This last patrol was memorable. On Friday, 21 June, the three tangled with a formation of eight Albatros D.IIIs based at Motta aerodrome, about 10 miles east of the Piave. Barker as he looked down from 10,000 feet spotted the scouts lifting off from the aerodrome. He elected to climb to 15,000 feet and fly northeast towards Pordenone, biding his time till the large enemy formation reached Oderzo to the west, and closer to the front lines. Will then turned his formation in a wide arc towards the west. By so doing he was placing his flight not only above his opponents with the morning sun behind (it was around 9:00 a.m.), but also east of it, a direction from which the Austro-Hungarian flyers would least expect to be attacked.

The tactic worked, and the three Camels clashed with the eight D.IIIs at 15,000 feet. Will immediately drove down one aircraft in a spin, and then manoeuvred onto the tail of a second Albatros which was firing at Gerry. This aircraft fell out of control for several thousand feet and then broke up in flight. Gerry then turned to fight a third Albatros at close range and, with two short bursts, destroyed it. "Mable" fought a D.III from 14,000 down to 9,000 feet, at which point the aircraft fell out of control. Will watched this machine crash south of the railway tracks at Sala di La.

Will then engaged a D.III, opening fire at 60 yards. But his opponent, showing good tactical sense, headed swiftly for low altitude. Barker pursued but could not overtake, eventually easing out of his dive at around 4,000 feet. Assuming that the Austro-Hungarian pilot did not want to fight, Will headed for home. The pilot of the D.III then attacked,

firing a few short bursts, but always maintaining at least 100 yards between his machine and the enemy. B6313's engine started to falter, and Barker was forced to break off the fight and head for San Pietro in Gu. He now had his 35th victory, Birks had his 12th, and Apps his 7th.

Birks was exhausted, but so was Barker, although he would not acknowledge the fact. He had logged 20 hours on B6313 in the week of 16 to 23 June. He had been engaged as a scout pilot, save for a few weeks of leave, for nine months. He had now been in the field for over two years.

Birks flew his 66th patrol on 24 June with Barker and Apps. They did not range far into enemy territory, being on a "close patrol," and the weather was not good. After Birks landed his Camel, D8101, for the last time, he methodically marked in his log book: "No EA seen. Weather poor. Vis poor. A.A. fire N&A. - TOTAL TIME (including practice flights etc.) 153 hrs 40 min - TOTAL TIME - WAR FLYING 146 hrs 30 min."

For Lieut Gerald Alfred Birks the fighting was over. He had 12 destroyed victories to his credit and was recommended for the Military Cross and Bar. After some weeks of leave he was on a ship heading back to his country. He put in about 20 hours of instruction in September on the JN4 at the RAF School of Special Flying, at Armour Heights in Toronto. That same month he was formally awarded his gallantry medals in a ceremony conducted by the lieutenant governor of Ontario.

Gerry ended the war physically unscathed with about 311 flying hours. He lived to be 96, but never flew as a pilot again. He became a successful investment banker with a dedication to education and art. He married twice and had several children. An avid amateur artist who was still taking art lessons in his nineties, he insisted on riding the Toronto subway at night by himself to the art school until the last months of his life. For a former Camel ace, the subway was nothing to be feared.

Time exposure photo of Gerry Birks sitting on his cot in the officers' quarters at 66 Squadron.

CHAPTER EIGHT

A HOSTAGE TO FATE

*"... I have been going to write for days past but I never seem to get time & if I do I feel too done in.
I think I have overdone it a bit as I have been feeling poorly lately ... I have got 37 Huns down & Major Richotfen
[sic] the German who is now dead claims 80. I am going to try to break this record if my health will only hold out.
After I have attained this I am coming home but not till I have done my best ..."*
MAJOR W.G. BARKER, 139 SQN, ITALY, AUTUMN 1918

By the time Barker left Italy he was well known outside the RAF. He had been decorated by the Italians, and he was the cheeky "Inglese aviatori" who had disrupted the King of Italy's awards ceremony. Along with other high-scoring Italian scout pilots like Baracca, Scaroni, and Piccio, Barker was a familiar name to aircraft manufacturing companies, and may have influenced their designs to some degree.

He was invited to the Ansaldo company of Turin to test fly one of their aircraft, the SVA (Savoia-Verduzio-Ansaldo), probably some time in May. On occasion manufacturers consulted with successful flyers about future designs. According to informal notes made by Barker after the war, he completed a test flight on 20 June at Genoa, and was photographed after the flight standing in front of an SVA (see photo on page 88). It was an elegant-looking, but rather mediocre scout, serving as a reconnaissance and bombing machine.

Newspaper articles in Manitoba claimed that the Italian manufacturer not only allowed Barker to fly their aircraft, but also gave him one as a gift, in recognition of his exploits. Presumably there was a little truth to the story because Barker received the nickname "Balilla" (the "hunter" in Italian) from the other pilots at 66. "Voss" Williams provided an uncorroborated story about the gift:

The Balilla company [i.e., Ansaldo] developed a Scout which they were giving him. He went down to the factory and flew this thing and told them to cut two feet off its length. I'm not too sure whether he did in fact ever get one but he was anxious to get a pair of Bosch magnetos for it. One day while on patrol he spotted an enemy two-seater that he knew was fitted with Bosch mags so he got underneath it as it was flying towards the lines. It was just over the lines when the observer looked down and saw Barker. Barker then had to shoot it down, or get shot down himself. The two-seater, though, fell behind the enemy lines and he didn't get his mags.

After returning from this interesting break at Ansaldo, Will was keen to further add to his victory total. Perhaps overconfidence, maybe misjudgement due to fatigue, prompted him to fly alone on patrol—something he had not done before, and which he lectured his own men against. Whatever the reason, on Tuesday, 25 June, he set out solo on an early-morning patrol, one that almost put an end to his fighting career.

Heading north for the Asiago plateau where there were reports of hostile aircraft, he found nothing, so he turned east towards the conspicuous landmark on the River Piave called "the twin bridges." Seeing a Berg D.I scout at 15,000, Barker gave chase towards Susegana, opening fire from astern at a distant 150 yards. Not his usually vigilant self, Barker was then bounced by what he described later as "one D.V. scout, painted red."

Instinctively turning towards his attacker, he was lucky not to have been hit on the enemy pilot's first pass. He fought fiercely for about three minutes against the red aircraft, in Barker's words, "manned by a very skilful pilot." Will managed to hit the hostile aircraft as the pilot pulled up into a climbing right-hand turn. Perhaps distracted by Barker's tracer bullets, or wounded, or possibly faking, the D.V pilot went down in an apparent out-of-control spin.

Mesmerized by the spinning red aircraft, Barker now came under attack by a mixed formation of eight Berg D.Is, and Albatros D.IIIs and D.Vs. With his left gun misfiring and the right gun jammed due to overheating, Barker evaded his enemies by spinning. He was able to clear his gun problems and fire two green flares over Susegana at 5,000 feet to alert other friendly pilots that might be in the vicinity about his predicament.

The flares were a call for help, something Will had never had to do. The sky was blue, innocent-looking, and empty. Like a novice, he had allowed himself to focus too narrowly. Now he swivelled his head in all directions, his situation awareness impaired after only five minutes of heart-pounding action. Will later received credit for a DDOOC (Driven Down Out Of Control).

But Major Whittaker was an insightful squadron commander, and a good judge of combat fatigue. He did not like what had happened to Barker during the mission, but he signed his combat report and sent it on up to Wing HQ. He also spoke to Joubert, who authorized a leave pass, and ordered his tired flight commander to go away for a week. Barker did not argue about it:

You will be surprised to hear that I am on leave & in Rome. I have 7 days & am visiting Rome – Naples – Florence – Genoa & Milan. On the morning of the 25th I got into a fight all alone with 9 Hun fighting machines & I need not say it was very hot for me. However, I engaged their leader & brought him down & got away myself. This fellow was one of the Austrian aces with 21 to his credit. He was killed & was hit 11 times. Speaks good for my gunnery

Eh!? On my return the Colonel packed me off on leave & I am glad as I was losing heart & getting tired. After this leave I am making one more effort & am going to try to bring my [number] of Huns up to 40 destroyed in ten days. 6 more to get & am then going home. I have now destroyed 34.

Rome is a splendid old city with many Historic places & monuments & I am taking full advantage of my stay here in seeing them all.

p.s.

Just before my departure from my squadron I rec'd a telegram informing me that I appeared in the list of the King's Birthday Honours & have been Mentioned in Despatches. I have not seen what it was for yet. We'll let you know later.

W.G.B.

Could the pilot in the red Albatros have been Godwin Brumowski? Not likely. The leading Austro-Hungarian ace had himself been sent on leave that morning, having flown his 438th operational mission a couple of days earlier. Brumowski was later promoted to command all the K.u.K. LFT scout squadrons attached to the Austro-Hungarian Army of the Isonzo, but he flew no more patrols.

It may be that another pilot of Flik 41J was flying the Albatros D.III (Oef), serial number 153.209, the famous all-red aircraft with the death's heads on the fuselage. But Linke-Crawford's Flik 60J also had five scouts airborne that morning, and they did have an air fight. "The Falcon of Feltre" flew both the Berg D.I and Berg D.II.

However, his aircraft (he had more than one) were not red, but various shades of olive, or strikingly painted with large hexagons. Each machine had a large letter "L" inscribed behind the cockpit, on each side, and on the top wing. Two pilots were listed as killed or missing on the 25th: Reserve Leutnant Wilhelm Pfeiffer of 43J, flying a Phönix D.II, and Feldwebel Josef Szwittek of 37P, in a Phönix D.I. Neither aircraft was painted red. How did Barker know how many bullets were in the pilot's body?

"HUNS AVOIDED BARKER"

After the war, a newspaper story claimed that Barker and some of his men had presented a challenge to the top aces of the Austro-Hungarian Air Service. This rather contradictory and possibly apocryphal tale was published in *The Toronto Telegram* in April 1920. The story became an enduring legend, repeated over and over for more than 60 years:

REFUSED TO FIGHT IN AIR

HUNS AVOIDED BARKER

Canadian V.C. Airman Dropped Note and Bombed

Airdrome so Huns Knew Where to Locate Them.

Lieut-Col. William G. Barker, V.C., D.S.O., etc., ... longed for aerial combats while on the Italian front, but his desires to fight the leading enemy officers were not fulfilled ... growing exasperated at the "yellow" fliers the colonel led his squadron over the biggest aerodrome dropping the following note, but the enemy avoided Barker:

Major W.G. Barker, D.S.O., M.C., and the officers under his command present their compliments to Captain Bronmoski [*sic*], Rither von Fiala [*sic*] and Captain Havratil [*sic*], and the pilots under their command, and request the pleasure and honor of meeting in the air. In order to save [the above] ... the inconvenience of searching for them, Major Barker and his officers will bomb Godigo [*sic*] aerodrome at 10 a.m. daily, weather permitting, for the ensuing fortnight.

Among the officers with Colonel Barker on this occasion were Lieut Gerald Birks of Montreal, and Capt McKeown[*sic*], D.S.O., M.C., from the west.

Apart from the spelling errors of the names and places, the newspaper account has other discrepancies. At the time Barker was promoted to major, Gerry Birks was on his way home, and "McKeown," most likely Clifford McEwen, was with 28 Squadron at another aerodrome. Barker may indeed have issued some kind of a challenge to his enemies in Italy, as it was certainly in keeping with his personality. But if so, would it not be with the members of his own flight or squadron?

One explanation of this apocryphal story is that Barker, or someone who had served with him, put a new spin on a wartime exploit, so as to include people who would benefit by their association with Barker. This legend about Barker's chutzpah was still being retold in speeches and booklets in the Second World War to new flyers, in particular by Billy Bishop, Director of Recruiting, as well as by the RCAF public relations branch.

Why did he make this claim privately when only credited with a DDOOC? Did the red D.V crash on the west side of the Piave? We don't know.

By this stage of the war most of the RAF scout pilots knew the names of their leading opponents, and their aircraft. It is likely that the Austro-Hungarians had the same information. Barker had received a letter from George Forder, in Salzerbad POW camp, describing how he had been shot down by Frank Linke-Crawford. Forder, who met the man who shot him down on 10 May, said "The Falcon of Feltre" knew Barker by name and achievements.

With the death of the Italian Ace of Aces, Major Francesco Baracca, on 19 June, and the extended leave of Brumowski on the enemy side, Barker was now the leading scout ace on the Italian Front, as well as the RAF Italian Expeditionary Force's most decorated pilot.

* * *

When Barker came back from a week of leave in Rome he learned in a letter from his parents that his grandfather, George Barker, Senior, had died and been buried in Riverside Cemetery in Dauphin. There would be no more friendly bets taken by Grandfather Barker at the shooting gallery on Main Street—his grandson had graduated to much more deadly stakes.

Barker's role in 66 Squadron was drawing to a close. He had achieved much in only three months, but his ambition was to command a squadron. He had much to recommend him, but his benign stubbornness, and habitual impromptu missions made his superiors edgy. Would the responsibilities of squadron command curtail Barker's impetuous streak? The man commanding 14 Wing was not sure, but had given it much thought in June.

Between 3 and 13 July, Will flew about nine times, his last two flights at 66 being on the latter date. On the dawn patrol that day he and "Mable" Apps fought a large mixed formation of Berg and Albatros scouts in the area of Godega aerodrome, the largest Austro-Hungarian military airfield, having more than 40 hangars.

Although fighting against eight, Apps accounted for one and Barker for two hostile aircraft. Will afterwards appraised this particular group of Austro-Hungarian pilots as poor flyers, with the sole exception of the pilot of a D.V, his aircraft painted with black and white checkerboards along the fuselage. This pilot evaded any attempt by Barker to get into a firing position. Barker eventually managed to drive the "checkerboard" machine down in a spin, but also saw it recover from the spin and land safely.

Good news arrived during this period. Lt Colonel Philip Joubert had managed to get his favourite Canadian promoted to major (temporary major, in fact) despite, rather than because of, Barker's colourful record. He was the first Canadian pilot on the Italian Front to achieve that rank. The question was what to do with him. He was overdue to be sent to Home Establishment, but the last time he had served in England had not been a great success.

Barker wanted command of his own squadron in the field, but he was unlikely to replace Whittaker at 66 or Ridley at 28. His best chance to command a scout squadron was in France, and he lobbied for a transfer, as he had done back in April. Unlike Italy, France had (so it seemed) pitched aerial battles almost daily, an abundance of ground attack missions for Camel pilots (most of whom loathed the work), and the cream of the German Air Service as opponents.

RAF pilots were racking up large victory scores there in relatively brief periods, most notably Barker's fellow-Canadians—Donald R. MacLaren, William G. Claxton, and Frederick R.G. McCall. By July, MacLaren was tied with Barker on the RAF unofficial scoring list after only four months of operational flying; and the brilliant duo of Claxton and McCall had about 70 victories between them in less than three months. These four men had never met, and may never have heard of each other, but nevertheless were in a race to surpass Billy Bishop.

Barker's best opportunity to command one of the RAF Camel squadrons in Italy came two days after his promotion, with the loss in combat on 16 July of a popular officer, Major A.M. Vaucour, commanding officer of 45 Squadron. He ignored the prohibition against crossing the front lines, flew on offensive patrols, was credited with several victories, and was decorated several times. He was shot down in error by Lieut Alberto Moresco, the pilot of a Hanriot scout from the 78a Squadriglia Caccia. A case of misidentification, Moresco was appalled at what he had done, and reported it to his boss. The Italian XV Group commander, Lt Colonel E. Visconti, apologized to his British counterpart.

This was not the first instance in Italy (or France) where friendly fire had eliminated the wrong aircraft. In fact, the Italians had lost aircraft to the British in just this way. The RFC pilots were amazed, shortly after arriving in the theatre, to find that the top wing surfaces of Italian two-seaters had no national markings. This led to unfortunate incidents, and possibly even deaths.

One would have liked to have been a mouse in the corner of Joubert's office, and heard the outburst when Major Barker was informed about his new assignment. He was ordered to take over the "Z" Flight of Bristol F2B Fighters, now redesignated as 139 Squadron by the addition of a second flight. Although not the usual three-flight squadron, 139 nevertheless holds the distinction of being the only RAF squadron formed in the field during the First World War. Years later Will mentioned this with pride in his lectures, but in July 1918 he was disgusted to be going back to two-seater operations.

Major William Barker on taking command at 139 Squadron, July 1918.

Library and Archives Canada

Perhaps as a condition of his acceptance, or as a consolation prize, Joubert allowed him to retain B6313. The Camel may have, only on paper, been sent to 7 Aircraft Park and then reissued directly to 139. It is unlikely this happened without official sanction, or the turning of a blind eye. Whatever the case, it was a unique arrangement in the history of British fighting squadrons.

As part of the transfer to 139 Squadron, B6313 received a strip-down inspection. Two new top ailerons were fitted, the cross-bracing wires were bound, controls were adjusted, and the whole machine was repainted. The polished metal finish of the engine cowling was painted to match the fabric, and Barker brazenly adopted more conspicuous non-approved markings.

Since the 139 markings were two white fuselage bands near the tail of the Bristol Fighters, Barker had not two, but four bands painted on his fuselage, separated by black. In addition, a red heart with an arrow through it was painted on the vertical fin. Two months later B6313 was modified again, with several more fuselage stripes, the heart symbol reversed, the aluminum cowling stripped once again, and once again polished.

This personalization of aeroplanes was not encouraged in the RAF, though it was common on the enemy side. By the end of the war, however, names and symbols and decorative markings were widespread. Training aircraft in England were the most colourfully painted. After the war, Camels, Bristol Fighters and Snipes proliferated with checker boards and stripes. Scouts with multiple fuselage stripes, perhaps in imitation of the famous B6313, or Barker's VC-winning E8102, became common.

Barker was so upset about his new assignment that he felt as if he had been stabbed. In a fit of pique, he had the arrow-in-heart painted on the tail of the aircraft, and told any pilot brave enough to ask that it was his own bleeding heart. He made sure that his 38 victories in B6313 were marked on the front wing struts. In another expression of individuality, he had a gargoyle-like, six-inch-long metal devil, thumbing its nose, attached to where the ring-and-bead foresight would usually have been on his right Vickers gun.

The new commanding officer of 45, Major J.A. Crook, arrived in Italy on 27 July. The head of 14 Wing possibly had an opportunity to switch assignment orders, and give 45 to Barker, and 139 to Crook,

129

Bristol Fighters of 139 Squadron over the Italian Alps, late 1918.

Library and Archives Canada

but did not do so. An alternative might have been to promote Capt A.A. Harcourt-Vernon, the head of "Z" Flight before expansion. Harcourt-Vernon, an engineer from Toronto, was as upset as Barker about the turn of events. He would have loved and clearly deserved to take command of 139. He did not appreciate, after months running the unit, having to report to a scout pilot promoted into the unit over his head. Harcourt-Vernon left 139 in August and went to France to another Bristol Fighter squadron.

Barker's life would have turned out differently had he taken command of 45 Squadron. It had the lowest accident rate and fewest casualties of the three Camel units in Italy, and the highest victory total. There were many talented pilots from the various Dominions. According to Crook, the squadron had only five British-born officers out of 23 when he assumed command. In addition to five or six Canadians, there were Australians, South Africans, New Zealanders, and three Americans. It was a unit well suited to Barker's style of leadership.

If Barker had been given 45, he would have taken the unit back to France in September, to be attached to the Independent Bombing Force. He would have returned to France, as he wanted, but as the boss of his own squadron. He is unlikely to have won the Victoria Cross, but his post-war life undoubtedly would have been less painful and traumatic.

It took Barker about 20 minutes on the evening of 15 July to fly northwest from San Pietro in Gu to his new aerodrome at Villaverla. What he saw when he looked down was an aerodrome much the same as the other RAF aerodromes in northern Italy. The Bristol F2B crews were housed in metal-clad Nissen huts. The squadron office looked rather like a small barn, with a tropical-climate thatched roof, instead of tar paper. There was a single row of canvas aircraft hangars painted a mottled green and brown. The

David Mackenzie collection

Barker (left) with Australian flight commander at 139 Squadron, Sydney Dalrymple, DFC.

139 Squadron was formed, and served till the end of hostilities. Of his eight victories, five were due to his own front gun, and three due to the shooting of his observers. He is credited by the American Fighter Aces Association as the first American pilot in any flying service to achieve five victories in a single mission. Simon tied with Barker for the most victories at 139, the squadron being credited with 27 in all, with Simon and Barker the only aces.

* * *

While Barker's B6313 was being overhauled and re-painted he flew the F2B. Occasionally over the next two months he flew the two-seater, but probably on no more than seven or eight patrols. His Canadian Armed Forces record of service indicates that he had 50 hours logged on the F2B, an estimate since there is no evidence that Barker kept a personal log book while in command of 139. In addition, he logged 54 hours in B6313 and flew at least 17 offensive patrols or ground attack missions, sometimes leading F2Bs, and sometimes flying alone. This was a substantial contribution for a CO, but it was well below Barker's usual pace.

He had no interest in being a paternalistic commander who did not fly. He paid scant attention to administration and, during his brief tenure, the squadron paperwork was mediocre, and nobody criticized the sloppiness of the Recording Officer. Will put the Barker stamp on 139 Squadron by dissipating his anger on the enemy. In his first 10 days he boosted morale, and led by example, achieving five victories in only three missions; two on the 18th, two on the 20th, and one on the 23rd.

The mission on 18 July saw Barker leading Simon and Smith in F2B (serial number C999), in an attack against two reconnaissance aircraft. One of these crashed and burned, the other was seen by Smith falling out of control as it passed through about 2,000 feet above ground. Barker's old friends at 66, Hilborn, Goode, and May, were also flying that morning in the same sector, and also tangled with a formation of Austro-Hungarians.

Willie Hilborn was credited with the destruction of a black Albatros D.III near Stoccaredo and

base of the hangars were protected by interwoven tree branches and shrubbery, as a shield against bomb shrapnel fragments. A short distance away was a farm house, the residence of the CO, and parked outside was his personal automobile.

"Z" Flight had suffered casualties between April and June. Three crews were shot down behind enemy lines, with only one of the six men surviving, and at least two other crews were wounded or had crash-landed. These losses demonstrated that the F2B could not perform its mission without escort, and successfully fight its way back home. Long-range reconnaissance rather limited the F2Bs other capabilities. When handled like a scout machine, many pilots and observers on the Western Front became aces on the Bristol Fighter.

In Italy, only one pilot achieved this level, an American, Lieut Walter Carl Simon, from New Orleans. He arrived in Italy only a few weeks before

Harry Goode with a D.III near Mount Baldo. Lieut Geoffrey May attacked a Brandenburg two-seater, killing the observer, and then driving the aircraft into the trees on Mount Mosciagh, his first and only victory with 66 Squadron.

Apparently, this two-seater came under fire from Barker as it reached low altitude. As a result, when the two combat reports from 66 and 139 arrived at Wing HQ, a decision was required on the entitlement. The Wing elected to credit Irishman Geoffrey May with the Brandenburg C.I, and allow only one victory to Barker. It was later speculated that May did kill or wound the observer, but that Barker administered the final shots that drove the pilot into the ground. Barker considered it a shared victory with May.

On the 20th, Will led two Bristol F2Bs, flown by Lieut Curtis and Lieut Wood (s/n C997), and 2nd Lieut Milburn and Sergeant Frow (s/n C916), on a morning patrol in the area of Motta. Noticing three Italian scouts in pursuit of six Albatros scouts, Barker and his men gave chase from Cessalto to Motta. In a strange twist, the Austro-Hungarians thought that the Camel and two F2Bs were friendly escorts, and their leader moved into formation next to Barker and company. This fatal error in identification offered Barker the chance to manoeuvre behind the rear Albatros, fire about 40 rounds, resulting in the aircraft's wings separating from the fuselage.

Curtis and Frow, between their two guns, destroyed an Albatros D.III, and Barker pursued and downed a third scout. Lieut Wood attacked yet another D.III but was interrupted by an Italian scout that thought the F2B was an Austro-Hungarian two-seater. Wood broke off his attack, and joined up on Barker, lucky not to have been shot down by "friendly" fire.

On 23 July, Barker shared a victory with Lieutenants Walters and Davies. He was credited with destroying an Albatros belonging to Flik 74J, in the vicinity of Godega. Barker's guns were overheating and misfiring, so the final blow was by Walters and Davies. Unfortunately, two other Bristols failed to return from their missions, having been shot down by Austro-Hungarian scouts. Killed were 2nd Lieut

William Watkins, from Wales, Lieut Van Dyke Fernand, a young American from San Francisco, and Lieut William Vorster, from South Africa. Lieut Max Ogilvie-Ramsay subsequently died of his injuries.

Will Barker had now achieved the goal he had promised his mother—he had destroyed 40 enemy aircraft and balloons, plus driven down out of control another three. But there was no home leave, as he had also promised, because he was obsessed with raising his score. Soon his fighting opportunities would end, and he would be sent to England, like it or not. The war had honed his abilities (as he himself had written) to kill as many as possible, and he now was so good at it, and so driven by it, that leave was out of the question.

But his inventive enthusiasm was needed by 14 Wing for a secret mission, unlike anything he had ever flown before. Given his history, it was hardly surprising that RAF staff officers thought of him if anything eccentric or dangerous was planned. He was asked to volunteer. Of course, he just couldn't turn it down.

*　*　*

It all came about only a week or so after taking command of 139 Squadron. He was telephoned by a staff officer at 14 Wing, somebody named Benn. Will had been called on the carpet a couple of times at Wing HQ, and he avoided rear-echelon types, those men with feet-on-desks, pens-in-hand, who assessed combat reports and planned dangerous, sometimes stupid operations. But this middle-aged gentleman with the smooth voice was not the red-tabbed martinet so despised and often lampooned in the squadrons.

Captain William Wedgwood Benn, MP, was a characteristic example of the many unconventional officers who thrived in the RAF. He was a Member of the British Parliament on leave to fight the war. "Will," as he was known to his family, had sat in the House of Commons since 1906, as had his father before him, Sir John Benn of Old Knoll. His age and position exempted him from military service, but he still volunteered, and eventually transferred from his regiment to the Royal Naval Air Service. He flew in the Middle East as an observer on seaplanes deployed from ships.

Will Benn had a keen intellect with little patience for conventional military thinking and, like Barker, did not suffer fools gladly. He was considered quite ancient by the young pilots with whom he flew in the RNAS. Qualifying for his pilot's wings at age 41, on the principle that all staff officers should know how to fly, Benn had crashed or damaged five machines during his training. This did not dampen his enthusiasm for aviation.

He never flew on operations as a pilot, but did occasionally fly as an observer. Motivated to keep his hand in, he attached himself to the Italian Army in July 1918 for one job. His mission was experimental and dangerous—parachute an intelligence agent behind enemy lines at night. This was irregular duty, and Benn thought: "Who better than Barker to pull this off?"

The French and British had used aircraft on the Western Front to land spies at night. However, these clandestine flights were never recorded in squadron record books, and pilots assigned to such missions were forbidden to mention them.

According to author Ralph Barker, the first spy insertions on the Western Front by the RFC took place in September 1915 with pilots of 3 and 4 Squadrons. By 1916 a Special Duty Flight had been formed by Lieut Jack Woodhouse of 4 Squadron, the first RFC pilot to parachute a spy successfully behind enemy lines in France. His aircraft was a BE12a, the lower wing of which was reinforced to allow the agent to lie across it in flight. The parachute, a C.G. Spencer design normally used by kite balloonists, was attached to the underside of the fuselage. Claude Ridley, under whom Barker would not serve at 28 Squadron, had been involved in this line of work as a pilot with 60 Squadron in 1916. Barker wrote about spy dropping after the war, referring to the units doing this work in France as "Hush Squadrons."

The Italian Alps and Venetian Plain were nothing like the French countryside, so a parachute descent was preferable to any night landing. In the First World War, unlike the Second, dropping secret agents silently from the night sky was a new idea.

Benn and Barker were the first British flyers in Italy to undertake such a mission. Benn wrote about the secret operation shortly after the war, but never revealed why the RAF was invited to assist. It may have been that the original Italian pilot selected had little experience in night flying, and Benn was given a green light to replace him with a pilot from the RAF.

Caproni bombers of the Italian Air Force flew night bombing missions and their pilots were experienced in night operations. Barker certainly had no experience in flying a twin-engine bomber by night or day. However, the experimental tests were being flown from Villaverla where Barker's squadron was based. Joubert gave permission to attach Barker to the operation, and Benn immediately appointed himself as flight observer and spy dropper. Benn was an unabashed Barker fan:

> He was the most undefeated optimist I ever knew, which was no doubt the spiritual secret of his success as an air fighter. Any enterprise on which he embarked ... became under the influence of his magnetism a glowing chance of glory, to be gratefully welcomed; and the imagination was set to work, not to reduce the dangers, but to improve the opportunity for gaining renown. When Barker joined the Board, so to speak, the whole thing got new life.

This was, of course, an Italian Army operation, commanded by an Italian officer, and assisted by at least 60 of their soldiers and airmen. Experiments had already been tried with a three-engine Caproni Ca.3, a large bomber having two engines pointing forward in the conventional way, but a third pusher engine mounted on the back of the fuselage. The propeller of the pusher engine chopped up the parachute and mannequin as soon as it was dropped overboard, and the debris caused serious damage to the aircraft.

A twin-engine Savoia-Polilia SP4 bomber worked better. Its bathtub-style fuselage had room enough for the observer in the nose, the pilot behind, and one agent in the tail. Two parachute descents had been made successfully by Italian soldiers from this aircraft before Benn joined the operation.

Barker's conversion to the twin-engine bomber was done in conjunction with the planning of and practice for the drop. He had never flown anything larger than a single-engine Dehavilland DH4 bomber, and that only briefly, but he converted to the Savoia-Polilia SP4 with no difficulty, almost certainly without dual instruction. Between 28 July and 12 August, Will flew only one offensive patrol in B6313, instead using his Camel to commute between 139 and 66 Squadrons. For two weeks there were no air fights. He had only one goal—to accurately drop a man by parachute on a moonless night over enemy territory.

Benn and Barker walked around the SP4, discussing how the machine could be modified so that they could control the release of the spy, rather than having the man climb over the side. The rear of the bathtub-shaped cockpit had to be restructured. What they fabricated was a trapdoor. The release mechanism was in the observer's front cockpit—a large wooden handle with wires connected to two bolts holding the trapdoor closed. The parachute itself was actually attached to the outside of the cockpit.

To evade capture if forced down on the east side of the Piave the aircraft carried two flotation vests called "Gieve waistcoats." Nervous about what might happen to them if captured with a modified aircraft for dropping spies, Benn and Barker packed 10 pounds of guncotton in a wooden box attached to the floor between their two cockpits. Twin detonators and a few feet of slow match cord were the simple ignition system. A ground test with the guncotton blew a sheet of corrugated iron several hundred feet into the next field, yet bullets that Barker fired into the guncotton failed to set it off. The SP4 had to be able to survive stray anti-aircraft fire.

Benn and Barker worked out a rather complex method of navigating and communicating, one that required the help of many Italian batteries on the ground. Positioned along the route of flight were six powerful anti-aircraft searchlights, some located at aerodromes. These lights were pointed in the direction of travel to help navigate, but were there to illuminate the landing fields if Barker had to put down suddenly.

To distinguish these lights from all the other anti-aircraft batteries, an Italian Army field wireless unit was located nearby, each with a distinct call sign. Benn, the wireless telegrapher, queried the units in

Savoia-Polilia SP4 used to parachute spy Lieutenant Alessandro Tandura at night behind enemy lines, August 1918.

succession from the cockpit of the SP4. As a backup plan, Italian Army motorcyclists stood by to transport messages should the wireless break down. If the mission had to be abandoned, red Verey flares were used to signal to ground units. The men below then turned on their powerful lights, tilting them towards the ground so Barker could see well enough to land.

To practise dropping the agent in different wind conditions, Benn and Barker rigged up a sand-filled dummy that they nicknamed "George." The SP4 was not the most robust aircraft, but that did not stop Barker from buzzing Grossa aerodrome. Benn was not keen on this stunt flying, although he was confident of his pilot: "His skillful handling of this unwieldy apparatus, the pretty play he made with the two engines and his insistence on a little visit to a neighbouring aerodrome just to show off the machine to his friends, all indicated the sheer enjoyment of the artist in the practice of his profession."

In the early hours of 29 July, Barker and Benn flew on a practice flight in a Bristol F2B to Nervesa on the west side of the Piave, near the twin bridges spanning the river. Following the railway track on the east side, which was dimly lit by moonlight, they navigated to a large field near the village of Serravalle, a few miles north of Vittorio. The straight-line distance from Villaverla to the village was less than 50 miles. A couple of searchlights on the Austro-Hungarian side picked up the F2B, and Barker decided to strafe the lights. This was not one of his better ideas because the tracer bullets from the Vickers gun illuminated a brilliant path right back to the aircraft.

On the way home, the aircraft became accidentally entangled in an anti-aircraft barrage aimed at an Austro-Hungarian bombing group. Benn, with British understatement, described what happened:

Archie by night has a much smarter appearance than by day. By day he is only a puffy brown ball, by night he is a scintillating diamond. We were soon forming part of a pyrotechnic display. The excitement was too much for my pilot, who immediately climbed into the thick of it, hoping that at last ... we

should be able to bring down one of the night raiders; a feat which on our front had only once been credited to an airman.

Barker had no luck in shooting down a bomber, but his efforts extended his time airborne. The men of 139 waiting by the hangars for his return had almost given up hope. Their CO was an hour overdue, and surely must have become a casualty. Soon, however, in the darkness they heard the drone of a Rolls Royce Falcon engine, and several fitters walked to the landing field, now brightly lit by an anti-aircraft search light, to watch Barker touch down. The successful dry run by Barker and Benn was encouraging. But the real mission demanded good weather on an otherwise dark, moonless night.

Unfortunately, an intense thunderstorm over Villaverla on 31 July and 1 August damaged the SP4, as well as 11 F2Bs. It took until Friday, 9 August, to repair it. Nervous about the secret mission being blown or cancelled, Barker decided to risk a flight that same evening, despite thunderstorms over the Alps. Sometime that day, the crew were photographed in front of the SP4. Barker took a picture with his own camera of an Italian Air Force mechanic standing beside a certain "Count Rossi," possibly the officer-in-charge. Benn recounted the story of the night mission in his autobiography, and Barker wrote about it in a 1921 article. The following description, presented in the first person, is based on their two accounts:

The Italian agent, an experienced soldier of an Alpini regiment, Lieut Alessandro Tandura, arrives at the aerodrome along with his "controller." The two men have dinner with Barker and Benn, study their maps, and wait around till about 1:00 a.m. The two Italians embrace and say goodbye, and Tandura then climbs into the rear of the SP4, and sits down looking aft.

The parachute is attached to a 12-foot-long hollow iron tube, hinged to retract along the bottom side of the fuselage. The chute is connected by a harness to the agent. Barker starts the engines, taxies out in front of the searchlight which is illuminating his takeoff path, turns into the wind, and brings the engines up to full power.

Lightning flashes from time to time over the mountains to the north and east. Due to the low clouds, Barker stays below 2,000 feet. Benn interrogates each searchlight unit by wireless code, the beams turn on in sequence, and Barker flies east towards Nervesa. Lightning illuminates the ground below, helping a little with the navigation. However, once across the Piave and into enemy-held territory, Benn rewinds the copper antenna, and Barker navigates by the glint of railway tracks.

Seated in the nose of the aircraft, Benn rests his hand on the wooden release handle as they approach the drop zone near Serravalle. The village is the home of Tandura's family, who will help conceal him from Austro-Hungarian soldiers until he can set up his communications network. Barker, seated ahead of Tandura, raises the nose of the SP4 and slows to just above stalling speed, then lifts his foot off the rudder pedal and taps his observer twice on the back.

This is the signal for Benn to pull the handle, dropping Tandura unceremoniously into the dark. Benn pulls the handle—nothing happens. He pulls again and the aircraft lurches as the agent plummets head over heels straight down. The chute works perfectly, but Tandura has little time to manoeuvre or brace himself, as he has been ejected at only 1,600 feet above ground. Barker banks steeply around to the southwest, retracing the path to Villaverla. To disguise the purpose of the mission, Benn throws two token bombs over the side, aiming at the railway track below. The SP4 lands safely, and the exhausted crew shake hands, and crawl off to bed.

Tandura worked undercover until the last days of the war, sending out valuable information by carrier pigeons that had also been dropped by parachute at night. Benn claimed that Tandura's information on enemy dispositions was used to plan General Armando Diaz's final blow against the Dual Monarchy's forces, the Battle of Vittorio Veneto. Barker was told that Tandura was on the verge of starvation when he finally connected with Italian soldiers on 25 October.

After the war, Tandura received the Gold Medal for Military Valour, for volunteering, as his citation noted, out of simple patriotism for an extremely risky mission that was accomplished with cool courage. The Barker/Benn/Tandura mission is one of the best-documented early uses of aircraft in warfare to support intelligence operations. It very likely was the first successful parachute descent behind enemy lines by an agent in Italy.

Both the pilot and observer received gallantry awards for their contribution to the Italian war effort. The highest medal granted to foreigners by Italy was the Silver Medal for Military Valour, roughly equivalent to the DSO. The "Medaglia d'Argenta Valore Militaire," with its bright blue ribbon, was Barker's second foreign award. Benn was presented with Italy's Bronze Medal for Military Valour and also the War Cross. Quite a few RAF officers received Italian decorations in 1917-18, but Barker was one of only four Canadian pilots to be awarded the Medaglia d'Argenta, and possibly the only RAF officer to receive it twice.

This came about after Barker received the Victoria Cross, and his exploit was publicized in Europe and North America. The King of Italy remembered Barker's flamboyant character, and initiated the award of another Italian Silver Medal, this one engraved on the reverse side: "Protector of the Air." This ninth gallantry medal was never formally presented by the King or gazetted in the UK, being sent to Will more than a year after his return to Canada.

In August 1918 Will also received a Bar to his DSO, putting him in select company among Canadian flyers. Only four—Billy Bishop, "Red" Mulock, Raymond Collishaw, and Albert Carter—had been awarded the DSO and Bar. The citation described him as:

A highly distinguished patrol leader whose courage, resource and determination has set a fine example to those around him. Up to 20 July 1918, he had destroyed thirty-three enemy aircraft—twenty-one of these since the date of the last award (second Bar to the Military Cross) was conferred on him. Major Barker has frequently led formations against greatly superior numbers of the enemy with conspicuous success.

* * *

Barker went back to leading 139, although his enthusiasm for the work was flagging. Apart from his deep-seated fatigue, Will was frustrated by the compromises. His outstanding skills as a tactical instructor and flight leader were wasted in 139, and more of his patrols turned into or started out as solo missions. By 1918 unescorted flying patrols were hazardous, because a solitary aircraft attracted immediate attention. Solo adventures that would have been unremarkable in 1916 were now frowned upon. Barker understood these rules, and had taught them to his wingmen.

Will Barker was an intense, emotional man, feeling the toll of almost three years of field operations: five months as a CEF machine gunner, then 15 months as an observer and pilot in Corps Cooperation, followed by 11 months on scouts. His trademark energy was draining away, although he still fooled most of those around him. Unable to lead a flight of outstanding scout pilots as he had in 66, he became even more obsessed with building up his own victory score. This obsession clouded his judgement, which was becoming impaired due to years of combat.

Most of Barker's letters from this period no longer exist, but the brief post cards that have survived speak in a banal tone of his leave, his fatigue, and his aerial victories. To family and friends Barker wrote about exactly the same things—his newest decoration, the number of bullets in his latest victim, and how hot Italy was in the summertime. Like most seasoned combat veterans, Will no longer felt connected to what American soldiers of the Vietnam War would later refer to as "back in the world." His boyhood farm home on the Canadian prairies, and the family he had not seen since May 1915 were faded snapshots. In Italy Will was in no position to say or do much about their declining fortunes.

His father had moved the Barkers into and out of various small Manitoba towns, working as a hard-scrabble farmer and grain agent, and struggling to rise above a subsistence living. Will knew that the Barker family no longer had a life rooted in community. When they had moved back to Dauphin from Russell in 1912, it took four railway cars to

Studio portrait of Major Barker after taking command of 139 Squadron in July 1918.

Provincial Archives of Manitoba

move their farm equipment and belongings. A few years after the Great War, when George and Jane Barker left for Chicago, their worldly goods fitted into a Model T Ford.

Barker knew he was the highest-scoring surviving ace still fighting on the Italian Front, after word spread through the RAF squadrons that Major Baracca had been killed on 19 June. With Godwin Brumowski, the leading Austro-Hungarian, on leave, that left the "The Falcon of Feltre," Frank Linke-Crawford. He was killed at the end of July, but *not* by Barker, as one enduring legend claims even to this day.

There is no convincing evidence that Barker ever fought one-on-one against any of the leading Austro-Hungarian aces. Nevertheless, authors since the 1920s have related a colourful story of Barker's triumphant aerial battle against Linke-Crawford, a story that has no foundation.

On the morning of 31 July, Linke-Crawford had fought two engagements. The first was against a three-plane formation of Camels from 45 Squadron, led by Capt James Cottle, and the second against Sergeant Ciampitti and Corporal Astolfi of 81 Squadron, Italian Air Force. The wings of his Aviatik D.I were seriously weakened in the dogfight, and Linke-Crawford was unable to evade the two Italian pilots in their Hanriot fighters. His aircraft broke up in the air and crashed in flames. Aldo Astolfi received his only victory credit of the war for this fight. Barker was practising parachute drops, and did no offensive patrols on 31 July.

Many of Barker's friends at 28, 45, and 66 had served their tours and been sent to Home Establishment. Three of his favourites—Gerry Birks, Harold "Chink" Hudson, and Tommy "Voss" Williams—had left by August, and he missed their company. "Mable" Apps, who had flown many missions with Barker and Birks, had been wounded by anti-aircraft fire and was in hospital. For his nine victories in Italy, Apps was recommended for and received the DFC. However, "Black Mike" McEwen and Stan Stanger were still flying patrols, as was "Mac" MacDonald, and these three aces survived the war and returned to Canada.

Another of Barker's protégés, Capt Willie Hilborn, had fractured his skull in a night flying accident. He lived on for a few days in hospital, but died on 25 August, and was buried, like many other RAF flyers, in Montecchio Precalcino cemetery. The idea to institute night flying for the Camels came from 14 Wing HQ. But there was no operational need to fly at night, and a few pilots, inexperienced and out of practice, had minor accidents.

Barker flew one noteworthy non-operational mission as CO of 139. On Monday, 16 September, Edward, the Prince of Wales, attached to the staff of the Earl of Cavan, drove by for a visit. Standing by the canvas hangars, Edward watched his equerry, Capt Lord Claud Hamilton, take off with Walter Simon. The Prince had flown at least once in France and thought aircraft much better weapons of war than tanks. Protected from most operational hazards

by his staff, being the heir to the British throne, he still insisted on flying when he could.

Barker took him up, but instead of circling the aerodrome, he pointed the Bristol (D8063) towards the front lines. By one account, the aircraft was gone for quite a while, frightening the staff officers and aides. Barker probably flew over the Austro-Hungarian lines, and the Prince may have fired the Lewis machine gun at enemy targets, but if so, neither man was going to admit it. But the Prince did show improved map reading knowledge after the flight, knowledge that could only have been based on some first-hand exposure to the enemy positions.

Although Barker's victory score was the highest in Italy, it was still behind other RAF pilots such as Bishop, Collishaw, Mannock, and McCudden. After the five victories in his first week with 139, he scored one last time before leaving Italy. It was his first triple victory against flying machines since becoming a scout pilot, and a great finale to his Italian tour.

On the morning of 18 September, flying just west of San Giustina, he sighted a large formation of nine enemy Scouts at 16,000 feet. All alone, Barker was able to attract the attention of an Italian formation of Nieuports. One of these, with a red fuselage, flew in formation on Barker's wing as he attempted to set up a successful attack. After a few minutes of manoeuvring, Barker fired a flare to alert his Italian partner, and then attacked two Albatros scouts at 17,000 feet. Neither aircraft was destroyed, but one spun down out of control.

Two enemy Scouts then attacked Barker who quickly rolled his aircraft upside down and, while diving to evade these two, opened fire on a third aircraft below him. The next to attack him was more experienced. He was Sergeant Ludwig Thaler of Flik 14D, who came at Barker head-on, not turning aside until they were 40 yards apart. When Barker manoeuvred onto his tail, Thaler attempted to outrun B6313, but Will was able to put a long burst into his Albatros just before it got out of range. It started to burn.

Thaler then rolled his aircraft inverted, smoke pouring from the fuselage. He released his seat belt, fell clear of the cockpit, and deployed his parachute. This was the first time that an opponent of

WILLIE HILBORN'S LAST LETTERS TO BROTHER CLARENCE

Willie Hilborn had only recently been promoted and transferred as a new flight commander to 45. He had just received his DFC for achieving six victories, and had put in nine months of field service. He might have survived the war but for the whim of the 14 Wing HQ to introduce night flying. His letters provide insight into the anxiety of young flyers of the First World War, not about death, but rather nervous breakdown:

My dear brother Clarence:-
... It is a good thing alright to do lots of time. I will have done quite a lot of time when I go back. I may have to go at the end of the month. You see I am starting to feel sick again. It is my stomach that bothers me. I would like to quit about the end of August.

A few days later Willie learned that Clarence was going back to England to instruct:
... You and I won't be very far apart in going back to England. If we can't get home we will at least try and get to the same aerodrome as instructors ... I was recommended for the D.F.C. a couple of days ago by the Wing. I am not supposed to know but somebody told me that knew. It will come through in a few days for sure. Decorations are very nice, but I don't believe in taking foolish chances to get them. I have just gone along, and done my work, and with a little luck have done pretty well.

Two days before his crash, Willie wrote Clarence for the last time:
... My captaincy came through last night or yesterday morning it was. I was in 28 and they didn't need me there so I came to 45. This is a much better squadron than 28. I am going to like it here very well. The O.C. is young but he is a nice fellow. I will get along fine with him. I have got a very good flight too. I was up with them this morning for the first time ...
I think that I will stay about two months and then go to H/E [Home Establishment]. Of course I may have to quit before then, but I will stay that long if I can. Two weeks of that will be in Italian leave. If you want any money I could let you have some for I have quite a bank account.
Well, I must close for this time. Hoping to hear from you soon. I remain your loving brother, Bill Hilborn.

On 31 August, Clarence received a telegraph at the Waldorf Hotel in Aldwych:
Deeply regret to inform you that Cpt. W.C. Hilborn, Royal Air Force, is reported to have died of wounds on August twenty-sixth. The Air Council express their sympathy. Sincerely Air Ministry.

Willie's death was a devastating blow within the family. From the ranch Josephine wrote Clarence:
... last Saturday we got the news of our dear son Willie's death. I could not write then. Oh, I can't tell you how we feel and I'm sure your own dear heart aches too. But we believe he has gone to a better world where there is no war and no more pain. Where everything is bright. He was a good boy & so brave & we are all proud of him. Only we wanted him home again, it was such a shock to us all. We must try & be brave too.

For Barker, attending Willie's funeral was a routine obligation done out of respect. His own squadron had had eight men killed in action or died of wounds since he assumed command. But this was nothing exceptional. Saluting Hilborn's grave at Montecchio Precalcino Communal Cemetery, Barker had yet another chance to think of his own mortality. Like most fighter pilots during a war he chose to think that Hilborn was one of "them," the dead, not like him, never going to be like him. It was just better that way.

Barker's had used a chute to save his life. (They had only recently been introduced into the K.u.K. LFT squadrons.) The sight of the white chute drifting down from the burning aircraft made a lasting impression on Barker. His experience dropping secret agent Tandura in August, followed by the dramatic escape of Thaler in September, convinced him, if he was not already convinced after more than two years of flying, that parachutes should be essential equipment for all military aviators.

Thaler's aircraft crashed in a riverbed, but he landed without much damage on his own side of the lines. In the afternoon, Barker photographed the wreckage from the cockpit of an F2B. The 14 Wing HQ gave him credit for a destroyed hostile machine, and also the two others driven down out of control. This raised his victory total to 46. There is no indication in the combat report whether the unidentified Italian Air Force pilot confirmed Barker's other claims, or in what squadron he was serving. This victorious fight, achieved with the protection of an Italian fighter pilot, was to be Barker's last in Italy.

Knowing that his days on that front would soon be over, Will flew over 15 hours of patrols, including two bombing raids, between 12 and 18 September. His combat fatigue increasingly evident to the commander of 14 Wing, orders posting him to Home Establishment were generated.

Billy Bishop, by his own account, had logged about 400 flying hours when he was posted to the UK in June 1918. Barker had logged over 900 hours when sent home in September. Six months in the field was typical for a scout pilot, but Will had been almost a year, and the odds were not always going to be in his favour. Joubert had ample reason to worry because Barker was well known not only as the RAF's best ace within 14 Wing, but also as the Wing's most valuable model of offensive leadership.

Barker had been able to keep one aircraft, B6313, for a year of operations. This was a remarkable and unique accomplishment. No RAF scout machine ever surpassed B6313's achievement—46 victories

Barker (centre) on leave at Lake Garda, summer of 1918; pilot Graham Curtis kneeling in front, others unidentified.

with one pilot. It may stand as a record in any air force, in any war. However, there was no way to transfer the Camel home. After flying it one last time on a one-hour test on Sunday, 29 September, Will handed it over to the flight sergeant in charge of B Flight's maintenance.

The aircraft had accumulated just over 404 hours since new, more than 80 percent of those hours on offensive patrols. Its Vickers guns were still the factory originals (serial numbers C3441 and C4488). Barker took off the metal devil attached to the foresight of the right gun. He had plans for it.

B6313 was not preserved. Later its log book was passed on to the Imperial War Museum in London, where it has been on display for decades. B Flight's fitters and riggers dismantled B6313 on 2 October, and transported it on a flatbed truck a few days later to 7 Aircraft Park. On receipt of the aircraft, the officer-in-charge of the Stores Section noticed that the timepiece was not in the cockpit.

Barker on leave posing with camera in hand.

RAF aircraft were fitted with a removable watch which was considered the most valuable cockpit instrument. Barker had lifted the watch from B6313 as a souvenir, but the Stores Section wanted it back. The watch was returned, although Barker was tempted to trade it for one of his medals.

Barker's ambition to add to his score pushed aside any notion of a well-deserved leave in the United Kingdom. It was the German "Ace of Aces," that he wanted to surpass, as he confessed to his parents:

I have been going to write for days past but I never seem to get time & if I do I feel too done in. I think I have overdone it a bit as I have been feeling poorly lately.

At last I am leaving this country. Orders have come through for me to proceed to England on the 15th October for a rest. I sure need it now but after it I am going to France & my ambition is to break all records. I have got 37 Huns down & Major Richotfen [*sic*] the German who is now dead claims 80. I am going to try to break this record if my health will only hold out.

After I have attained this I am coming home but not till I have done my best.

Many accounts say that he was posted to, or ordered to take command of a School of Air Fighting at Hounslow, but his RAF service records show no such posting. As soon as Barker arrived in the UK, he fast-talked his way back to France. He must have been his most persuasive, claiming a need to assess the style of air fighting on the Western Front. The senior officer at RAF HQ in London who granted the request was taking a great risk letting this fatigued pilot back into action. But he put Major Barker on a short leash. Permission was granted for only a 10-day roving commission.

Sopwith Snipe - E8102 by Robert William Bradford.

CHAPTER NINE

AN APPOINTMENT WITH FAME

"Major Barker's wounds are, one in the left arm, the elbow joint having been shot away, leaving only a muscular connection; one through the upper part of the muscle on the inside of the right leg, and one through the left hip, passing down through the muscles of the left leg, the bone of the hip being slightly fractured where hit."
CAPTAIN JOHNSTON, CANADIAN SECTION, G.H.Q., B.E.F., JANUARY 1919

Barker was authorized to have any aircraft from the St Omer Aircraft Supply Depot, and attach himself to any squadron he wanted. He chose the machine he had lusted after while in Italy—a Sopwith 7F.1 Snipe. He did not choose Major Raymond Collishaw's squadron, 203, belonging to 13 Wing on the St Quentin front. The Canadian ace from Nanaimo, BC, recalled many years later that he welcomed Barker during a flying visit, but warned him against operating solo now that he was back in France. Will was in no mood to take advice from a former Royal Naval Air Service pilot, and opted for another squadron, 201, also in 13 Wing.

Only one man at this squadron had an appreciation of Barker's fighting ability and character. He was Major Cyril M. Leman, the commanding officer. Leman had been Barker's pilot when he was just a green observer at 9 Squadron back in 1916, and they had become friends. Barker picked 201 mainly because he knew Leman, and would have a dinner companion in the evenings in the Officer's Mess.

The men flying their tired Camels at 201 wanted to get their hands on the RAF's newest scout machine, but who there had the pull of Major Barker, DSO and Bar, MC and Two Bars? When he arrived at Beugnatre aerodrome on 17 October, there were fewer than 100 Snipes in France.

The pilots of 201 felt no comradeship at all with the visiting major, and most resented that he was allowed to fly where and when he wanted in his own personal

aircraft. Will Barker was an outsider and would remain so for his 10-day tour. At a reunion of 201 pilots in the 1970s nobody had a kind word for Barker. Some considered his Victoria Cross action just a vainglorious act of grandstanding.

Barker was just another hotshot who had scored big against a second-rate enemy, the Austro-Hungarians, in an Italian side-show. That was the opinion of these Western Front veterans hounding the retreating German Air Force in the last weeks of the war. Will had not lived through Operation Michael when they had been mauled in the spring retreat with the rest of the BEF; he had not tangled with the multi-coloured Fokker Dr.I Triplanes flown by the aces of the Richthofen Circus, or their formidable Fokker D.VII. He was a nobody in terms of the Western Front, and a flashy paint scheme on his machine changed nothing in the eyes of 201's pilots.

Will had his Snipe painted like B6313, with five white stripes around the rear fuselage. His was an early production airframe, serial number E8102, which had been slated to go to 43 Squadron. Later versions had a bigger vertical fin and rudder, and horn-balanced ailerons to improve handling, but not E8102. Although quite manoeuvrable, the Snipe was heavier on the controls than the Camel, lacking its hair-trigger responses. Some pilots considered the Snipe a truck by comparison.

By the standards of the day it was sophisticated, being the first RAF scout machine to have an electrical heating system for the cockpit, and oxygen equipment for the pilot. It was more docile to fly, and it had an adjustable horizontal tailplane, making it less fatiguing on long missions. The Bentley engine was more powerful than the Clerget, but the Snipe weighed 600 pounds more at takeoff than the Camel, and its performance was only slightly better. From a distance, in the heat of battle, German pilots could not distinguish between the two Sopwith machines, and victories against Snipes were "Camel" victories.

According to *The War in the Air*, the German Army could have been more harshly dealt with if the weather had been better in October: "For about ten days, while the Germans were going back as fast as they could, rain and mist made relentless air attacks impossible." This miserable weather during Barker's roving commission curtailed his opportunities to close with the enemy, setting the stage for a tragic conclusion to his tour, one brought on mostly by his own fatigue and short temper.

He flew three offensive patrols between 21 and 23 October, but had no combats. He took off with the pilots of 201, but did not integrate with any of their patrols, preferring to take advantage of the Snipe's better high-altitude performance by flying thousands of feet above the Camel formations. The others could see him suspended, hawk-like, above them, waiting for targets of opportunity that never showed.

Bad weather then grounded him for three frustrating days. Already on a short fuse, shunned by the other pilots, and with time running out, he felt like some trapped animal. The abbreviated roving commission that had been granted by RAF HQ was very frustrating. He needed more time. He received orders on the 26th to return E8102 to the Aircraft Supply Depot so it could be signed over to its proper squadron. He was then expected, without delay, to return to London.

A British pilot, Capt Ronald Sykes, later recalled how angry the Canadian was at the Saturday evening dinner: "Major Barker was furious in the Mess saying that the Air Ministry must be fed up because he had not been able to report a victory on the Western Front (as his score shows, he was full of confidence

and aggression). He said he intended to go to the Lines and have a fight the next day with the Snipe enroute for 1 A.S.D."

What happened early Sunday morning changed everything. Had he followed orders and delivered E8102, instead of crossing the lines on one last patrol, his life would have been so different.

Edna Barker had never wanted her dear brother Willie to go overseas. She could not go to the train station to see him off. She just wanted him safe and sound back on the farm. What her brother did that Sunday changed him, and changed the Barker family forever: "... he was home free after Italy; all he had to do was come home. He didn't have to go to France. Why didn't he come home? Maybe he was just bloodthirsty."

Barker shook hands with Cyril Leman, who wished him good luck in his new command in England. For the others his departure was unimportant, and no pilots waved goodbye. The aerodrome was busy, and formations had already taken off on dawn patrols. The sun was not up, but the sky was brightening. The rain had ended in the night, and there were only a few clouds against the blue sky.

His Snipe lifted off easily, and climbed quickly through 10,000 feet, reaching that altitude in less than 10 minutes. Will felt the sunshine on his shoulders, the vibration of the engine through the throttle and control column. He pulled back the cocking lever on his Vickers machine guns, and briefly pressed the thumb triggers on the control column. Cordite stink mingled with burning castor oil. He had smelled that mixture for over a year, and it never failed to wake him up.

His eyes searched ahead and above to the east. The Snipe climbed effortlessly through 15,000, then more slowly. The town of Valenciennes was behind him now, the dark green Mormal Forest was directly below. The watch in the cockpit read twenty-five past eight. The sky seemed empty, but then Barker saw what he was hunting for—a German machine. It was white against the brilliant blue, a two-seater reconnaissance aircraft. It was well above him, 21,000 feet, perhaps even higher. The German flyers were confident that altitude was their protection against attack. What scout machine could reach them, let alone dive out of the sun?

The pilot and his observer were not daydreaming, however, and one or the other spotted E8102 climbing towards them from the west. The Snipe had little speed advantage, and the German pilot pushed his throttle forward. Barker fired several short bursts, and the observer fired back. The pilot manoeuvred his machine so his observer's rear gun was well positioned to protect them both. This was not going to be an easy victory. Will was impressed with the pilot's flying, and the observer's shooting. He was going to have to kill the observer, and at long enough range to avoid being hit himself.

Each turned for advantage, the two-seater with its higher-aspect-ratio wing more stable at this altitude than the Snipe. To turn tightly in the thin air and not stall demanded that both pilots descend. But shooting rather than turning was what mattered here,

and at a range well beyond 100 yards, likely from below and behind, Barker managed to wound or kill the observer. He was now free to close in, firing burst after burst into the pilot's cockpit, the engine, and the wings.

The white machine started to break apart, and one of the two airmen fell free, his chute blossoming. Will was mesmerized by the scene. He was fixated on his target, no longer thinking as a predator. He had lost his situation awareness, and instantly became the prey of a German pilot in a Fokker D.VII, who had seen the drama above him, and started climbing at a steep angle. Will had never fought against one. It was reliable, well-powered, tight-turning, stable at high altitude, and able to hang on its propeller at low speed, shooting upwards into the belly of the unaware. The first Barker knew of his stalker was a sledge-hammer punch to his right thigh.

David Mackenzie collection

Crew of 29 Kite Balloon Section who rescued Barker from his Snipe on Sunday morning, 27 October 1918.

He threw the Snipe into a spin, either by instinct or, in shock, simply letting go of the controls, with the same result. When he came out of the spin several thousand feet lower he ran head on into a large formation of Fokker D.VIIs. In the vernacular of today's fighter pilot, Barker had put himself "in a world of hurt."

In a descending, whirling battle for survival, Will gave as good as he got. At least two more bullets struck him, one in the left hip, one through the left arm, destroying his elbow. In shock and pain, he knew he could not escape, and must fight on. He had no parachute.

Believing he was done for, he tried to ram into a German machine, his guns firing as he closed in. But the D.VII either fell apart or spun away, and Will saw a familiar sight on the horizon—observation balloons. By instinct, barely conscious, he sped at low altitude towards the front lines, and crash-landed near a British balloon.

The balloonists of 29 Kite Balloon Section ran to the Snipe, tipped over on its back, and lifted Barker out of the cockpit. Pulling open his Sidcot suit, a young officer saw the bright red arterial blood pumping from Barker's groin. He applied pressure to the wound while the unconscious aviator was bundled into a motor tender, and rushed to the nearest field dressing station.

The kite balloonists had no idea who this RAF major was, but he certainly had plenty of ribbons on his chest. Lieut Frank Woolley Smith washed the blood from his shaking hands at the field dressing station. It was a hell of way to start a Sunday morning. Whoever the poor devil was, it did not look good. The surgeons went to work on him as soon as Smith and his men had laid him on a gurney. But he had lost a lot of blood, his Sidcot suit was drenched in it, and he was not moving at all. Smith walked back to the tender, hoping to God this war was going to end soon.

He never received, nor expected any credit for saving Barker's life, and by 1969 when he finally told his story (see Appendix One), Frank Woolley Smith, OBE, DFC, wanted only to pass along the photograph he snapped of E8102 many years before.

Barker certainly would have bled to death had he crashed in No Man's Land. He was lucky to have survived at all, given the devastating power of the enemy guns that had been aimed at him. The 7.92 mm copper-jacketed rounds from the Fokker D.VII's Spandau machine guns were high velocity, more than 2,500 feet-per-second. As Woodman has written, in the Great War, the severity of wounds suffered by Allied airmen, that sometimes included the amputation of limps, was attributed, mistakenly, to the use by the Germans of explosive bullets. In fact, the severe damage inflicted on Barker's left arm and legs was caused by the characteristic instability and cavitation of high-velocity rounds.

Such bullets tumble and yaw, transmitting greater kinetic energy as they move through the body. The shock wave generated in front of each bullet, and the cavitation in its wake, forces tissues to stretch and recoil, resulting in damage some distance from the wound track. A transient, water-vapour-filled cavity forming around and behind the bullet, but much larger in diameter, sucks in foreign material, skin and bone fragments, and bacteria.

The medical personnel at the field dressing station stopped his bleeding and covered his wounds, but then loaded him aboard an ambulance tender for 8 General Hospital in Rouen. On arrival there Barker was laid on an operating table and given anaesthetic. By this stage of the war, medical treatment for traumatic gunshot wounds had been refined due to the experience gained on hundreds of thousands of soldiers. According to Stout, the torn flesh around the wound was

> ... radically excised; then small rubber tubes with lateral holes were inserted freely into the wound, and gauze placed over it. The wound was not drained, but left like an open trough so that the Dakin's solution could lie in the wound and get longer contact with the tissues ... solution was then introduced into the tubes four-hourly by means of a syringe ... In large wounds trays were placed under the limb to catch the overflow.

Barker was fortunate to be treated within a couple of hours. With no antibiotics to fight bacterial infection, gas gangrene was the leading cause of death in the wounded of the Great War. His doctors could cut away dead flesh, and nurses could keep his wounds open, and change his dressings. They could also amputate. But if that did not stop the spread of the toxaemia, there were no other alternatives.

After a week in critical condition, Barker improved. By 7 November he was able to write a short note in a shaky but optimistic uphill scrawl to his only friend at 201 Squadron:

My dear Leman: -
I arrived here fairly well & am progressing. Please send all my mail on here.

By Jove I was a foolish boy but anyhow I taught them a lesson. The only thing that bucks me up is to look back & see them going down in flames. I wish some of you could have been with me & we would have got more.

My elbow is a bit septic other wise I am about the same

Best of luck to all. I hope to see you again soon.

W.G. Barker

By the time Will wrote his letter to Leman it was known throughout the hospital that the Canadian major had been recommended for the Empire's highest gallantry award, the Victoria Cross.

Four days later the Great War ended—at the 11th hour, 11th day, 11th month. The news spread quickly. Men cried, or shook hands, or sat up in their beds, saying nothing, just thinking. The patients at 8 General Hospital's recovery ward knew most of them would survive—even the now-famous RAF pilot lying by the window. But Will was unable to sit up for three months, and was not even moved from Rouen until January 1919.

Telegrams of good luck and praise arrived at the hospital almost daily—from His Majesty the King; from Edward, Prince of Wales; from the general staff of the CEF; from Billy Bishop, VC; and from the prime minister of Canada, Sir Robert Borden: "The inspiring story which has just been told in the press has thrilled the hearts of all Canadians. I trust you are making good progress toward recovery from your injuries and I send every good wish."

To Borden, a man like Barker was a symbol of what Canadians had contributed to the defence of the British Empire. He had visited Canadian soldiers in hospital, a self-imposed duty that often brought him to tears.

* * *

The phrase "60-against-1" or "1-against-60" was part of the lead in most of the newspapers. *The London Times* headline was "The Great Air Fight"—*The Daily Telegraph* labelled it "Marvellous Air Fight," and, after learning that Barker was Canadian rather than British, *The Daily Mail* trumpeted, "Canadian Major's Triumph." Major General Trenchard praised the performance of the Snipe to designer T.O.M. Sopwith, not mentioning Barker by name, but endorsing the sturdiness of E8102 in its last action. Lieutenant General Sir Richard Turner, VC, the Canadian commander in England, wanted the pilot promoted. The Boer War Victoria-Cross-recipient scribbled the ringing newspaper phrase "60-against-1" on his memorandum that requested Barker's promotion to lieutenant colonel, an example of officialdom adopting an exaggerated journalistic account and, thereby, conferring legitimacy on it.

It is very unlikely that 60 German aircraft were chasing one Snipe, and the fight did not last 40 minutes. Some newspaper stories credited the pilot with the destruction of a dozen enemy aircraft. Such exaggeration partly explains the historical claim that it was the greatest one-sided aerial fight of the war.

When journalists asked Barker for interviews in the 1920s about the action, he would not grant them, simply commenting, "It's all down in the Gazette." Some have recorded this as evidence of his modesty. In fact, Barker was proud of his war record, and bragged about other episodes, but not the action that conferred on him the VC, because it revealed him making a crucial mistake.

AN ANALYSIS OF OCTOBER 27TH, 1918

The awarding of gallantry medals in war is rarely a simple, unequivocal process. Many factors can influence who receives a medal, who does not, and what medal is handed out. Many brave men never receive recognition, or die courageously without witnesses. The winning of a nation's highest award for bravery in war, whether Great Britain's Victoria Cross, or its United States equivalent, the Medal of Honor, forever changes the person who receives it. The high regard in which such medals are held inevitably colours how we see a recipient, and creates a legendary aura that almost nothing can dispel. Receiving such a medal can be more stressful in certain ways than the winning of it. Some have observed that the wearing of the medal, over a lifetime, is a strain, due to the high expectations of others.

The military bureaucracy that took care of gallantry awards in France in 1918 had responded quickly when Major Leman filled out Barker's combat report for 27 October. The official citation of what happened to Barker has been published many times in the last 90 years (see page 5), but the mandatory paper trail of recommendations and approvals which led to the awarding of his Victoria Cross is unavailable. We do not know exactly who suggested to whom that Barker was deserving, perhaps Leman, perhaps Leman's superiors at Wing or Brigade HQ, and maybe all of them.

What we think we know about that Sunday morning comes from other men, none of them witnesses to or participants in the aerial combat itself, plus many accounts, none of them written by Barker himself. The man from Manitoba later summarized his dramatic struggle in one sentence: "I was severely wounded and shot down." That is all he ever said in any public way about 27 October.

There had, of course, been witnesses on the ground. The finale of Barker's aerial battle was seen by many soldiers along the front lines south of Valenciennes, but most of what is described in the VC citation could not have been seen looking up from the ground. Indeed, nobody could have seen and comprehended all that is described. For several days following the combat Barker was unconscious, and in no shape to provide an explanation of what had happened.

There were two eyewitnesses who later wrote of their memories of that morning. One was Lieut Woolley Smith, the other, Brigadier General Andrew McNaughton, head of the Canadian Corps heavy artillery, who provided a dramatic description of his view of the aerial battle.

It has been suggested by one aviation historian that McNaughton could not have seen Barker's fight. This is based on the distance (more than 15 miles) from McNaughton's ground position somewhere between Bellevue and the town of Valenciennes, and the Forêt de Mormal, the forest to the southeast over which the battle took place. However, that Sunday morning was clear and bright, and any aerial activity below 10,000 feet would have been visible, if one looked up. But distinguishing friend from enemy from the ground was not easy even for a knowledgeable observer.

McNaughton learned a few days after the fight that the hero was a Canadian, and a farmer's son from the Prairies, as was McNaughton himself. That parallel helped reinforce McNaughton's memory of the aerial battle. At the end of a long military career, in old age, he recalled that:

> The spectacle of this attack was the most magnificent encounter of any sort which I have ever witnessed. The ancient performances of the gladiators in the Roman arenas were far outclassed in the epic character of the successive engagements in which enemy machines, one after the other, were taken on and eliminated. The spectators, in place of being restricted to the stone walls of a Roman arena, had the horizon as their bounds and the sky as their stage. The hoarse shout, or rather the prolonged roar, which greeted the triumph of the British fighter, and which echoed across the battlefield, was never matched in Rome, nor do I think anywhere else or on any other occasion.

The official history, *The War in the Air*, even published the description of Barker's action. Jones was cautious to note, however, that the commanding officer of the squadron, not Barker, had written the combat report:

8.25 a.m. Observed enemy two-seater at 21,000 feet N. E. of Forêt de Mormal. Enemy aircraft climbed east and Major Barker following fired a short burst from underneath at point-blank range. Enemy aircraft broke up in the air and one of the occupants jumped with a parachute. He then observed a Fokker biplane 1,000 feet below stalling and shooting at him, one of the bullets wounding him in the right thigh. He fell into a spin from which he pulled out in the middle of a formation of about 15 Fokkers, two of which he attacked indecisively, both enemy aircraft spinning down. He turned, and getting on the tail of a third which was attacking him, shot it down in flames from within 10 yards range. At this moment he was again wounded in the left thigh by others of the formation who were diving at him. He fainted and fell out of control again. On recovering he pulled his machine out and was immediately attacked by another large formation of 12 to 15 enemy aircraft. He got on the tail of one and from a range of less than 5 yards shot it down in flames. At this moment he received a third wound from the remainder of the formation who were attacking him, the bullet shattering his left elbow. The enemy machine which wounded him closed to within 10 yards. He again fainted and fell out of control to 12,000 feet, and recovering was at once attacked by another large formation of enemy aircraft. He then noticed heavy smoke coming from his machine and, under the impression he was on fire, tried to ram a Fokker just ahead of him. He opened fire on it from 2 to 3 yards range and enemy aircraft fell in flames. He then dived to within a few thousand feet of the ground and began to fly towards our lines, but found his retreat was cut off by another formation of 8 enemy aircraft who attacked him. He fired a few bursts at some of them and shaking them off dived down and returned to our lines a few feet above the ground, finally crashing close to one of our balloons.

The combat report is breathtakingly dramatic and detailed. But was it Barker who provided all the facts? Who else could have known that one of the airmen in the two-seater had bailed out? Who was counting all those enemy aircraft, more than 30 in all? Were they the same or different formations, all attacking one Snipe, or did Barker simply spin down through their formations, firing at targets of opportunity and being fired upon? Did he really shoot down three of his four enemies at ranges of five yards or less?

It was not uncommon in the First World War for citations to be written for heroes who had been taken prisoner, or were unconscious or deceased. Leman at some point presumably interviewed Barker in hospital. But it is also possible that he wrote the combat report before talking to him, relying on unidentified witnesses, and with the tacit support of his superiors at HQ. By 5 November, stories were already being published in British and Canadian newspapers, describing how Barker fought alone against 60 enemy aircraft. Had King George the V, who had final approval on the award of the bronze cross with the maroon ribbon, already assented to Barker's award?

Whatever the case, the combat report became the basis for the Victoria Cross citation that credited Barker with destroying four enemy aircraft, three in flames. The citation also credits him with torching the enemy scout that first attacked and wounded him, which the combat report does not do. The many magazine stories written over three generations rely heavily on the official citation, embellishing here and there to create a more legendary account of a cockpit awash with blood, an aircraft in tatters.

However, there is little evidence of bullet holes, and none of bloodstains, on the fuselage section of E8102, shipped to Canada in 1919. This priceless and unique artefact of a VC-winning fighter pilot is on display at the Canadian War Museum in Ottawa.

Sykes at 201 wrote in his diary at the time that the three bullets that struck Barker in the arm and legs must have been lucky shots since he could not find any other holes in the fuselage when he walked around the Snipe. Will was later photographed for publicity standing next to, or sitting in the fuselage of his Snipe, first in London and then Toronto, but the look on his face in these photos seems grim or haunted.

All his leadership and tactical brilliance demonstrated in nearly three years of field service paled to insignificance against the lone-wolf legend created on 27 October. He would always be remembered as the pilot who had fought single-handedly against 60 German machines. For someone so proud of his achievements, it was especially galling to know he had been the agent of his own undoing. His long fighting career was trivialized by a solo action in which he had been defeated. The fight returned in flashbacks, in occasional dreams, and his physical wounds became a constant reminder of that failure.

What is the truth behind the legendary fight? We will probably never know (see analysis of the events of that combat on pages 148–49). But, from

his record, we do know that Barker's gunnery skills were exceptional. All but three or four of his targets had burned or broken up in the air. If any pilot was skilled enough to fight his way out of a corner, it was Barker.

However, there are no surviving German records to confirm the loss of three Fokker D.VIIs. Aviators named Wattenburg, Mack, and Scheffler were killed in action that day. But other RAF pilots, including those of 29 and 74 Squadrons, also claimed victories over the Forêt de Mormal. The German Air Force was very short of aviation petrol, and had been rationing it to its best squadrons, allowing them to fly two missions a day. The most likely units to have launched offensive patrols that morning were

150

Snipe E8102 on its nose after the crash on 27 October 1918.

Jastas 2, 26, 27, and 36, all belonging to Jagdgeschwader III and/or Jastas 1, 57, 58, and 59, all belonging to Jagdgruppe 10.

It is the pilots of some or all of these units who are most likely to have fought against Barker. The diary for Jagdgeschwader III did not survive the war, and the diaries of the other German units are typically sketchy due to the rapid retreat in the last weeks of the war. There is little likelihood, 80 years later, that any undiscovered German documents will surface that could clarify or correct the events of that morning.

The RAF no longer has Barker's medical records, but his own and other letters provide a graphic description of his condition. The most detailed account comes from a Capt Johnston, in January 1919, who wrote that Barker said there were 15 Huns below him after he shot down the two-seater (see his written report in Appendix Two):

Major Barker's wounds are, one in the left arm, the elbow joint having been shot away, leaving only a muscular connection; one through the upper part of the muscle on the inside of the right leg, and one through the left hip, passing down through the muscles of the left leg, the bone of the hip being slightly fractured where hit.

By this time Barker was a public figure. Even the doctors and nurses paused during one of his many operations so that they could be immortalized by a photograph, operating on a VC recipient. In the photo, Barker is anaesthetised, his shattered arm hangs down limply from the gurney, and his legs are suspended from pulleys.

Will was moved to England that month, crossing the English Channel in the H.M. Hospital Ship, *Grantully Castle*. In London he was operated on several more times. Billy Bishop once asked Barker how many times he had received an anaesthetic, to which Will replied, "Not so often," but Bishop later learned that it had been 17 times in two months. A surgeon, Robert Dolbey, recalled the challenges faced: "... he was under my charge in London, after the war. I

operated on his elbow joint, after which—though it was no fault of mine, but an inevitable result of the destruction of the bone—he was never able to have any power in his arm, unless he had a retentive apparatus, so that Barker, from that time onwards, flew entirely with one arm."

Barker was on the road to physical recovery but had, inevitably, to cope with a flood of emotions arising from trauma. In 1918 such mental distress was called neurasthenia, or hysteria, but today is labelled post-traumatic stress disorder (PTSD). There is inferential evidence suggesting that Barker suffered from PTSD, based primarily on the changes in his behaviour observed by family and friends.

Certainly, his psyche was ill prepared to handle the consequences of defeat. He was an emotional man who controlled his emotions through self-discipline. A perfectionist who set high standards, he had rarely made mistakes in the heat of combat. Barker's helplessness in hospital, and the knowledge of his shattered left arm, resulted in withdrawal, denial, anger, and depression. His Methodist upbringing ensured that the guilt of failure would linger long after the event. Will did not forgive others easily, but was the last to forgive himself. At the same time, the good opinion of others was very important to his sense of self-worth, and in the eyes of some experienced scout pilots his final action was more reckless than brave.

There was little treatment for the emotional trauma of burns or gunshot in 1918. Only the most severe kinds of shell-shock elicited any sympathy from military medical officers, and often not even then. Flyers were simply expected to rebound to robust "up-and-at-them" health, without psychotherapeutic intervention. Men like Barker were expected to fit the stereotype of manliness, and any display of nerves would have undermined the heroic archetype.

For British and Canadian journalists this epic story had everything going for it. The first accounts in Canada did not identify Barker by name or nationality, stating only that he was a British pilot. But when Carmen Alguire read the story in the Winnipeg papers, he said to George Barker: "I'll bet you a nickel that's our Will." George rather doubted it with so many pilots in France, but Carmen knew his nephew and retorted: "Well, it just sounds like something he would do."

There were 19 Victoria Crosses awarded for gallantry in the air, but only nine of the recipients were alive at war's end, and three were in hospital (Barker, Anthony Beauchamp Proctor, and Ferdinand West). The "60-against-1" story was published in the Manitoba papers on 7 November, four days before the Great War ended, and one day after 19-year-old Alan McLeod, of Stonewall, died of influenza. McLeod had earned his Victoria Cross the previous March flying an FK8 with 2 Squadron. The Barker family knew Dr and Mrs McLeod, and knew that Alan was their only son. They were heartbroken to see the obituary printed right next to the story of another VC hero.

The Barker family, having received a telegram that their eldest boy was badly wounded, was unable to find out how he was progressing. On 16 November, George sent a telegram to Ottawa asking about the condition of his son, "Major W.G. Barker, DSO, MC." The Department of Militia was apparently not paying attention to the front pages of the daily newspapers. They knew he was a former CEF private, serial number 106074, but beyond that their inquiries failed.

It took until December for the Barkers to learn where their son was hospitalized, and how he was doing. What added to the confusion was that Will apparently did not write to his parents while in France. He was a long way from full recovery when he scribbled on 4 February:

I am in England at last & in a fine hospital [the Anglo-Chilean, 6 Grosvenor Square] where the food & treatment is [sic] splendid ... I have made good progress & will soon be able to sit up. My wounds are not healed yet. The one in the right thigh is much smaller —But my left hip is still troublesome & I had an operation on it last week—my left elbow is progressing but will take a long time yet. However, my general condition is much better.

Awfully glad to hear Howard is back. I wish I could have seen him.

Lance Corporal Howard Alguire had been convalescing in the UK after having two inches of his left leg, and his kneecap, blown away by a random artillery shell. Jessie Hacksley, Howard's sweetheart in Manitoba, brought him up to date on the big story back home: "Say, Billie Barker has become a demigod in the eyes of Dauphinites. The *Free Press* gave him a whale of a write up on Saturday ... Billie is some boy. He takes after you, but he hasn't got quite up to you in my estimation. I don't care if he has brought down the whole German air fleet. I mean it ... I love you in the same old way."

Will was too weak to walk any distance, and could not leave his hospital to see Howard before his uncle was shipped home to Canada: "I am still improving & am at present learning to walk. I find it a bit painful as so many of my thigh muscles & tendons were severed in operations & by the bullets. However good substantial progress is being made in that direction ... The Duke of Rutland was in to see me today & the Earl of Hardwicke is coming on Sunday. I am also going up before the king for my decorations soon. It will be the big show—VC (1), DSO (2), MC (3) ... will let you know all about it later on."

The press looked for a modest hero who would be a credit to the British Empire. Inevitably, Barker fell into the stereotype that public relations demands. His first major profile was written by a Canadian, Arthur Beverley Baxter, later the editor of *The Daily Express*, which was owned by a fellow-Canadian from New Brunswick, Max Aitken, better known as Lord Beaverbrook.

It was Beaverbrook who had established *The Canadian Daily Record*, a publication for CEF soldiers. He had also written a couple of books about Canada's fighting in the war. He loved a good story and he loved heroes. Barker's photo was featured on the front page of the *Daily Record* in December 1918. The editors labelled William Barker of Dauphin as the Canadian holding the record for the most fighting decorations in the war.

The medals of William Barker, donated in the 1980s by his family to the Canadian War Museum.

Photo by author Wayne Ralph; courtesy of the Canadian War Museum

Gripped by hero worship, it was not sufficient for journalists and press officers that Barker was just about the most decorated soldier of the British Empire. They had to make sure that he had received one of everything. If he had one award and Bar, they would add a second Bar. Baxter wrote that Barker had two Bars to his DSO, plus a French Legion of Honour. Other writers would mistakenly confer upon him the Distinguished Flying Cross, the new RAF gallantry medal equivalent to the MC, introduced in June 1918.

Will did not help in clarifying any of these exaggerations. Credited with feats he himself never claimed, he made little effort to deny them. He was affable with journalists, but apparently did not much care if they got it wrong. This just fuelled the legends about him. Asked by Baxter about his aerial victories, he responded "between forty-five and fifty," but his public relations handler, Capt Lloyd Lott, chirped in "Fifty—confirmed." Yet Baxter was sensitive enough to recognize a wounded man struggling for his composure:

We did not mention his V.C. exploit, because it was obvious that the strain of that classic battle had not left him ... Canada is a young country, but she starts rich in heroic tradition. Major Barker's last fight will rank with the epic battles of all history.

Towards the end of February, Will could walk well enough with a cane to leave the hospital, but he had to rest frequently. On Saturday morning, 1 March, he went to Buckingham Palace to receive his medals in a formal ceremony. King George V wrote in his diary: "Held an investiture at 11:00 when I gave 344 decorations, including 6 VCs & 3 Albert Medals, it lasted till 12:30." The first Victoria Cross conferred was on Lt Colonel William Clark-Kennedy, of Montreal, commander of the 24th Battalion, CEF.

Major William Barker's name, service, and feat were then read aloud. Will did not march, but rather walked slowly the ten yards into the middle of the room, leaning heavily on the cane in his right hand.

He turned left, bowed, and stood to attention. King George pinned on his decorations and talked briefly to him. Will described it this way:

... last Saturday I went to Buckingham Palace where the King presented me with 6 decorations. The former record was 4 so I raised it to 6. He mentioned the fact & also talked to me for about 5 minutes. He also thanked me for taking his son the Prince of Wales up so often & when I left the throne I met the Prince who took me about the Palace & we had a very friendly talk together. I can walk about 200 yds now so am improving & getting stronger but my wounds are still open.

Will Barker was the 18th and second-last air VC of the First World War. The former student at Dauphin Collegiate Institute was one of 7,200 RAF airmen who had been wounded in action or injured in crashes. He and his Uncle Howard were now faced with the same challenge—how to get past their crippling wounds, adapt to being a civilian, and make a living. Barker had no formal skills other than the military had provided, and he had no entitlements under Canadian law, being a member of Imperial Forces. The Canadian government was not obliged to provide a ticket home, a civilian suit, a discharge bonus, or medical care.

Howard received a 50 percent disability allowance of $17.50 a month, and a soldier's grant of 160 acres of second-rate farm land. Barker was not even

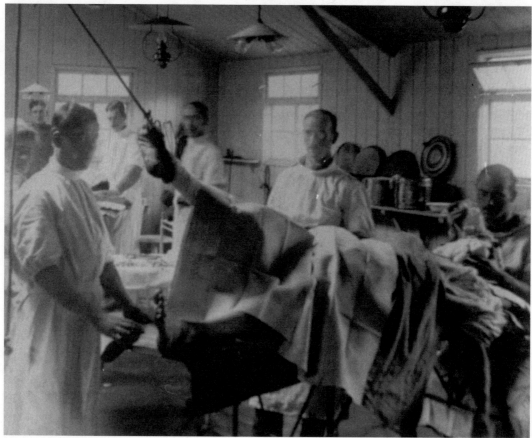

William Barker unconscious in the operating theatre at Rouen General Hospital in France; this was one of more than a dozen operations that he required to repair gunshot wounds inflicted on 27 October 1918.

Wayne Ralph collection

entitled to the annual tax-free annuity of £10 given to enlisted men who had been awarded the VC. His future as a scout pilot or squadron commander in the post-war RAF was limited—it was being reduced to one-tenth of its wartime size, eventually sliding to 30,000 from a wartime peak of 290,000.

But Barker took no counsel of his fears. He had always promised his family that he would make a fortune in civil aviation after the war, and he started

planning while still in hospital. Someone with a similar optimism about the future, and an even higher profile, came to visit him. Lt Colonel Billy Bishop, VC, DSO and Bar, MC, DFC, walked into Barker's life at a time when they were both wondering what adventures they could have without a war to fight.

Howard Alguire on crutches at the Manitoba Military Hospital in 1919.

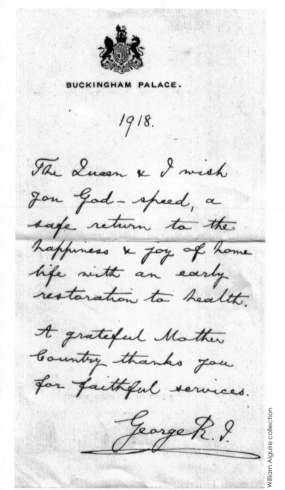

BUCKINGHAM PALACE.

1918.

The Queen & I wish you God-speed, a safe return to the happiness & joy of home life with an early restoration to health.

A grateful Mother Country thanks you for faithful services.

George R.I.

Letter from King George the Fifth and Queen Mary to Howard Alguire in hospital.

Billy Bishop, VC, with William Barker, VC (in uniform), outside the offices of the *Ottawa Evening Telegram*, May 1919.

CHAPTER TEN

A Scheme on for Flying

"Evidently ... there is some misunderstanding. I repeatedly told you all in my letters & telegrams that I was working
& organizing two companies & not playing & spending money. Now I have been successful & when I do come home I
will be of some use financially."

WILLIAM BARKER TO HIS MOTHER, OCTOBER 1919

Barker was the most decorated Canadian of the Great War, and Bishop was the second-most decorated. To the delight of journalists their names harmonized beautifully. Since Bishop was called "Billy," not William, Barker ended up being labelled "Billy" as well. His school friends and family had called him Will, and he had been Bill Barker to his comrades-in-arms in the war, but that was a minor detail. Since Bishop had many more victories than Bill Barker, 72 versus 50, they were always listed accordingly, in a one-two ranking.

Bishop's position as the highest scoring ace of the RAF, and Canada's first air VC, has put him in all the Canadian history books, in every general summary of the Great War, and in every retrospective of Canada's century. Bishop became the archetype of all scout pilots, and his achievements put all other heroes in his shadow, with the sole exception, at least through the 1920s, of Barker.

Journalists always wrote about the parallels between Billy and Will, but men and women who knew both remembered the contrasts. For these two men were more about contrast than similarity. Bishop was short, cool, and aloof; Barker was tall, gregarious, and emotional. Bishop was a graduate of Royal Military College, the son of a lawyer, married to the niece of a millionaire. Barker, a high school dropout because of the war, was descended from three generations of cobblers, blacksmiths, and farmers.

Barker had been elevated out of the working classes by his achievements in the war, whereas Bishop had simply been confirmed by his achievements within the affluent middle classes to which he had been born. Barker had to come farther, thereby making his achievements all the more remarkable. Bishop certainly thought so. In his speeches and books during World War Two, Bishop compared Barker's family upbringing to America's Ace of Aces, Major Richard I. Bong, who grew up in rural Minnesota.

Billy and Will wanted to stay in aviation, but there were few choices. They were not enthusiastic about the military, even assuming that the RAF might have them. The provisional CAF in the UK was soon to be disbanded. Not men to do things by half, they immediately started an international aircraft importing and sales company, an aviation services company, and also a passenger and cargo airline. The American import and sales division of Bishop-Barker Company, Limited, was probably one of the first in North America, if not the first in New York City. Their short-lived airline was one of the earliest in Toronto, or anywhere else in Canada.

What other choice did they have than to be bold? How does a Victoria Cross winner get a job after the war is over? What kind of civilian job could match what these two had experienced? The most decorated American of the Second World War, and Medal of Honor recipient, 1st Lieut Audie Murphy, once complained that the US Army "took Army dogs and rehabilitated them for civilian life. But they turned soldiers into civilians immediately and let 'em sink or swim." Bishop and

157

William Massey Birks, with sons Henry, Gerald, Noble, and Victor (left to right). Photo was taken 28 August 1918 at St Bruno, Quebec.

Barker, entitled to nothing from the Canadian Army, would have endorsed Murphy's assessment.

For Barker, the most useful skill the military had provided was how to fly. Like most, he had been transformed by the experience, and believed there was a great future in aviation. With characteristic confidence he wrote to his mother: "I have a scheme on for flying or attempting it at least ... my left arm will be in a sling for 8 or 10 months more—However having done so much flying, I can fly with one hand so it will not prevent me."

Most pilots who had survived the war were not looking for a career in aviation. The barnstormer immortalized in movies was the exception who had neither the patience nor the temperament to settle down.

For a generation of young men born in the 1890s, the war was the defining experience in their lives. But it was also a transient experience, and for some it had been quite traumatic. Many quite suc-

cessful military pilots never flew again, and took no interest in recreational flying. Medals and log books were thrown into a drawer, and seldom looked at. Those who had survived aerial warfare rarely spoke of that experience with their families. A reunion dinner with other veterans was the place to reminisce, among companions who could understand.

Integration back into polite society could be protracted and turbulent, and some men never made it back into the world. Tommy "Voss" Williams, having survived 200 offensive patrols, was typical of many veterans in his attitude: "I didn't care about flying. Most Canadians didn't. Canada took quite a drubbing in the First World War. Lost a lot of people. As far as I was concerned, I didn't care if I ever flew again." He returned to his hometown of Woodstock, Ontario, and took up farming.

Gerry Birks agreed with Williams. He knew he had been lucky to survive. There were few opportunities in a post-war recession for a scout pilot, and

Virginia and Michael Alexander collection

Gerry was thankful he could work in his grandfather's business: "It didn't matter that there weren't many jobs. I was a Birks ..." He never flew again. His first job was as manager of Birks stores in Winnipeg, then Halifax. He left behind the family business in the inauspicious year of 1929 to establish his own investment bank with a friend. Birks was of the same social class as Bishop—an affluent family, established in the business community, provided a leg up.

Barker's father could offer little, and wrote his son asking him to come back home and farm. In a macabre foreshadowing of Will's gunshot wounds, George had been injured in 1918 in a fall from the loft of a barn. The elbow of his right arm had been shattered, and later the elbow joint had to be amputated in hospital in Winnipeg. A leather harness was made to provide support to and additional mobility for his arm. During his lengthy convalescence he learned to knit, so as to keep his fingers from atrophying. In one of those coincidences that happen more often in fiction than in life, George's physician was Dr McLeod, father of Alan Arnett McLeod, VC.

With the demand for wheat plummeting after the war, and both he and his father handicapped, almost anything was more attractive to Will than farming. A flying business had many unknowns, but it was also a chance to build on the skills learned in the war.

The first meeting between Will Barker and Billy Bishop was an important turning point for Will, but his surviving letters make no mention of it, and provide no descriptions of Bishop. The exact date and location of their first face-to-face meeting is not known, but it was most likely sometime in January or February of 1919 in a London hospital. Billy Bishop's books and articles, as well as Arthur Bishop's biography of his father, suggest that the two aces met for the first time in Toronto in the summer of 1919. In fact, the foundation for Bishop-Barker Company and Bishop-Barker Aeroplanes was completely laid out by the two even before Barker sailed to Canada.

Since both young men had won the Victoria Cross, they had little difficulty in attracting the attention of entrepreneurs and investors. However, it was Bishop who had the best network of business

Alan Arnett McLeod, VC, who died of influenza at Winnipeg in November 1918, at age 19.

Provincial Archives of Manitoba

contacts. He was better known to Canadian and American readers than Barker. The book, *Winged Warfare*, written about Bishop's exploits in 1917, was popular, especially after Bishop became the highest-scoring ace of the British Empire.

Since neither flyer had a private income, they both needed other people's money to launch their company. While Barker was still recovering from his wounds, his new partner looked for ways to make money. He was offered a substantial fee to give speeches in the United States, talking about his war experiences.

He returned to Canada in February and started a whirlwind tour, lecturing in Chicago, Louisville, Cincinnati, New York, and several southern cities, including Nashville, and Roanoke. It was in this latter city that he collapsed with appendicitis, and was hospitalized on 16 March. But Bishop had made connections in the US that would benefit Bishop-Barker Company, Limited. At the same time Barker did the lobbying in the UK that would provide the link to British manufacturers and underwriters.

Bishop-Barker Aeroplanes, Limited (BBAL) was the Canadian branch of a three-country venture. BBAL has never been taken seriously by Canadian aviation historians, receiving only a passing mention. It has been unfairly dismissed as an inconsequential footnote in the history of aviation in Canada. In fact, the company was little different from all the other upstarts—ambitious in its scope, but ultimately a failure that was neither better nor worse than many other flying companies of the 1920s.

BBAL lasted less than three years, and was much better known for its founders, than for its extensive network of routes, and comfortable, reliable aircraft. Bishop, much later in life, described the venture in casual terms:

> Barker and I decided to become the pioneers of commercial flight soon after we returned home. Although we couldn't make a dollar, we had a lot of fun ... such capital as Barker and I had consisted of our own resources plus all that we could coax out of the pockets of friends—the latter moneys probably regarded as charitable donations made to a couple of pleasant lunatics who sooner or later would break their fool necks and so rid their friends of further expense.

At 50 it was easier for Air Marshal Bishop to treat his first corporate venture lightly, noting that, "he and I were happy partners in one of the first and most amusing commercial aviation enterprises ever undertaken by foolish young men." But, at age 25, as Bishop and Barker were in 1919, their emotional investment in the company was huge. For Will Barker

it was unquestionably a make-or-break effort. His character would entertain nothing less.

When he was released from Shepherd's Bush Hospital in April 1919, Bishop's mentor, Lady St Helier, took Will into her home, Portland Place. She charmed him as she had Billy: "… she is a wonderful old lady and I am very much at home here." Lieut General Sir Richard Turner, head of the Overseas Military Forces of Canada, who had earned his Victoria Cross as a mounted rifleman in the Boer War, had also adopted Barker, seconding him to the OMFC Headquarters at Argyll House, London. Before leaving for Canada in May, Barker was given plenty of help to establish his company from senior OMFC officers in London, as well as British businessmen, and Canadian expatriate millionaires like James Dunn.

Will's career handicap was that he had been an enlisted man. His discharge papers from the CEF were as Trooper Barker. He had never held a commission in the Canadian Forces and, therefore, was a member of the RAF, not simply attached to it from his former regiment, as was Bishop. Recognizing the importance of regimental tenure on the Militia Lists, Turner pulled some strings. He drafted a letter to Colonel G.S. Harrington, the Deputy Minister of the OMFC, asking for Will to be promoted after his resignation from the RAF, and transfer to the Canadian Forces:

> It is suggested that upon such transfer Major Barker be granted the rank of temporary substantive Lieut-Colonel in the O.M.F. of C., as a special case based upon the excellent and gallant work done by him while flying, to the great credit of the Canadian Forces ...
>
> Major Barker resides in the Province of Manitoba, and I think, by reason of his excellent work, that no objection could possibly be raised by any Officer of the rank of Lieut-Colonel in the Manitoba regiment to his receiving that rank and being posted to the Manitoba Regimental Depot.

It is unlikely that anyone would have opposed Turner's recommendation, but it helped that the

Manitoba Regiment was little more than a paper unit. This administrative sleight of hand, done with the best of intentions, did not help Barker. Turner's letter makes no mention at all of the Canadian Air Force (CAF), but Barker believed he was moving from a flying position in the RAF, to an equivalent flying position in the two-squadron Canadian Air Force based in England. This was not the case.

His rank was that of an Army officer belonging to a dormant regiment, his pay was as a non-flying lieutenant colonel, and he was placed on the Army retired list in September 1919. Preoccupied with his civilian future, Barker paid no attention to the military fine print.

He had always been willing to go right to the top during his service in France and Italy. Now that he was a public figure, he approached the prime minister, Sir Robert Borden, looking for help and also offering it without a moment's hesitation. Borden was in Europe that spring to attend the Versailles Conference and Barker asked for an interview to discuss his new company. He was interested in what Bishop-Barker Company could do for Canada and, more importantly, what Borden could do for two heroes.

He wanted his new company to be a consultant to the government on military and civil aviation. What he proposed to Borden was rather similar to, and competitive with, the planned Air Board. Barker may not have known that the parliamentary approval for the new Air Board was far along, with the Air Board Act coming into law on 6 June 1919, less than two months after he wrote Borden. According to Barker's letter, and newspaper reports at the time, Bishop-Barker Company was intended to be, among other things, an insurance underwriter. Another goal was to act as an importer for British-manufactured aircraft, in particular the Sopwith and AVRO lines.

It is unlikely that the prime minister gave Barker's suggestions much thought, given his more pressing concerns about Canada's humiliating status at the Peace Conference. Nevertheless, from the Hotel Majestic in Paris, where the British delegation were staying, Borden drafted a letter to the acting prime minister in Ottawa, Sir Thomas White, enclosing Barker's letter and attachments, and also

sending copies to Sir A. Edward Kemp, Minister of the OMFC in London, Major General Mewburn, Minister of Militia and Defence, and Charles Ballantyne, Minister of the Naval Service.

It was an assistant deputy minister of the OMFC who arranged for the incorporation of Bishop-Barker Company, Limited. He was Lt Colonel Thomas Gibson, 44, who had served in France with the 4th Labour Battalion. The colonel's civilian occupation was law partner with his brother, Joseph, in the Toronto firm of Gibson and Gibson.

He had taken an interest in Barker shortly after the VC was gazetted. He instructed a staff officer, Capt Lloyd Lott, to get him more information about the Canadian flyer. Gibson chatted frequently with Will whenever he visited HQ, and the two men hit it off. A few months later, Gibson and Gibson became the law firm for Bishop-Barker Company. Lott became Barker's handler during press interviews, and Barker asked him to become the secretary in his new venture.

Barker turned his formidable powers of persuasion on one of Britain's best known aviation entrepreneurs, Tommy Sopwith, and gained his permission to fly the new prototype Dove, a two-seater version of the Pup. His passenger on this flight was Edward, Prince of Wales. A film crew was at Hounslow aerodrome to mark the event (as far as we know, the first time Barker was ever filmed).

Still photographs of Barker, the Prince, and an unidentified civilian in a bowler hat have been reproduced many times in books and magazines. The civilian was an anxious Tommy Sopwith, not at all sure that a pilot with his shattered arm in a sling should be flying the heir to the throne in a Sopwith prototype. Edward, later the Duke of Windsor, recalled to author Alan Bramson how the flight came about: "I met Barker at some Canadian dinner in London. Anyway, we all had a very good time and he said: 'Why don't you come and fly with me tomorrow morning. Let us renew our acquaintance with the air.'"

When the flight featured in *The Daily Mirror* ("Prince of Wales stunts with one-armed VC"), King George called his son to account: "... he gave me absolute hell. He said: 'What are you doing flying with this man?' and I said: 'Well, you know, Father,

Barker with Edward, the Prince of Wales, in the Sopwith Dove prior to flight in April 1919.

he is a very gallant man and you gave him the Victoria Cross so I supposed it was all right for me to fly with him.' "

* * *

This flight with the Prince of Wales was Barker's parting salute to Britain and his RAF career. He requested convalescent leave from Colonel Gibson so he could return to Canada, and booked and paid for passage on the *Mauretania*. When he got off the ocean liner in Montreal, he immediately hopped a train to Ottawa to meet with government officials who, he felt certain, would help his new company. Bishop joined him in Ottawa, and the lobbying started in earnest, as well as the newspaper stories.

Barker's family, and many Manitobans, expected him to travel by train from Ottawa to Winnipeg. This did not happen. Amazingly, Will did not go home, and made no effort to go home for nearly six months. As compulsively driven to succeed in

business as he had been in combat, he could not pull himself away, not even for his mother. He put his heart and soul into his new venture.

He kept promising to come home to Manitoba soon, any day now, next week, or next month. But he had promised his family he would make a fortune in aviation after the war, and was going to keep that promise. As consolation and reassurance to his family, he mailed off newspaper clippings about his business activities, and a few letters: "… although my left arm is useless I can do a lot & dance quite a bit, only am a bit weak about the hips where I was hit."

The town of Dauphin wanted a formal homecoming with speeches and bands, despite the fact that the Barker family was no longer living there. Months before, Will had sent a note of thanks from his hospital bed to Mayor Bowman: "I am, of course, anxious to get back to Canada and Dauphin again and hope to be able to travel in about three months time if no complications set in." The local branch of

Barker on board SS *Mauretania* coming home to Canada in May 1919.

train for Warren. What ever you do don't publish this letter as it might ruin my plans.

* * *

Billy Bishop and Will Barker made exciting copy for newspaper reporters. They were good-humoured, and could always be counted on for an opinion. The aviation magazines of the day, including *Aerial Age Weekly*, *Aviation and Aircraft Journal*, *Aviation and Aeronautical Engineering*, and *Flying* frequently reported on their flights, and their plans. They also published their wildly optimistic advertisements.

While staying at the Ritz-Carlton Hotel in early July, Barker assured a *Montreal Daily Star* reporter that England and Canada had the capability to monopolize aerial service in Europe and North America, being well ahead of the United States in aeronautical developments. Photographed outside the offices of the *Ottawa Evening Telegram*, Bishop in a three-piece business suit, Barker in his RAF uniform, the headline above the photo read: "Canada's Most Famous Airmen." In a reverential story, Bishop was described as the premier ace among the aviators of the Royal Air Force, but Barker, it was also noted:

the Great War Veterans' Association wrote to Ottawa for further information about Barker's arrival back in Canada: "... we would appreciate it as Major Barker is a resident in this town and naturally his return is eagerly looked for by the residents."

Dauphin's veterans received the same treatment as Will's family. They had to wait till he had made his fortune. He wrote to his mother in early July from the Chateau Laurier Hotel in Ottawa:

Am so sorry that I have not been able to get home but hope to be able to get away soon. I am trying very hard to get the gov't to take an interest in civil aviation. I was down to New York last week getting information regarding American aviation & then back to Toronto, then here and then I went to Montreal & have just come back from there. I have a very big deal in hand & think it will go through as soon as I know & get it settled then I will catch a

... has had in some respects the most remarkable record of any aviator in the world. Perhaps his most astounding feat was his defeat of 60 German airplanes single handed and his later successful landing although severely wounded ... in returning to his home [he] is probably the most frequently decorated Canadian and it is believed has only one equal in the British Army in the number of decorations won. The story of his fight against a horde of enemy planes constitutes the most astounding individual aerial battle on record.

Just as before the war, the most common place to see an aeroplane was at an agricultural or industrial exhibition. But the long-distance flying and racing craze of the Roaring Twenties was already underway. In April 1919, Billy Bishop donated the "Ace of Aces" Trophy for the pilot who achieved the fastest flying time between Toronto and Atlantic City, New Jersey.

163

Barker sitting in Snipe E8102 with Dominion Archivist Arthur Doughty looking at the camera, summer of 1919.

Library and Archives Canada

In June, the non-stop trans-Atlantic flight of John Alcock, and navigator, Arthur Whitten-Brown, from Newfoundland to Ireland, was world-wide news.

Barker wanted to win air races, too, and also fly in exhibitions. He needed a fast machine. With the assistance of Arthur Doughty, Dominion Archivist, he was able to get his hands on several Fokker D.VII scout machines. Doughty had been appointed the Director of War Trophies in the CEF. He regarded the War Trophy machines he had collected in Europe as something akin to personal property, and saw them as a public relations tool for the Canadian government. He loaned them not only to Barker, but also to cities and universities across the country for public display and education. At least 36 German aircraft arrived in Canada after the war, but only three have survived.

Barker met Doughty in Ottawa and proposed a non-stop Toronto-to-New York flight in a D.VII.

Will had met with the Aero Club of America in New York City, and some of its members were keen to see this famous German scout machine on Long Island. He proposed to Doughty that the flight be made between 1 and 4 August. Since the D.VII was relatively short-ranged, Will offered to install additional fuel tanks to ensure nine hours endurance. The machine, thus modified, could then be flown to other parts of the Dominion for flying demonstrations. The Aero Club of Canada in Toronto was particularly keen on this idea. However, the flight did not take place, being overtaken by a grander project, a race of many aircraft between the two cities, flown by military and civilian pilots.

Barker was photographed that summer in the same type of German scout that had shot him down the previous October. He even founded his own flying team of four War Trophy scout planes, the first such team in Canada. Lt Colonel Barker led

Kenneth Molson collection

Barker in Fokker D.VII in Toronto prior to his departure in the Toronto-New York City-Toronto air race, August 1919.

the D.VIIs flown by Captains L.B. Hyde-Pearson, W.R. James, and V. Dallin, all RAF veterans. Based at Leaside, these four men put on the first public exhibition of formation flying in Canada, making it the forerunner of all the Canadian military aerobatic teams to follow. They were the premier attraction at the 1919 Canadian National Exhibition (CNE) near the Toronto waterfront. *The Globe* had praise for the team's performance:

> "Stunt" Flying Thrills Crowd - Spectators at Exhibition Gasp at Feats of Daring Airmen - Exhibition visitors Saturday evening saw about the best series of "stunts" the Fair patrons have ever witnessed ... the four flew in squadron formation with Col. Barker in the lead ... flying well up the four airmen turned and wheeled, changing formation. They flew far out over the lake, and then turned and came over the grounds.
>
> After this Col. Barker and Capt James led off with trick-flying in pairs ... During a good many of the 'stunts' the spectators were breathless. They thought the airman was plunging down to destruction ... on one occasion two of the machines approached each other. People below gasped with apprehension thinking that a smash-up was coming. But just before they came together one smartly dived under the other ... In the stunt flying all four airmen appeared to perform equally well.

Remarkably, Doughty not only provided six D.VIIs for the team, but also paid some of the costs, including the hangar rented from Ericson Aircraft, a BBAL competitor that leased Leaside aerodrome. Ericson was already storing 28 German aircraft in

Barker seated on the fuselage of Fokker D.VII with air mail bag prior to his departure in the Toronto-New York City-Toronto air race.

another hangar at the field on behalf of Doughty's department. Barker estimated to Doughty that he had spent $1,500 for an automobile, and the salaries of three pilots, four mechanics, and two helpers, all of which he expected to recover from the CNE directly.

Over the summer Bishop and Barker had operated their corporate affairs on an *ad hoc* basis, by dint of their reputation and connections. Bishop-Barker Company, Limited was formally incorporated under the Ontario Companies Act on 20 September, and Bishop-Barker Aeroplanes, Limited, on 17 November 1919. BBAL's corporate charter allowed the company to carry passengers and goods, set up schools, establish a registry of pilots for hire, organize aviation and flying meetings, as well as repair, sell, buy, and lease aeroplanes of all kinds.

W.A. Bishop was the president, and W.G. Barker, the secretary-treasurer. The capital of the company was $300,000 Canadian, consisting of 3000 shares of $100 each, one thousand being preferred shares paying 7 percent. The largest holder of common shares was Billy Bishop and his wife, Margaret Burden, with 937, followed by Barker with 794. The largest outside holder of shares was Margaret's uncle, Sir John C. Eaton, president of the T. Eaton Company, with 140. Next was Edward Beatty, president of Canadian Pacific Railway Company, with 70. The Gibson brothers, Lott, and the employees of Gibson and Gibson also held some shares.

The cachet of being attached to the modern and romantic lured investors. The smaller shareholders represented an impressive cross-section of Canadian business. They included, among others, Lt Colonel Sir Hugh Allan, president of Merchants Bank of Canada; Sir Joseph Flavelle, former head of the Imperial Munitions Board, and president of National Trust Company; Brig General Frank Meighen, president of Lake of the Woods Milling Company; Lt Colonel Herbert Molson, president of Molson's Brewery Limited; and Sir Vincent Meredith, president of the Bank of Montreal.

A Curtiss JN4 was the first aircraft purchased by the company. It was powered by a 90-hp OX-5 engine, and in RAF service it had been C-628. Later the company registered the trainer as G-CAAT, and bought several dozen more machines from the Canadian government, selling most of them in the United States. Barker's extensive experience in war photography was a natural lead-in to industrial photography, and G-CAAT made the first money for BBAL as a photographic platform.

He approached Queen's University at Kingston, and photographed the campus from the air. The company also tendered a proposal, with sample photos, to the Toronto Harbour Commissioners, offering to take aerial views of the new construction along the waterfront. Barker also flew as far west as Stratford, taking aerial views of the town. These were made into postcards with advertising printed on the bottom. Will had a personal interest in the town, since his great-grandparents were buried there, and his great Uncle Henry's family were still living on Hibernia and Caledonia Streets.

Will could not do all the aerial photography, and two of the first employees of BBAL were Sidney Bonnick and John Victor Dallin. As an RAF pilot of 54 Squadron, Dallin had ferried D.VIIs out of Germany to France. He solved one of Barker's problems with the machines, blown spark plugs, and, in gratitude, Will offered the Englishman a slot on the new flying team, and an irregular-paying photography job.

Dallin and Bonnick used war-surplus cameras to photograph golf courses, factories, and real estate. When aerial photography was slow, Dallin ferried JN4s to US buyers in New York and Philadelphia from their company hangar at Armour Heights. This had been one of the busy RAF training fields during the war, sprawled over 180 acres bordered by Wilson Avenue and Bathurst Street.

Doughty asked Barker what they would charge to store War Trophy aircraft at Armour Heights. A fee of $100 a month per hangar, for two hangars, was discussed. The Dominion Archivist liked the idea of moving his German machines from Ericson Aircraft at Leaside, but others, including Capt George O. Johnson, had reservations about Barker.

An argument broke out on one occasion between Barker and Johnson over a de Havilland DH6 (serial F2323) that Johnson claimed he, as officer-

BARKER IN THE TORONTO–NEW YORK CITY–TORONTO AIR RACE

Barker flew his own D.VII to New York and back in the first post-war international air race. The route was between Leaside aerodrome and Roosevelt Field, at Mineola, Long Island. The round-robin, staged over four days, 25-29 August, was entered by 69 pilots, the majority being Americans, of whom 55 got airborne, and 29 completed the two-way, 1,044-mile flight.

The aircraft were diverse, almost all being ex-military, including a Caproni Ca.3 bomber (the largest); several Dehavilland DH4 bombers (the fastest); the SE5a scout; the Curtiss Oriole; and many Canadian and US-built JN4s. Barker finished the race in almost a dead heat for last place. Despite this low standing, he received the most publicity of any Canadian pilot in *The New York Times*, partly because of his physical condition:

Barker, Canadian ace, arrived at Roosevelt field, Mineola, L.I., to-day with his left arm frozen, and started back before noon.

The Canadian made the flight without a compass, and using his right arm only, due to the disability of his left arm, which froze because it was disabled and hanging limp after war wounds ... Col. J.G. Carmody, who commands the Roosevelt field and Col. Archie Miller went out on the field to greet Col. Barker as soon as he stiffly hobbled out of his machine. They at once saw the condition of his left arm and hand, and called for a medical officer.

"No, no, no," he said. "Don't bother, really. It's been that way for a long time. Ever since last fall."

"But, man, it's frozen," said Col. Carmody.

"Just a bit stiff," said the Canadian, with a rueful grin. "It was a bit chilly up there to-day. It was a very satisfactory trip; I enjoyed it immensely."

The American Colonels hurried Col. Barker to Col. Carmody's quarters, and ice water was applied to his arm, and it was brought back to life.

He had a particularly hard time all day yesterday, the Colonel said, encountering snow and freezing rain in the upper air between Buffalo and Syracuse. He brought letters from Toronto to New York newspapers, and a bag of mail for Washington, in which was included a letter from Sir Robert Borden, Premier of Canada [*sic*], to President Woodrow Wilson.

Col. Carmody himself took the mail pouch and threw it into the tonneau of a mail plane for Washington which left at 11:19 o'clock ...

Col. Barker started back for Toronto at 11:15 o'clock. The Fokker plane started a riot among the spectators by shooting out a cloud of red flame and smoke as it moved from the field, and ambulances were started from two stations toward it, but the airship sailed into the air long before they reached the spot where the explosions started.

Barker's enthusiasm or, perhaps, pig-headedness, had not been dampened by the outbound flight, but his flight home was even more daunting. The Fokker D.VII was powered by a 180-hp Mercedes having an engine-driven pump to pressurize the fuel tank. The pump failed on the ground at Roosevelt Field, put he pressed on, pumping fuel manually with his good right arm, all the while squeezing the control stick between his legs. An exhausted Barker told *The Globe* after the race was over that, "The chief significance of this race is that it has demonstrated the danger of small airdromes and fast-landing machines. The need of roomy airdromes was amply illustrated at Albany, where five machines crashed on the small field ... What we must have for commercial flying is a machine that will make about 125 miles per hour in the air, and will land at a speed of 65 miles per hour."

in-charge of War Trophy aeroplanes, owned, and Barker said BBAL had purchased. While Johnson turned beet-red with anger, Will proceeded with removing the engine from F2323, ignoring the protests. Johnson stormed out of the hangar; he then telegrammed Doughty asking for direction, but we do not know how the conflict was resolved. This particular machine was unique, being the only DH6 built in Canada during the war.

Johnson recommended that the War Trophy machines be stored at the War Trophies Building at the CNE grounds, at no cost to the government. Johnson, who later rose to the rank of Air Marshal in the RCAF, complained bitterly about Barker's actions:

I would not recommend that the aeroplanes be stored in a private aerodrome, especially in this case, when it is the obvious purpose

of Col. Barker to fly the machines while in his charge. In this respect I might add that, although the six Fokkers which were loaned to Col. Barker for use during the Exhibition were to be handed back to me, this has not yet been done and the machines are still being flown occasionally.

It is not certain that Barker ever gave back all the Fokker D.VIIs. At least one was still in the company hangar at Armour Heights in the fall of 1920. But the decision to keep them seems to have been tacitly approved by Doughty. There is no evidence money changed hands between BBAL and Doughty.

The demands of setting up a two-country operation meant many trips for Will between Toronto and New York City. A subsidiary or affiliate of Bishop-Barker Company called Interallied Aircraft

Barker was vice-president of a New York-based company, Interallied Aircraft, and is seen sitting on a JN4 offered for sale.

Joe Barker collection

Corporation had offices at 185 Madison Avenue. It was mainly an importing and purchasing agent for British aircraft, but may also have had flight operations in the NYC area.

Barker never offered much information about Interallied, beyond telling his family he was working very hard on its behalf. A US magazine painted a rosy picture of its financial stability. It noted that the president was Bishop, "the famous ace of aces"; first vice president was Barker, "who brought down sixty-eight enemy planes"; second vice president was Major Reed G. Landis, "second ranking American ace"; and the manager was Lieut Charles H. Payne, formerly of the US Navy. According to *Flying*:

> These aces formed this corporation ... when they found that American manufacturers could not supply the increasing demand for aeroplanes. They arranged to import to the United States aeroplanes of famous makes like the "Sopwith" and "AVRO" machines. They readily obtained the financial backing necessary from New York bankers to purchase 2,000 British machines, and Colonel Bishop went to Europe to arrange the purchase and supervise the shipping, while the other members of the firm attended to the selling end. Within a month after the formation of the company they had received prospective orders for close to 500 aeroplanes, and as the shipping strikes in England prevented the shipping of machines to the United States, they bought fifty second-hand training machines from the Canadian Government which the company sold to waiting customers. But shipping conditions have improved and deliveries are now being made.

Interallied Aircraft Corporation ran advertisements for their new and used aircraft, mentioning that they had distribution outlets in Boston, San Francisco, and Estherville, Iowa.

They were looking for more sales distributors, as well as pilots and mechanics who were "familiar with AVRO and Sopwith machines and LeRhone motors."

A "slightly used" AVRO 504K sold for $3,000 F.O.B., New York, a JN4 Canuck for $2,600 to $3,000, the latter "in first-class condition and inspected and tested by Lt. Col. W.G. Barker." The most creative advertisement from Interallied trumpeted:

> Service is our middle name. We want our customers perpetually with us. It is selfishly good business. If you want a job as pilot or mechanic—or want to hire either one—or have any worry on Aviation, write us about it. ... For undiluted pleasure a red blooded man will always pick an AVRO or Sopwith "Camel." Their reliable, up-to-date, easily accessible, rotary motors make flying simple—stunting comes as second nature—and repairs and overhauls are like play.

Barker's obsession to return home as a successful businessman was mystifying to his parents. As the months went by, Will kept writing that soon he would arrive. This was followed by an apology in his next letter for his failure to show up in Warren. He had promised his mother in July that he would be home within weeks, but in October he was apologizing yet again. On letterhead emblazoned with: "The Bishop-Barker Company Limited (Operators of Air Services - Manufacturers and Agents for Aircraft - 93 Spadina Avenue, Toronto)," he lamented: "I suppose by now you will think I have disappeared altogether. Well, I have been so busy that I have not even had time to write. ... I have now got my business firmly established and am making money. I can now take time for a little rest and at last will be able to get home. I cannot understand not hearing from you once in a while."

Jane and George seldom replied anymore to their son's letters. Friends of the Barker family visiting Toronto, Muriel Cassy and Mrs Ferguson, took a taxi to Armour Heights to visit their famous friend, and both women went flying. They spoke to Barker about his parents' unhappiness, and he sent off a disapproving note: "Evidently, there is some misunderstanding. I repeatedly told you all in my letters & telegrams that I was working & organizing two companies & not playing & spending money. Now I have been successful & when I do come home I will be of some use financially."

It is possible that George and his wife had heard about Will's social life in Toronto, his partying and drinking. He had never been a party animal during the war, when it was to be expected. He did not abuse alcohol, and was remembered by other flyers in the RFC as a temperate man.

However, Barker's likeable personality changed for the worse after being wounded. He was occasionally moody, angry, and paranoid. Such feelings were by no means unique to Barker, but were characteristic of many wounded men re-entering civilian society. The understandable lack of insight by family and friends, the patriotic jingoism of non-combatants, drove many veterans into a rage or a sulk. The feelings of alienation from society could be very powerful, and usually were alleviated only in the company of other war veterans.

Bishop was in the best position to observe the re-entry problems of his wounded business partner. The two spent many hours and days together between 1919 and 1921, performing air-show stunts together for crowds at the Canadian National Exhibition (CNE), and flying as pilot and co-pilot in the HS-2L flying boat. Inevitably, anti-social episodes by these two men were winked at because of their fame.

Bishop related to his son, Arthur, a story of the two wrecking their automobile on a concrete embutment intended to block traffic at the CNE. Barker and Bishop abandoned the vehicle and headed for the fairway shooting gallery. A fellow standing ahead of Barker in the line was wearing a bowler hat. Barker grabbed the hat, threw it behind the counter and fired six shots into it. The man called the police, but they shrugged their shoulders and smiled: "Hell, it's only the two colonels, you get used to them."

On another occasion, Barker and Bishop took to racing cars in the wrong direction around Queen's Park in Toronto and eventually crashed into a car leading a funeral procession. When the driver complained "Don't you know we're going to a funeral," Barker snapped, "Don't you know it might have been your own."

The CNE committee fired the two pilots for performing stunts at a dangerously low altitude over the crowds, with aircraft painted conspicuously with the Bishop-Barker name. Will was outraged that these lily-livered civilians had no stomach for a good air show, and attempted to punch one of the executives while Bishop restrained him.

Dozens of traffic tickets had been issued by the police to the two men for speeding. Bishop arranged a party for the Toronto legal community, in Barker's apartment. Most of the infractions were paid for by those who attended—one ticket for one drink. But Barker was evicted for having a drunken, noisy party. Whispered accounts about chorus girls playing strip poker with the two heroes, passing out on the bed, and jumping out of windows, did nothing to add lustre to Barker's business image.

Receiving the Victoria Cross had thrust Barker into a public role, and a social milieu, that he was not well equipped to handle. Fame or wealth conferred impunity from social consequences and, despite Prohibition, alcohol was still the drug of choice. Will began to drink. He drank far more than he had during the war, firstly to be social and then, later, to numb the pain. The gradual onset of painful arthritis in his arm and legs was a constant reminder to him of his last battle.

*   *   *

The stunts performed by Barker and Bishop at the CNE, as well as by other flyers after the Great War (and also the Second World War) were sometimes the result of post-traumatic stress disorder (PTSD), but often were just a craving for a peak experience. Risk taking, what might be labelled the "flying low" syndrome, was the war pilot's way to recapture the intense rush felt only in combat.

Flight Surgeon Dr. Douglas Bond wrote about Second World War aviators in his case studies, the men of the US Army Air Corps but his findings also ring true for World War One flyers:

... less concern need be shown for the civilian adjustment of those men who 'broke' in war than for the adjustment of those who enjoyed war too much. The liberal use of primitive drives, condensed and rewarded, had very destructive consequences ... it made "stale" less violent forms of expression and no doubt accounted in part for the bursts of unlicensed behaviour following the war. One need only look at the records to see that the men most successful in combat are unlikely to be so in civilian life, that many of the men highly decorated for heroics in war would not be considered deserving of medals in time of peace.

Alienation from the life of the ordinary was not unique to Barker. Many other heroes of his and later generations have had similar problems, suffering especially because of the unrealistic expectations held by the public. War hero and Hollywood movie star Audie Murphy articulated very well why warriors adjust poorly to everyday existence: "War robs you mentally and physically. It drains you ... Things don't thrill you anymore. It's a struggle every day to find something interesting to do."

What was surprising about Barker was not that he occasionally behaved recklessly, or was socially inept, but that he retained the regard of his peers and most of the public in spite of it. He was the hero of heroes to his own generation. He was the hero even the most egotistical of scout aces could admire and praise un-

THE WAR HERO IN THE WORKS OF FAULKNER, FITGERALD, AND HEMINGWAY

In this media-saturated era, where fame has been reduced to little more than 15 minutes on a television talk show, it is difficult to appreciate the reverence with which brave deeds and famous heroes were held some 85 years ago. In the 1920s, men divided into two clear categories—those who had fought or served in the war, and those who had not.

If one's war record was indifferent, one might embellish, or even fabricate stories. This was done to fit more easily into society's stereotype of honour, duty, and courage. Yet, at the same time, a new kind of literature developed in the 1920s that offered either a tragically damaged ex-hero suffering existential despair, or an anti-hero, opportunistic and cynical.

Examples include William Faulkner's wounded RAF pilot in *Soldier's Pay*; F. Scott Fitzgerald's war hero turned bootlegger, Jay Gatsby, in *The Great Gatsby*; and Ernest Hemingway's neutered ex-soldier, Jake Barnes, in *The Sun Also Rises*, and deserter, Lieut Henry, in *A Farewell to Arms*.

Of all these fictional characters, it is Jay Gatsby who most closely approximates William Barker, especially in his hopes and dreams for love and success following heroism in battle. The post-war story of Barker is a common war veteran's story, and so is that of fictional war veteran Jay Gatsby; above all it is a story of social class and the gulf separating the wealthy from the working classes, however heroic they may have been in battle. Gatsby, had he lived, would have learned the emptiness of crossing that gulf, in just the way that Barker did after his marriage to the girl of his dreams.

Faulkner and Fitzgerald had missed out on the "Big Show" as Fitzgerald called it, and, therefore, were not members of "the greatest club in history." This had so aggravated Faulkner, who was in training with the RAF as a pilot on 11 November 1918, that he left Toronto for Oxford, Mississippi, wearing an RAF officer's uniform and pilot's badge that he had not earned. He later learned to fly, just to help validate his fraudulent claims of fighting experience in France. It was after receiving the Nobel Prize following the Second World War, and the attendant publicity, that Faulkner was forced to confess to his modest record as a cadet.

Only Hemingway could speak from direct experience about war, that on the same front as Barker. But he, like Faulkner, wore a uniform after the war to which he was not entitled. He had been wounded by mortar fire and machine-gun bullets in July 1918 at Fossalta, near the River Piave, only about 30 miles from Villaverla aerodrome.

reservedly. In an occupation with inevitable jealousy and professional rivalry, Barker inspired a remarkable degree of unalloyed admiration. If one had directly asked Bishop or MacLaren, for example, who their hero was, they were very likely to answer, "William Barker." He was in a very profound sense the hero's hero, the man that the other heroes held in awe.

This regard for Barker was demonstrated by the Aero Club of Canada when they elected him their honorary president in the fall of 1919. When their new club room was opened at 32 Yonge Street in

October, many well-known flyers attended, and quite a few had speeches to give. But when Barker got up to speak, the reaction was profound:

The colonel received a thundering ovation and the near 500 airmen and guests present cheered again and again for the popular hero of the Royal Air Force. When Col. Barker concluded another burst of applause greeted him, followed by singing 'He's a Jolly Good Fellow,' and then more cheers.

Chafing against his lowly status as an American Red Cross ambulance driver, and a field experience measured in weeks, Hemingway embellished his respectable service by claiming membership in an elite infantry unit, and command of a company of the Italian Army in battle (at the youthful age of 19).

Hemingway was a hero, but not a fighting hero. He was decorated with the same Italian medal as Barker, the "Medaglia d'Argenta," and also received the "Croce di Guerra," the War Cross. Both were awarded for tending to other wounded men before having his own wounds dressed at a casualty clearing station. While working in Toronto in 1919, Hemingway showed his "gongs" to *The Toronto Daily Star* journalist, Gregory Clark. Clark had won his Military Cross as a member of the 4th Battalion, CMR, at Vimy Ridge, and was sceptical about cub-reporter Hemingway's war record, until he saw the medals.

After every war in the 20th century there have been men who claimed heroic deeds that were entirely bogus, or gilded the lily of respectable service. After the First World War, a few ambitious men were driven to actually sew on the ribbon of the Victoria Cross without having earned it. *The Toronto Daily Star* reported in a photo-story in October 1921 that a couple named Beese had been arrested after three years of cheque forgeries ("Long Honeymoon Ended By The Police"). Charles Sidney Beese said he was an officer of the 11th Hussars, and "a winner of the Victoria Cross." The proof of manly heroism was in the medals, and what greater medal than the VC?

Hemingway himself once referred to the publication of an early short story as the equivalent of receiving the Victoria Cross. Did Hemingway meet Barker and Bishop in Toronto? It certainly was possible. He had been befriended in 1918 by a British Army officer stationed in Milan, Capt (later Major General) Eric Edward Dorman-Smith. Was it he who told a convalescing Red Cross driver about Barker's Christmas Day raid, or did Hemingway read about it in a 1935 pulp edition of *War Birds* (Chegwidden, *Barker's Christmas Party*)? We don't know, but both are likely sources for Hemingway to have used.

The portrayal of Barker is not flattering in *The Snows of Kilimanjaro*, but Hemingway often combined factual material with fiction to produce a more dramatic effect, in this case squadron pilots who were appalled by Barker's brutality. Hemingway combines facts and speculations in this brilliant story to diminish what many saw as a heroic act into an act of murder.

Paradoxically, Barker's high reputation was solidly based on the truth, but his legendary war achievements read like pulp fiction. He might have survived longer and suffered less had his war record actually been made up, as was Hemingway's.

Barker (left) with Bishop in cockpit of HS2L at Muskoka, circa 1921.

CHAPTER ELEVEN

THE FLYING DOLDRUMS

"The flying boom which developed in Canada following World War I had passed its peak by the end of 1920 ...
the flying doldrums set in ... Canada lost several valuable years during the lull, and the development of commercial
aviation in Canada was much slower than it should have been."

FRANK ELLIS, PILOT, ENGINEER, AVIATION HISTORIAN

Barker's reluctance to return home immediately after walking down the gangway of the *Mauretania* was a terrible blow to his mother and father, and created a rift between him and his family that never healed. After four years of war, and more than three in the front lines, Barker was not the naive, likeable 20-year-old kid who had climbed aboard the train for Brandon. He wanted to be more than just a figurehead at public ceremonies. He was obsessed with making his fortune in aviation. But as the post-war recession deepened, BBAL in Toronto and Interallied in New York struggled to find more buyers for their used aircraft, more charter passengers, and more aerial photography contracts.

Will boarded the train on a cold November day for the trip from Toronto to Winnipeg. The City of Winnipeg honoured him with a standing ovation at an evening session of the City Council, and Mayor Charles Gray welcomed him with a patriotic tribute:

> ... your splendid and heroic achievements will be handed down in Canadian history as an inspiration to future generations, that Winnipeg and Manitoba did their share in producing men like you. We hope that your duties now that you have come back to private life will not take you far from us, as we need men like you to help build up our country. Long may you be spared to wear the laurels you have won.

Barker responded that he had not made the sacrifices of others, all those men, including some of his friends, who would never be coming home. Self-conscious about his long absence from his home province, he offered a brief apology: "I am sorry to have disappointed my friends so many times, but I had to stop in the east to get business settled. I am real glad to get home."

Will could not have come at a more sobering moment in his mother's life. Jane's 10th child, Ross, born in the town of Warren, northwest of Winnipeg, had died only a few days before his arrival. For Orval, five years old, the homecoming of his famous brother was *the* event of his young life. Having heard so much about him, Orval was expecting a superman, and was disappointed with the man standing at the Warren train station. He was not wearing the uniform or Sidcot flying suit that Orval had seen in all the photographs. He was a stranger in a racoon-skin coat and fur hat, his left arm unnaturally straight and limp against his side.

Orval had no memories of Will, and Leslie, seven, Roy, 10, almost none. The brother who stepped down from the train was familiar only because of postcards and letters that had been read around the kitchen table during the war. They knew he was famous because the newspapers said so. Edna, Ilda, Percy, and Lloyd were overjoyed to see him, but had little sense of who he was anymore, or how the war had changed him.

Blessed with exceptional eyesight, Will was unhappy to see Edna wearing eyeglasses. When he was unpacking in the bedroom at the top of the house, he complained to her about how cold it was. Manitoba was having one of the coldest Novembers in living memory.

She teased: "You're just soft. It's not that cold. You're just not used to it any more." He asked her if she was too grown-up to sit on his knee, and do her school work.

Edna watched her favourite brother shave in the mornings, handling the razor with his good right hand. She stared in horror at the angry scars on his left arm. His forearm was connected only by sinew and muscle, and the cramped fingers of his left hand barely moved. When he needed to use that arm, he reached across with his right hand, and placed his left hand next to the shaving brush. Willie had always been so physically poised that it was heartbreaking for Edna, and she was scarcely able to watch.

Around the dinner table, he talked about the war, and Lloyd bombarded Will with question after question. His mother asked if it was true that he and his friends had dropped a wreath at the funeral of an Austro-Hungarian scout ace. Will said that it was. He also talked effusively about his new company, but his father said nothing, still hoping that Will would come back to farming. The bond between Jane and her son remained strong, but Will felt judged by George, who seemed to lack confidence in his son's plans. From time to time after Will's departure, George said, "I hope it works out for him," but not really believing it would.

Dauphin invited Barker to a homecoming ceremony which he either turned down, or, according to some, actually failed to attend, after accepting an invitation. In one version of the story, Will was expected to fly in from Russell, but no aircraft arrived. Standing up the town fathers after a band had been hired was not endearing behaviour, and Dauphin's citizens did not forget this "slap in the face." Will never returned to the town, but Jane Barker felt the criticisms keenly for many years. More than 75 years later, there were still old-timers in Dauphin who remembered Barker's insulting behaviour.

Lt Colonel Barker had no difficulty at all with public ceremonies in Winnipeg, however, and gave a speech to the women's division of the Canadian Club. Interviewed by newspaper reporters and the editors of war veterans' newsletters, he made a provocative forecast:

There will be another continental war in Europe within 30 years and it will be fought entirely in the air ... A person does not want to go by train to Brandon if he can get there in an hour by air. The thing will be to get to the enemy's territory in the shortest possible time.

The war just ended was gradually becoming one to be fought out entirely in the air. At the last aeroplanes played by far the most important part more than the general public are aware.

This exaggeration of air power's significance in the Great War was not unusual. He shared this opinion about the omnipotence of aircraft in future wars with better known air power advocates such as Trenchard of the RAF, and Brigadier General Billy Mitchell, deputy chief of the US Air Service.

After a few days at Warren, Will left for the east, and his departure was no happier than it had been in 1915. He plunged back into business with a vengeance, but he still wrote his mother from time to time: "Financially I am just making things meet but by mid-summer I will be much better off—you know sales have been very slow during this bad winter and consequently business is bad ... I am very anxious to know what you have done re, another farm ... I really have too much to do & may resign as Vice President of this Corporation [Interallied Aircraft]."

* * *

Struggling to make money over the winter of 1919-20, Barker learned that being a war hero did not always open doors or people's wallets. His shattered left arm was gradually healing, but needed another operation. He had been so advised by his doctors before leaving Shepherd's Bush Hospital in London. Will wanted the operation done by Dr Sir Robert Jones, who had performed some of his previous surgery.

He soon learned that the Canadian military had no interest in or obligation to repair his wounds. During the summer and fall of 1919, he believed himself to be a member of the Directorate of Air Services (i.e., the CAF attached to the OMFC), sent home on sick leave to Canada. When Barker requested transportation from the Department of Militia and Defence, everything proceeded smoothly until early December, when a Colonel Clarke, Director of Supply and Transport, asked the Personnel Services if Barker was entitled to paid transportation. It turned out that he was not. Clarke then asked the vice chairman of the Air Board, Colonel Oliver M. Biggar, if Barker was a member of their organization:

Referring to your minute of the 5th, the Air Board has no official knowledge of this officer, who has never had any official relation of any kind with the Board. I have personally been informed by the officer that he has been in Canada on sick leave, and that he has always intended to return to England for a further operation on his arm. Beyond this, my information does not extend.

Barker was still just another name, rank, and serial number to the Canadian military. He was outraged to discover that he had no status with the OMFC in the UK, or the Directorate of Air Services. His commissioning into the Manitoba Regiment had only been an administrative sleight of hand. He received a chilling letter from the Adjutant-General's office in February 1920, outlining his limited rights as a retired officer:

... in view of the fact that you should have returned overseas within four months of the date you sailed to Canada, they are not in a position to recommend return transportation, as you would have been struck off strength of the O. M. F. of C. under the Four Months Clause (see para. 11 of route letter which was furnished you as authority to return to Canada) ...

I cannot hold out any prospect of your being granted transportation at public expense ... I would suggest that you see Lieut Col. Morrison, D.S.O., District Representative, Dept. of Soldiers' Civil Reestablishment in Toronto; who could inform you if that Department is

in a position to grant you transportation to England in order to have necessary operative treatment on your arm completed in England, as it appears that further treatment should be an Imperial claim.

Barker had been wounded in the service of the RAF, and neither the Canadian government nor the Department of Militia and Defence had any obligation to provide medical care. The insensitivity of the establishment to his medical needs was a blow, and Barker felt humiliated. Fortunately, the Department of Soldiers' Civil Reestablishment did agree to an operation at the Dominion Orthopaedic Hospital in Toronto.

Barker was contemptuous of the Department of Militia and Defence, but his opinion of the new Air Board was lower still. He had had running disputes in the summer of 1919 with the Board, in particular Oliver Biggar, the vice chairman and chief executive officer. It was this long-time bureaucrat, with no flying experience, who had recommended to Arthur Doughty that Barker be forbidden to fly any of the War Trophy machines. Biggar got his information from Lt Colonel Robert Leckie, a Scotsman with a brilliant war record with the RNAS, who was seconded from the RAF to the post of superintendent of flying operations at the Air Board.

Leckie said the Fokker scouts were unsafe to fly. He recalled the death of Major Albert Carter, a 29-victory ace, following the in-flight break-up of a D.VII at Shoreham on 22 May 1919: "Every machine showed signs of stress, and one would not have withstood another flight. The fitting which connects the inter-plane struts with the top-main spar is weak. As a result of the above finding I issued an order forbidding all stunting on Fokkers."

Lt Colonel G. C. de Dombasle, who had been involved in the acquisition of War Trophy machines, told Biggar that the British had orders never to fly the German machines. He wrote that Britain's donation to Canada had been made on condition that the machines never be flown, but used only for exhibition or training aids.

THE PREVALENCE OF RNAS PILOTS IN EARLY CANADIAN AVIATION

There was a history of RFC-RNAS antipathy going back to the earliest days of the Great War. Within the RFC, up to 1917, there was resentment that the RFC had done the tough fighting, and suffered the majority of casualties. The RNAS (with the exception of units at Dunkirk) was safe in southern England, and lost few flyers to enemy action. Inter-service resentment was still a factor in 1919, despite a unified RAF.

What particularly rankled Barker, Bishop, and many other RFC flyers was that the affairs of Canadian civil and military aviation were dominated by former RNAS personnel, or ex-Naval bureaucrats, and/or RAF staff officers from training organizations.

Few of the senior positions in the Air Board, or the newly authorized non-permanent Canadian Air Force, were held by ex-RFC Scout pilots. Ex-RNAS pilots, however, had a distinct advantage in competing for positions, simply because of their flying boat experience. As Air Vice-Marshal Ken Guthrie recalled to the author: "There were no bloody airports, and every damn senior position [in the new air force] was given to RNAS types ... Leckie, to me, was a bit of a pompous ass, and he looked on us Canadians as colonials. He didn't know anything about Canadian civil government operations, although that was what he was in charge of ... Lindsay Gordon was the officer who saved Leckie while he was seconded to us."

The *éminence grise* of the Air Board was John Armistead Wilson, a 50-year-old Scottish-born engineer, and former assistant deputy minister of the Naval Service. He had well-reasoned theories of how Canadian civil aviation should lead the way for military aviation, and was unquestionably the most influential bureaucratic player in the development of post-war aviation in Canada. What Wilson recommended usually came to pass.

Major Clarence C. MacLaurin, an ex-RNAS pilot who served as the acting Director of the short-lived Royal Canadian Naval Air Service, worked with Wilson during the war. Both men wrote about the future of aviation in Canada, favouring seaplanes over landplanes, partly because of the abundance of lakes, rivers, and coastline, and also because of the high cost of building a national system of airports.

Neither man was strongly motivated to form Scout, Bomber, or Corps Cooperation squadrons, even had the budget been provided by the Canadian government to do so. Wilson wanted to see military representatives with good administrative skills appointed to the Air Board: "These two officers might well be chosen from Canadian Officers at present in the Imperial Air Forces and should have good records, not merely as fighting pilots with big scores to their credit, but rather on account of their record for administrative capacity and varied experience in operations on a large scale."

Very few Canadians met Wilson's requirements, and almost none were high-scoring Scout pilots. One of the few was Colonel Redford F. "Red" Mulock, a McGill University engineering graduate who had been a versatile pilot and commanding officer during the war, but had no ambition to head up a peacetime air force. He, like Bishop and Barker, had his sights set on making a prosperous living in civil aviation. He twice turned down an offer to command the CAF.

Barker and Bishop had nothing to do with the CAF when it was formed in 1920. Bishop had been put forward in April 1919 by an MP named Lemieux to sit on the Air Board. The members in the House of Commons were misinformed that Bishop was making $30,000 a month in the United States, and was unlikely to accept.

Billy and Will did not lobby for a job on the Air Board, and they were not offered, and were unlikely to have accepted, any subordinate position in the CAF. They were outsiders, "fighting pilots with big scores," with little enthusiasm for the new air policies of the government.

Barker thought the members of the Air Board were too full of themselves. Apparently, Doughty felt the same way, since he favoured Barker, and ignored the Air Board concerns. But the D.VII dispute served as a useful warning to Will that the Air Board was no friend, and was unlikely to help Bishop-Barker Aeroplanes, Limited.

Bishop and Barker lobbied through 1919 with cities and towns across Canada to build "air harbours" (as they were then called) so that Canadian civil aviation could develop at the same pace as the United States. The Air Board, largely for economic reasons, preferred flying boats over land planes. What money they spent on infrastructure went mainly for seaplane bases.

Canada was one of the first nations in the world formally to regulate aviation, licensing pilots and certifying aircraft. Pilots had to qualify for a certificate for flying machines, and aircraft had to be certified airworthy in order to receive registration letters. Everyone had to take a flight test, regardless of previous experience, then fill out an application form, include a photograph, and sign up as a member of the CAF, available for military service. It was this last stipulation that irritated Barker and Bishop, who needed commercial certificates to fly their company aircraft, but had no intention of being obligated to the CAF. The two young heroes advised the Superintendent of the Certificate Branch of their feelings.

Lt Colonel James Stanley Scott, of Roberval, Quebec, was an experienced pilot and talented staff officer. He had received his MC in the RFC while serving in France with 5 and 6 Squadrons. After about four months in the field he was injured in a night landing accident and invalided home. He made his administrative reputation as the wing commander of 44 (North Toronto) Wing, part of the RFC/RAF Canada training organization, and received the Air Force Cross (AFC) for valuable contributions to the development of winter flying training.

As the recently appointed head of the Certificate Branch, "Jimmy" Scott signed the certificates of all private and commercial pilots. He had exercised his new authority by issuing himself the first Private Air Pilot's Certificate (Flying Machines), on 24 January 1920. An ambitious bureaucrat, Scott was efficient and conscientious to a fault, and heartily disliked by many war flyers.

Combat veterans of the Great War found it aggravating that their competence was being assessed by inspectors who may never have flown on operations, or spent the war in training establishments or prisoner-of-war camps, or (even worse) as staff officers. For scout aces to be messed around by such rear-echelon types was, as Williams recalled, ridiculous.

"Voss," after an unhappy time as a farmer, decided to go back flying. During the course of his refresher training, Williams took an instant dislike to Air Board Certificate Branch inspector A.T.N. "Tom" Cowley. Here was this ex-RNAS seaplane pilot who had spent most of the war in a German prisoner-of-war camp, who had never fired his guns at, let alone killed any Germans, refusing to give Williams a flying certificate!

This conflict between combatant flyers and non-combatant instructors is inevitable after any war but in 1920 regulation was not readily accepted, or seen as an obvious sign of progress and maturity. The Air Board that did not know, at least officially, who Barker was six months earlier, now demanded that he show that he could navigate cross-country in an aircraft much like the one in which he had survived over 150 offensive patrols.

Unlike today, flight tests, other than for three landings (the so-called "alighting tests"), were flown solo—i.e., the examiner did not go with the candidate in the machine. Will had to fly a round-robin in BBAL's Sopwith Dove from Syracuse, New York, via Rochester and Hamilton, and west to Armour Heights aerodrome in north Toronto. "Jimmy" Scott signed his test report as satisfactory, without ever having flown in the Dove.

Barker also had to prove he could take off and "alight" at night. This test was conducted on 9 July 1920 in a JN4. Lloyd Breadner, a future Chief of Air Staff of the RCAF, was the examiner. Breadner had been an RNAS ace on Pups and Camels. He and Will got along well. Barker went flying at 10:00 p.m. and landed four minutes later. Breadner thought the exercise was a waste of time, and needed to see only one takeoff and landing to satisfy himself that Barker could fly in the dark. The night flight test, according to Air Regulations, should have taken at least 30 minutes.

However, Barker's and Bishop's certificates did not arrive in the mail after their flying tests were completed. They still refused to sign the following agreement: "I understand that upon issue to me of the certificate asked for, I become a member of the Canadian Air Force and liable to perform such military training and other duty as may be prescribed."

Their temporary certificates were due to expire on 7 October, and Scott advised them by mail that they must sign the CAF agreement or permanent certificates could not be issued. Scott was angry about an accident to BBAL's flying boat on 10 September, and Air Commodore Arthur Tylee, the CAF's Air Officer Commanding, agreed to a court of inquiry to investigate the prang.

Unfazed by this two-pronged Air Board assault, Barker and Bishop asked Thomas Gibson, their lawyer, to write directly to Biggar, Scott's boss:

As was to be expected in a pioneer industry, [my clients, Bishop and Barker] are having quite a hard time to get their business on a sound footing. There are innumerable difficulties which have to be surmounted by anyone who is attempting to make civil flying a commercial success, and I think you will agree that they are to be encouraged in every possible way by the Government ... While they have no objection whatever to rendering themselves liable for military service in the event of war, they very naturally feel that in view of the distinguished position which they attained in flying during the war, they ought to be relieved from the necessity of annual or biannual training which, I understand, is to be prescribed for pilots ... can you see your way clear to relieve them of this duty, in view of the exceptional services which they performed for Canada, and the high state of efficiency which they attained in flying.

Biggar could not find his way clear to do any such thing, and made an appeal to Gibson that the two men obligate themselves for military service to set an example for others. He also pointed out that all commercial pilots have the same challenges to face in getting a business started, and the Militia Act makes every man liable for military service with the land forces.

Barker and Bishop did not surrender, and this precipitated a lengthy discussion at an Air Board meeting on 21 October. The Inspector-General, Air Vice-Marshal Sir Willoughby Gwatkin, realized that it was not going to be easy to force the issue. It could have caused embarrassment to the Board and the infant CAF if the newspapers picked up the story, and questions were asked in the House of Commons about the two famous pilots who would not serve.

Scott agreed with Gwatkin that it would not be appropriate to coerce commercial pilots into military service: "the great majority of Commercial Pilots would undoubtedly join the Canadian Air Force, but as long as there was an element of compulsion there would be difficulties." Shortly thereafter, Bishop received Commercial Air Pilot's Certificate 54, and Barker, 55. The matter was closed, but not forgotten by Scott.

Commercial aviation had scarcely existed before the war and therefore had to be invented in the 1920s. In Canada, two of the earliest commercial applications were aerial survey, using a sketch artist or camera to bring back images; and the transport of workers and tools to remote locations, usually in support of forestry, or mining and oil exploration. Occasionally an aircraft might be hired to fly a businessman, or a policeman.

Air mail in Canada had been confined to a few experimental flights, and there was nothing of a regular public service until 1927, unlike the United States, which instituted air mail routes in 1918. However, flying the US Mail was riskier than any war service. A US Mail pilot's life expectancy was four years. Of the first 40 pilots hired by the Post Office Department, 31 lost their lives in government service, for a salary of $250 per month, paid only if they flew.

Pleasure flying was almost exclusively barnstorming; 10-minute flights for $10. Aerobatic stunts and wing walking at fairgrounds were typically by one-pilot, one-aircraft operators, often with the company's only mechanic sitting on the lower wing or hanging from the landing gear. Parachute descents (sometimes by the same mechanic) were popular with spectators, but jaded audiences looked for new thrills, and this led to some dangerous stunts, and several fatal crashes.

Barker and Bishop flew air shows on the Toronto waterfront until the CNE fired them for painting advertising on their Martinsyde aircraft, and also for repeatedly diving directly at the crowds in the grandstand. They were not cowed by the rebuke. Their plans extended far beyond stunt flying.

In addition to importing and selling British machines, and trading in war-surplus Canadian JN4s, they wanted to start a proper airline with scheduled flights and paying passengers. The Curtiss JN4s were not good machines for regular passenger service, and the dehavilland DH4 and DH9 bombers in Canada, that might have been converted to cabin-class machines (as happened in the UK), all belonged to either the Air Board or the CAF.

Moreover, all of BBAL's competitors had JN4s, including companies like International Aerial Transport located near BBAL's hangar at Armour Heights aerodrome; Ericson Aircraft Ltd at Leaside aerodrome, which was still building the JN4 from surplus parts; McCarthy Aero Service, also at Leaside; Canadian Aero Film Company at

DND DHist Biographical file

Fighter aces Clifford "Black Mike" McEwen, RFC, and Alfred William "Nick" Carter, RNAS, flew HS-2Ls with the CAF's Civil Government Air Operations; they are shown here with ground crew at an unknown location.

Burlington; Allied Aeroplanes, Ltd, in Brantford; and Clifton Aero Company Ltd at Niagara Falls.

BBAL needed a more capable machine to set it apart from these other outfits. A large flying boat made sense because it could lift three or four passengers, and did not need grass runways to land or takeoff. There were many lakes to use, at least until they froze up in the fall. The best of the flying boats, the HS-2L, all belonged to the Air Board, or had been loaned by the Board to Laurentide Aviation in Quebec. This US Navy single-engine anti-submarine patrol aircraft was designed by the Curtiss Aeroplane and Motor Company. About 1,000 had been manufactured.

Powered by a 360-hp Liberty engine, the 6,500-lb HS-2L managed a cruising speed of about 65 mph, and could not make it up to 10,000 feet fully loaded—its rate-of-climb rarely exceeded 150-200 feet per minute. Flown normally by a crew of two or three, the machine was a state-of-the-art anti-submarine patrol machine in 1918.

Shortly after the war ended, the US government brought its USN detachment home from Dartmouth, Nova Scotia. It generously gave its seaplanes to the Canadian government. The Air Board had appraised its 12 free Curtiss HS-2L flying boats and 10 extra engines at $175,000, a high price based on replacement value. For a country with few aerodromes, and to a government that was tight-fisted, the HS-2Ls were of immeasurable value.

Fortunately for BBAL, the US Navy was selling off war-surplus machines. In June 1920, Barker, while in New York City, walked over to the Times Building and checked out the deals being offered by Inglis M. Uppercu, and his Aeromarine Engineering and Sales Company. When the Navy decided to sell off its HS-2Ls, Uppercu's company was the go-between, offering stock or modified machines. A stock HS-2L at the Brooklyn Navy Yard was priced at $6,160, and an enclosed-cabin "flying limousine," $9,000.

Barker opted for a stock airframe, US Navy serial number A-1727. The machines were bought in an "as-is" condition. Barker, co-pilot Russell McRae, and air engineer Charles Mount took off, circled the Brooklyn Bridge, and followed the Hudson River

north to Troy, where the engine died and they descended to a safe landing by the shore. The three men worked for days to get the HS-2L back into the air. When the machine finally touched down in Toronto harbour at noon on 8 July, waiting to greet them at the Hanlon ferry dock at the foot of Church Street were Billy and Margaret Bishop, and Toronto mayor Tommy Church.

The BBAL flying boat was registered as G-CADB on 12 July. Bishop and Barker christened their first big machine, "The Gin Rickey," perhaps in honour of their favourite summer drink. It fit the company's image in that its two owners were known to drink occasionally while on the job. Barker's left arm was useless to overcome the seaplane's heavy controls, so Bishop or other BBAL pilots assisted him during the takeoffs.

All the early flights in Canada by HS-2Ls were pioneering. It was Canada's first bush plane. Moving people and cargo by air was entirely new, and many of the wilderness sites that companies like BBAL flew into had never seen a flying machine. These HS-2Ls were expensive to operate, but reduced a week's journey by train or boat into the Canadian north to only five or six hours. As for passengers, a certain sense of adventure was needed to squeeze into the front cockpit of an HS-2L.

As the flying boat was difficult to launch into the air, a pilot could not fly it unaided. An air engineer or a general purpose "grease-monkey" was needed for the start-up and taxi. Without him the aircraft could not even get off the water. Its limitations as a passenger transport can be gauged by the recollections of a former CAF airman, Gerald LaGrave, in *Roundel*:

> ... the rudder did not have enough surface to counteract the swinging of the aircraft in a cross-wind. So they furnished you with a pair of running shoes and, if you know the HS-2L, they have a bar which comes between the cockpits on a slant. Your job was to stand there ready, as the aircraft taxied out and, if the pilot wanted to swing, he'd give the engine more power and point to the wing and you got up

No. 386

Good for
One Aeroplane Flight
• $10.00 •

Subject to conditions set forth on back hereof.

THE BISHOP - BARKER COMPANY

HOLDER of this ticket hereby releases The Bishop-Barker
    Company from all liability for injury or damage resulting
from any action of said Company, its representatives or employees,
or from defects of any nature in the machines or equipment used
by said Company.
    Purchase price of this ticket will be refunded on demand of
purchaser, or if for any reason flight is made impossible.
    This ticket redeemable for $10.00 cash at the office of
The Bishop-Barker Co., 93 Spadina Ave., Toronto, Ont.

Holder

Stephen Heinemann collection

Aviation companies and barnstormers offered free coupons to encourage flying; this is one issued by The Bishop-Barker Company.

and walked the entering edge hanging on to the struts and wires. Then the float would hit the water and swing the aircraft around. But if the pilot over controlled you'd be running like hell to get to the other wing. After a while, you'd get quite agile ... Half the time you'd still be out on the wing when the pilot gunned the engine for take-off. Then you went like hell to get back to your cockpit.

* * *

Shortly after its arrival in Toronto, G-CADB inaugurated an air service between Toronto harbour and the Royal Muskoka Hotel on Lake Rousseau, 130 miles north of the city in the Muskoka Lakes. This region of Ontario was cottage country for some of Canada's most affluent families.

The BBAL air service, albeit somewhat irregular and short-lived, was probably the first by an air transport company based in Toronto, and possibly the first in Canada. The company hoped to make money from rich people, offering sight-seeing flights, and shuttling prosperous businessmen back and forth to their offices on Bay Street.

Bishop's relatives, the Eaton family, were obvious charter passengers. On one of the early BBAL flights in mid-July 1920, Billy talked his aunt into flying down to Toronto. The trip was an exciting first for Florence McCrea, Sir John Eaton's wife. She recalled it fondly in her memoirs:

I seldom get into one of the comfortable big planes without remembering my first

experience off the ground. It began in Muskoka, where the famous Billy Bishop, V.C. (Jack's niece's husband) and his equally famous flying friend, Colonel Billy Barker, had started an air service to Toronto ... I sat in the open cockpit for almost two hours as we made our "lightning" trip to the city. Jack was waiting for me at the Toronto waterfront, and never have I seen a more perturbed husband! "You, a mother of five children, risking your life in a thing like that!" On the way up Yonge Street, his driving was so erratic that I finally burst out, "Look, dear, I may have been taking a risk when I went in the plane, but that is nothing compared to the danger I am in right now!" He couldn't help laughing, so the tension eased.

Sir John Eaton must have been inspired by his wife's daring. He went flying on 26 July in the HS-2L with his niece, Margaret, Billy Bishop, and co-pilot McRae. Eaton is reported to have said that "the sensation of danger is sadly lacking." *The Globe* reporter also noted that the aircraft had taken 50 passengers for flights in "the cool upper air breezes" in the first two days at the Muskoka Lakes.

The first full-time pilot of BBAL, Russell Fern McRae, was a former Camel pilot who had served with 4 Squadron, Australian Flying Corps. Transferred out because he was not Australian, just before King George was due to inspect the squadron, McRae arrived at 46 Squadron, during the time Donald MacLaren was at the peak of his fighting career, and stayed with the unit almost till war's end.

David Mackenzie collection

Billy Bishop assists a passenger with her helmet while Barker adjusts his goggles. The woman standing is believed to be Bishop's wife Margaret Burden, the other may be Sir John Eaton's wife, Lady Florence McCrea Eaton.

BBAL needed more pilots in addition to McRae, and there were quite a few to choose from. According to *The Globe*, by July 1920, about 135 flying certificates had been issued by the Air Board, including 48 commercial, 46 private, and 41 air engineer. In addition, 52 aircraft had received registration certificates, and 25 air harbour licences had been issued.

Bishop and Barker interviewed and hired Philip C. Garratt, Forde W. McCarthy, and Stanley H. McCrudden. Garratt was an ex-70 Squadron pilot, with over 400 flying hours. He had received the AFC for his contributions as an RAF instructor at Northholt. He later became the general manager of de Havilland Aircraft of Canada, and was twice awarded the McKee Trophy for his contributions to the development of Canadian aviation. McCarthy had worked for Ericson Aircraft before joining BBAL. McCrudden was a graduate of the Curtiss School in Toronto and had served in 1917 with 8N

Squadron, RNAS, until wounded in action.

Working at BBAL called for patience, a sharp eye, a sense of humour, and an alternative source of income. The pilots did not remember the experience with fondness, and most erased it from their CV, or mumbled about it in passing. Vic Dallin left for Philadelphia, and later founded his own successful aerial survey company. McRae recalled that it was tough getting paid, and months went by without remuneration. The two owners partied too often and drank too much on the job.

McRae was a temperate man, and his girlfriend wanted him to quit flying altogether. Many wartime pilots discovered it was a rare female who would marry a pilot in the 1920s, and a proposal inevitably led to: "You're going to stop flying, aren't you?" McRae did, and had a safer career as an electrical inspector. What focused his mind on a career change was a crash in BBAL's "Gin Rickey."

Unidentified employees of Bishop-Barker Aeroplanes in Toronto, likely at Leaside aerodrome.

On Friday afternoon, 10 September, enroute from Orillia to Toronto, the Liberty engine failed, and McRae was forced to land in the tree tops of Bickle's Wood outside Brooklin, northeast of Toronto. The newspapers liked the flying boat's nickname, and ran a photo of the HS-2L that had been taken in Toronto harbour, with Barker and his crew standing up in the cockpit. Above the photo was this headline: "The Gin Rickey Lights on a Tree."

While the HS-2L glided down, Baker had climbed behind McRae in an attempt to work on the engine, and eyewitnesses on the ground said afterwards that the passengers were all out on the wing helping keep the hydroplane in balance. Baker suffered a broken wrist and a couple of broken teeth in the impact, and was released after being patched up, but McRae was kept in hospital at Oshawa for several days. The two passengers were lucky. William

Thompson broke a rib, and Leonard Cairn was cut up and bruised by the trees.

Faced with a serious public relations crisis, Bishop did his best to minimize the accident. He invited Thompson and Cairn to spend Friday night at his residence at 50 Poplar Plains Road. *The Globe* on Saturday morning had large headlines on page one:

MEN CLING TO WINGS AS AIRPLANE CRASHES – Bishop-Barker Machine Falls Into Tree Tops—Occupants Narrowly Escape Death—Take Desperate Chances to Make Landing.

But Bishop had been able to talk to *The Toronto Daily Star* reporter at greater length and reassure him that the accident was a complete anomaly. Their story was published on an inside page, with Bishop quoted: "To point out how safe flying is as compared with other modes of travelling, I might say that since May 1 we have carried 2,450 people and have flown 30,500 miles without a breakage of any sort or kind ... In contrast to this the other day I read an account of five people being killed by motors in Toronto over one week-end."

"Jimmy" Scott, now titled the Controller of Civil Aviation, did not like the two men operating a flying boat passenger service between Toronto and Muskoka, and other points, without so much as a lean-to on the shore:

> They were operating one flying boat, but evidently had no fixed base and certainly no building which could be licensed. After discussion it was decided that it would not be possible to licence any piece of water without some fixed shore base as an air harbour and that it would be permissible for them to operate without an air harbour licence so long as no building was habitually used as a base.

It was these kinds of fine bureaucratic distinctions discussed *ad nauseum* at Air Board meetings in Ottawa that drove Barker into a frenzy. He and Bishop had, by this time, developed a strong antipathy to Scott, who seemed dedicated to destroying their future.

Within weeks of the crash of G-CADB, Barker picked up a second war-surplus HS-2L at the Brooklyn Navy Yard. He flew G-CADM (serial number A-1721) back via Albany and Montreal on 2 October 1920, setting a 2 hr, 5 min, flight record between the two cities. But winter was now setting in, and the lakes were freezing over. This was the time when the Air Board and other operators completed engine and airframe overhauls. Barker and Bishop moved the company's flying boat operations to Palm Beach County, Florida.

Located about 70 miles north of Miami on the Atlantic Ocean side, Palm Beach County was another version of the Muskoka Lakes, well suited to flying boats. It had Lake Worth and Clear Lake parallel to the Atlantic Ocean, large hotels, many tourists, and many boats. It was going through a

period of explosive growth due to land speculation. Most importantly, it was the latest fashionable place to be if you were rich, or wanted to be rich.

BBAL had plenty of competition in Palm Beach, mainly from Uppercu's Aeromarine West Indies Airways. It had seven flying boats and, according to one source, flew 95,000 miles and carried nearly 7,000 passengers in the first year of operations, 1920-21. The company published a schedule and carried passengers between Miami and the Bahamas, Key West and Havana, and Miami and Palm Beach. The BBAL operation could not compete, and its Florida venture of 1920-21 was short-lived and unprofitable.

Will's anxieties about his flying company that winter were compounded by his concerns for the hardscrabble existence of the Barker family. Despite his promise, he was no more able to help them financially in 1921 than in 1918. But he was not ready to give up and return to farming:

> I have just arrived back from Florida and leave again on the 24th for Palm Beach ... where our flying boats are in operation. This means that I will spend Xmas on the train. I am indeed disappointed that I cannot get home for Xmas but sincerely hope that I will be able to next year. I will try to get up to see you all in March on my return from the south.
>
> How is everybody and everything? I have not heard from you or any of the family for ages and am anxious to know how you all are. I am most anxious to hear from you—write care of this office & the letters will be forwarded to me.

Will and his family were drifting further apart, and the occasional letter he sent to them went unanswered. George Barker's farm at Warren had not turned out well, and he moved the family yet again, this time to south-western Manitoba. He farmed just a few miles north of the Manitoba-North Dakota border near the town of Waskada. He was also a part-time grain elevator manager at a railway whistle stop at Deloraine.

* * *

Despite his worries and workload, Barker had found time to fall in love. Her name was Jean Kilbourn Smith, a granddaughter of John and Maria Kilbourn, and a cousin of Billy Bishop via his maternal grandmother, Sarah. Jean's mother and father were Helen Maud Kilbourn and Horace Bruce Smith, the latter a successful Owen Sound lawyer. She was born, an only child, in October 1896, and attended school in Owen Sound with Billy. The two were close enough to write letters to each other during the war, and afterwards, Billy and Margaret occasionally visited Jean at her father's estate home in Toronto.

Jean had heard and read about her cousin's handsome business partner, but they had not met. A few months after the establishment of BBAL, Bishop and Barker were invited to a party at 355 St Clair Avenue West. A rather proper, but strong-willed young woman, Jean watched quietly from the far side of the living room as Will walked in with Billy.

She later described the experience to her grandson, David Mackenzie, as love at first sight. She knew, there and then, that he was the man she wanted to marry. Apparently, the feeling was mutual, and the two hit it off immediately. Will told his parents: "Jean is a wonderful girl. ... She is about five feet four inches in height, rather slight, large blue eyes and fair hair, and the best person in the world."

They may have been smitten, but Horace Smith was appalled by his daughter's choice in suitors. Smith was, in that Roaring Twenties phrase, "a captain of industry." His father, William Henry Smith, was a master mariner and owner of a shipping company at Owen Sound that served Collingwood and North Shore communities. Horace grew up immersed in the shipping business. He became a lawyer with the same firm that John Kilbourn had once worked for and, building on his legal experience, became a successful entrepreneur between 1894 and 1914.

When Barker first met him, Smith was president of the Northern Navigation Company, and Collingwood Shipbuilding Company, as well as Halifax Shipyards Limited, Davie Shipbuilding and Repairing Company, and the Steam Navigation Company. Northern Navigation had been bought out by Canada Steamship Lines before the First World War, and Smith sat on its board of directors until his death in 1939.

Balding and bespectacled, sober and restrained, Smith was a 56-year-old, self-made millionaire. Horace was not impressed by Will's soldierly bearing or medals. He had nothing in common with Barker. Very few men were good enough for his only daughter, but Barker didn't even come close. He was a farm kid with no education, he had no sensible means of financial support, he was known to drink, he was known to be reckless (his medals were evidence of that), and he was in partnership with another man cut from the same cloth.

Smith had a heart-to-heart talk with Jean, but, at 23, she did not need his permission to marry. In any case, she was certain that nobody as ardent and persistent as her "Billie," as she fondly called him, would ever let her down. Moreover, in addition to being a famous war hero, he knew the Prince of Wales. There was no better endorsement in 1920. Jean was *not* reckless, like "Billie," and had given her parents little cause for concern growing up. To some of her friends, however, she hardly seemed an ideal match for a man so energetic, so sexy. If Jean was attracted to the rogue in him, so were many other young women.

When her father could not change her mind, he begged her to wait 12 months before marrying. She agreed to this, confident that their relationship would survive the test, even with "Billie" flying down in Florida. Barker knew Horace's feelings, and believed that he would stop the marriage if he could. In a rare private letter to his father, just a month before the wedding, Will outlined his worries:

> ... You know I am getting married soon and I must now tell you that her father is objecting and doing all in his power to stop it. He "Mr. H.B. Smith" is a very unreasonable man and just because he is worth four or five millions he thinks I am marrying his daughter Jean for her money.
>
> He asked me for your address, etc. which I gave him so I suppose he will be either sending someone to see you or else writing to you. So I thought I would tell you in advance. If he

Wedding portrait of Jean Kilbourn Smith, June 1921.

writes you a personal letter I wish you would send it on to me. I will attach my remarks and return it. Then you answer it. My reason for asking you to do this is that he is a lawyer and is grasping for something to use as an argument against me. So I think it would be better for you to let me advise you on it ...

On 1 June 1921, Will and Jean were married by the Reverend James Broughall at Grace-Church-on-the-Hill in Toronto, in a family ceremony attended only by a handful of relatives and close friends. Billy Bishop was the groom's best man. The wedding rated a headline "Canadian Ace Weds," and short narrative, in the "Woman's Daily Interests" section of *The Toronto Daily Star*:

... The bride, who was unattended, was given away by her father. She was wearing a lovely wedding gown of shell pink kitten's ear crepe, with rose point face panels, over which hung a veil of filmy tulle caught with a bandeau of orange blossoms. She carried a white ivory prayer book, the gift of the groom and wore a string of pearls given her by her father and mother ...

Barker did not invite any of the members of his own family. By any conventional measure, the gulf between the Smiths and the Barkers was huge. Will's marriage to Jean moved him upward in society, into a chauffeured-limousine class in which he was never entirely at ease. As Edna Barker expressed it:

We were just ordinary folk ... we didn't travel in those days ... Jean was a society girl. She was presented at court in England. She sent us a photograph of herself in her gown with the feathers in her hair. That was not our world ... I would not have wanted that life ... It was an awful life for him ... without anything of his own.

Will promised to bring his new bride out west, but he never did. Jean met her in-laws for the first time at her husband's funeral. But in 1921 they were very much in love:

Jean and I had a very nice marriage and all went very well. We are now at Footes Bay in the Muskoka Lakes district on our honeymoon and are very happy ... we are going to live in Toronto after our honeymoon. Here we have a very nice cottage on the lake with large verandahs [*sic*] to the lake front ... We have about a mile to go for our mail and supplies which is only a few minutes in the launch.

I hope all your troubles have righted themselves and that all is now well. My advice is to retrench yourselves well this fall if the crops are good. I will have a pretty hard time making things go but with hard work I will succeed. The most important thing is that we are very happy.

George and Jane wished him well, but the fun-loving Willie they had raised was gone, replaced by a public figure they did not know. An occasional letter, or newspaper article, a photograph, or Christmas card was hardly an emotional connection. Will made one final visit to his family during an autumn business trip to Winnipeg.

He had been friends during his teenage years with Fred Ferguson, who now worked as the secretary to Mayor Charles Gray. Ferguson arranged for Will to borrow a JN4 that was owned by the city, but looked after by Canadian Aircraft Company on McDermott Avenue (see photo on page 191). Fred and Will flew 155 miles south-west to Waskada in a tired machine that had received little maintenance. The town's school children, including Edna, Orval, Leslie, Roy, and Lloyd, were let out of classes to watch the famous William Barker, VC, land in a field near the town.

Will stayed only a couple of days. Waskada was in the hottest, driest, and flattest patch of south western Manitoba. This was the region farmers had left during the drought in the 1890s, crossing over the Riding Mountain to the Dauphin Valley. In Will's eyes it was a giant step backwards for his family.

Barker in uniform holding his daughter Jean Antoinette Barker, fall of 1922.

Waskada was no comparison to Russell or Dauphin in looks or fertility. Nothing his father could possibly offer would alter the parched, board-flat landscape. This was a town figuratively and literally at the end of the line—in fact, the CPR tracks ended there.

On the flight home, the engine of the JN4 failed over Pilot Mound. Fred was not only impressed with how well his old friend handled the forced landing, but also with his mechanical ability. Will checked the Curtiss 0X5 engine, had parts sent in on the train, installed them, did a test run, ordered Fred to hop in, and took off for Winnipeg.

* * *

To raise the profile of the company, Barker had flown a couple of pioneering cargo flights between New York and Toronto. To promote BBAL, he gave talks to the weekly meeting of the Rotary Club in Toronto, and handed out pencils that had been carried across the border. The speeches were so entertaining that the Rotarians gave Barker a standing ovation. According to *Aerial Age Weekly*, these flights in January 1921 were the first to carry "merchandise" from the US into Canada.

Billy Bishop had, sometime in the fall of 1920, lost his pilot's medical validation after he had crashed the Sopwith Dove on landing. This was the same machine that had flown the Prince of Wales over London in 1919. Bishop suffered serious head injuries, a broken nose, and a broken toe, but the impact had also broken the back of his passenger, Andrew Maclean, of the Maclean Publishing Company, seated in the front cockpit. Bishop recovered, but young Maclean had to wear a brace for some period. Billy was grounded in February 1921 due to problems with his vision, and did not fly an aircraft again until the 1930s.

David Mackenzie collection

Barker during a visit to Manitoba flew this JN4 of Canadian Aircraft Company from Winnipeg to visit his family at Waskada; he repaired the JN4 after a forced landing at Pilot Mound, and returned it safely to Winnipeg.

Fokker D.VII brought to Canada after the war, now preserved in a museum; it is similar to those on loan to Bishop-Barker Aeroplanes in 1919-20.

Airforce Magazine collection

The safety record of BBAL after 18 months of operation was not great, but was by no means the worst. Unlike some operators, the company had not killed any passengers. Quite a few of the early post-war Canadian flying companies had accidents that proved fatal for the passenger or passengers (often seated in the front cockpit), while leaving the pilot with minor injuries. Newspapers were quick to publicize these tragedies.

Historian Frank Ellis, a Canadian "early bird" who knew first-hand the challenges of making money in the Roaring Twenties, labelled the period from 1921 through 1923 as the flying doldrums: "Although there were a number of notable achievements during the doldrums, the regrettable fact remains that Canada lost several valuable years during the lull, and the development of commercial aviation in Canada was much slower than it should have been."

Barker was learning the hard way that the riches he had forecast in his wartime letters were ephemeral. His company was ahead of the times. It completely lacked not only the aircraft to provide reliable service, but also the mature management necessary to inspire customer confidence. As the winter of 1921-22 set in, Bishop-Barker Aeroplanes only occasionally met its payroll, and was unable to continue the 7 percent dividend on its preferred shares.

Toronto-Muskoka was a seasonal summer operation, and the company could not expect much flying revenue in the winter. The Palm Beach venture had not paid well, and the market for AVRO and Sopwith sporting machines in the US had dried up. By this time, nobody could be enticed into buying a JN4. If one could not make money barnstorming, there was even less to be made by running a used aircraft lot. Will described his company's grim situation to his mother:

> I have been going to write you many times but have sadly neglected. I got a letter from Percy a week or so ago. I was glad to hear from him. How are you all? Has the farm paid this year? I hope it has and that you are in better circumstances now ...
>
> We have had a bad season and it is possible that our company will not weather the winter. In that case I will have to take a position with a company I know quite well here. However I hope it does not come to that ... We are having quite a time to make things go but are confident all will be well.

All did not go well, and BBAL did not survive the winter. While Barker flew some cargo flights, Bishop hustled up some non-aviation contracts. He submitted a winning bid for a contract with the city of Toronto to paint streetcars which, according to his son, Arthur Bishop, earned the faltering company $30,000, enough to pay off the bills owing, but probably nothing for its shareholders.

It is unlikely that any company aircraft were flying by the spring of 1922. Bishop decided to return to England, and soon became a sales executive for an iron pipe manufacturer. He came back to Canada for the special general meeting to surrender the charter of BBAL. This took place on 28 December 1922, by which date Barker was back in uniform.

Barker, over several months, disposed of all the remaining BBAL aircraft. The solitary flying boat, G-CADM, and an AVRO 504K, G-CABD, flew or were shipped to unknown destinations and owners. One JN4, G-CABB, was sold in August 1923 to a man named Peel, in Ford City, Ontario. Since Will was searching for a Mercedes engine from the Air Board as late as November 1920, he may have had one or more Fokker D.VIIs stored in the Armour Heights hangar. If so, their ultimate fate is a mystery.

Barker in cockpit of HS2L, Bishop standing on cowling; women passengers possibly Lady Flora McCrea Eaton, Margaret Burden; unidentified young man in front cockpit, Muskoka, circa 1921.

David Mackenzie collection

Barker (centre) with US Air Service deputy chief, Brigadier General Billy Mitchell (left), and W/C Christie, RAF, on visit to Camp Borden, February 1922.

CHAPTER TWELVE

BARKER AND THE
FOUNDATION OF THE RCAF

"I found Barker to be a very fine person; he was one of the finest officers I ever served under. His arm was practically useless ... but he played tennis one-handed, he could just throw the ball up with his left hand, and he golfed one-handed, and he shot skeet, and he'd knock down 24 out of 25 most of the time, though his left hand was just barely able to hold the gun ... he was a terrific man, anything he set out to do, he was bound to do it ... we all loved him."

AIR-VICE MARSHAL THOMAS A. LAWRENCE

Will did not want to join the Canadian Air Force, but was forced to it when no civilian flying position came his way after Bishop-Barker Company closed its doors. His physical condition did not allow him to take a bush flying job, and there were no outfits looking for operations managers or chief pilots in 1922. To get into the CAF he had to go through his old nemesis, the Air Board. On 30 March 1922, therefore, he had an interview in Ottawa with Major General Sir Willoughby G. Gwatkin, the inspector general.

After two months of soul searching, he applied in writing on 3 June. Gwatkin turned his request over to the Chief of the General Staff, Major General James H. MacBrien. He told MacBrien that the Air Board was in agreement with commissioning, but "that there was no position to which Colonel Barker could be appointed immediately."

MacBrien became Barker's mentor during his four years in the CAF and RCAF. He was considered a soldier's soldier. He had been at the centre of any action since joining the Militia in 1897. He had commanded the 12th Brigade of the 4th Canadian Division for more than two years in the Great War, from September 1916 to December 1918, during which time he was twice wounded in action, six times mentioned in despatches, and awarded the DSO. According to legend, the hotter the action, the cooler MacBrien was. He was popular and also had a sense of humour.

He was not a sophisticated bureaucrat in Ottawa, and could be impatient, petulant, and short-tempered. Nevertheless, when it came to matters of personnel, he

was very attentive, and few positions were filled, and few promotions or transfers effected without his involvement. The 44-year-old Chief of Staff may have recognized in Barker a kindred maverick. Like everybody else, he admired his war record. Only two Victoria Cross recipients, Milton Gregg and George Pearkes, were serving in the Permanent Forces in the 1920s. A third one for the CAF was a plus.

While waiting for a reply from the CAF, Barker and his wife went on a holiday to the United Kingdom, during which Jean got one of her most cherished wishes. She met the Prince of Wales and was presented at Court to his father, King George the Fifth. This was a happy time for Jean, since she and Will were expecting their first baby. She was not so keen on her husband's career plans, however, as nothing in her background had prepared her for the nomadic life as a military officer's wife.

MacBrien knew Barker was overseas, and smoothed the way for his re-entry to military service. He had him commissioned immediately without a job to go to:

Dear Sir Willoughby -
With reference to your draft letter to Lt.-Colonel Barker: I know that this officer is anxious for appointment to the Non-Permanent establishment of the Canadian Air Force. He is at present in England, and there would therefore be considerable delay in referring to him.

In the circumstances I should be glad if action could be taken to appoint this officer a Wing Commander in the C.A.F. with seniority in that rank as from the 3rd June, 1922, and am quite sure that such action will be agreeable to Colonel Barker.

The ranks of lieutenant colonel and wing commander were equivalent, and used interchangeably in the CAF until November 1922 when the RAF system was implemented. After some administrative training at Kingston and Ottawa till late August, Barker was posted to Training Depot Station Camp Borden, 50 miles north of Toronto. He got acquainted with the large station and flew the AVRO 504K, his first military flying since Hendon aerodrome in May 1919.

On September 14 he was granted leave and immediately drove home to Toronto. His wife was in the maternity ward at Wellesley Hospital and, two days later, their daughter, Jean Antoinette, was born. At this time Jean and Will were living in his father-in-law's large grey estate house on St Clair Avenue West, and for the next few weeks Will stayed close to home, getting used to the unfamiliar role of parent.

In October General MacBrien ordered the acting director of the CAF in Ottawa, Lt Colonel James Lindsay Gordon, to transfer Barker to Camp Borden to take command on 1 November. As commanding officer, Barker had his own residence, but Jean did not want to take an infant to the sand dunes of Camp Borden. Will commuted on weekends to Toronto. However, Jean soon hired a nanny, and by the end of November was spending some time at the station, which for the rest of her life she referred to wryly as "Camp Boredom." Getting there in the 1920s was an adventure. The train station at Angus was several miles south, and through much of the winter the road to the aerodrome could be travelled only by horse and sleigh. It was not on the frontier, but it seemed like it.

Wing Commander Barker established his own unique style at Camp Borden. His personal automobile was, according to Air Vice-Marshal Lawrence, a Rolls-Royce which he drove as fast as the roads allowed, and which occasionally had to be retrieved

Barker's wingman at 28 Squadron, Clifford "Black Mike" McEwen, commanded 6 Bomber Group, RCAF, in 1944-45; his was the most successful military career of all of Barker's pilots.

from a snow-filled ditch by one of the junior officers stationed at the aerodrome.

He inspected the aerodrome not on foot or in a truck, but on horseback. One of the more striking sights of 1923 at the air station was Barker, dressed in midnight blue CAF uniform, with silver buttons and a gleaming black Sam Browne belt, astride a large white mare. He was the first station commander to claim forage for a horse. In those days of balanced budgets, such an unusual request generated paperwork right up to the deputy minister of defence, George J. Desbarats.

Chief accountant R.P. Brown agreed with Barker that conditions at Camp Borden might warrant a horse, unlike other stations, and he suggested that a flat rate of 50 cents per day to cover forage and stabling for Barker's mare was preferable to specific invoices. Desbarats scribbled his approval across the memorandum.

Training Depot Station Camp Borden was the home of the CAF. It was the largest flying station in Canada, and the centre for virtually all the military flying. At the time Barker took command, Camp Borden had a staff of 14 officers and 120 airmen, more than 50 percent of the whole air force.

In addition to Camp Borden, there were six air stations across Canada—at Jericho Beach, in Vancouver, British Columbia; High River, Alberta; Victoria Beach, Manitoba; Rockcliffe, Ontario; Roberval, Quebec; and Dartmouth, Nova Scotia. They were small by comparison, Rockcliffe being average with a staff of about 18. The stations were managed by the Air Board, and their personnel had all been hired through the Civil Service Commission, and were paid as civil servants.

It was common for wartime flyers to be hired through a Civil Service Commission competition for occupations such as clerk, storesman, or apprentice air mechanic. There were few flying positions. A veteran wearing the DFC or MC below his wings might have to work in a hangar or an office, but would be first in line for any new flying slots. Barker's friend from 28 Squadron, Lieut "Black Mike" McEwen, MC, DFC, started out as a clerk.

Men moved back and forth between the CAF and the so-called Civil Government Air Operations (CGAO) branch, being put on leave without pay in the organization they had left behind. Although the CGAO was a civilian body, and its budget presented as a separate item in the House of Commons, virtually all of its staff were ex-military.

Camp Borden aerodrome had been built in the first four months of 1917, on an around-the-clock schedule, the largest of several RFC/RAF Canada training establishments. The site for the aerodrome

McEwen in the characteristic bush pilot's attire while serving in the CGAO branch of the CAF in the early 1920s.

DND DHist Biographical file

spread over 1,000 acres of sand, scrub-brush and trees, adjacent to the Militia camp of the same name. More than 55 buildings and 18 hangars were built, and during wartime the aerodrome was capable of supporting 500 cadets-in-training, 122 officers, 120 senior NCOs, and another 900 fitters, riggers, and office staff. When flying training shut down at war's end, the station was given to the Canadian government. It was used as a storage facility for the more than 100 of the so-called "Imperial Gift" aircraft shipped from the UK, until a CAF work team resurrected it for service flying in the summer of 1920.

Unfortunately for Barker, he was taking command of the country's largest air station at one of the quietest periods in its long aviation history. In 1921 there had been over 7,200 training flights at Camp Borden, and more than 2,800 flying hours were logged by former World War One flyers on refresher courses.

On a once-every-two-year schedule, former RFC, RNAS, and RAF veterans with civilian jobs got a chance to fly aircraft at Camp Borden, or work on or around them for 28 days. A few were granted extensions and served for two or three months, and in rare cases got a full-time job. The cost to run 190 pilots through a 28-day-refresher course was $380,000. The cost to train 400 mechanics for three months was $240,000. The total of $620,000 represented 70 percent of the entire CAF budget.

The RAF had been dramatically reduced to 10 percent of its wartime strength, and the British government had slashed its operating budget. In the United States, the Air Service was a tiny part of the US Army and struggled throughout the 1920s for survival. The lack of funding, the inadequate aircraft, eventually forced the flamboyant Brig General Billy Mitchell to talk to the newspapers, leading to his court martial. Budgetary famine was just as severe in Canada as in the UK and US.

The new government of Prime Minister Mackenzie King, elected in December 1921, had reduced the Air Board's total budget for both civil and military flying by about 40 percent for 1922-23, and the program of refresher training was shut down on 1 April 1922. More than 800 flying hours had been

logged in the first quarter at Camp Borden, but for the remaining nine months it was only 131 hours. The $825,000 approved for CAF work in the 1921-22 year was reduced for 1922-23 to about $440,000. In 1923-24, fewer than 600 flying hours were for military training, with another 90 hours being combined training exercises.

There had been no less than four commanding officers before Barker, and that was just in 1922; this high turnover had done nothing to improve the efficiency of the sprawling aerodrome, which had many problems. As historian Wing Commander F.H. Hitchins observed:

> The great air training centre at Camp Borden ... was beginning to prove something of a white elephant. The temporary war-time buildings were becoming increasingly costly to maintain and repair, and the whole establishment ... was much larger than the small requirement of the peace-time RCAF.

Barker's paramount interest was to build an operational capability to fight. He was the only senior flying officer to persist in this personal obsession despite the antipathy of the newly elected Mackenzie King government to any military expansion. He was not prepared to go along with policies he thought were misguided. Many of Barker's colleagues who had been with the Air Board or CAF from inception had come to accept that military aviation was secondary to aid to the civil powers.

A member of His Majesty's Loyal Opposition was the solitary voice in the 14th Parliament against the military flying cuts:

> ... the Air Force, as a defensive force, is practically going to cease to exist ... the only body of, I will not say men, but of anything savouring of military training in this country, which body is going to be maintained and for which the estimate has been kept up, is that of the Boy Scout movement in Canada. Is it possible that the people of this country are going to depend on our Boy Scouts as a body of national

Barker being photographed with Brigadier General Billy Mitchell, US Air Service, during Mitchell's visit to Camp Borden, Ontario.

defence in the future? The minister may smile. But this is a serious matter ... Why should men who are acting as fire rangers throughout the country be listed as part of the defence forces of the country? Yet that is what the minister is doing ... If national defence in the future is to consist of an air force for forest ranging and the detection of smugglers, I think the House should know it.

Dr Donald M. Sutherland, MP, defence critic and a future minister of defence, had commanded the 52nd Battalion, CEF, in the war. He and Barker shared similar worries about Canada's lack of military capability, and by 1923 Will had a much better sense of how limited the CAF was. He was angry when nobody wanted to know about, let alone use, any of

his ideas about air power. Two months after taking command of Camp Borden he had written a memorandum to Lindsay Gordon detailing his worries:

In my opinion the efficiency of any part of the Air Force should be judged by its striking power and its ability to turn out in the case of a national emergency Flying Officers who are capable of performing any or all of the duties performed by aircraft in war. This, of course, could not be done with our present organization.

... if a number of bombing machines were required, or machines fitted with machine guns, to settle some disorder, it would be practically impossible to provide them from this Station, owing to the fact that there is no

199

Officer here who understands the installation of bomb racks and bombs, or machine guns ...

I do not want it to appear that I am desirous of carrying this to the extreme, but it seems to me very advisable that we have at least a very small striking force ready in this country. Our condition might be compared to that of the Artillery if they were without shells or sights for their guns.

Gordon knew that Barker's proposal for a strike force, and a school of aeronautics to teach the fundamentals of aircraft weapons and tactics had no chance in Ottawa. He told him that any money left after paying the overhead of the CAF went to support civil operations. Barker was not easily dissuaded, however, and he kept up a steady flow of criticisms that did nothing to endear him to his boss.

Will was a popular commanding officer because of his contagious enthusiasm for all aspects of station life. Just as in the war, he poked his nose into hangars, talking to fitters and riggers one-on-one. There was little about airframes and engines that he did not understand, and he was always ready to listen to the opinions of his air mechanics.

He had an abundance of ideas of his own, on engines, airframes, weapons, and parachutes. He was keen on experimentation and it was this creative streak that Flight Lieut George V. Walsh, the station adjutant, admired the most. Not being the most patient administrator, Will was fortunate to have him to take care of the paperwork. Air Vice-Marshal Walsh remembered Barker:

... as an officer of brilliant ideas, particularly in the field of air armament ... For aerial gunnery practice he suggested equipping the AVRO trainers with a shotgun fitted with Constantinesco synchronization gear, and with his armament officer he worked out the designs for its installation. The plans were all destroyed in the second fire at Camp Borden in October of that year, and the idea was never revived. Another of his proposals (which was later to

become standard practice on fighter aircraft) was to mount machine guns on the wings of the aircraft where they would be outside the propeller arc ... while serving with the RCAF, he was instrumental in introducing the use of parachutes into the Canadian service and may also have played a part in their adoption by the RAF.

* * *

It was a tradition at Camp Borden for the officers to do some shooting every week, either skeet shooting, or target practice on the range. During his 14 months in command, Will was almost invariably the highest score on the station.

He was familiar with the aircraft types at Camp Borden because most had been transferred from the RAF wartime inventory. By 1923 these fighters and bombers were more and more difficult to maintain. They had been built for a short service life and a quick death. The temperature extremes in Canada, as well as the dryness in winter, and the winds and turbulence in summer, were brutal on wooden and fabric structures built on wartime assembly lines. Most of these machines had been given by Great Britain at the end of the war to Canada as part of a program to help foster aviation in the British Empire.

When Camp Borden was reactivated there were three flights in 1 Wing at the station, a refresher training flight with AVRO 504Ks, one flight of SE5as, and one of DH9as. But it was hard to keep the scout and bomber aircraft serviceable, and there were only two flights when Barker took command. Most flying was on the 504, it being the most common type in the CAF. Some 62 504s were included in the Imperial Gift allotment, but many had been written off in accidents since 1920. There were also solitary examples of the Bristol F2B Fighter, the Sopwith Snipe, the Martinsyde F6, and one or two Dehavilland DH4s.

Camp Borden was snowed in on several occasions over the winter of 1922-23. After one particularly heavy storm in late February, Barker received a telephone call from Billy Mitchell, deputy chief of the US Air Service. Mitchell wanted to fly into Camp Borden with two DH9 bombers from

Selfridge Field, outside Detroit. Barker said that was just fine, but he cautioned the American flyer to equip the aircraft with skis.

It appears that Mitchell wanted to come to Camp Borden, in the dead of winter, mainly to meet Barker. He had been on an inspection tour in the US since January, and his interest in CAF winter flying operations had to do with planned long distance flights with US Air Service aircraft to Asia via Alaska, and to Europe via Labrador and Iceland.

The two men may have previously met during the war but, if so, there is no record of it. However, Brig General Mitchell's bombing demonstrations against submarines, destroyers, and battleships in the summer of 1921 were well publicized. Will had taken a keen interest in these successful exercises, and knew Mitchell by reputation, as did Mitchell, Barker.

The airmen at the station levelled off the snow and marked the landing threshold with a large black circle, not unlike a bull's eye. Mitchell had not taken Barker's advice, and when he touched down, right on the bull's eye, the wheels of his DH9 dug into the snow, and the bomber tipped up on its nose, breaking the propeller and radiator. The pilot in the second bomber, an RAF officer named Christie, thought that a strip of high sweet clover was a runway. When he touched down, his machine was also damaged.

Will was relieved that nothing worse had happened, but he ribbed the Americans for their undignified arrival. They were now stuck in Camp Borden until replacement propellers and skis could be sent up. When the skis arrived the Canadians shook their heads in amazement, since they looked almost identical to those used by people for downhill skiing. While waiting for the aircraft to be repaired, Barker, Mitchell, and Christie travelled by horse and sleigh to the railway station at Angus, and on to Ottawa for a visit. Mitchell put the blame for the landing accident on his own shoulders:

[Wing] Commander Christie and I went, in February, 1923, to Camp Borden, Canada, having flown there from Detroit. The cold was intense. Our airplanes were equipped with wheels when skis should have been used on account of the deep snow. As a result, the machine was thrown forward on its nose but no serious damage was done. From Camp Borden we proceeded to the railroad station by horse and sleigh, a distance of about eight miles. It took us as long to cover the eight miles by sleigh as to traverse the two hundred miles from Detroit to Camp Borden by air.

While in Ottawa, Barker was called into the Chief of Staff's office for his personal congratulations. MacBrien had recommended him to become the honorary Air Force aide-de-camp (ADC) to the Governor-General, Baron Byng of Vimy, and the appointment had been approved. The honourary Royal Canadian Navy ADC was its commander, Commodore Walter Hose. There were about 20 honourary ADCs from the Army, including Colonel Peck, VC, and Major Pearkes, VC. Since Byng had five full-time ADCs working for him, the position meant simply that Barker could write the letters "adc" after his long list of decorations.

Barker and Mitchell shared many similar views about military aviation, and wrote each other after their Camp Borden meeting. Mitchell had high praise for Canada, exaggerating the percentage of Canadian flyers in the war, while describing them to his boss, Major General Mason Patrick, as blessed with flying talent:

The Canadians are particularly adapted to air work ... at the end of the war close to seventy percent of all pilots and observers serving in the British Air Force on the front against the Germans were Canadians. Some of these, however, were Americans who had joined the Canadian forces. The two great British air heroes of the war, Bishop and Barker, are Canadians (I stayed with Colonel Barker while at Camp Borden). This gives a prestige to aviation throughout the Dominion which is very great ... Our trip has resulted in an excellent understanding between ourselves and the Canadian authorities in every way and we have laid the foundation for cooperation along lines that are materially advantageous to us, particularly concerning winter flying in all its phases. When the time comes for establishing commercial lines in the North the Canadians are not at all adverse to the influx of American capital. The only thing they desire is to be able to control it.

Unlike Mitchell, Barker did not seek the limelight, and did not publish his views on air power very often. His first lecture on the subject for a military audience was at Royal Military College, Kingston, in 1922. His first essay on aircraft in war was in a book for boys.

He always drew directly on his war experience, particularly tactical air support to troops on the ground. He did not place much emphasis on aerial fighting in his lectures, and seldom mentioned anything of his own air fights. Barker differed from better

known air power advocates in his focus on the tactical over the strategic and on the specific over the abstract. His military hobby-horses were the development of the aircraft as a weapons platform; the tactics of air-to-surface attack; the value of long-range, low-level interdiction both day and night; and the role of aerial reconnaissance for the battlefield commander.

Unfortunately, this focus put him on the wrong end of the air-power spectrum for the age in which he lived. In the 1920s and 1930s it was strategic air power, the use of large bombers against major centres that consumed most of the attention and resources. It was a common belief in air forces at the time that the next war would be entirely aerial, dominated by bomber forces attacking military and civilian targets. Barker shared Mitchell's frustration about the slow pace of developments in aircraft technology in North America. Like Mitchell he was vocal in his disagreements with authority, and like him, he rarely compromised.

Airforce Magazine collection

Photo by Wayne Ralph

Air-Vice Marshal Thomas Lawrence in 1927 with the Hudson Strait Expedition, and in 1991 during an interview with the author.

It did not take a court martial to get Barker to leave the RCAF, but both he and Mitchell were no longer serving officers by the time Charles Lindbergh gave aviation a much-needed boost. Mitchell was resurrected by the US Congress as an important figure in air power after World War Two. It arranged by a special act to promote him to major general retroactive to his death in 1936. Barker's contributions in the 1920s have not been so honoured. His entire post-war career in the RCAF rated only one paragraph in the 800-page, *The Creation of a National Air Force*, Volume II of the official history of the RCAF.

Five years after the war, the CAF was forced to look beyond the pool of Great War veterans and think of the future. Pilot candidates were recruited from the Canadian Officer Training Corps (COTC) units at civilian universities, and from the gentlemen cadets at the Royal Military College. Barker was naturally involved in these plans for the first post-war, ab-initio pilot training. In April 1923 he wrote a letter to Gordon, outlining the deficiencies at Camp Borden. He requested an increase of 10 "labourers" at the station, five to be used as batmen for the new trainees:

... in this connection, it is pointed out that when the cadet training takes place, there will be somewhere in the neighbourhood of 45 officers to be looked after, and the request of one batman for 8 officers appears to be very reasonable ... in the RAF one batman per Squadron Leader, and one to every three officers is allowed ...

The condition, owing to lack of establishment, in the officers mess is disgraceful, and in the interest of the RCAF, this situation should be remedied ... it is doubly necessary to have a first-class mess, in view of the fact, that these cadets should be taught a good deal in the Officers Mess, and impressions they take away with them will either be for the good, or to the detriment of the RCAF.

At the beginning of 1923, the Department of National Defence replaced the Department of Militia and Defence, and the CAF became a directorate of this new government department, reporting to the Chief of the General Staff. A request was made to King George, through the Governor General, that the CAF have conferred the preface "Royal," which the Australian Air Force had been granted in 1921.

This was approved in March 1923, and routine orders and documents reflected this change, although the official birthday of the Royal Canadian Air Force was not celebrated until 1 April 1924. The blue-grey RAF uniform with gold buttons, and the motto of that service were adopted. But the midnight blue CAF uniform, with silver badges and buttons, could still be seen on air stations as late as 1926.

Barker was not an aviator who believed in specialization, and he felt that if one could fly, one ought to fly anything that came one's way. The fact that you were not formally trained to do something should never be a hindrance. With this philosophy in mind, he appointed one of his pilots, Pilot Officer Thomas Albert Lawrence, to be the head of the Engine Repair Section at Camp Borden.

Lawrence was born in 1895 in Creemore, Ontario, and attended school only a few miles from Camp Borden. After several years in the CEF, he finally got his long-awaited transfer into the RFC in 1918. He was on his way to 24 Squadron on the SE5a when he came down with influenza. By the time he had recovered the war was over. After surviving a crash in an SE5a on a ferry trip, he returned to Canada in July 1919 to his family's farm at Cookstown, a few miles south of Camp Borden. He recalled to the author how his life took on a new direction:

I never thought about flying anymore. It was gone out of my head ... I stayed on the farm that winter and following spring. I didn't know what I was going to do. I knew I wasn't going to farm, that was for sure. But I had no intention of what I was going to do with my life. I was sitting on a fence, giving the horses their wind, we were doing some ploughing. I was having a cigarette, and I heard an aeroplane overhead. I knew what it was right away, the rotary engine of an AVRO trainer. It was right over my head at about 1,000 feet ... we were directly on a route from Camp Borden to Toronto ... right then I said, "Aviation."

Lawrence was accepted by the CAF as air mechanic trainee, but managed to gain a flying position after a few months. He met Barker for the first time when he was sent to Camp Borden in the spring of 1923 for a flying instructor's course. Despite some experience in the repair shops, Tommy was taken aback by Barker's order to manage the Engine Repair Section. By deferring to the guidance of an excellent fitter, Flight Sergeant John Brims Boyd (later group captain), his section ran smoothly and Tommy liked working for the new station commander:

I found Barker to be a very fine person; he was one of the finest officers I ever served under. Keen, he was keen at flying, and he was willing to talk to any of his people and tell them things. Now I knew Bishop; Bishop was entirely different. He didn't have that capability of getting down and talking to his lower people. Now I wouldn't blame him for it, he was just a different makeup, that's all, but Barker was that makeup ... his [left] arm was practically useless ... but he played tennis one-handed, he could just throw the ball up with his left hand, and he golfed one-handed, and he shot skeet, and he'd knock down 24 out of 25 most of the time [although] his left hand was just barely able to hold the gun ... he was a terrific man, anything he set out to do, he was bound to do it ... we all loved him, he was a good mixer with anyone.

Lawrence remembered Barker's experiments with an aircraft shotgun installation as a touch bizarre, but full of his characteristic energy:

Air-Vice Marshal Kenneth Guthrie in 1917 as a 16-year-old pilot in training, and in 1991 during an interview with the author.

As you know, in those days they used to do a lot of aerial fighting by camera gun, and there had been many, many accidents and he was all against this, and he was trying to find a [better] way. In the meantime, he was also trying to get a shotgun to fire through the propeller, instead of bullets. He tried to get Ottawa to approve buying a repeating shotgun ... He and a sergeant/armourer at Camp Borden were going to put this in an AVRO trainer themselves, the two of them. Ottawa said no, you can't have the money, so he bought it himself, and they put it in, and they flew it, and it worked ...

Barker then asked, "What will we do for targets?" They started first with pigeons. Somebody in the back seat would keep the pigeons, and when he got to 3,000 feet he would toss the pigeon overboard. Well, a pigeon would go straight for the ground. That was no good. So his next step was seagulls ... which were a protected bird in Ontario. He got permission from the Ontario government to capture some live gulls and use them to test this out ... he knew people in Toronto.

He had eight or nine gulls by the side of his house at the station. But in all his trials Barker never shot one himself. His adjutant, George Walsh, took a bet with Barker that he could shoot one from the back seat with a shotgun before he [Barker] could shoot one with the mounted gun. Once, more by accident than anything, Walsh managed to shoot one. I went up with George Brookes ... and the AVRO 504 could just overtake the gull ... and I managed to run one down—it died more from a heart attack than anything else.

Barker encouraged his officers and men to compete in shooting competitions. He, Lawrence, and another junior officer on temporary duty at Camp Borden, Kenneth Guthrie, were members of the station skeet shooting team. Guthrie was a "visiting fireman," doing equipment research for the CGAO branch.

Kenneth McGregor Guthrie was born in 1900 in Guelph, Ontario. His father, Reverend Donald Guthrie, was for several years the minister of the First Presbyterian Church on Park Avenue in Baltimore, Maryland. Ken spent his winters there, and his summers in the Gatineau Hills near Ottawa. He used to memorize his father's sermons, and could mimic his delivery. One of Ken's Sunday school teachers in 1912 was a young man a few years older, Gerry Birks, the same man who was Barker's right-hand sidekick a few years later at 66 Squadron.

Ken got interested in flying when he saw his American cousin, John Blair Guthrie, in the attractive RFC "maternity" uniform. John Guthrie was killed in action on 10 May 1918 in Italy. A Bristol Fighter pilot of 34 Squadron, he and his observer, H.V. Thornton, were attacked by four enemy aircraft at 16,000 feet. Their F2B fell in flames behind enemy lines, and the credit went to Frank Linke-Crawford, who also shot down another American, George Forder of 28, later that same afternoon.

Guthrie took his RFC training in Texas over the winter of 1917-18 (he was a witness to the fatal crash of Capt Vernon Castle). Arriving in the UK in May 1918, he flew Short seaplanes at Calshot for the last months of the war. On the ship home to Canada he played craps and poker, and accumulated winnings of $2,000. After a spell as a car salesman and quartermaster in a military hospital he was accepted as a storesman with the Air Board's CGAO branch.

He met Tommy Lawrence when they worked together at Roberval, Quebec, building seaplane docks. Like Tommy, Ken keenly wanted to get back into the cockpit of a flying machine, any flying machine: "I couldn't fly landplanes worth sour apples ... but I knew how to fly seaplanes." Lawrence and Guthrie took the manual labour in stride, stuck with the CAF/RCAF through the lean years, and were Air Vice-Marshals during the Second World War.

When Barker learned of Guthrie's love of cards, he invited him as a fourth to the evening bridge games with Jean, and the station's armament officer, Flight Lieut Arthur C. Snow. Guthrie quickly noticed that Barker was easy to read because he used his atrophied left hand to sort his cards by suit.

One day an ailing friend of Ken's asked him to stand in as station Orderly Officer for the day, although Ken was only on attached duty. Regimental Sergeant Major Leonard J. Dyte, also on attached duty at Camp Borden as the disciplinarian, was unhappy with the deportment of the fitters and riggers, who had a habit of wearing black socks on their hands, in lieu of regulation black gloves, which presumably cost too much money.

The RSM asked Guthrie to accompany him on the morning parade, and every time Guthrie made a comment to an air mechanic about his choice of hand covering: "Where are your gloves; on your feet?" Dyte wrote the man's name for a punishment parade: "I've got his name, Sir." The scrutiny resulted in the engine repair and airframe repair sections being nearly deserted, most of the fitters and riggers bashing around the parade square.

The officers-in-charge of the Engine Repair and Airframe Repair Sections complained to Barker, who shouted at Ken: "What the hell are you doing upsetting the calm of my happy station?" Guthrie wasn't bothered by this outburst—he always figured that Barker knew that it was Dyte's idea. Dyte asked to stay on with these inventive airmen, rather than return to the army, and retired with the rank of squadron leader, by then a living legend to the pre-1939 generation of RCAF flyers and airmen.

* * *

There were two fires at Camp Borden in 1923, the first on 29 August, destroying the aircraft repair section, No 8 hangar, dope shop, paint shop, and latrine; and the second on 16 October that destroyed the technical stores building. The shotgun-equipped AVRO was consumed in the second fire. Barker either lost interest or did not have the money to pay for a second shotgun. A military Court of Inquiry was convened twice, but its findings were inconclusive. The incidents were raised in the House of Commons several months afterwards, when a Member asked about the value of losses, and the findings of the investigators.

Defence Minister E.M. MacDonald reported that the first fire had destroyed $230,000 of assets, and the second $30,000, with both buildings being

destroyed. The cause of the fires was unknown, but the second blaze suggested perhaps an "incendiary origin."

Quite a few of the Imperial Gift aircraft were burned up, including several of the SE5s, and some of the German machines. Many of the CAF's officers were happy to see them burn, including Guthrie, believing that no new aircraft would ever be ordered for the CAF as long as an inventory of Great War relics survived. The aircraft were difficult to maintain, and as they aged, more hazardous to fly. It is possible that some enterprising airmen took the initiative to accelerate the replacement aircraft program.

Two Great War flying boats, Curtiss H16s, had sat outside the hangars at Camp Borden from fall 1919 until spring 1923, over four Canadian winters and summers. The twin-engine machines were patterned after the British Felixstowe F3, but powered by United States Liberty rather than Rolls-Royce Eagle engines. At the direction of CAF headquarters, one of the H16s was restored to airworthy condition, and put in the water at Barrie. The plan was for the commanding officer of the Winnipeg station to fly it out west. He was the famous Basil D. Hobbs, the only Canadian flyer of the Great War to be credited with the destruction of a Zeppelin, *and* the sinking of a submarine.

Hobbs did not like the flying boat, and on his first and only flight he ripped away the step below the hull on landing. He refused to have anything more to do with it, and caught a train home. Not long after, Tommy Lawrence was called to the station commander's office. According to Lawrence, Will began the conversation:

"I have a wire here, and you are to fly that boat to Ottawa, to Rockcliffe, right away."

I told Barker: "I have never flown a twin-engine aircraft before."

"Oh, well," he said, "we'll never learn later."

Away I went. I had two excellent men, a flight-sergeant rigger, and a flight-sergeant fitter. Ten days later Barker calls me in and says: "You are to go back to Ottawa and fly that boat to Winnipeg. I don't know why the hell some of them can't fly it out there." …

I had one helluva trip. I had engine trouble here and there … once just west of North Bay … I had to dodge around an electrical storm … one engine didn't respond, the throttle control wasn't connected, and I had to run it full out so as to avoid getting into a flat spin because it was a very poor aircraft to fly on one engine … I had flown practically across Superior about 10 feet off the water … terrible weather … I knocked the wing-tip float off the wing, [looked] like it had been cut by a jack-knife … I managed to recover from that. I was very lucky really.

After 12 days unserviceable at Port Arthur during which repairs were completed at the local shipyard, Lawrence was ready to leave with his two crewmen for Kenora and Winnipeg. To his surprise, Barker and his family stepped off the steamship just arrived at the dock. As Lawrence related it, Will laughed and said:

"Is this as far as you've got?"
I said: "I've had lots of trouble."
"Is it flyable now?"
"Yes," I said.
"I want to fly it," he said.
I near fainted, because I knew his physical problem with his arm … he wouldn't let me go with him. I was really very afraid, not because of his ability to fly it, but because it was such a dog-gone big machine. Getting it off the step and off the water would be most difficult, because it was underpowered … he shouldn't have done it, you see, putting me on the spot, because I was working for Headquarters and was in charge of the H16. But I couldn't say no to him … immediately after getting it off the water he turned back, flying low directly over the hotel at the head of the docks … Actually the Port Arthur papers wrote it up the next day—"Dangerous Flying"—and *it was*. I was scared to death really. [I thought] my God, I

don't know how that man is flying that aircraft that way. He came in and landed and taxied back, and went off with his wife and father-in-law … I was astounded … I guess you could call him stubborn.

Despite this harrowing experience, Lawrence remembered Will with affection: "I liked the man. I had tremendous respect for the man. If I had been in a squadron with him, I would have followed him anywhere."

* * *

The RCAF finally included parachutes in their aircraft in 1925, something Barker had been lobbying for ever since his war experiences in 1918 had made him a believer. Flying Officer Albert Carter and Corporal A. Anderson trained in Illinois with the US Air Service as parachute riggers, and they in turn trained another 16 on how to pack a chute, at Camp Borden, High River, and Vancouver. The first parachute descents in the RCAF were by Carter and Anderson. It was not mandatory to jump after learning how to pack a parachute, but 35 jumps were made in 1925, many by pilots who might one day have to use a parachute in earnest.

Barker was unquestionably the most knowledgeable person at Camp Borden about artillery cooperation, and a great advocate for army support. Therefore, it was to be expected that the most extensive practical course on "shoots" was held at his station. Thirty-eight flying hours were devoted solely to this tactical training between 19 November and 5 December 1923. This was more than one-third of the total military flying hours logged in 1923 by the CAF.

However, in the winter of 1923-24 there was almost no authorized flying at Camp Borden, and Barker was relieved to move to Ottawa in early January to replace Lindsay Gordon as acting director of the CAF. In the first three years of the CAF's existence, several officers held the so-called "acting director" position. Since the CAF was not a permanent military formation at the time, there was no such position as "director." The switch in names from CAF to RCAF did not change this; the first permanent "director" did not take command of the RCAF till 1925.

Gordon was sent over to the Canadian High Commission in the UK in mid-February pending his appointment to RAF Staff College to attend Course 3. "Jimmy" Scott was finishing up there, the first CAF officer to attend and graduate. With Gordon on his way over to the UK, and Scott not returned, Barker was the most senior wing commander in Ottawa, other than Ernest Stedman, who was assistant director for supply and research.

It was General MacBrien who appointed Barker to his new position. By so doing, he guaranteed that Canada's most decorated war hero held the senior post in the new RCAF on its official birthday, 1 April 1924. In his characteristic way, Barker threw himself into every aspect of the job, official or unofficial.

He hatched a scheme to obtain several Camels, aided and abetted by the RAF exchange staff down in Washington, DC. His ultimate goal was to have some or all of the machines re-fitted with more tractable in-line engines. The Camels, 2F.1 ship-variants, arrived in the summer of 1925 to be spares for three Imperial Gift machines located at Camp Borden. They probably never flew in Canada, but served as training devices for the RCAF. The particular Camel that was, for several decades, on display at the old Canadian War Museum on Sussex Drive in Ottawa, is the lone survivor from this batch that he scrounged in 1924.

As part of the birth of the RCAF that year, everybody in the old CAF was discharged and most, though not all, were re-enlisted or commissioned in the RCAF. The salaries were actually lower in the RCAF, and that explained some of the personnel losses. A new set of serial numbers was issued for airman and officers, and the allocation for the officers appeared to follow no particular logic, being based neither on seniority, nor on position held, nor on location.

Even from the UK, Scott managed to get the first serial number for officers, "C1," assigned to him (perhaps due to his higher seniority in rank). Barker was C2," Stedman "C3," and Gordon was well down the list, despite his rank, at "C13." The Weekly Or-

ders for the RCAF, issued on Tuesday, 1 April 1924, were signed by Barker as acting director.

Barker and Scott had not patched up their differences after Will came back into the military. They were complete opposites in personality and character, and were remembered that way by those who served under them. Neither man was likely to forgive previous slights. But conflict had been alleviated because Scott was out of the country for over a year.

Scott's military career progress had always been a bit ahead of Barker's. He had been the first superintendent of the Certificate Branch, the first Canadian private pilot licence holder, the first Controller of Civil Aviation, and so it was no surprise that he received the first serial number in the RCAF. Scott wanted to become the first permanent director of the RCAF.

When Barker left for the United Kingdom in late May, Scott replaced him. Within six weeks he was promoted to temporary group captain, the first RCAF officer to hold this rank. He was appointed the RCAF's first permanent director and confirmed in rank on 1 April 1925. Volume II of the RCAF official history had this to say about Scott:

As a former commander of the Canadian Air Force and the first Canadian officer to attend the RAF Staff College, Scott was a logical choice as director. A no-nonsense commander —tough, forceful and direct—his somewhat arbitrary manner was more apt to generate respect than affection during his four years as the RCAF's senior officer.

There were many, including Guthrie and Lawrence, who felt that Barker was a better man for the job. Both held the view that, for all his rough edges, he could have done more to advance the interests of the junior service. However, being the commander of an air force involves more than just operational competence. In Camp Borden, Barker's free-wheeling, spontaneous style worked well, but in Ottawa he was required to be restrained, diplomatic, even polished. This he was not, as Guthrie sadly recalled to the author:

Barker was a completely different character [from Scott and Bishop] ... a farm boy from Dauphin ... he didn't have the *savoir faire*, the social knowledge ... he didn't have the social graces. His wife did. A husband does not like a wife telling him, "Use the other fork," or having to do it. And she didn't like doing it ... In the capital city here everybody is watching you ... Those jobs are snooty jobs because you are under the glare ... If you don't put down your knife and fork properly on your plate when you're finished [well, people take notice].

I liked him ... but as I say, he couldn't handle social responsibility ... Now Jimmy Scott was a very good looking fellow ... had a lot of girl friends ... and a nice guy. But I disliked him heartily at first. I thought he was a stuffed up old poop ... When I met him down here in Ottawa he was a social dandy ... He came from a very old Quebec City family ... he was a Scott of Quebec City, which put him ahead of any Scott in Montreal.

Barker had expected Scott or Gordon to replace him as the head of the RCAF, and had written a confidential memorandum to the Chief of Staff, voicing his unhappiness. He claimed that other station commanders, knowing he was leaving, were anxious about the future. The station commanders at this time included "Black Mike" McEwen, Winnipeg; Pat Cuffe, High River, Alberta; Earl Godfrey, Vancouver; Lloyd Breadner, Camp Borden; and John Tudhope, Dartmouth, Nova Scotia.

It was risky to write such a blunt memorandum. However, Will had never been one to hesitate before going to the top of the ladder, and his carefully crafted communication to MacBrien on 26 March 1924 laid it all on the line:

What I am about to outline and endeavour to convey to you is most difficult. It seems impossible to avoid personalities. This is regretted very much, but there is no other course open, if I am to submit to you my views as clearly as possible.

During the Conference last week with the Station Commanding Officers there was some discussion concerning the officer who would succeed me as Acting Director ...

I was asked who would succeed me, and in reply stated that in all probability the officer would be Wing Commander J.S. Scott. Each Station Commanding Officer expressed a lack of confidence in this officer, the reasons put forward being –

(a) Wing Commander Scott's arbitrary manner and his method of dealing with all ranks junior to him.

(b) His short flying service in a theatre of war.

(c) His lack of ability from a flying standpoint.

The records show that Wing Commander Scott served for four months in France, of which three months as a flying officer, and one month as a flight lieutenant. He then crashed and was admitted to hospital, and his subsequent service together with his subsequent promotions, was all in Canada or the United States.

Barker went on to note that Gordon's war service was all in England or near the English coastline, rather than on the continent. He concluded:

So far as I am concerned, I do not lay claim to this appointment on the grounds of war record, length of service at the Front, experience in flying since the war, or on any other grounds, but I only respectfully wish to point out that I cannot see my way clear to at any time serve in the Royal Canadian Air Force as junior to either of the two officers mentioned above ...

My one desire is to serve the Department to the best of my ability, and to state my own case clearly, and if I am to return to civil life, I do not think the Department would be justified in incurring the expense of sending me overseas, much as I desire to go.

Barker's memorandum was somewhat disingen-
uous. Did he receive any reassurance from MacBrien
and, on that basis, depart for the UK? There is nothing in Barker's surviving military record to support
this idea, or even that MacBrien read and responded
to his memorandum.

MacBrien was distracted by his own conflicts
with Desbarats and MacDonald, MacBrien and
Commodore Hose had been hostile to each other
for years, and by early 1927 it was clear that Hose
had won the bureaucratic battle, and MacBrien had
lost. In frustration, the general volunteered to take
a reduction in rank and go to China on any mission
the head of the Imperial General Staff in the UK
might wish. He was not taken up on his offer.

* * *

Barker started his new job in the UK in June 1924.
He was granted $6.00 *per diem*, $2.00 less than
he had requested, which combined with his wing
commander's salary of $3,700, and allowances of
$400 for dependants, $200 for rations, and $500 for
quarters, gave him a gross annual income of $7,300,
or about £1,500.

As liaison officer he kept informed on all aspects
of aviation in the UK, attended functions as the
RCAF's representative, and handled administrative
inquiries from Ottawa. The work was not strenuous,
and his position and income permitted a social life
on a loftier scale than Toronto or Ottawa. Paradoxically, Will's stature in London and with the RAF was
considerably higher than back home. Memories of
the war had faded somewhat, but not to the same
degree as in Canada, and Barker's record was legendary. His acquaintance with Edward, Prince of Wales,
was a distinct plus in some circles.

For Jean Barker it was probably the first time
that being an officer's wife seemed to have something
to recommend it. She was in her first home away
from her father's sphere of influence; she had household servants to manage, and an energetic daughter
to care for. Dinner parties included some of the public figures of the day in London, including her cousin
Billy, who was becoming a successful expatriate, following in a long line of Canadians in Britain such as

Max Aitken, Bonar Law, and James Dunn. Bishop
even had his own polo team, and played occasionally
with Sir Winston Churchill.

After settling into Room 296 at Adastral House,
the Air Ministry headquarters on Kingsway, Barker
immediately wanted to get out. He travelled as much
as possible to military events, flying stations, and
aircraft manufacturers. He spent 21 July at Farnbor-
ough, and a week later attended the Naval Review at
Portsmouth. In October he was invited by Sir Sefton
Brancker, at the time head of civil aviation in the UK,
to a four-day meeting of the International Commission for Air Navigation in Paris.

During his two years in the UK he frequently
ran afoul of the tight-fisted rules governing Canadian officers on overseas duty. Capt B.J.W. Spink,
paymaster at DND Headquarters, and R.P. Brown,
the chief accountant, took their financial responsibilities very seriously. Barker got no sympathy when
he complained how much it had cost him to move
his family to England. He attempted to claim tips
and gratuities, without receipts, but had no success.

Certainly, £1,500 was a healthy income in the
UK in 1924, but did not go far in London. Will
spent almost £25 to have a Wimpole Street dentist
take care of his teeth, when the annual allowance
laid down by DND regulations was only around
£4. Desbarats approved the expense, but the deputy
minister also scribbled a cautionary note that RCAF
officers should be directed, as Army officers were, to
have their teeth attended to before leaving Canada.

The RAF was generous in letting RCAF liaison
officers fly its machines, but Will was horrified to learn
that parachutes were not universally used. He wrote to
Desbarats in January 1926 requesting one:

> Owing to the fact that there have been a num-
> ber of accidents in the R.A.F. which evidently
> cannot be explained, I do not feel inclined to
> fly in the future without being equipped with
> a parachute ...
>
> I am making arrangements for some
> flying prior to attending the Staff College in
> May, and of course while there shall be doing
> a good deal of flying, therefore it is requested,

please, that I be issued with one parachute complete for my own use.

A few weeks later an Irving "Service Seat, Pack Type Parachute" arrived at the Air Ministry, and Will took it with him everywhere, and always wore it in the air.

Inevitably, Barker found the duties of a liaison officer too administrative. In his search for excitement, he made a proposal in January 1925 to MacBrien and the RAF Air Ministry that he visit the Near East, in particular, Cairo, Egypt, and Baghdad, Iraq. The RAF had several squadrons engaged in a frontier police action on behalf of the Iraqi government, suppressing rebel chieftains, and tribes such as the Bedouin and Kurdish.

BARKER – MITCHELL CORRESPONDENCE ON THE VALUE OF PARACHUTES

William Barker thought that all RAF and RCAF pilots should have parachutes and he lobbied for a change in RAF policy. He enlisted Billy Mitchell as a supporter, writing him in April 1925 for data on US Air Service experience:

Would it be possible for you to provide me with some information which I require rather urgently for a campaign I am conducting in this country.

I have always been a great believer in the parachute, and while in Ottawa about 8 months ago, I manage [sic] to gain approval for the purchase of a number of your Service parachutes, and have carried on the propaganda here until the Air Ministry has now placed an order for some sixty of your parachutes.

Of course this number will only cover the test pilots, and as I am very anxious to press the matter to a point where it would be compulsory for all pilots to wear parachutes, I would like some figures to support my contentions.

I have noticed from time to time that lives have been saved in your Service through their use, and if you could have your Intelligence Department despatch to me a rough outline of how many lives have been saved since [your] parachutes came into use, I should be most grateful.

One of these parachutes has recently been issued to me, and I do not intend to go into the air in future without one. We have had some very nasty accidents, due to collisions where, undoubtedly, parachutes would have saved the lives of the personnel ...

I would like to say that your Engineering Division has rendered the greatest possible service to aviation as a whole, in my judgment, in the perfecting of your parachute. There is nothing to compare with it in Europe.

Mitchell responded within a couple of weeks, indicating that all the pilots and passengers flying with the Army Air Service equip themselves with a seat-pack chute:

So far as I know or can find out, there has never been a failure of functioning of the parachutes except where weights have been dropped to test certain defects that were previously known. To date the lives of twelve of our Air Service men have been saved by the use of parachutes. The use of parachutes greatly increases the confidence with which pursuit pilots fly in the squadrons. They are no longer afraid of collisions. During the past year, every pilot who has collided with another has been saved by his parachute. In attacking also the pilots will close in much more readily when equipped with parachutes. I have found no deterrent elements in their use. You will remember that many of us thought it would lead to pilots' abandoning their ships before they should, and a whole lot of other things. While this may be so to a limited extent, I don't think it makes much difference. If we had had parachutes during the war, as you know, many a good man would still be with us.

REPORT

OF

WING COMMANDER W/G. BARKER, V.C., D.S.O., M.C.

ON VISIT TO IRAQ, MARCH 1925.

R.A.F. Staff College,

Andover, Hants.

13th July 1925.

Subject:-   Report on Iraq.

Sir,

I have the honour to submit the following report on Iraq.

I visited that theatre of operations in March in accordance with your instuctions.

This report was ready for despatch shortly after my return but was held up pending the receipt of photographs and information from Iraq.

The photographs showing the effect of bombing operations against tribes and the report on the operations against the Wahabi were furnished by the Air Ministry on the understanding that both would be treated as "Secret".

I have the honour to be,

Sir,

Your Obedient Servant,

The Secretary,

Wing Commander.

Cover letter for Barker's report on a two-week visit to the war zone in Iraq in March 1925.

It was a trial balloon by Barker but, surprisingly, Scott recommended the trip as a good preparation for Barker's year at Staff College. Desbarats approved the mission, despite the estimated travel cost of over $450 for the three-week deployment. The RAF had already agreed to absorb any cost in the theatre. Barker left London in the first week of March by the "Orient Express." From Trieste, Italy, he caught a boat to Alexandria, Egypt.

Early on 12 March, in Cairo, he boarded a Vickers Vernon twin-engined transport, belonging to 45 Squadron, the same unit that flew Camels in Italy in 1918. The Vernons flew a weekly mail-run between Cairo and Baghdad, carrying miscellaneous cargo, soldiers, and visiting airmen. At Hinaidi aerodrome outside Baghdad, Barker met Squadron Leader Corballis, the commanding officer of 55 Squadron.

With the exception of the Vernons, all the other aircraft in Iraq were well known to Barker, since he had flown them during the Great War. They were DH9 bombers (8, 30, and 55 Squadrons), Bristol F2B Fighters (6 Squadron), and Sopwith Snipes (1 Squadron). According to Barker, the aircraft were tired, overloaded for a hot climate, and 15 mph slower than their wartime best. As an observer in Corballis's DH9, he visited several outposts, including Mosul, Kirkuk, Erbil, Rowanduz, Amadia, and Zakko, and flew a reconnaissance trip along the Iraqi frontier, escorted by two Bristol F2B Fighters.

The mountainous terrain in Iraq was somewhat reminiscent of northern Italy. Barker was greatly impressed with the airmanship of the RAF pilots, particularly in such tired, overburdened aircraft. Any forced landing put the British flyers at great risk.

Photo of Barker's Staff College Course at Andover, England. Barker is in the back row, third from left.

The tribes against which they flew bombing and strafing missions could bring down aircraft with rifles, and the RAF had lost an F2B in flames the week before Barker arrived.

He was pleased to see close ongoing cooperation between air and ground forces, pointing out that troop transport by air took a few hours instead of many days by rail and foot:

> During these operations [in Kurdistan, 1923] the closest cooperation was maintained between the ground forces and air intercommunication was maintained between the columns by means of pack wireless sets and by aircraft dropping and picking up messages ...
> On May 4th, 1924, serious disturbances broke out in Kirkuk ... The nearest unit was ... at Baghdad, 150 miles from Kirkuk. For a detachment ... to have proceeded by ground would have meant a 12-hour rail journey and a four days' march ... As it was, however, by the use of aircraft 66 officers and other ranks arrived at Kirkuk within 8 hours of the outbreak of the trouble.

Barker told Mitchell in his April letter, that he had just been in Iraq, and he may have passed along a copy of his report, since the US Air Service deputy chief used the example of air power in Iraq in his book published during his 1925 general court martial: "The aeroplanes fly over the country at will, are able to put down uprisings quickly, transport troops to places where they are needed on the ground, and to cover much more country with less effort than is possible by any other means."

Barker filed a 44-page report on his visit to the Middle East with the Deputy Minister of Defence. It was classified "Secret" because of attached RAF documents on specific bombing missions.

The Barker report was a well-reasoned analysis of the utility of air power against rebel forces, illustrated by the RAF's and Barker's own photographs. But it had little relevance to RCAF operations, and it is doubtful that it was given anything other than cursory attention. Between 1925 and 1945, the report was drawn from Central Records only twice. It sat in a locked DND filing cabinet, until being declassified in a routine administrative way, more than 60 years after being sent from London to Ottawa.

* * *

At the beginning of May 1925, Barker and his family packed up and moved to the village of Chilbolton, not far from Andover, home of the RAF Staff College. The commandant at Andover was Air Vice-Marshal H.R.M. Brooke-Popham. Will attended Course 4, graduating on 5 March 1926. The 29 students on course with him were an interesting cross-section of junior and senior officers of not only the RAF and RCAF, but the RAAF, the Royal Navy, and the British and Indian Armies.

It was, not surprisingly, a seasoned group of students, with ranks ranging between flight lieutenant to wing commander or equivalent, with 21 of the 29 being decorated. Some on this course rose to RAF air rank, including T.L. Leigh-Mallory; C.E.H. Medhurst; the Honourable R.A. Cochrane; H.P. Lloyd; as well as S.J. Goble of the RAAF and A.E. Godfrey of the RCAF.

All students on course at Staff College were expected to deliver lectures on prepared subjects. Barker's lectures drew on his extensive Great War experience in artillery support, reconnaissance, and tactical bombing. But his thinking about the next war showed not only imagination, but also a thorough appreciation of what had not worked in the Great War. Raymond Collishaw had been a classmate of Lindsay Gordon's on the previous course. His appraisal of RAF Staff College, and Navy and Army attitudes, as related to historian Ronald Dodds, gives a good sense of what Barker faced in presenting his own air power requirements:

> The planning section of the Air Staff used the Staff College to examine problems and plans but little inspiration was forthcoming. There was a tendency at Andover towards stereotype thinking and an absence of any stimulus to use the imagination when evolving staff solutions.

Conservative solutions were normally the only acceptable answers to a problem and although they had the merit of being based on practical experience they lacked the vision and concept of a broader use of air power ...

The Naval Staff seemed unable to conceive any need to develop an air striking force capable of sinking the enemy's battleships and regarded their big ships as quite immune from anything that an enemy's air force might undertake against them. The General Staff of the Army considered reconnaissance as the main contribution of the air force and gave little serious thought to the development of effective air support.

Barker forecast a future, two-seater, close-air-support aircraft, not yet designed. Its capabilities, including good top speed, and very short takeoff and landing capability, match pretty closely that of a modern attack or reconnaissance helicopter:

... [the] type of machine for the future ... should be capable of a normal speed of over 200 and capable of a diving speed greatly exceeding this ... At once this question will arise—Can a pilot gain information at that speed? I feel sure that he can. The method to be adopted should, in my opinion, be along these lines:

(a) The observer to act as gunner and to be concerned with defence only.

(b) The pilot to carry out the actual reconnaissance.

(c) That the situation should be fairly well defined from above 1000 feet; the pilot should then confirm his information at the greatest speed possible and at a height where uniforms are easily distinguishable.

This type of machine should be able to land in small spaces. I believe that regardless of intercommunication development, that to able to land to land at a Formation Headquarters will always be of the greatest value.

Due to his experience in northern Italy, Barker believed that the bombing of aerodromes and army facilities should be conducted at very low altitudes, to avoid detection and the hazards of anti-aircraft fire:

... it becomes increasingly important to evade anti-aircraft fire and search-lights ... I also believe that there is a great future for long distance low daylight raids. The advantages would be:

(a) Avoidance of anti-aircraft fire.

(b) Surprise.

(c) A greater weight could be carried with engines throttled down.

(d) No heated clothing, oxygen, etc., need be carried; a great saving in weight.

Barker also said that effective bombing and artillery shoots demanded the direct suppression of enemy anti-aircraft batteries—something he had practised on his own shoots during the war. The development of aircraft and missiles specialized to attack enemy anti-aircraft and radar installations (in the US military, so-called "Wild Weasel" squadrons) certainly would have met with Barker's approval.

Much of what Barker spoke about does not sound provocative today, but was well ahead of its time. While on course he had opportunities to view various exercises and war games, and had a sharp eye for stupid practices that would not work in wartime, or were dangerous to airmen. He was critical of an RAF torpedo attack by four three-plane formations that he witnessed on 14 September 1925 against the Royal Navy battleship, HMS *Hood*. He wrote that such badly planned and executed attacks "make the Royal Air Force appear ridiculous in the eyes of the Navy." Barker was aboard the *Hood*, and wrote a four-page analysis of what he saw and heard:

The method of attack was very crude and would have proved a failure in actual warfare ... Except for the second three machines the flying was very poor. I did not see any other machine even execute an ordinary turn ... During my attachment I failed to meet any

Naval Officer who believed in the effectiveness of the present aircraft and ... the torpedo and bomb ... It appears to me that, if progress is to be made, conclusive demonstrations should be carried out in conjunction with the Navy.

Barker advocated the use of large fragmentation bombs in preference to torpedoes, delivered at very low altitude, and designed to inflict maximum damage to the fire-control and superstructure of capital ships, and the landing decks of aircraft carriers:

I am ... firmly convinced that bombs of three or four thousand pounds, not intended for penetration, would make a shambles of the deck and would destroy the Central Gunnery Controls and do other damage to the signal arrangements which would reduce the efficiency of a capital ship by at least 50%.

Perhaps his most lasting idea, and the one that was later introduced in the Hawker Hurricane and Supermarine Spitfire, was multiple guns for fighters, installed within the wings. He may not have been the first to propose the idea, but his RCAF colleagues always remembered Barker for advocating that future fighter designs eliminate synchronization gear and have all guns outboard of the propeller so as to increase the fire power of the machine.

In addition to prepared assignments, students were permitted a random lecture on a subject of their own choosing once a month. To the chagrin of the Staff College's directing staff, Barker delivered the same lecture month after month. His subject— multiple gun armament. For years after, students from the RCAF who attended the College or worked at the Air Ministry heard this story about Barker's obsession. He persisted with the idea with any aircraft manufacturers he met while in the UK, and Air Vice-Marshal Lawrence, for one, believed Barker influenced their thinking on the subject.

When Barker graduated from his course, Robert Brooke-Popham gave him the most accurate assessment he ever received:

A strong character, self-possessed, and has the courage of his own convictions. Sociable, good-natured and cheerful. Expresses his views forcibly in speech, but often does not carry conviction in paper work. Takes an interest in all practical subjects on which his opinions have been of considerable value. In practical work his self-confidence and determination can be relied upon to carry him through any difficulty. He is more suitable for command than work in an office. Recommended for P.S.A.

Wing Commander Barker had been advised by Group Captain Scott in February that, upon graduation in March from Staff College, he would be appointed to command No 1 Flying Training Station, Camp Borden. Barker may have got drunk on his last day at Staff College, out of anger and frustration about his stalled career. He had been asked to be a dinner speaker at the graduation ceremonies, but was "indisposed" that evening.

He moved back to the Air Ministry for a few weeks until his replacement, Squadron Leader Walter Kenny, arrived in late May or early June. Barker probably had made up his mind to resign from the RCAF before Scott's order assigning him to Camp Borden. In a note scribbled circa 1925 to a former Camel pilot, Lieut H.N.E. "Daddy" Row, ex-66 Squadron, who was looking for a flying job, Will wrote: "Sorry to hear that you are having not the luck you deserve. I am afraid I cannot promise anything in the C.A.F. as it is so small and over establishment. It is not much of a show and as a matter of fact I am leaving it soon myself."

Will, Jean and their daughter, left for Canada on the *Minnedosa* on 17 June 1926. At Will's request, he was granted a month's leave of absence until the end of July, which he spent at his father-in-law's home in Toronto. At that time he asked Scott for a leave extension to 10 August, and an interview with General MacBrien. It is not known whether the interview took place. MacBrien was himself miserably unhappy as Chief of Staff, and by the end of the year he was on the retired list. On 19 August, Barker submitted his resignation. It was approved by Mac-Brien and gazetted a week later.

Depressed though he was by the failure of his RCAF career, Barker did not entirely close the door on a military future. A few days later he wrote MacBrien, asking for his name to be placed on the "Reserve Air Force" list, which did not then exist, but was anticipated: "I would very much like to be definitely informed in this connection for it has a bearing on my future plans. Again thanking you for your many kindnesses and with best wishes from my wife and myself."

MacBrien assured him in writing that as soon as the regulations for the Reserve Air Force were promulgated, his name would be included. This did not happen, and in 1929 Barker requested a second time. However, his name does not appear on any published list of RCAF reservists.

Wing Commander Barker had two final duties. He was required to pay £1, 2s, 3p to the RAF for two blankets it claimed he had signed out in Cairo, and not returned. Will said he never had been issued with blankets, having slept in his Sidcot flying suit through two cold desert nights. Nevertheless, he wrote a cheque, shipped back the parachute he had been loaned and said goodbye to his RCAF career.

A Vickers Vernon on the Cairo – Baghdad air mail flight nearing Baghdad.

DND DHist Biographical file

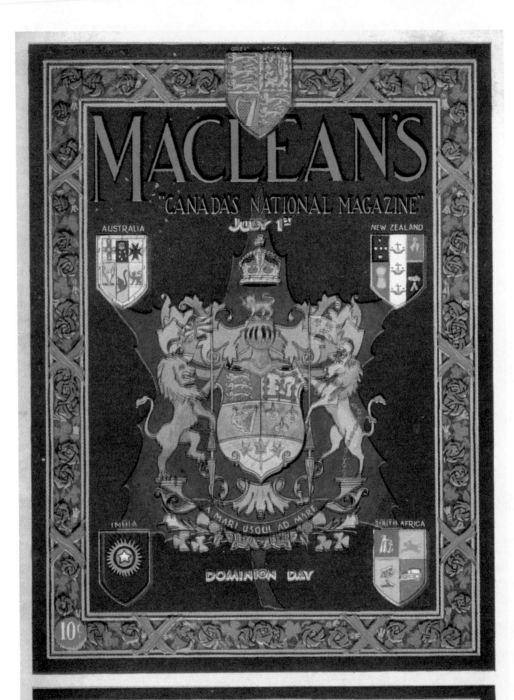

Cover of pamphlet reprinted by *Maclean's Magazine, The Truth about the War,* by George Drew, July 1928.

CHAPTER THIRTEEN

HUMILIATION AND REDEMPTION

"On the way up Jarvis Street his car skidded and turned upside down. He showed up in the dressing room, clothes torn and covered with blood, and didn't give a bad speech, at all, on the importance of morale. I don't know how much it actually helped morale, but it probably did make a few guys think about the dangers of drinking and driving."

CONN SMYTHE, COACH AND OWNER OF THE TORONTO MAPLE LEAFS

For the first time in his life, Barker felt like a complete failure. He had been a bankrupt in commercial aviation, and thwarted in his ambition to be the head of the RCAF. Group Captain Scott was always remembered by Jean Barker as the man who stole her husband's job. Will might have swallowed his pride and bided his time, but it was not in his nature. If he had been patient, he might well have succeeded Scott, who retired less than two years later to take up a different career as a salesman in stocks and bonds. MacBrien's successor, Major General Andrew McNaughton, would have enjoyed Will's company in Ottawa.

For months, Barker drifted along. A combination of physical pain, caused by arthritis due to gunshot wounds, and emotional distress due to the lack of any meaningful future turned him into a steady drinker, and a sometimes binge drinker. In the Roaring Twenties, this was not a unique character defect, especially among war veterans. Men who had survived the war sometimes disappeared from home and family for days at a time—to party, drink, and reconnect with their past. Barker had plenty of former flying buddies in Toronto, Montreal, and New York ready to party with him at a moment's notice.

The phrase coined by Gertrude Stein in that period about 1920s young men being "a lost generation," was particularly appropriate for Canadian war veterans, who had received little help in re-entering society. In some senses the First World War was Canada's equivalent to America's Vietnam War, at least in its psychological impact on a generation of young Canadian war veterans. If it was hard for an average soldier to adjust to civilian life, it was even harder for such a heroic figure as Barker.

Jean Barker saw how shattered her husband was by his loss of status, and the attempts by her father to assist Barker only added to his own sense of worthlessness. Will had been given an office at his father-in-law's Toronto corporate headquarters, 1103, Royal Bank Building, and a supply of stationary imprinted with his name. But the world of business meant nothing after the RCAF, and much of his characteristic intensity and enthusiasm was gone.

Despite his private grief, self-flagellation, and occasional drunkenness, many people still held him in the highest regard. Others saw in him enormous potential as a public relations symbol. Barker's wartime fame led to an honorary position courtesy of a former RFC Corps Cooperation pilot. How well Constantine F.C. "Conn" Smythe knew Barker, the man, as opposed to Barker, the legend, is debatable. But Smythe was looking for ways to enhance the profile of a National Hockey League team recently renamed the Toronto Maple Leafs, formerly the St Patrick's.

The team had finished last in the 1926-27 season, and Smythe was not happy. Over the summer he traded or sold the players that had not measured up, and brought in nine new men. He pushed with the Leafs' board of directors for a man of legendary stature to become president:

... one other part of the new set-up didn't work out exactly as I had planned. I insisted on Billy Barker being the Leafs' first president because of the gallant man he had been in wartime—Lt. Col. W.G. Barker, V.C., as he appeared on our first list. I thought that maybe a speech now and again from him in the dressing room would be good. Most of the players had missed the war, but certainly knew its most-decorated heroes. Many of the other directors had been in the war as well, but Barker was by far the most famous. However, he had trouble with alcohol. Trying to stay away from it he carried a case of ginger ale with him wherever he went, and when the impulse came he'd grab a ginger ale. But one night when I'd lined him up to visit the dressing room before an important game, he had to go to Hamilton. On the way he reached down for a ginger ale. There wasn't any. He went into a hotel instead and got plastered, then headed back to Toronto hell-bent for Maple Leaf Gardens [the Gardens was built in 1931—Barker was actually heading for the 8,000-seat Mutual Street Arena]. On the way up Jarvis Street his car skidded and turned upside down. He showed up on time in the dressing room, clothes torn and covered with blood, and didn't give a bad speech, at all, on the importance of morale. I don't know how much it actually helped morale, but it probably did make a few guys think about the dangers of drinking and driving.

Barker is not even a footnote in the history of the Toronto Maple Leafs. No recent history of the hockey team mentions him even in passing, and his name is not recognized in the Hockey Hall of Fame. His connection to the sport was tenuous; he had not played hockey himself since childhood.

Smythe wanted Barker for his heroic image and for his public relations value. Dealing with a man in a lot of pain, rather than an enduring legend, was more than Smythe had bargained for. The founder of the Leafs neither smoked nor drank, and The Leafs probably had the best reputation of any of the original NHL teams for clean living and discipline. Smythe was utterly ruthless about cutting his losses, and Barker did not last.

About this period, Horace Smith decided to get into the tobacco business 90 miles south-west of Toronto in Norfolk County. This was the heart of Canada's tobacco growing region, a new type of farming in Ontario that had been expanding rapidly through the 1920s, with the help of southerners from the tobacco regions of the United States. Smith bought eight farms, each farm having between 20 and 40 acres of land, and named them the Lynedoch Plantation, after the village a few miles south of Delhi.

A tobacco farm could generate $20,000 of revenue, and about $6,000 in profit from one year's crop, assuming the Canadian cold or hail from a passing thunderstorm did not destroy it. A land owner received 50 percent of the profits, and the farmer who grew this risky crop, the other 50 percent. Smith's plantation manager was Henry Fair; he and his wife managed the day-to-day work. Barker was offered the position of president. But it was not an authentic job, and for a war hero who never smoked and had never wanted to farm, this sorry outcome was especially ironic.

The Barkers moved to the village of Lynedoch, but their marriage was falling apart. They had travelled a very long way since those happy days when Jean had met the Prince of Wales. The war hero she had fallen in love with was so full of confidence, despite his physical challenges. His wounds had not faded, and were an ongoing source of pain, but what was making Will drink was more than physical pain.

He had deliberately closed the door on his working-class origins, and had little, if any, contact with his family. But as his sister, Edna, and brother, Orval, saw it, he had nothing to offer that mattered a damn to the social class into which he had married. There was no one in his wife's family circle in whom he could confide, and no one who understood the complexities of his character.

Jean had been patient with his alcoholic binges, and kept him sequestered from their daughter "Tony" when he was particularly sick or hung over. The police in Simcoe and Toronto had an arrangement where they called Jean, and she would come and pick up her husband at the station, and no charges would be laid.

But on Wednesday, 5 September 1928, Barker's car was pulled over yet again by the Simcoe-area police, and he was taken to jail. In the police file he is identified only as "W.G. Barker, farmer." He went before provincial magistrate R.E. Gunton, and this time his behaviour was not winked at. He was sentenced by Gunton in police court, and committed to seven days in the Simcoe jail for driving his car while intoxicated. The newspapers either did not know about or, more likely, chose to censor the fact that Canada's most decorated war hero was in jail for impaired driving. For Jean this was the final humiliation, and she and her daughter left Lynedoch for Toronto.

King George the Fifth is believed to have said that a Victoria Cross holder convicted of murder had every right to wear his decoration on the gallows. But there had been a few men who had the award rescinded because of their subsequent criminal acts, and going to jail might place a VC at risk of that additional humiliation.

Barker's life was in a spiral dive, and he was in real danger of self-destructing. He was becoming unacceptable to the affluent class that had adopted him. Every year since 1921, Barker had been listed in *Who's Who in Canada*, but the 1928-29 volume deleted his biography.

However, because of the direct or indirect actions of several influential people, Barker did not drop out of sight. He was rescued from a life as a social outcast by Major George Drew, lawyer and politician; Wing Commander Lloyd Breadner, acting director of the RCAF, and the former RNAS fighter ace who had endorsed Barker's certificate for night flying back in 1920; John Wilson, the Controller of Civil Aviation; and Sherman Fairchild, an American businessman.

Consolidation in air transportation and new aircraft manufacturing in Quebec were the events that allowed Barker to return to aviation, three years after he had left. But undoubtedly the most important event in Barker's rehabilitation was a magazine series by Drew.

George Alexander Drew was a wounded war veteran, and the commanding officer of a volunteer Militia unit, the 16th Artillery Battery, in his home town of Guelph. He later commanded the 11th Field Brigade that was headquartered there. In addition to his law practice, Drew served as an alderman, and then became mayor of Guelph in 1925 (he was even better known in the 1940s as the premier of Ontario, in the 1950s as the head of the national Progressive Conservative Party, and after that Canada's High Commissioner to London).

In response to articles in *The Cosmopolitan* and *Liberty* magazines by Brig General Henry J. Reilly, US Army, Drew wrote a rebuttal in *Maclean's Magazine*, entitled "The Truth About the War." The essay was featured on the front pages of the 1 July 1928 edition.

Reilly had argued that the British Empire had simply not used the forces available to it and by 1918 the United States had almost the same number of troops facing the Germans as the Empire. His proposition was that the United States armed forces had been crucial in defeating the Germans. Drew's rebuttal touched a national chord, and letters poured in congratulating the magazine. *Maclean's Magazine* reprinted the essay as a free pamphlet, and thousands requested it. General Reilly was given an opportunity to respond, and Major Drew provided a second rebuttal.

The editor of *Maclean's*, Napier Moore, seeing this patriotic response, took the opportunity to tell Canadian readers much more about the contributions of the nation in the Great War. From November 1928 through into 1930, the magazine serialized the stories of Victoria Cross recipients, and famous Canadian war pilots. All the profiles of the flyers were written by Drew, starting with Bishop, then Collishaw, and then Barker, followed by MacLaren. Drew was the first author to write at length about Barker, and the first author who could claim to know him personally.

He had been friends with Will since the days of Bishop-Barker Aeroplanes, when Billy and Will would drop by his law office in Guelph. When writing Barker's biography he visited his Toronto home

221

frequently, spending afternoons in Will's study, having a few drinks, and reliving the adventures of the war. Although the portrait Drew sketched of Barker is generally accurate, there were a few legends created by it (the killing of Linke-Crawford being one), and a variety of other errors, due to Will's embellishments and/or Drew's enthusiasm. It is difficult to know where Barker's contribution leaves off and Drew's begins.

The *Maclean's Magazine* serial on Barker ran from May through August 1929 in five instalments. It was the longest profile in the magazine, the most laudatory, and well illustrated. The profiles on Bishop, Collishaw, Barker, MacLaren, McLeod, McCall, Claxton, and the others, was turned into *Canada's Fighting Airmen*, an illustrated book published shortly after Barker's death, by The Maclean Publishing Company, Limited.

The Drew profile did more to promote the Barker legend than any other story. It was read by thousands who recognized the name, but knew little else. For aviation enthusiasts it was the first detailed account of Will's brilliantly diverse war career. This biography of about 23,000 words has become the basis of every subsequent narrative on Barker's life. Bishop relied on the Drew story, as did the RCAF in the Second World War, and several generations of journalists.

As we have seen, Barker had never done much to polish his own image. But the *Maclean's Magazine* series was a notable departure for him in that he actively helped Drew to tell the story of his war exploits. Drew's narrative was a personal source of satisfaction at a time when his life seemed little more than an alcoholic haze. Best of all, however, was that Jean had agreed to live together again for a trial period, but with the clear understanding that he had to stop drinking.

They spent the summer of 1929 at the "Yule-Log Cabin," near Lakefield, north of Peterborough, and Will devoted many hours to his daughter. During that summer he decided to teach her how to shoot, but the recoil from the gun knocked the six-year-old over. This provoked a sharp exchange between mother and father. He also gave driving lessons,

and she would sit on his lap and steer the car down country roads. That summer was her most vivid and positive memory of her father, but for her mother, Jean, it was to become an especially sad and poignant memory.

By 1929, Will felt that the world of flying had left him behind. Much had happened since 1926, and he had played no part in any of it. Aviation in North America had expanded at a dramatic rate, spurred on by public enthusiasm for one man and one event—Charles Lindbergh's trans-Atlantic flight in May 1927. It was the event of the decade, and arguably one of the most important catalysts for aviation development ever.

Governments that had been lukewarm to aviation revisited their policies in the wake of public enthusiasm for Lindbergh's achievement. Prime Minister Mackenzie King, no visionary when it came to aviation, was captivated by the trans-Atlantic solo flight, confiding in his diary: "[Lindbergh] was like a young god who had appeared from the skies in human form." "Lucky Lindy" flew to Ottawa in his Ryan monoplane, *The Spirit of St. Louis*, to help celebrate Canada's Diamond Jubilee in July 1927, and was a guest at Laurier House.

King's infatuation, reinforced by the United States policy of actively encouraging airlines via airmail contracts, motivated his Liberal government, for a little while at least, to look at air transportation as a useful instrument of national will. The US Congress had authorized $2 million in 1928 to encourage the development of international airmail, and as one journalist expressed it:

The Post Office Department of Canada has been almost forced into the air mail game because of the vigor with which the United States has gone into the business ... Canadian cities were in danger of becoming terminals and feeders for the United States air mails. It was imperative that Canada act. In view of this, our modest appropriation of less than $400,000 for air mails this year appears to be the least we can do.

CHILD STORY

...ded an airmail contract from the federal government. This was
...-old American businessman, who had invented an electrically
...that it rapidly became the standard around the world for map-

...he K-3 for some of the earliest aerial photography in Canada.
...a hostile climate, this company, headed by two ex-RAF pilots,
...d grown into the most successful company of its kind in North

...mingdale, Long Island, also designed and built a modern en-
...e aerial photography with the K-3 easier and more comfortable.
...that replaced the tired HS-2L, and by late 1929 more than 50
...ansport companies.

...vice, Sherman Fairchild wanted a large chunk of that lucrative
...smore and Saunders flew experimental airmail flights in the fall
...r from ocean liners on trans-Atlantic service.

...l for a regular mail service. However, two higher bidders were
...Airways, for Ottawa-Rimouski, and Canadian Airways, for Mon-
...Airways then subcontracted to Fairchild because only the FC2
...t.

...s still no closer to a government mail contract. Tired of bush
...Island, and proposed to Sherman Fairchild that his company
...he idea, and had a high regard for Martyn. He appointed him
...ory, and the establishment of a Canadian-owned manufac-
...d.

...Quebec, the headquarters of the aerial survey operations, in
...7-year-old Calgary-born accountant of the survey company,
...hore selected for the factory was on the south shore of the St.
... Green's Island.

Barker was searching desperately for ways to get back into aviation. He had written to the Secretary, Department of National Defence, requesting that his name be placed on the RCAF Reserve "as and when it is formed." He also wrote to Wing Commander Lloyd Breadner offering his services as an unpaid teacher at RCAF Station Camp Borden, where he could give a series of lectures on "Air Fighting" to the advanced pilot training class.

Breadner thought the world of Barker, and saw an opportunity to bring the war hero, a miserably unhappy tobacco farmer, back into the RCAF community. He told Major General McNaughton that Barker's lectures were "extremely interesting and instructive," and recommended his offer be accepted. Breadner also recommended that Barker be allowed to fly service aircraft.

The mutual interests of Pasmore and Barker were about to intersect, in a way that Pasmore could not have anticipated. He and his accountant Ronald Irvine had travelled to Ottawa early in the establishment of the new company, and were aghast to

223

discover that the RCAF wasn't the least bit enthusiastic about their new company. As Irvine later wrote:

> Our most important customer was the RCAF. They had already bought a number of our planes and everyone (i.e., us) took it for granted that they would be pleased to have a manufacturing and servicing plant set up in Canada close to home …
>
> To our astonishment and fright we were received coldly and with obvious distaste. It was a most difficult interview. I suspect they enjoyed going down to New York to take delivery of planes and didn't want these pleasures stopped. On the other hand, they may have had experience with other Canadian subsidiaries and from experience distrusted such offshoots … in time we made friends and our association for years was pleasant.

Irvine does not identify who they met with in Ottawa, but it was likely Breadner and Squadron Leader Earl Godfrey. Breadner had assumed command as the acting director of the RCAF on 15 February 1928, immediately after Group Captain Scott's resignation. He held that position until 1932, in addition to keeping his current job as assistant director for another 22 months.

Godfrey was a superintendent in the CGAO branch of the RCAF. Since he and Will had graduated from Course 4 at RAF Staff College, Earl had made quite a name for himself as a long-distance flyer. The flying records Earl had set between Ottawa and Vancouver had all been in the new Fairchild FC2.

The third man in Ottawa that Pasmore and Irvine met was John A. Wilson ("J.A." as he was called in the bureaucracy), the head of civil aviation within the Department of National Defence (all aviation in Canada, civil and military, was then run by the DND). Almost nothing happened inside or outside the RCAF that Wilson did not know about, influence, or shape in some way.

At the celebrations marking the opening of the 38,800-square-foot factory of Fairchild Aircraft

Limited at Longueuil in September 1930, the only individual from the government cited for his contribution was Wilson. Ernest Robinson, vice president of Fairchild in New York, said that Wilson's confidence, cooperation, and patience were largely responsible for the existence of the plant.

However, in 1929, when the factory was being built, the frosty reaction from Breadner, Godfrey, and others in the RCAF was a worry for Fairchild. The RCAF was the single-most important customer for Fairchild machines in Canada. The question was how to build rapport with the RCAF? It was Breadner and Wilson who answered the question by recommending, either independently or in unison, that Fairchild Aircraft hire Lt Colonel William Barker, VC.

The benefit to the new company was that it would then have a recognized public figure, recently profiled in a national magazine; a man who was well liked in the RCAF and on a first-name basis with every senior officer. It is impossible to know how subtle or otherwise the RCAF was in its recommendation, but certainly the wishes of the military at this critical stage of Fairchild Aircraft's birth would have received serious consideration.

When Sherman Fairchild interviewed Martyn Pasmore in the 1960s about the foundation of the company, as part of a larger Fairchild corporate history, Pasmore implied that Barker had been hired for his contacts in Ottawa. He was given the nominal position of president (the *Canadian Aviation* press release said "vice president and general manager," while newspaper accounts usually said "president").

Nevertheless, it was Martyn Pasmore who ran the day-to-day affairs at the factory. Sherman Fairchild appears (judging from 1960s interviews) to be entirely ignorant of Barker, but it is virtually certain, as the chairman of the Canadian board of directors, that he approved Barker's appointment.

Pasmore and Irvine, as founding officers of Fairchild in Quebec, were not enthusiastic about the appointment. Barker was an outsider. It was they who had been pioneers in the development of Fairchild in Canada. They had suffered the frost-bitten fingers, the balky cameras, the many aggravations of

Hubert Martyn Pasmore, Victoria, BC, at the age of 98.

Photo taken by author Wayne Ralph

aerial survey. What had Barker done to create this new company? What did Barker even know about aircraft manufacturing

Pasmore has been described by one author as a "sober, powerful personality," a man who never smoked, and for much of his life drank no alcohol. He had to accept Barker's appointment, but he had no intention of approving of his lifestyle. In January 1930, the famous war hero was formally taken on the payroll of Fairchild. Irvine recalled that he was not well served by his old friends:

> For sales manager, the Air Force recommended a Colonel Barker, a Canadian war ace whose fame was only eclipsed by Billy Bishop himself. Since the end of the war, he had been engaged in growing tobacco in Ontario and had developed a distaste for tobacco growing and a taste for whiskey. He was only with us a few weeks. His old friends welcomed him to Montreal and to celebrate his return from the tobacco growing waste land they gave many parties which I am sure greatly worsened his already serious alcohol problem.

Several ex-RAF Italian campaign pilots lived in Montreal, including Gerry Birks; Stan Stanger, recent co-founder, with his brother, of the Guardian Trust company; and the Foss brothers, Joe and Roy.

* * *

On 27 January, Will went to Dr Howard Reilly on Drummond Street for his medical. The doctor noted on the pilot's application form that Barker's physical challenges were "due to Service, recovered from except left elbow. This on record at HQ. Disability does not interfere with his ability to handle any type of aeroplane." Barker claimed that he had a total of 3,500 flying hours solo, and had flown 300 hours since his previous examination, likely an optimistic estimate, given his occupation since 1926. Dr. Reilly assessed him as "Fit, Category A-1." A temporary pilot's certificate was issued on the same day.

Within a couple of weeks, possibly right after a flight test in a Fairchild KR-34, Barker's commercial certificate (No 637), was issued by Squadron Leader A.T.N. "Tom" Cowley, Superintendent, Air Regulations.

The KR-34 and the smaller KR-21 biplanes were not original Fairchild designs. The company had bought a controlling interest in a small manufacturer in Hagerstown, Maryland, called Kreider-Reisner Aircraft Company, Inc., named for its two founders, Ammon Kreider and Lewis Reisner. It had been producing three types of machine, the three-seater Challenger C2 and C4, and the two-seater, the Challenger C6.

Unfortunately, Ammon Kreider was killed in a mid-air collision in April 1929, only days after Sherman Fairchild had bought his company at the All-American Aircraft Show in Detroit. This death prompted Sherman Fairchild to renumber the sports-utility biplanes using only the initials of the Kreider-Reisner Company. Thus, the C2 became a Fairchild KR-31, the C4, a KR-34, and the C6, a KR-21. Both the latter machines were sent up to

Fairchild FC2 of the RCAF in Manitoba in 1928.

Montreal, and offered for sale to flying schools, provincial governments, and the RCAF.

The particular KR-21 airframe delivered to Fairchild in Canada on 8 March 1930 had been built in 1929, the 12th aircraft in this series. It was never assigned a U.S. registration number. There are no colour images of the biplane, but it likely was painted in shades of blue-grey and silver, with the Canadian registration, CF-AKR, displayed on the fuselage, and the wings.

Pasmore and Barker believed that the KR-21 had good sales potential as a sporting machine, but the best customer was obviously the RCAF. A demonstration was immediately scheduled for them. On Tuesday, 11 March, Fairchild's demonstration pilot, 25-year-old Donald Campbell Shaw, flew the machine to RCAF Ottawa Air Station at Rockcliffe. This was to be the first sales visit by the new company to market an open-cockpit biplane. It was Barker's first opportunity to pitch the RCAF on the KR-21 as a replacement for the aged AVRO 504.

He arrived in Ottawa on the train, and stayed across the street from Union Station at his usual hotel, the Chateau Laurier. Will met there with Earl Godfrey, and invited him to fly the KR-21 at Rockcliffe on Wednesday morning. It was Godfrey who threw a welcoming party for Will that Tuesday evening at his home on the south side of Ottawa. Many officers and their wives attended, all wanting to shake hands with the famous hero. Will was made to feel that he had returned to the bosom of the RCAF after long exile.

Nineteen-year-old Sylvia Graham, F/O Stuart Graham's step-daughter, talked enthusiastically to Barker that evening about learning to fly. Will encouraged her to take lessons, and he promised to take her up the next day. He also promised her sister, Peggy, and their friend, Jessie, the daughter of an MP, that all would get a flight. But Sylvia felt especially honoured to be singled out by the Canadian ace. Colonel Barker was a Victoria Cross recipient, and yet had chosen her, over everyone else in the room,

Mary McKee Selby collection

to go aloft with him. She did not know that he had never flown the KR-21.

At lunch in Montreal with Gerry Birks just a week before, Will had described a manoeuvre he had witnessed at the air show in Detroit. A pilot had landed his aircraft off the back side of a loop. He knew he could do the same, and was itching to try it out. Birks was now an investment banker, and had not flown since 1918. He was hesitant to give his old flight commander a lecture. But he wanted to say: "Now, Bill, you go up to 5,000 feet, and practise that landing loop on some clouds before you do it down low."

About 11:00 a.m. on the 12th, Earl picked Will up at the Chateau Laurier. He drove a few miles north along Sussex Drive, following the south shore of the Ottawa River. The weather was warming, but the river was still frozen. They arrived at Rockcliffe just as the KR-21 lifted off.

At about 12:40 p.m., Shaw flew the machine around the Rockcliffe aerodrome, landing after 10 minutes. There was no need for Will personally to demonstrate the KR-21. But he was unhappy with Shaw's demonstration, and knew he could do better. The staff at Rockcliffe aerodrome had seen the biplane fly several times that morning, and several RCAF pilots had taken it up. A talented test pilot on exchange from the RAF, Flight Lieut Neil Ogilvie-Forbes, who was in charge of the Test Flight at the station, had put the machine through its paces, by looping, rolling, and spinning it.

But Barker was back in the flying business, the company definitely needed more sales, and this graceful biplane just might fill the bill as the new RCAF trainer. He had to show what it could do.

Kenneth M. Molson collection

Fairchild KR-21 with Canadian registration CF-AKR prior to leaving the American factory in early March 1930.

William Barker's coffin is lifted on the carriage outside 355 St Clair Avenue West; note the well dressed crowds in Toronto on this Saturday afternoon, 15 March 1930.

CHAPTER FOURTEEN

DEATH AND MOURNING

"… unaccustomed to the 'dive' and 'feel' of the plane the famous pilot did not have time to bring experience to bear when instinct could not function."

NEWSPAPER REPORTER

Barker had logged about 14 hours since joining Fairchild. He had a few hours on the KR-34, and was confident that the lighter KR-21 would present no difficulties. Shaw argued that he should go up with him for a couple of circuits around Rockcliffe. But Will's entire flying career had been self-taught. He had learned how to be an observer on the job. He went solo in less than an hour at Netheravon. Why should he now have to take training on this light aircraft? Who was going to argue against a Victoria Cross recipient, if he wanted his own way? Asserting his authority with Shaw, Will brushed aside his attempts to help.

The Rockcliffe Air Station orderly officer, with considerable courage and presence of mind, took Barker aside, and suggested he not take any passenger up on his first flight. Barker had nodded in agreement. He then walked over to Sylvia Graham and told her he'd be back soon, and she would fly next.

Climbing into the rear cockpit, Will asked AC1 Chapman, the weekly timekeeper for aircraft movements, which switch was the "spark" for the engine, i.e., the ignition. Chapman had no idea, and turned to Shaw, who briefed Barker and fastened his seat belt, while Godfrey looked on anxiously. With the warmer weather, Earl was worried about the surface conditions of the aerodrome. He cautioned Barker to be very careful when landing, to which Will replied, "All right, old man, I'll land all right."

LAC Jack Hunter and his friends were walking down the hill from the mess hall when they saw Barker taxi the aircraft away. It was a little before 1:00 p.m., and the fitters and riggers had just finished lunch in the Airmen's Mess. The weather was good and they could see the aerodrome, the hangars by the shore, and the ice-covered Ottawa River below them.

Barker added power, and pulled away from Godfrey and Shaw. The surface of the turf aerodrome was soft, with the mud showing through the patches of snow. The small biplane gained speed, its tail bouncing almost too high in the air as the tailskid struck patches of crusted snow. Chapman thought that the aircraft might tip forward on its nose. Although the wind was blowing out of the west, Will had pointed the aircraft in a southerly or south-westerly direction for his first takeoff. He did not climb away across the Ottawa River to the Gatineau Hills on the Quebec side to check out the biplane's handling by practising a few loops and rolls.

Instead, Will banked the KR-21 soon after he was airborne, cranking it around in steep turns a few hundred feet above the spectators. As an ex-Camel pilot he felt at home immediately with the aircraft's light and beautifully responsive controls. On each diving pass towards the two RCAF hangars near the south shore of the river, Will pulled the machine into a steep climb to demonstrate its ease of handling. Each climb was steeper than the one before, followed by a sharp wingover and a dive to regain airspeed.

The KR-21 weighs about the same as a Sopwith Camel. Considerably more docile than the Sopwith fighter, it has 40 hp less engine power. It also has distinctive tapered wings which give it a graceful profile, but a more abrupt stall than an aircraft with wings having a constant-chord from root to tip. A tapered wing (all other things being equal) is more likely to stall first at the wingtip, creating a higher risk of the aircraft entering a spin.

But Barker had no experience with the tapered-wing KR-21 and, what was more crucial, he overestimated the energy available at the bottom of each dive. To enter a looping manoeuvre with this light aircraft he needed an entry speed of 120 mph, and this required a pretty steep dive. But the low-powered trainer, as one owner describes it, "pays off its speed" quickly during the pull up, not gaining much altitude as the airspeed decreases.

On his final pass, Will flew the trainer from the north to the south side of the Ottawa River, aiming directly towards the slipway, building up airspeed, and then pulling up just over the shoreline into the steepest climb of all. He may have planned to loop—perhaps even land off the backside of the loop. For one endless moment, the aircraft hung on the prop, silhouetted against a milky winter sky. Godfrey, intently watching Will's flying from the slope above the river, swore aloud, "My God, he's stalled."

Flight Sergeant Duncan Black and Corporal Benjamin Flesher started running down the slope towards the wood slipway that projected out into the river, Black shouting as he ran for other men to accompany them. A group of young RCAF pilots had witnessed the flight demonstration with their hearts in their throats. To them it seemed that Barker was trying to prove that the KR-21 was a fighter rather than a trainer, pushing it far beyond its small engine. A future Chief of Air Staff of the RCAF was watching Barker perform. As the aircraft hung at the apex of the climb, Flying Officer C.R. "Larry" Dunlap murmured to his friends, "He's gone." The others nodded mutely.

At an altitude of about 250 to 300 feet above the ice, the aircraft started to slide backwards on its tail, but instead of nosing over gently to recover from the stall, the KR-21 flopped inverted onto its back. With its 90 hp engine still roaring at full throttle, the Fairchild rolled quickly to the left and pitched down steeply towards the frozen Ottawa River, disappearing from view behind the trees along the river bank.

Perhaps 100 feet more altitude would have made all the difference for Will, because the KR-21 has good aileron and rudder control right through the stall. It also has excellent spin characteristics, rotating rapidly, but not losing much altitude, and recovering easily and quickly just by neutralizing the stick, and applying opposite rudder. But Will had run out of airspeed, and had precious little altitude. Some eyewitnesses recalled later that he made no effort to stop the spin.

Corporal Flesher and Flight Sergeant Black arrived within seconds of the impact. The fuselage was sitting upright on the ice near the end of the dock. The wings and undercarriage had collapsed

The airmen of Rockcliffe Air Station gather around the Fairchild KR-21 shortly after the crash, Wednesday, 12 March 1930.

on impact, and the engine had been torn from its mounts, and hurled further out on the river. After cutting through the fabric on the side of the fuselage, the two airmen attempted to remove the motionless pilot from the cockpit.

Will's head had been smashed on impact, and he had been thrown forward in the cockpit, his mouth resting on a ledge below the cockpit dash. His left arm and right ankle were broken, and his left leg was broken and twisted, protruding out of the fuselage.

A group of officers and air mechanics quickly gathered around the wreckage. Ogilvie-Forbes looked down at the broken body. Seeing that Barker was dead, he told the mechanics trying to lift him from the wreckage to wait until he could be removed without further mutilation. He stopped Godfrey as he approached the wreckage, telling him that Barker's head was badly smashed, saying: "Don't look." Shaw pulled up near the slipway in an automobile, ready to rush his boss to hospital, sick at heart as he heard the news.

The RCAF flyers who knew Barker, who had attended his welcoming party the night before, who had, a bit apprehensively, watched him climb into the small biplane, were in shock. It was simply awful to have this hero, of all heroes, die in such trivial circumstances, and to have it happen at an RCAF station. Many of the flyers, who witnessed the accident, including Godfrey, Cowley, and Grandy, were war veterans. They had seen many crashes. But this one was different—more shattering and more tragic because it seemed so unnecessary. For the fitters and riggers at Rockcliffe Barker was a legend; a few of them had worked for him at Camp Borden, and they felt lost and sad that afternoon as they worked on machines in the hangar.

Sylvia Graham never forgot the horrific sound of the impact. She, Peggy, and Jessie were immediately hustled away to a private room, and told to stay there. They were forbidden to talk to the newspaper people who showed up a few minutes later. Sylvia would often wonder as to what might have been. If she had gone flying with him, would he have performed such wild stunts? Perhaps he might have lived if she had been in the plane too.

* * *

The death was a front-page news story across Canada. The description of his fatal accident, followed by an obituary and/or eulogy, was published in major newspapers in the United Kingdom, and the United States. Known by reputation to virtually all military flyers in Europe and North America, the circumstances of his death were especially poignant. The man who had fought against 60, and lived, was gone.

A typical front page headline announcing the death of William Barker for Manitoba residents.

231

Many commented on the tragic waste of such a valiant human being, while others shook their heads upon hearing about it. What an irony—brought low in a docile training aircraft! Some who were closer to the man were overcome. Kenneth Guthrie was travelling on the afternoon CNR train between Ottawa and Toronto. He was on his way to Winnipeg, to take command of the RCAF sub-station at Lac du Bonnet. In those days the CNR had its own radio station, and broadcast music and news in the radio car.

Guthrie was enjoying this mobile entertainment when a broadcaster interrupted the music, announcing: "Colonel Barker, the Victoria Cross winner, has been killed in a flying accident in Ottawa." Ken thought he might faint: "I leaped up and tore the phones off. 'Jesus Christ!' I said. Everybody looked at me who didn't have phones on. I said to them, 'I just had lunch with Colonel Barker.'"

Billy Bishop was near tears. He had difficulty talking to the journalists who came to his Chester Terrace home in London, England. He told one: "It is a most terrible shock to me. He was one of my dearest friends and one of the finest men I have ever met. There has been no bigger man in the air business either during the war or since. I really cannot express what I feel."

Jean Barker was devastated by the news of her husband's death. That Wednesday afternoon, "Tony" was playing in the garden at her grandfather's St Clair Avenue West home. Mrs Barker asked the butler to bring the child to her bedroom. Barker's daughter remembered that a sense of unease hung over the day. Seeing her mother crying on the bed, she blurted out: "My daddy is dead." Her mother nodded mutely.

After Will's body had been placed in a wicker laundry basket by Sergeant Stan Greene, it was escorted by Ogilvie-Forbes to the funeral parlour of Gauthier and Company on St. Patrick Street in Ottawa. Dr J.E. Craig, the coroner for the city, convened an inquest at 4:00 p.m. at the funeral parlour. After examining the body, he decided against an autopsy, and gave permission for it to be moved to Hulse Brothers on McLeod Street.

Late that evening, the coffin was put on board the overnight train to Toronto. An informal voluntary group of pall bearers wanted to be at the station to see Barker off. They were J.A. Wilson, Colonel "Red" Mulock, Lt Colonel Eberts McIntyre, Lt Colonel R.F. Parkinson, Flight Lieut Neil Ogilvie-Forbes, and Donald Shaw.

J.A. Wilson had obtained permission from George Desbarats, the deputy minister of defence, to appoint a Court of Inquiry. All accidents in those days were investigated by the RCAF even if the aircraft was on the civil register. On the afternoon of the accident, President of the Court, Flight Lieut Alan Ferrier, and his board members, Flying Officer W.R. Brookes, and Flying Officer G.B. Holmes, filled out RCAF form "D6," listing six witnesses to be interviewed.

By today's standards, the investigation into Barker's death was very rapid and superficial. All documents and witness testimony had been submitted to Wilson by the following day, and signed as approved by George Desbarats on 14 March. That same day a press release was sent out to the Parliamentary Press Gallery, *The Ottawa Citizen*, and *The Ottawa Journal*. The cause of the crash seemed quite obvious to the many knowledgeable eye witnesses. No one wanted Rockcliffe remembered for this sad event, and the RCAF probably did not want any lingering connection to the death of a legend.

The members of the Court of Inquiry examined the aircraft wreckage. They confirmed that the control surfaces moved freely, that the magneto switch was in the "On" position, and the safety belt had broken away from its anchor bolts. The aircraft had not burned. Photographs were taken of the aircraft sitting at the edge of the wood slipway, with the engine at least one hundred feet to the east and farther out on the river. However, there is no way to know if that was its impact point, or if the aircraft was dragged to the slipway to prevent it being lost through the ice.

On the day of the crash, CF-AKR's journey log showed only 10 hours and 15 minutes on the airframe, and just over 12 hours on the Kinner 550 five-cylinder radial engine. The Court of Inquiry concluded that the aircraft was airworthy prior to flight, and this did not change during the time

Barker flew it. Witnesses were in general agreement with each other as to what happened just prior to the accident, although their estimates of the altitude of the aircraft at the apex of the climb varied from 250 to 400 feet above ground.

There was disagreement, however, about Barker's physical capabilities to deal with what appears to have been an unexpected stall and subsequent tail slide. Shaw did not want Barker to fly solo, because "As far as I know he had never flown this type of aircraft (K.R.21) before and owing to the lightness of control and his left arm being partially disabled and the bad condition of the aerodrome, I thought it advisable that he should have had a dual circuit."

He did not believe that Barker was capable of recovering from the inverted position because the Kreider-Reisner machine had no shoulder harness, and the "waist belt" would not restrain him adequately while upside down. Without a seat belt or harness, it would be more difficult for the pilot to reach the throttle on the left side of the cockpit. During the interviews, Alan Ferrier asked: "Do you think that after coming off his back and in the resulting dive he could have used both control column and throttle in sufficient time to recover control of the machine before striking the ground?"

Shaw replied: "In my opinion a skilled pilot with full use of his limbs could have prevented a similar accident."

Two RCAF pilots gave testimony: Earl Godfrey and R.L. "Bill" Grandy, the commanding officer of Rockcliffe Air Station. The RAF exchange officer, Ogilvie-Forbes, side-stepped whether the aircraft could have been recovered: "As the machine went out of my sight and I did not see the end of the dive, I cannot express an opinion." He did say that his flight in the KR-21 had been normal, and there was no difficulty in pulling out of high speed dives with the stabilizer set in the neutral position. The machine was "moderately stable on all axes and light on controls."

Squadron Leader Grandy indicated that from his position standing on the bluff above the river, just outside the Officer's Mess, there seemed to be plenty of altitude for the light aircraft to pull out of

its dive. Godfrey believed that the position of the aircraft wreckage, resting upright on the ice and facing north, as well as the attitude just prior to impact, suggested that Barker may have already initiated a recovery, but simply ran out of altitude.

The Court asked Godfrey about Barker's physical condition: "Do you think that the known disability of Wing Commander Barker's left arm would have any effect on the control of the machine under any circumstances?" Godfrey replied: "Not in the least as he has demonstrated the strength of that arm while wrestling with me on a number of occasions and I have driven with him in a Buick car which was rather heavy on the steering, when he has driven for hours on end controlling the steering with that hand only."

The Court did not ask any other questions about Barker's ability to use his left arm, apparently content to accept Godfrey's version over Shaw's.

Two military witnesses who did not testify, Flying Officer Dunlap, and LAC Hunter, both told the author six decades later that the steepness of the climb was far beyond what such a low-powered machine could manage. Both men recollected that there seemed to be little effort by the pilot to recover, and Hunter remembered that the KR-21 completed about one-and-a-half turns of a spin before hitting the ice.

The findings and recommendations of this RCAF Court of Inquiry were unequivocal:

The cause of the accident was in our opinion–
(1) Primary Cause - an error of judgement on the part of the pilot in that he performed aerobatics at too low an altitude.
(2) Secondary Cause - Loss of control due to too steep a climb without sufficient height to recover from the resultant dive ...
Following are our recommendations for prevention of a repetition of this type of accident–
That the dangers of aerobatics at low altitudes be more strongly impressed upon all pilots.

The press release for the Parliamentary Press Gallery added that "the aircraft was airworthy, [and]

233

the pilot was a commercial pilot in good standing and physically fit and well at the time of his flight."

Newspapers published the findings of the Court of Inquiry, some along with photographs and accounts of the funeral. One Ottawa journalist reporting on the accident expressed his personal, but insightful opinion that: "unaccustomed to the 'dive' and 'feel' of the plane the famous pilot did not have time to bring experience to bear when instinct could not function."

The following week, Squadron Leader Cowley replied to an insurance company, Air Investors, Inc, at 20 Pine Street, New York City:

> The accident was in no way due to a defect in either engine or aircraft but to the pilot having insufficient altitude to come out of a vertical dive following a "rocket zoom." Actually, at the top of the zoom, the aircraft hung on its prop for a moment and then fell off backwards.
>
> The accident can, therefore, be directly attributable to an error in judgment on the part of the pilot in carrying out aerobatics in a low powered aircraft without sufficient altitude for a safe recovery in event of a stall.

* * *

Arrangements had to be made quickly about the funeral. Jean was consoled in her grief by her father, who had supported his only child wholeheartedly despite his past misgivings about her husband. The two decided that, despite Barker's public profile, his remains should be interred in the Smith family crypt at Mount Pleasant Cemetery.

But Jean was the wife of a hero who, despite his recent difficulties, was still an iconic figure for thousands. The Department of National Defence wanted a military funeral for such a legendary man. The Smith family acquiesced. The Barker family was not asked their opinion.

Barker's widow would have preferred to entomb his remains on Friday, but the thousands of military participants were not in place and ready to parade that day. Moreover, Barker's mother, and two sisters,

had to travel from Winnipeg to Toronto by train and had not yet arrived.

Will Barker had not seen his mother and father or brothers and sisters for eight or nine years. Most of the Barkers were living in a three-story, six-apartment walk-up in south Chicago. Percy owned the small building at 6117 Ellis Avenue, and a couple of others like it in the Woodlawn area. Almost all the family were working to bring in money. Lloyd was driving a bread truck for a bakery, Cecil was a fireman in the Conway Building, Roy was a bricklayer, and Orval worked at the A&P grocery store.

Jane Barker learned of her son's death the day after the funeral of her youngest sister, 33-year-old Lola Louise Buchannon, who had died of a gall bladder infection. Auntie Lola, Will's childhood companion, was buried at Riverside Cemetery at Dauphin on 11 March. Jane wired her husband, and then took the train to Winnipeg, where her two daughters lived and worked.

Ilda and Edna were cashiers at the Eaton's Department Store on Portage Avenue. The store manager escorted the two grieving sisters out of the store, and asked the doorman at the entrance to flag down a taxi for them. Jane Barker, having lost a son and a sister in the same week, needed her daughters' help to make the travel arrangements.

George Barker, and three of the boys, Orval, Lloyd, and Percy, and Percy's wife, got into Lloyd's Kissel car for the trip north. The Barkers congregated at 355 St Clair Avenue West on the afternoon before the funeral. The Smiths and the Barkers had never met. The Barker family was in no financial position to assist with the funeral arrangements, even had they been asked. They had no say in the details of this public event. They were mute observers to a state ceremony paying tribute to a war hero.

Barker's sudden death struck an emotional chord with thousands of people in the US, UK, and Europe. A flood of telegrams and letters of sympathy were received by Barker's widow, from relatives in Toronto, and from strangers as far away as Egypt. Official letters of condolence were sent to the government of Canada from the political and military leaders of England, France, and the United States.

The rhetoric of a senior official of the United States Post Department was characteristic of the flood of emotions:

> Such an irreparable loss as this can ill be afforded by our Governments ... The record of Colonel Barker is so outstanding that it reads like fiction and none braver has ever faced the enemies' guns. Of course, the King and the Dominion are glad to have had a man of the type of this brave soul who was so unfortunate as to come to the end of the trail in such an untimely manner.

General Sir Arthur Currie, at the time the principal of McGill University, was fulsome in his praise:

> ... he was a gallant fighter who never deserted a friend nor feared a foe ... I am sure his courage and resourcefulness will prove an inspiration to all young Canadians. He died as he would have wished to die—in that realm where he reigned supreme. His name will live forever in the annals of the country which he served so nobly.

The head of the Royal Air Force, Sir John M. Salmond, observed in a telegram: "His achievements in late war will remain as an example to British Air Forces for all time." The head of the French government aeronautics branch, M. Laurent Eynac, telegraphed condolences from Paris, and Wilfrid Lamoureux, president of the Association Nationale des Vétérans in Montreal, wrote to say that

> The former combatants of [our association] have been shocked to hear of the tragic death of one of the most distinguished officers, as well as one of the cleverest airmen in Canada, Lt Colonel W.G. Barker. I have been requested by the Association to transmit to you, and to the bereaved family, our deepest condolence for the great loss sustained by our dear country.

A young man from Trois Rivières, Quebec, Jean Baptiste Duchesneau, wrote to the RCAF asking for a photograph:

> How shocked I was to hear of Colonel Barker's death! It dealt me a blow as if I had lost a relative of mine or a friend. I met him in Montreal two years ago, and I have read of his deeds during the war ... aviation is my ideal, and my aim is to become a pilot.

American Ace of Aces, Capt Eddie Rickenbacker, said "the science of aviation and the citizens of Canada have lost a great soldier and patriot." The president of Curtiss-Wright Flying Services, C.S. "Casey" Jones, agreed: "To United States aviators his deeds were an inspiration. Memories of his gallantry in action will last permanently in all records of the Great War. He died fittingly with his boots on in the cause of aviation."

Dr. Robert Dolbey, a former medical officer of the RFC who had served with Barker in Italy, and had operated on him in 1919, wrote to the Barker family from Cairo: "... he was one of the finest young men that I ever met and I think his death is a terrible loss, not only to Canada, but to the whole of the British Empire."

"J.A." Wilson summarized the feelings of many Canadian flyers: "His personality endeared him to all who knew him and Canadian aviation has lost in him an outstanding personality, whose energy, courage and enthusiasm cannot be replaced."

The Daily Express and *The Daily Telegraph* in London both wrote retrospective columns on Barker's life and character, *The Daily Telegraph* noting that:

> ... though essentially of the type to which the American adjective 'tough' might be applied, he was a very loveable fellow ... [Bishop] tells me that Colonel Barker was the one man to whom he would willingly have handed over sole control in a moment of emergency. That is no small tribute to his courage and skill.

RSM Leonard Dyte from Camp Borden Air Station holds William Barker's medals outside the Mount Pleasant Cemetery Mausoleum, Saturday, 15 March 1930.

Correspondent Thomas Champion, reporting back to the Canadian papers from London, offered the following personal anecdote:

The gallant airman, when you met him on leave in London was, in one sense, often an exasperating character. He was always glad to meet you even if you were a newspaperman, but the most patient efforts usually failed to get him to talk about his exploits. He could not be induced to say there was anything to talk about. "It's all down in the Gazette," he would say, and then would speak of something else.

The Smith family did not want a church service. Jean Barker had decided that the remains would rest at the home of her father, and that mourners could come there to pay their respects. In an unusual departure for a victim of a flying accident, the dark-stained oak coffin was open for viewing.

The coffin rested at one end of the long, dimly lit drawing room "surrounded by a sloping bank of flowers stretching from wall to wall and almost to the ceiling." A Royal Canadian Air Force Regimental Sergeant Major (probably Leonard Dyte of Camp Borden) stood guard at the foot of the coffin. Through the afternoon people came in twos and threes to the house to pay their respects. Barker's high school sweetheart, Mabel Buchannon Disney, travelled from Oshawa to see him one last time.

More than 60 wreaths and floral arrangements arrived from people who had known or served with Barker, as well as many from those who simply knew the legend. Tributes came from the Governor General and Lady Willingdon, Colonel "Red" Mulock, Squadron Leader "Black Mike" McEwen, Dr. Willard Box, and the directors of the Toronto Maple Leafs; as well as many veterans' associations, military units, airlines, and flying clubs.

The Mail and Empire assigned two reporters to cover the event. Guy Cunliffe focussed his story on Barker's seven-year-old daughter:

A slender blonde child in a simple white dress, silhouetted against a phalanx of the highest dignitaries of the nation's civil and military life, chattering unrealizingly in a sweet, clear voice amid the hush of the last rites ... delicate, fair face tinged with a shy, proud smile; hands clasped behind her back, slim legs apart, she watched while the mourners took a parting

Globe and Mail collection, City of Toronto archives

Barker's funeral cortege awaits the order to march away from 355 St Clair Avenue, Toronto.

glance of that shattered young face in the casket, crushed in the accident which wrecked his plane at Ottawa on Wednesday.

Orval Barker sat next to Jean on a bench in the drawing room, watching the stream of visitors. He taught her simple coin tricks to while away the time. The two were still young enough to be awed, yet curious about the ceremony, more sobered than sad. At one point, Jean asserted to Barker's sister Edna that perhaps angels or fairies might bring her daddy back. Edna considered it a foolish observation by a naïve child, and, at a time when her heart felt so bereft, it upset her.

Barker's only child remembered vividly being lifted by her grandfather to kiss the heavily-made-up cheek. There was a brief eulogy by Reverend Canon James Broughall. The service commenced at 3:30 and was over in less than 15 minutes.

The Commander of Military District 2, Major General Ernest C. Ashton, had instructed Stanley Barracks that he wanted the RSM of the Royal Canadian Dragoons to act as Garrison Sergeant Major for the procession. The coffin was carried from the house

at 3:45, and strapped to a black wooden platform on a two-wheeled caisson, towed by an olive-drab RCAF aircraft tender. The dress of the day for Army personnel was full field service dress, and for the RCAF, winter dress, with greatcoats. A black crepe arm band was worn on the left sleeve by all officers and warrant officers.

William Barker's funeral procession had a mythical quality befitting a great warrior, or even a head of state. Probably the last funeral of comparable pomp and circumstance in Canada had been that of Prime Minister Sir Wilfrid Laurier more than 10 years before.

A famous American had died just a few days before Barker. He was former United States President, and Supreme Court Chief Justice, William Howard Taft. The account of Taft's funeral was published the day Barker died, pushing Barker's fatal crash to page three in *The New York Times*. The lying-in-state in the rotunda of the Capital had been viewed by more than 6,000 mourners. Taft had requested a military funeral and burial in Arlington National Cemetery, and his interment ceremony on 11 March included an honour guard of 1,000. The newspaper reporter

Majors General "Andy" McNaughton, Chief of the General Staff, (left) and Ernest Ashton walk towards Mount Pleasant Cemetery Mausoleum.

Globe and Mail collection, City of Toronto archives

estimated that a thousand or so spectators stood quietly in the rain to watch the service.

Impressive though it was, Taft's military funeral paled in comparison to Barker's, which was reported to be the largest in the history of Toronto, attracting an estimated 50,000 spectators, with a cortege of more than two thousand soldiers in uniform, from all the garrisoned regiments of the city and surrounding district, plus another thousand military personnel wearing civilian clothes. The military ranks stretched for almost a mile behind the official mourners.

Along the one-and-a-quarter mile parade route from 355 St Clair Avenue to Yonge Street the sidewalks were lined with spectators, with the greatest number waiting around Mount Pleasant Cemetery. People crowded on balconies, and stood on roof tops to get a better view. The sun was bright, but it was cool and there were patches of snow here and there. Men in uniform who were not part of the procession saluted as the caisson passed, others removed their hats. In the crowds surrounding the house at St Clair Avenue were many well-dressed men and women, who knew Barker only by reputation. Nevertheless, they had come out on a Saturday afternoon just to pay their respects.

An honour guard and firing party of 35 RCAF airmen from Camp Borden Air Station, their rifles reversed, led the cortege at 60-paces-to-the-minute. The band of the Toronto Scottish Regiment, its drums covered in black felt, were directly behind them, playing the dirge, "Dead March in Saul." An officer's sword and dress hat rested on top of the Union-Jack-draped coffin. Immediately behind the caisson the same RCAF RSM that had stood guard inside the house now carried a purple silk cushion supporting all the hero's decorations.

Behind the RSM were five Victoria Cross recipients, one carrying a wreath of poppies in the shape of the patée bronze cross. They were Corporal Colin Barron, 3rd Canadian Infantry Battalion (Toronto Regiment); Chaplain Benjamin Geary, formerly 4th Battalion, East Surrey Regiment; Private Thomas Holmes, formerly 4th Canadian Mounted Rifles; Private Walter Rayfield, 7th Canadian Infantry

Battalion (1st British Columbia); and Private Henry Robson, formerly 2nd Battalion, The Royal Scots (The Lothian Regiment).

Barker's coffin was escorted by the most important military officers in the nation, including at least four generals. The Chief of the General Staff, Major General "Andy" McNaughton, who witnessed Barker's VC action, and Brig General Victor Williams, who had interviewed William Barker for the RFC marched in the parade. There were six honorary pall bearers, including the four most senior flying officers of the RCAF. They were the acting director, Wing Commander Lloyd Breadner; the head of civil government air operations, Group Captain Lindsay Gordon; the commanding officer of Camp Borden, Wing Commander George Croil; and Squadron Leader Earl Godfrey. The two Army pall bearers were Lt Colonel Eberts McIntyre and Lt Colonel T. Wendell MacDowell, VC, DSO.

Prime Minister Mackenzie King sent two members of the Liberal Cabinet: the Minister of Trade and Commerce, James Malcolm, and the Minister of Health, Dr J.H. King. Representing the province of Ontario were Lieutenant Governor W.D. Ross, Premier Howard Ferguson, and several members of his Cabinet. Representing the city were Mayor Bert Wemp, himself a decorated RNAS pilot, and some of his city councillors, as well as former mayor Sam McBride.

The company that Barker had briefly worked for was struggling with their worst public relations nightmare. A famous man had been killed in one of their aircraft, an aircraft they had hoped to sell to the Canadian government. Still, they sent official mourners. Ernest Robinson, vice president of Fairchild on Long Island, and Martyn Pasmore and Ron Irvine from Montreal walked in the procession.

The Barker women, Jean, Jane, Ilda, and Edna did not go to the cemetery. The Barker men, George, Percy, Lloyd, and Orval walked beside Horace Smith. Orval had never experienced anything like this. The only funerals that could remotely compare with his brother Willie's were those he had seen in Chicago, as rivals of the Al Capone gang went to their final rest.

The Toronto Flying Club had provided an aerial escort, and pilots from other clubs in the region had travelled to Toronto to do a flypast, 10 men in six aircraft. In the bright skies above, the two three-plane vee formations circled. They had taken off from Leaside aerodrome, and several times they descended over the long procession, scattering rose petals. All the light aircraft were flown by ex-military flyers who had known Barker.

Two of the pilots, including the leader of the formation, had served with him in Italy, and five others were Great War veterans (the latter were R. Carter Guest; P A. Hutton; J.G. Crang; C.W. Dingwall; W.T. Wrathall). The two Italian front veterans were Earl McNabb Hand, and "Voss" Williams. Williams was sick-at-heart about Will's death, and his mind was flooded with wartime conversations and memories as he flew above Toronto. Hand told reporters that: "Barker enjoyed the most colourful career of all Canadian pilots serving in the Great War—he was, in my opinion, the finest that Canada has produced."

On a Saturday afternoon, there were thousands of school boys running beside and ahead of the cortege. They pointed at the aircraft, and followed the coffin with solemn eyes. This was an event to remember. They scrambled ahead of the procession, up Warren Road, east along Heath Street, and north up Yonge Street. Most of the boys knew who Barker was, how many German planes he had shot down, and how many medals he had won. They wanted to see his coffin lifted from the gun carriage, and they wanted to hear the trumpets and rifles.

Spectators stood shoulder-to-shoulder on the lawn of Yorkminister Church, near the Yonge Street gate to the cemetery. There was a police cordon around the Mount Pleasant Mausoleum, and policemen on horseback, cantering up and down the path leading to the Mausoleum, shouted at the crowds to stay back. But lots of boys, and some men and women, broke through the cordon, even climbing over the cemetery fence, to get a better view of the cortege coming through the entrance gate.

The gravel on the pathway crunched under the wheels of the aircraft tender and gun carriage,

as the honour guard slow-marched in time to the muffled drum beats. As the cortege pulled up to the mausoleum, the drum beats stopped. The coffin was unstrapped from the gun carriage.

The RCAF rifle party fired three volleys, and then two buglers sounded the Last Post and, after a silence, Reveille. The eight airmen assigned to carry Barker's remains moved cautiously up the shallow steps, the coffin digging into their shoulders. Earl Hand then descended low enough so that people looking up could clearly read the registration letters on the underside of the wing. The last rose petals were thrown out, and they floated down like a pale pink cloud. The five aircraft that followed behind him each left a shower of pink.

The pallbearers turned to the right, past the chapel inside the entrance, conscious of the heavy weight on their shoulders, and the slippery marble floor beneath their cleated boots. They turned left, then right again, into the centre hall. At the end was an unlocked bronze door to a white marble chamber.

Waiting by the high window at the end of the hall was the Bishop of Toronto, the Right Reverend J.F. Sweeny. He delivered a final eulogy. The coffin was then lifted well off the ground into a slot, designated as Crypt B, on the right interior wall of Room B. Orval Barker watched intently. Never having seen a crypt, he could not understand why they were putting his brother Willie inside a closet.

The city of Toronto had seen nothing to match the Barker funeral in a long time. The pink cloud of rose petals and the fading drone of aircraft engines were signals to the spectators: "The spell was broken. The crowds began to dissolve, traffic stopped for more than an hour, resumed its way. It was over. Canada had buried her Barker but a gallant soul lives on."

The RCAF guard shouldered arms and marched away. The men had come to the funeral by train and street car to honour their former commanding officer. They rode the street car back to Union Station. They had been told to bring their own lunch, but the adjutant-general in Ottawa authorized a 65-cent dinner at the Union Station restaurant. The train pulled out for Barrie just before 10:00 p.m., and since the men of Camp Borden had been up since before

6:00 a.m., many of them dozed on the trip home.

The Smith and Barker families, and a few members of the funeral cortege, including Godfrey, sat down in the large dining room of the Smith home for dinner. Horace Smith presided at the head of the table, serving up slices of rare roast beef to his guests. Godfrey sat next to the youngest Barker boy, and talked to him about the accident, saying that Will should never have taken the trainer up, being unused to the low power.

After dinner, demitasses of strong coffee were served in the drawing room. The banks of flowers and wreaths were still in place. The men sat around speaking in subdued tones and the atmosphere was somewhat more than sad, it was tense. The Barkers were particularly conscious of the gulf between their own lives and social position, and that of the man who was their host.

At some point in the conversation, Smith made some disparaging comment about his late son-in-law. This precipitated a quarrel. Lloyd leaped up to hit him, and it was due only to Percy's fast reflexes that Horace didn't end up on his back. Feeling like a lost soul, Orval drifted away, and found his way "below stairs" to the butler's pantry. Sitting with the family chauffeur and a house boy, he was regaled with stories about his famous brother, who had left behind only good memories for the servants.

Nowadays, posthumous poems are a rarity when a public figure dies. But, without a trace of parody, several poems were composed in memory of William Barker and some were published in the newspapers. One woman who had sat near Will in class at Russell, Edna McDougall, wrote:

It seems to me twas yesterday,
Yet eighteen years have passed away,
Since he sat in school amongst us all,
With keen brown eyes, slim and tall, ...
We little tho't that "His" life was meant to
share the lives of famous men,
To us he was just 'Bill' Barker then, ...
And we as a class would like to meet our hero
who sat in the second seat,
But alas we read of an awful crash.

Michael Delaney in Winnipeg recalled his Victoria-Cross fight: "You felt the Spandau's lash, and reeling came back to rout the black-cross kings." Canon Frederick George Scott, former military chaplain of the CEF's 1st Canadian Division, wrote:

Up to the regions of battle
Where broods invisible Death
On the broad white wings of morning
Fanned by the winter's breath.
Our comrade rose, light-hearted
With eyes that gazed afar
Till the arrow of Fate's bow struck him,
And he plunged like a falling star.

Will's death, in what seemed a freak accident, effectively erased the last 11 years of his life. Unable to justify such an untimely end, journalists and historians pushed back the climax of his life to 27 October 1918. It was that event that made him legendary, and it was more comfortable to freeze his legendary reputation at its apex. After such a battle, any life would seem ordinary, and any death an anticlimax. No one wanted to know about Barker's personal problems, his pain, or his dark night of the soul.

Every sketch of his life, every magazine article of his war career, every propaganda piece, every obituary, either started or ended with the winning of the Victoria Cross. Barker was inducted into Canada's Aviation Hall of Fame solely on the strength of it, rather than for any post-war accomplishment.

For the men who had served with him, it was like a white-hot light had been extinguished. This hero left few untouched. No more need be said than "I knew Barker, I flew with him in the war." to gain deference from other men. One need not even know him personally to be affected by his death. As young Duchesneau had written: "It dealt me a blow as if I had lost a relative of mine or a friend."

The bronze door to the Smith family crypt was closed and locked. Jane Barker never visited the crypt at the time, or later. Her faith told her that her boy was not there.

William Barker's daughter, Jean Mackenzie, as a Royal Canadian Navy officer during the Second World War; she deliberately chose the RCN over the RCAF to avoid publicity concerning her famous father.

EPILOGUE

"Like Barker? I liked him. Jesus, more than liked him, I practically adored him!"

AIR VICE-MARSHAL KENNETH M. GUTHRIE, 1991

The wreckage of CF-AKR was never returned to the company, and after a few days in the corner of a hangar, was placed in the dump at Rockcliffe. A legend had died in the machine, and men were drawn to the remains. Rockcliffe's airmen removed a few bits and pieces from the KR-21 as keepsakes. Jack Hunter took the No 1 cylinder of the engine, added a walnut base, and converted it to a lamp. Someone else kept the control column from the front cockpit. The RCAF never bought the trainer, and no more than 45 or 50 were ever built. A few Fairchild KR-21s have been painstakingly restored, and are highly regarded by their owners for their beautiful handling traits.

Stories were exchanged within the flying community about Barker's fatal accident for many years after. Some believed that no one as talented as Barker could make such a simple flying error. One legend was that he had killed himself, unable to cope with his severe physical and emotional pain. This myth endures despite the history of other First World War veterans who had come to a similar end. In Great Britain, Anthony Beauchamp-Proctor, VC, had been killed during a practice flight in a Sopwith Snipe in June 1921.

Three months after Barker died, his widow grieved for their friend, Major John Leach, killed in a crash at Port Arthur, leaving his wife to raise three small children. A couple of years later Barker's friend from the war, Flight Lieut "Mable" Apps, was killed in his RCAF Fairchild FC2 at Peterborough, on takeoff for a routine navigation training flight. Jean Barker wrote Jane Barker from Lakefield, Ontario: "It was hard for me when we first came up here, as I was reminded of Billie at every turn, and all the people round about were eager to talk about him. However, I think it did me good, and I feel closer to him and happier and more contented than I believed possible. Everyone in this vicinity had such a high regard for Billie, even the Indians knew and liked him and it is nice to be surrounded with that sympathy."

Arguing against the possibility of suicide was the fact that Barker's life had taken an encouraging turn upward. He was no longer a tobacco farmer, he was an aircraft salesman. However, for some, it was easier to believe that he had chosen to die, rather than been rusty after years away from flying.

The other rumour was that alcohol had been a contributing factor to the accident—that Barker had been

·LIEUT-COLONEL·WILLIAM·GEORGE·BARKER·V.C·D.S.O·M.C·
·BELOVED·HUSBAND·OF·JEAN·KILBOURN·SMITH·
·NOVEMBER·3·1894 — MARCH·12·1930·
·IN·MEMORIAM·

Inscribed marble facing in front of Barker's coffin inside the Smith family crypt.

Photo by Wayne Ralph

drinking before going flying. Grandy, Ogilvie-Forbes, and Chapman were specifically asked during the RCAF Court of Inquiry if Barker appeared normal in appearance and conversation prior to flight. The three men said he did. If Barker had been drinking, they were in the uncomfortable position of allowing him to go flying, knowing he was unfit. Sylvia Graham remembered him as alert, sober, and quite enthusiastic about the new aircraft, as did Grandy and Ogilvie-Forbes.

Barker left behind no last will and testament. He had few assets to give anybody. His clothing was shipped by Jean to his parents in Chicago. Jean commissioned a stained-glass window for the back wall of the Smith family crypt to honour her husband. Lily, the wife of the family cook, went to Mount Pleasant Mausoleum to leave fresh flowers through the summer of 1930.

Perhaps because of her feelings about the RCAF and "Jimmy" Scott, Jean had the marble facing over her husband's coffin engraved with his rank as a lieutenant colonel, rather than the equivalent RCAF rank of wing commander. The pilot's wings engraved into the marble inside the crypt are those of the RFC, not the RCAF.

There is no evidence in the Mausoleum that any member of the Barker family is entombed there. No-one from William Barker's immediate family, the Barkers or the Alguires, has been to the crypt since March 1930. There is nothing on the door of the crypt or the marble walls of the Mausoleum to commemorate Canada's most decorated war hero, or mark his connection to the military history of the nation. Barker's remains lie in anonymity in Room B, seldom visited, and far from the Great Plains on which he was born. (*Author's note in January 2007: the Mackenzie family will erect a memorial to their famous grandfather at Mount Pleasant Cemetery in the near future.*)

Jean had never been enthusiastic about military life, but she took an interest in preserving her late husband's reputation. Days after his funeral, she requested from the DND a service medal called the "1914-15 Star," to which Barker was entitled, but did not wear, and apparently had never received. The DND obtained his medal from England and forwarded it to her. Some years later, she protested to Ernest Hemingway's publishers about the portrayal of her late husband in *The Snows of Kilimanjaro*.

On 6 June 1931, an aerodrome of 220 acres on the west side of Dufferin, north of Lawrence Avenue, which had been in use since 1927, was named Barker Field. The dedication ceremony, in pouring rain, was attended by Bishop, Jean and Antoinette Barker, Horace Smith, the new Mayor of Toronto, W.J. Stewart, and Canon Baynes.

Earl Hand was master of ceremonies, and his company, National Air Transport Limited, which was already located at the aerodrome, demonstrated its new sales line of Buhl Bull Pup aircraft. An autogiro was brought up from the United States for the occasion, and Flying Officers Davy, Wray, and Edwards from Camp Borden did a formation demonstration. At an evening dinner at the Royal York Hotel, "J.A." Wilson gave a speech recommending that every city in Canada have a municipal airport, a proposal that Barker and Bishop had made back in 1919.

Barker Field thrived through the 1930s and the Second World War, and thousands of young men and women learned to fly there. The growth of the city made the land so valuable that, by 1953, Barker Field had been closed to flying, but opened to real estate development.

Jean remarried, to Gerald E. D. Greene, an engineer, architect, and farmer, with various business interests, including a dairy farm in Toronto on York Mills road. They had no children, and when Greene died in 1974, Jean entombed his remains above those of her first husband.

She maintained a small shrine in her living room to the first love of her life, including his portrait, and his framed medals above the mantle. She was a member of the Imperial Order of the Daughters of the Empire, and flew only the Union Jack at her garden parties. Jack Hunter, who retired as the head of Transport Canada's flight operations department, lived next door to Mrs Greene. She liked to talk to Jack and to Air Vice-Marshal Tommy Lawrence about her "poor Billie." Unhappy with the Canadian governments of the 1960s and 1970s, she refused to give the government her husband's unique set of gallantry medals. They were not formally gifted to the nation till after her death.

Jean died in December 1983, and was the last to be entombed in the crypt. Her marble facing was inscribed "Jean Kilbourn Barker Greene—Beloved Wife of W.G. Barker and G.E.D. Greene." The Smith family crypt is now full.

* * *

On the outbreak of World War Two, the unblooded Royal Canadian Air Force was faced with a propaganda challenge. It had no war history as a fighting service, yet hundreds of Canadians had brilliant records in the Great War with the RFC, RNAS, and RAF. Using as a basis the George Drew biography, the Chief of Staff authorized a booklet in 1940 titled *Canada's Air Heritage*. It was distributed within the service and handed out to some graduating classes of pilots to remind them of their lineage and congratulate them on their achievement.

Only four men were featured in the booklet: Bishop, Barker, Collishaw, and McLeod. The profile on Barker altered certain aspects of his CAF/RCAF career. It has him joining sooner and leaving sooner, and does not say he was the RCAF's first acting director in 1924. As to his death, the booklet declared: "A stalled engine had done what the combined skill and intent of thousands of enemy pilots in many skies had hitherto been unable to accomplish." In World War Two, the RCAF wanted to forget that they had attributed his death to pilot error. The Chief of Air Staff wrote: "Today we are at war again—and once more Canadians are in the front rank of airmen ... Thus Canada's air traditions, nobly begun, are being carried on."

To further cement the relationship between the Canadian flyers of the First World War and those of the Second, RCAF Headquarters had oil paintings commissioned of the four heroes. Copies of the paintings were distributed in large numbers to flying schools and stations across Canada. A few Canadian Forces Bases, Schools, and Messes today still have on their walls the gold-framed portraits that were commissioned to promote these four fighting legends more than 60 years ago.

In the Second World War, Billy Bishop was elevated to the honorary rank of Air Marshal. As the Director of Recruiting he gave many speeches, attended graduation parades to pin on wings, showed up for public relations events, and even played himself in a James Cagney movie released in 1942 called *Captains of the Clouds*. Bishop never forgot Barker, and was still promoting his legend in 1944-45. He used his war career as a model of courage for the new generation of RCAF flyers. He especially wanted the Canadian public to remember him and when he wrote *Winged Peace* in 1944 he devoted an entire chapter to his former business partner. Bishop died in 1956, and his funeral in Toronto rivalled Barker's for size and drama, including flypasts by RCAF jet aircraft. His remains were interred in the family plot in Owen Sound.

During the Second World War, Barker's daughter, Jean, decided that she did not want a spotlight on her just because she was the offspring of a famous hero. Concerned that this might happen if she was in the RCAF, she joined the Women's Division of the Royal Canadian Navy, eventually becoming a commissioned officer in the RCN, and a plotter for North Atlantic convoys.

George and Jane returned to Dauphin in 1932 and lived out the rest of their days in the town. Cecil also came back to the district to farm. George died in 1950, Jane in 1962, Cecil in 1989. These Dauphin pioneers are buried in Riverside Cemetery. Percy died in Van Nuys, California, sometime in the 1960s. Howard Alguire died in 1966, still an active farmer and keen gardener, and a much-admired member of the Barker-Alguire clan. Edna Barker Buchannon died in 2002 and Orval in 2003.

The writing of this book was sustained by the respect and love felt by four old warriors for the greatest warrior of them all. It was because of Thomas F. Williams that I first learned of William Barker, VC. "Voss" died in 1985, just a few weeks short of his 100th birthday. He was still flying in his own aircraft until he was 87, and had made it into the record books as the world's oldest licensed pilot. He never stopped paying homage to Barker.

Gerry Birks outlived all his friends at 66 Squadron and when he died in May 1991, aged 96, he held the distinction of being Canada's last surviving scout ace of the Great War. He was proud of his war record and especially his gunnery skills, saying to me, "I shot down 12, six in flames." I met him on the last day possible in his life for one precious, magical afternoon, less than two months before he died. His words, "six in flames," echo vividly in my memory today. Air Vice-Marshal Tommy Lawrence passed away less than a year after Birks and Air Vice-Marshal Ken Guthrie a few months after Lawrence.

For these four men born in the 19th century, life had been full of adventure and, above all, comradeship. Williams once said that nothing he experienced after the First World War matched the camaraderie of flyers in a fighting squadron in the Royal Flying Corps. Men were judged by the abiding virtues of courage, character, and honesty. Nothing else mattered if you had them, and nothing could redeem you if you didn't. For Williams, Birks, Lawrence, and Guthrie, William Barker was a shining example of those virtues—a fine breed of man, of pioneer stock, above all a patriot. He was remembered in their hearts long after he had been forgotten by his country.

I had only a few visits with these old men, scrambling as I was, so late in the day, to recapture their past. There are many, many questions I wish I had asked, but one in particular I was glad I did. On my last visit with Guthrie, our dinner over, Ken shook my hand and said: "All old men, we like to talk about the past. We don't give a damn about the future ... and, in the present in Canada there is too much fighting and arguing, and NO decision-making." On that political note, we said goodbye.

As I turned to leave I asked him if, beyond respecting his courageous achievements, he had actually liked William Barker. Guthrie growled: "Like Barker? I liked him. Jesus, more than liked him, I practically adored him!"

It is now more than 110 years since Barker was born in the log house on the northern Prairies, and more than 75 years since his death. Few legends live more than 100 years. We should not be surprised

in the 21st century that the story of our most decorated war hero, of one of the British Empire's most decorated heroes, in our first Great War, is no longer remembered. The bloody and cruel Battle of the Somme is a name that now echoes like Agincourt or Gettysburg.

A common question I am asked by young people when I speak about Barker's achievements is: "What is a Victoria Cross?" They can hardly be expected to know, since Canada's history as a Dominion of the British Empire is no longer taught in Canadian schools, and our history as warriors within that Empire is now politically and socially irrelevant and, in some eyes, horrific and contemptible.

Unlike Britain and the United States, Canada did not build a "Tomb of the Unknown Soldier" immediately after the Great War. It took us 19 years to put up a national war memorial in Ottawa, and

Photo by Wayne Ralph

Orval Barker, William's youngest brother, in Dauphin, Manitoba, 1991.

our most evocative and dramatic memorial to the Great War is in France at Vimy Ridge. Due to our policy of burying our war dead where they fell, Canada never created a cemetery like Arlington in the United States. It was only about five years ago that a section of Beechwood Cemetery in Ottawa was set aside as the "National Military Cemetery of the Canadian Forces."

If it is true, as Canadian philosopher Northrop Frye has noted, that Canadians seem to like their heroes *smaller* than life, then Barker is sadly irrelevant. Outside of Canada, however, he is still occasionally remembered. Almost all the magazine articles and narratives about Barker in the past 20 years have been written by American writers who still like their heroes *larger* than life, and don't mind them having a darker, more complicated side.

Canadian historians and writers quickly erased everything that made Barker a human being, especially his physical and psychological pain. We were left with this cartoon image of a warrior—his life before and after 27 October 1918 only a footnote. His interment in the private Smith family crypt, without even a bronze plaque to mark his place, was the final footnote.

Our most decorated war hero gradually became our unknown soldier, except, most importantly, in the hearts of the men and women who had loved him. My greatest reward was to meet some of those men and women and, with their help, resurrect Barker, the man and the hero, from his tomb.

Barker's father and mother, George and Jane Barker, are presented with a painting of their son by Air Vice-Marshal Kenneth Guthrie (on right) at the end of the Second World War.

Airforce Magazine collection

Dedication ceremony for Barker Field, 6 June 1931; left to right, Horace Smith, Jean Barker, Reverend Baynes-Reid.

Dedication ceremony for Barker Field, 6 June 1931.

There were Germans everywhere. The sky was a mass of red. Still Barker fought on, pulling a surprise every minute.

"Greatest Fighter Pilot the World Has Ever Known"

... is what Billy Bishop called Bill Barker the Ace of the Alps. Was this a case of one Canuck boosting another or did he rate this? Here's the evidence — see what you think

Every generation of writers since 1930 has resurrected the Barker legend; example above was written in 1960 by William W. Walker for *Cavalier Magazine*.

Barker standing by B6313 at 28 Squadron, Italy, 1917.

APPENDIX ONE

LETTER FROM FRANK WOOLLEY SMITH, OBE, DFC

Croft House
Weavers Ring
Angmering, Sx.
7-1-69

The Defence Attaché,
Canada House,
Trafalgar Square.
London SW I.

Dear Sir,

For the 50th Anniversary of the formation of the R.A.F. I was asked by the Station Commander, R.A.F. Thorney Island if I had an 'vintage photos' which might be of interest in their exhibition which they are putting on at the Station.

Amongst several I lent them was the one I now enclose herewith (with relative [*sic*] press cuttings) and which they have now returned to me. I personally took the photo of the upturned "Snipe" as it landed after Barker's epic sortie in which he won the V.C.

At the time (some date in Sept [*sic*] 1918) I was serving as an observer with 29 Kite Balloon Section, R.A.F.

Very early in the morning on the date of Barker's fight we were roused by the sound of a fighter plane of unusual type circling round overhead and gradually descending; obviously looking for a place to land. Something appeared to be wrong as the engine seemed either to be at full throttle or else completely cut out.

After a couple of circuits the plane came in to land at considerable speed, struck some strands of barbed wire and up-turned onto its back. It was only about fifty yards away and with men of my section I rushed to extricate the pilot before a possible fire took place. He was pinned underneath, obviously badly wounded and only partially conscious.

On cutting away his Sidcot flying suit we were astonished to see his tunic bore the ribbons of the D.S.O., M.C., Croix-de-Guerre & the Italian Medal for bravery.

I personally took him into the nearest Field Dressing Station in our Crossley Tender and, during the trip, applied pressure to an artery in the groin to stop bleeding.

I later visited him in the Air Force hospital in Grosvenor Crescent. He then told me the reason for his full-throttle, off-and-on landing was because the bullet through his left elbow prevented him getting at the throttle on the port side of the cockpit. At the time he was hit the throttle was full on, and the only means of controlling the engine was by means of the cut-out button on the top of the control column.

He recovered fully, returned to Canada and, I believe, was regrettably killed in some quite trivial accident in a light plane. I do not know the circumstances.

The scratch marks on the print occurred because the negative was in the camera for several weeks in very damp conditions.

Cameras were banned to any serving personnel under penalty of a court-martial and I was in the somewhat invidious position of having to read out the order and penalties to my section all of whom, of course, knew quite well I had one and had taken interesting photos in which they were included!

Perhaps the scratches can be taken out by a photographic expert?

If you wish to keep the photos and attached cuttings for your historical records please do so with my best wishes. I think I would prefer them to go to Canada than be lost in jungle of the R.A.F. Museum, Henlow.

I have visited Canada three times and have cherished memories of fishing holidays amid the glorious mountain country of British Columbia where I have many good friends. I would dearly like to make a fourth visit before I become too antique to do so!

Yours faithfully
signed – F. Woolley Smith

ENC: – Letter from Stn. Commander, Thorney Island.
(return of this not required.)

Canadian Section,
General Headquarters,
Third Echelon, B.E.F.

January 6th, 1919.

TO: D.A.A.G., Canadian Section,
        G.H.Q., Third Echelon.

Sir,

As instructed, this afternoon I went up to No. 8 General Hospital to see Major W.G. Barker, VC, DSO, Royal Air Force, and to ascertain his condition.

I found Major Barker was making excellent progress and the Medical Authorities were very well satisfied and pleased with his condition and progress towards recovery. It is expected that he may be transferred to England by about the middle of the month.

Major Barker's wounds are, one in the left arm, the elbow joint having been shot away, leaving only a muscular connection; one through the upper part of the muscle on the inside of the right leg, and one through the left hip, passing down through the muscles of the left leg, the bone of the hip being slightly fractured where hit.

The arm wound is healing very satisfactorily and Major Barker will have a certain amount of use of the arm; he is now able to move the thumb and all the fingers except the little one. The second is in good shape. The wound in the left hip is doing well, but will be rather a long time in healing, particularly on account of the injury to the bone.

He was very bright and cheerful, eating well and getting quite a lot of sleep.

I had over an hour's talk with him, during which he gave me a good description of his last encounter with the Huns. It began by him going up to 22,000 feet to get a two seater. He told me that when going after this one, he did not act with his usual care in seeing that there was not a trap laid, and when he had downed the Hun two-seater, he found fifteen Huns below him. Two machines came after him and he got the first wound through the left hip. He attached [sic] the Hun who had wounded him bringing him down, then bringing down the other machine which was attacking with the second machine, which was brought down. He was later wounded in the left arm and fell quite a distance before regaining control of his machine. After doing so, he brought down the Hun who gave him his last wound. During this latter action he had only the use of his right arm, guiding the machine and using his right machine gun at the same time. He was unable to shut off the engine which was controlled from the left side.

His chief regret is that he will be unable to play Hockey, Baseball or Water Polo again, on account of his left arm.

signed – B. Johnston, Captain. Canadian Section.

Column by Barker in the London *Sunday Express*, 1922,
in response to author John Galsworthy

Shall We Abandon the Air?

by Wing-Commander W.G. Barker, VC, DSO, MC etc.

In the closing days of the War the whole world was thrilled by the story of Wing-Commander (then Major) Barker's single-handed fight against sixty Hun machines. It was as great an epic as that of Sir Richard Grenville and the Spanish Armada.

He has just reached London from Canada and has some significant things to say to "Sunday Express" readers.

When I arrived in London last week from Canada it was with a natural excitement that I found England discussing the future of her Air Force and of the aeroplane generally.

Naturally, I did not expect to take part in the discussion at all, but when the Editor of the "Sunday Express" showed me a letter from Mr. John Galsworthy to the Press advocating the complete civil and military abandoning of the air, I felt that if an author can encroach on matters of defence, perhaps an airman might be excused for invading the territory of an author.

Mr. Galsworthy always deserves respect. But his opinions on the air are not practical. To say "Stop!" to the conquering of the air is to order the incoming tide to recede.

LONDON'S ONLY DEFENCE

It is true that the air is a dreadful menace in war. It is true that the next war will be hideous beyond description; but war is made by men and nations, not by machines. Stop war by all means—but you cannot stop scientific progress.

Therefore, aeroplanes must remain and multiply, and since every civilian aeroplane is a potential bomb carrier, and since the nations have not yet put out the fires of hatred, we must be prepared for war.

Let us assume that some time in the future Germany and England duplicate the situation of August 1914. An ultimatum is given. It expires. Three hours later a huge fleet of aeroplanes are over London.

And London cannot be defended

To my mind there can never be any defences adequate to repel the aeroplane. The only defence is offence. While they bomb London we put Berlin in ruins. Apparently a very good argument for Mr. Galsworthy.

THE NAVY'S PART

As a matter of fact, it is the biggest possible argument for a tremendous air force. Great Britain must assume the role in the air which she has played in the past on the sea—control without tyranny, domination with justice. Great Britain must be so powerful that war will be impossible.

Now I come to a delicate subject. I know how England loves her Navy and all the glorious traditions of the sea, but without prejudice I am convinced that the Navy must dwindle and dwindle in importance.

When I say this I do not mean to belittle the Royal Navy. Every British subject knows that it was the Navy that made victory possible. But conditions have changed, and we must change to meet present-day developments.

In 1914 an enemy could only disturb our shores after defeating our Grand Fleet, but that is not true to-day. A powerful fleet of commercial seaplanes hurriedly converted into bombers could cause terrific havoc in this country, and it is a question whether or not our Navy would be aware of their presence.

INADEQUATE LAND GUNS

And again, a fleet can only engage coastal targets, and that with questionable effect, since the perfection of the submarine and the mine, while a force of aeroplanes can strike at the heart of industry.

My experience in the war proved conclusively to me that ground or land defence was not a success. No number of land guns could prevent a determined and resourceful airman from attacking his target.

The finest battleship, escorted by cruisers and destroyers, cannot be protected from an aeroplane. An expert pilot could manoeuvre to an absolutely certain range and by torpedo attack blow the ship and the millions it represents to atoms. And if an aeroplane or two is lost in such an attack, the taxpayer will never notice it.

A SECURITY FOR PEACE

With Mr. Galsworthy's opinion that we cannot continue to muddle through, I am in the heartiest accord. It would be the most dreadful folly to continue the existing paralysing policy towards both the civil and military branches of the air. Most of us who have flown in other days will soon be reaching the time when we shall be discarded like the good old omnibuses of 1914 that went rattling and wheezing into the air to meet the rattling and wheezing omnibuses of the enemy. But where are the pilots to follow us? How will they be trained?

No one but a madman wants to see another war, but there is no greater guarantee of war than an air policy of indifference on the part of Great Britain. And there is no greater guarantee of peace than to make the British Air Force the trustee of the air for Europe.

The world knows such a trust would never be abused.

GENERAL

Transcription copies of original RFC/RAF documents, including combat reports and communiqués, and the excerpts from Barker's personal letters, are quoted exactly as they were written or typed, without editorial correction, other than the noting of spelling and syntax errors. The most useful archives in the preparation of this book were:

> National Archives of Canada (NAC)
> NAC Personnel Records Centre (PRC)
> The Directorate of History (DHist), DND
> The Stewart K. Taylor collection
> The Provincial Archives of Manitoba (PAM)
> The RAF Personnel Management Centre (PRC)
> The Imperial War Museum (IWM)
> The Canadian War Museum (CWM)
> The Library of Congress, Manuscript Division, USA

The references for individual holdings in each archive, with file numbers when applicable, are listed in the bibliography.

The author did not review the original RFC/RAF documents at the Public Records Office (PRO) in England, but has drawn from the RCAF and Canadian Forces transcriptions and photocopies gathered over five decades by Canadian military historians.

Wise, *Canadian Airmen*, Jones H.A., *The War in the Air*, Shores, Franks, Guest, *Above The Trenches*, and O'Connor, *Air Aces of the Austro-Hungarian Empire 1914-1918* were invaluable references. The best summary of Barker's victory record is in *Above The Trenches*, and this has been used in conjunction with DHist and NAC files, and Dodds, *The Brave Young Wings*, and *High Flight*.

The articles in *Cross & Cockade* (UK), *Cross & Cockade* (US) and Over The Front have been extremely useful, particularly those by Boksay/Guttman, D'Ami, Grosz, Haddow, Kerr, Robinson, Sapru, Scheimer; and also Peball's and Warner's essays on the ground war, Vol. 9 of Young, *Marshall Cavendish Encyclopaedia*.

Previous to this work, the longest Barker biography was in Drew, *Canada's Fighting Airmen*. Regrettably, due to a dispute about ownership and the authority to release, Volume 409 of the Drew collection (MG30 C3) at National Archives, about the research for *Canada's Fighting Airmen*, was unavailable to the author.

My interpretation of Barker's personality and actions are based on interviews with relatives, and people who knew him, as well as his letters and lectures. A 1994 scriptoanalysis of Barker's hand-written letters by Susanne Shaw offered useful insights. Medical and psychological discussion was based on several surgical and PTSD books, all listed in the bibliography. I owe a big intellectual debt to James Jones, *Whistle*, and Neil Sheehan, *A Bright Shining Lie*, which fired my early interest in the subject of war heroes and trauma.

Any questions about Barker, sources, and chapter notes are welcomed. The author can be reached via the Internet at the following email address: *wayneralph@telus.net*

INTRODUCTION: THE WAR HERO IN THE CRYPT
Archives: NAC, NAC/PRC, City of Toronto.
Books: Filey, Graham.
Correspondence: Filey, MacInnes.
Interviews: Filey, Hawkins, MacInnes, Mount Pleasant Cemetery staff.
Magazines, Journals, Newspapers: *Mail and Empire, Globe, Evening Telegram, Toronto Daily Star*, 15, 17 Mar 1930.

CHAPTER ONE: A MAN OF PIONEER STOCK
Archives: Alguire collection, Barker collection, Fort Dauphin Museum, IWM, PAM, Taylor collection, Hitchins List/ Dodds collection.
Books: Dauphin Historical Society, Dauphin Rural Municipality, Duguid, Ellis, Fuller/Griffin/Molson, Gray, Little, Morton/Granatstein, Regehr, Russell's Women's Institute, Shores/Franks/Guest, Singh, Stegner, Tascona, Thompson.
Correspondence: Hull, Naylor, Shaw, Wray.
Interviews: Alguire W., Barker O., Buchannon E., Ferguson, Ledingham, Sainsbury E., Tascona, Taylor.
Logbook/Barker: Oct 1917.
Logbook/Camel B6313: page 6.
Combat Report: 26 Oct 1917, 28 Squadron.
Magazines, Journals, Newspapers: *Cross & Cockade* (UK), Winter 1975, *Over The Front*, Winter 1986, *Liberty Magazine*, 29 Aug 1931, *Dauphin Press*, 1 Dec 1914, *Manitoba Free Press*, 14, 22 Jul 1911.

CHAPTER TWO: MACHINE GUNNER IN THE CANADIAN MOUNTED RIFLES

Archives: Alguire collections, Barker collections, DHist/DND, NAC, NAC/PRC, PAM, Reg't Museum/LSH, University of Victoria.

Books: Bishop Billy, Bishop W.A. (*Courage of The Early Morning*), Bennett, Drew, Duguid, English, Fussell, General Staff/War Office, Hogg/Weeks, Kludas, Marteinson/Greenhous/Harris, et al, McCaffery (*Billy Bishop*), McAskill, McWilliams/Steel, Meek, Morton, Morton/Granatstein, Nicholson, Rawling, Reid, Roy, Stegner, Tascona, Winter (*Haig's Command*).

Correspondence: Christie, Rawling, Cooke, Tascona, NAC, NAC/PRC, PAM.

Interviews: Alguire E., Alguire W., Barker O., Buchannon E., Marsh, Tascona.

Letters/Barker/NAC MG30 E195: 4,10,19 Mar; 22 Sept; 22 Oct; 3, 20, 24, 27 Nov; 25 Dec 1915; 17, 21, 25 Jan; 2, 9 Feb 1916; 4 Feb 1919.

Magazines, Journals, Newspapers: *Brandon Weekly Sun*, 20, 26 May 1915, *Dauphin Press*, 11 Mar 1915.

Regimental War Diary, 1st CMR: NAC RG9, Vol. 4946, Folder 464.

CHAPTER THREE: CORPS COOPERATION DUTIES ON THE SOMME

Archives: NAC, DHist/DND, Hitchins List/Dodds collection, PAM, RAF/PRC, Taylor collection.

Books: Armstrong, Barker R., Cooper, Drew, Dodds, Edmonds, Greenhous, Grinnell-Milne, Hawker, Hallion, Insall, Jones H.A., Kilduff, Lewis (*Farewell to Wings*), Mead, Winter, Wise, Woodman.

Correspondence: Phillips, Taylor, Williams T.F.

Interviews: Alguire W., Barker O., Barker E., Dodds, Taylor, Williams T.F.

Lectures: Wing Commander Barker's lectures on his war experiences, RAF Staff College.

Letters/Barker/NAC MG30 E195: 9, 27 Mar; 12, 19, 23, 25 Apr; 8, 14, 26 May; 15 Jun; 12, 26 Jul; 28 Aug; 26 Sept; 21 Oct; 3, 9, 12, 26 Nov; 2, 9 Dec 1916.

Magazines, Journals, Newspapers: *Cross & Cockade* (US), Spring 1968, *Dauphin Press*, no date (circa Dec-Jan 16-17), *London Gazette*, 10 Jan 1917.

CHAPTER FOUR: A PILOT AT LAST

Archives: NAC, DHist/DND, Hitchins List/Dodds collection, RAF/PRC, Taylor collection.

Books: Bean, Bishop Billy, Bishop W. Arthur, Bowyer (*Ball, VC*), Dodds, Drew, English, Fussell, Grinnell-

Milne, Hallion, Jones H.A., Kilduff, King, Lewis (*Sagittarius Rising*), Macmillan (*Memoirs, Brancker/Into the Blue*), Mead, Nicholson, Shores/Franks/Guest, Springs, Thompson, The Trail Makers Boys' Annual, Travers, Wise.

Correspondence: Creagen, Taylor.

Interviews: Alguire W., Barker O., Birks, Creagen, Dodds, Mackenzie D.W.G, Sainsbury, Taylor.

Letters/Barker/NAC MG30 E195: 20 Dec 1916; 18 Jan; 5, 9, 14 Feb; 6, 28 Apr 1917.

Magazines, Journals, Newspapers: *Clickety-Click*, Jun 1918, *Profile Publications* No. 85 (Bruce, 'The R.E.8'), *London Gazette*, 18 Jul 1917.

CHAPTER FIVE: FLIGHT COMMANDER IN A SCOUT SQUADRON

Archives: NAC, DHist/DND, Hitchins List/Dodds collection, IWM, RAF/PRC, Taylor collection.

Books: Armstrong, Bond, Bowyer (*Camel – King of Combat*), Chant, Dodds, Drew, Hemingway (*A Farewell to Arms/The Snows of Kilimanjaro*), Jones H.A., Kennett, Macmillan (*Offensive Patrol/Into the Blue*), Molson (*Canada's Nat'l Av. Museum*), Musciano, O'Connor, Shores/Franks/Guest, Singh, Smythe, Springs, Sturtivant/Page, Tredrey, Winter, Wise, Woodman.

Correspondence: Creagen, Taylor.

Interviews: Dodds, Taylor.

Lectures: Barker's lectures on his war experiences, RAF Staff College, 1925-26.

Letters/Barker/NAC MG30 E195: 29 Sept; 2, 10, 15 Oct; 1, 15, 1, 26, 30 Nov 1917; 1 Jan 1918.

Logbook/Barker: Sept-Dec 1917.

Logbook/Camel B6313: pages 1-10.

Magazines, Journals, Newspapers: *CAHS Journal*, Vol. 1, No. 4, *Cross & Cockade* (USA), Winter 74, Spring 76, *Cross & Cockade* (UK), Winter 75, *Over The Front*, Fall 1986, Winter 86-7, Summer 1987, *Popular Flying*, Jun 1935, *Profile Publications* No. 1 (Bruce, 'The S.E.5A'), Profiles in Vol. 7, 8, *Aircraft In Profile* (Haddow, 'Phonix Scout,' 'O. Aviatik (Berg) D.I.'), *The Sunday Express*, 1 Apr 1962, *War Birds*, Vol. 31, Oct 1935.

CHAPTER SIX: AIR WAR OVER THE ITALIAN ALPS

Archives: DHist/DND, Hitchins List/Dodds collection, IWM, NAC, RAF/PRC, Taylor collection.

Books: Allen, Barker R., Bond, Bowen, Corley-Smith, Dodds, Drew, Jones H.A., Joubert, Kennett, Macmillan (*Offensive Patrol*), Mead, Pariseau, Singh,

Shores/Franks/Guest, Spick, *Trail Makers Boy's Annual* (Barker's essay), Winter, Wise.

Correspondence: Taylor.

Interviews: Birks, Dodds, Sawyer, Taylor, Williams T.F.

Letters/Barker/NAC MG30 E195: 3 Feb 1918.

Logbook/Barker: Jan-Apr 1918.

Logbook/Camel B6313: pages 10-18.

Magazines, Journals, Newspapers: *Cross & Cockade* (US), Autumn 1967, *Liberty Magazine*, 29 August 1931, *London Gazette*, 18 Jul 1918, *Monitor*, circa 1960s, *Over The Front*, Fall 1986, Winter 86-7, Summer 1987, Profiles in Vol. 7, 8, *Aircraft In Profile* (Haddow, 'Phonix Scout,' 'O. Aviatik (Berg) D.I.'), *Sunday Express*, 1 Apr 1962, *Weekend Magazine*, No. 21, 1963.

CHAPTER SEVEN: SPRING OPERATIONS AT 66 SQUADRON

Archives: C.Av.H.Fame, DHist/DND, Hitchins List/Dodds collection, IWM, NAC, RAF/PRC, Sawyer collection, Taylor collection,

Books: Corley-Smith, Dodds (unpublished MS on US pilots), Jones H.A., Kilduff, Macmillan (*Offensive Patrol*), O'Connor, Pariseau, Winter, Wise, Young (essays by Warner, Peball).

Correspondence: Sawyer, Taylor.

Interviews: Alexandor, Birks, Blatherwick, Dodds, Sawyer, Taylor, Williams T.F.

Logbook/Birks: Mar-Jun 1918.

Logbook/Camel B6313: pages 18-32.

Magazines, Journals, Newspapers: *Clickety-Click*, Jun, Jul 1918, *Cross & Cockade* (US), Winter 1974, Spring 1976, *Cross & Cockade* (UK), Spring 1975, Spring 1993, *London Gazette, Over The Front*, Spring 1987.

CHAPTER EIGHT: A HOSTAGE TO FATE

Archives: DHist/DND, Hitchins List/Dodds collection, IWM, NAC, NAC/PRC, RAF/PRC, Taylor collection, Sawyer collection.

Books: Apostolo/Begnozzi, Barker R., Benn, Blatherwick, Burke's Peerage, Jones H.A., Macmillan (*Offensive Patrol*), O'Connor, Pariseau, Shores/Franks/Guest, Winter, Wise, Zeigler.

Correspondence: Taylor.

Interviews: Blatherwick, Dodds, Sawyer, Taylor.

Letters/Barker/NAC MG30 E195: circa Sept-Oct 1918.

Logbook/Camel B6313: pages 32-37.

Magazines, Journals, Newspapers: *Toronto Telegram*, 17 Apr 1920, *Canada's Air Heritage*, 1940, *Cross & Cockade* (UK), Autumn 1973, *Cross & Cockade* (US), Spring 1976.

CHAPTER NINE: AN APPOINTMENT WITH FAME

Archives: Alguire collection, CWM, DHist/DND, Hitchins List/Dodds collection, IWM, NAC, RAF/PRC, Royal Archives, Taylor collection.

Books: Bishop W.A., Blatherwick, Bliss, Blumenfield/Schoeps, Bond, Bowyer (*History of RAF*), Bramson, Cooksley, Dodds, Drew, Dufour, et al, Graham, Healy, Jones H.A., Stout, Swan/Swan, Swettenham, Trimble, Whitehouse (*Decisive Air Battles*), Winter, Wise, Woodman.

Correspondence: Bowyer, Cheesman, Franks, Markham, Taylor.

Interviews: Barker O., Blatherwick, Buchannon E., Dodds, Markham, Mackenzie C.J.G., Mackenzie D.W.G., Mackenzie J., Taylor.

Letters/Barker/NAC MG30 E195: 7 Nov 1918; 2, 13 Feb; 2, 25 Mar 1919.

Magazines, Journals, Newspapers: *Aircraft In Profile*, Vol. 3, (Bruce, 'Sopwith 7F.1 Snipe'), Canada, 29 Mar 1919, *Canadian Daily Record*, 5 Dec 1918, *Cross & Cockade* (UK), Autumn 1973, *Daily Mail*, nd Nov 1918, *Daily Telegraph*, nd Nov 1918, *The Times*, nd Nov 1918, *High Flight*, Vol. 1, No. 3, 1980, *Liberty Magazine*, 29 Aug 1931, *London Gazette*, 30 Nov 1918, *Manitoba Free Press*, 7 Nov 1918; 13 Mar 1930.

CHAPTER TEN: A SCHEME ON FOR FLYING

Archives: C.Av.H.Fame, DHist/DND, Fuller collection, NAC, Ontario Provincial Archives, Richardson collection, Taylor collection, Toronto Harbour Comm.

Books: Bowyer (*Hist. of RAF*), Burrill, Collard, Dodds, Eaton, Ellis, Fitzgerald, Fuller/Griffin/Molson, Graham, Harrison, Meyers, Milberry, Molson (*Pioneering in Can. Air Trans.*), Sutherland.

Correspondence: Dubé, Hotson, Taylor, Williams T.F.

Interviews: Bishop W.A., Dubé, Hotson, Mackenzie J., Mackenzie D.W.G., Molson, Taylor, Williams T.F.

Letters/Barker/NAC MG30 E195: 4 May, 6 July, 2, 19 Oct 1919.

Magazines, Journals, Newspapers: *Flying*, Apr 1919-May 1920, *The Gazette*, 25 Dec 1919, *Globe*, 25-30 Aug 1919, *Manitoba Free Press*, May/June, Nov 1919, *Montreal Daily Star*, 5 Jul 1919, *Ottawa Evening Telegram*, May-Jun 1919, *Veteran, GWVA Man.*, Nov-Dec 1919.

CHAPTER ELEVEN: THE FLYING DOLDRUMS

Archives: C.Av.H.Fame, City of Winnipeg, DHist/DND, Fuller collection, NAC, Ontario Provincial Archives, Richardson collection, Taylor collection.

Books: Bishop W.A., Collard, Collishaw/Dodds, Douglas, Eaton, Ellis, Fuller/Griffin/Molson, Greene, Greenhous (*Rattle of Pebbles*), Griffin, Hitchins, Jenkins, Milberry, Molson (*Canada's Nat. Av. Mus.*), Palmer, Parker, Solberg, Sutherland, Wise.

Correspondence: Mackenzie J., Mackenzie D.W.G., Molson, Taylor.

Debates, House of Commons: 29 April 1919.

Interviews: Alguire E., Barker O., Buchannon E., Dickins, Mackenzie J., Mackenzie D.W.G., Marsh, Molson, Taylor, Williams T.F.

Letters/Barker/NAC MG30 E195: 8 Mar 1920, 9 May 1921, 2 Sept 1921, 17 Oct 1921.

Magazines, Journals, Newspapers: *AAHS Journal*, Spring 1979, *Aerial Age Weekly*, 14 Mar 1921, *Canadian Defence Quarterly*, Apr 1927, *CAHS Journal* booklets ('First 500 Pilots' and 'Civil A/C Reg'), 1980-82, *CASI Journal*, Sept 1970, *Gazette*, 3, 17 Jan, 5 Oct 1920; 10 Jan 1921, *Globe*, 2, 9, 14, 20, 28 Jul, 10, 11 Sept 1920, *Montreal Daily Star*, 11 Sept 1920, *New York Times*, 12 Jan 1921, *Roundel*, Jul 1994, *Saturday Night*, 2 Jul 1921, *Toronto Daily Star*, 11 Sept 1920; 1 Jun 1921, *Toronto Evening Telegram*, 17 Apr 1920.

Meetings, Air Board: No. 61, Oct 1920, No.139, No.196, May, Nov 1921.

CHAPTER TWELVE: BARKER AND
THE FOUNDATION OF THE RCAF

Archives: DHist/DND, Library of Congress, NAC, NAC PRC.

Books: Bercuson/Granatstein, Bishop W.A., Blatherwick, Bishop W.A., Collishaw/Dodds, Dodds, Douglas, Dupre, Eayrs, Griffin, Hitchins, Kennett, Molson (*Can. Nat. Av. Mus.*), Mitchell W., Stedman, Sturtivant/Page, Sullivan, Sutherland.

Correspondence: Donaldson, Dunlap.

Debates, House of Commons: 12 May 1922, 24 Apr 1924.

Interviews: Blatherwick, Dickins, Dunlap, Guthrie, Hunter, Lawrence, Mackenzie J., Mackenzie D.W.G.

Magazines, Journals, Newspapers: *Canadian Defence Quarterly*, Apr 1927, *Gazette*, 6 Jul 1922, *Journal of Canadian Studies*, Autumn-Fall-Winter 1981, *RMC Review*, 1922, *RCAF Logbook (Silver Jubilee)*, 1949.

Meetings, Air Board: No. 245, 271, 273, Mar, June 1922.

Reports, DND; Militia Lists: 1924-1930.

CHAPTER THIRTEEN: HUMILIATION AND
REDEMPTION

Archives: Library of Congress, NAC/PRC, Ontario Provincial Archives, Ontario Tobacco Museum.

Books: Batten, Barker J/Kennedy, Drew, Duplacey/Romain, Fuller/Griffin/Molson, Hitchins, Houston, Irvine (unpublished MS), Juptner, Mitchell K.A., Molson/Taylor, Molson (*Pioneering in Can. Air Trans.*) Smythe.

Correspondence: Medina, Mitchell K.A., Richardson, Taylor.

Interviews: Guthrie, Lawrence, Mackenzie J., Mackenzie D.W.G., Medina, Molson, Pasmore G., Pasmore D., Taylor.

Magazines, Journals, Newspapers: *Canadian Aviation*, February 1930, *CAHS Journal*, Summer 1971, *CASI Journal*, Feb 1967, *MacLean's Magazine*, 15 Jul, 1 Nov, 1 Dec, 1928; 1 May-1 Aug, 1929; and *Ottawa newspaper*, 12 Mar 1930.

CHAPTER FOURTEEN: DEATH
AND MOURNING

Archives: Alguire collection, Barker collection, City of Toronto, NAC, NAC/PRC.

Books: Blatherwick, Filey, Juptner, McCaffery (*Air Aces*), Mitchell K.A.

Correspondence: Dunlap, Fuller, Holloway, Medina, McInnes, Pasmore G., Rex, Richardson.

Interviews: Alguire W., Alguire E., Barker O., Buchannon E., Dunlap, Gray, Guthrie, Hunter, Holloway, LaGrave, Lawrence, Mackenzie J., Mackenzie D.W.G., McGrath, McInnes, Medina, Pasmore G., Rex, Taylor, Woollett.

Letters/Barker/NAC MG30 E195: 3 Apr, 18 Aug 1930.

Magazines, Journals, Newspapers: *AIR International*, June 1996, *Canada's Air Heritage*, 1940, *Canadian Aviation*, Oct 1930; Jan, Jul 1931, *Canadian Defence Quarterly*, Apr 1930, *Daily Telegraph*, 15 Mar 1930, *Daily Express*, 15 Mar 1930, *Evening Telegram*, 13, 15, 17 Mar 1930, *Gazette*, 13 Mar 1930, *Mail and Empire*, 17 Mar 1930, *Manitoba Free Press*, 13, 16, 17, 18 Mar 30, *New York Times*, 12, 13 Mar 1930, *Ottawa newspaper*, 13 Mar 1930, *Saturday Night*, 22 Mar 1930, *Toronto Daily Star*, 13, 15 Mar 1930, *Winnipeg Evening Tribune*, 12, 13, Mar 1930, *Winnipeg Free Press*, 22 Nov 1930.

BIBLIOGRAPHY

BOOKS

Allen, Warner. *Our Italian Front*. London: A.& C. Black, 1920.

Armstrong, Dr Harry G. *Principles and Practice of Aviation Medicine*. Baltimore: The Williams & Wilkins Company, 1939.

Baker, David. *William Avery 'Billy' Bishop*. London: Outline Press, 1990.

Barker, Judy, Kennedy, Donna, et al. *The Tobacco Leaf Yesterday and Today*. Delhi: Delhi Public Library, 1979.

Barker, Ralph. *The Royal Flying Corps in France – From Mons to the Somme*. London: Allen & Unwin, 1994.

Batten, Jack. *Hockey Dynasty – The Inside Story of Conn Smythe's Hockey Dynasty – A fascinating history of the Toronto Maple Leaf Hockey Club*. Don Mills: General Publishing, 1969.

Bean, C.E.W. *Anzac to Amiens – A Shorter History of the Australian Fighting Services in the First World War*. Canberra: Australian War Memorial, 1961.

Benn, Captain Wedgwood. *In The Side Shows*. London: Hodder and Stoughton, 1919.

Bennett, Captain S.G. *The 4th Canadian Mounted Rifles 1914-1919*. Toronto: Murray Printing Company Limited, 1926.

Bishop, Billy. *Winged Warfare – The Illustrated Classic Autobiography of Canadian World War I Ace Billy Bishop*. Montreal: McGraw-Hill Ryerson, 1918, 1990.

Bishop, Air Marshal William A. *Winged Peace*. New York: The Viking Press, 1944.

Bishop, William Arthur. *The Courage of the Early Morning – A Son's Biography of a Famous Father*. Toronto: McClelland and Stewart, 1965, 1985.

Bliss, Michael. *Right Honourable Men – The Descent of Canadian Politics from Macdonald to Mulroney*. Toronto: HarperCollins Publishers Ltd., 1994.

Blumenfield, Dr Michael, Schoeps, Margot M. *Psychological Care of the Burn and Trauma Patient*. Baltimore: Williams & Wilkins Company, 1993.

Bond, Dr Douglas D. *The Love and Fear of Flying*. New York: International Universities Press, Inc., 1952.

Bowen, Ezra, and the editors of Time-Life Books. *Knights of the Air*. Alexandria: Time-Life Books, 1980.

Bowyer, Chaz. *Albert Ball, VC* London: William Kimber & Co. Limited, 1977.

———. *History of the RAF*. Greenwich: Bison Books Corp., 1977, 1984.

Bowyer, Chaz. *Sopwith Camel – King of Combat*. Falmouth: Glasney Press, 1978.

———. *For Valour – The Air VCs*. London: William Kimber, 1978, 1985.

Bramson, Alan. *Pure Luck – The Authorized Biography of Sir Thomas Sopwith, 1888-1989*. Somerset: Patrick Stephens Limited, 1990.

Burrill, William. *Hemingway – The Toronto years*. Toronto: Doubleday Canada Limited, 1994.

Collard, Edgar Andrew. *Passage to the Sea – The Story of Canada Steamship Lines*. Toronto: Doubleday Canada Limited, 1991.

Collishaw, Air Vice-Marshal Raymond, with Dodds, R.V. *Air Command – A fighter pilot's story*. London: William Kimber and Co. Limited, 1973.

Cooper, Malcolm. *The Birth of Independent Air Power – British Air Policy in the First World War*. London: Allen & Unwin, 1986.

Corley-Smith, Peter. *Barnstorming to Bush Flying – British Columbia's Aviation Pioneers 1910-1930*. Victoria: Sono Nis Press, 1989.

Cosgrove, Edmund. *Canadian Portraits – Canada's Fighting Pilots*. Toronto: Clarke, Irwin & Company Limited, 1965.

Dauphin Historical Society. *Dauphin Valley Spans the Years*. Dauphin: Dauphin Historical Society, 1970.

Dauphin Rural Municipality. *History of the Rural Municipality of Dauphin*. Dauphin: Rural Municipality, 1987.

Dodds, Ronald V. *The Brave Young Wings*. Stittsville: Canada's Wings, Inc., 1980.

———. *Americans in the British Flying Services WWI*. Ottawa: unpublished manuscript, 1979.

Douglas, W.A.B. *The Creation of a National Air Force – The Official History of the Royal Canadian Air Force, Volume II*. Toronto: University of Toronto Press and DND, 1986.

Drew, Lieut-Colonel George A. *Canada's Fighting Airmen*. Toronto: The MacLean Publishing Company, Limited, 1930.

Dufour, D., Jensen Kroman, S., Owen-Smith, M., et al. *Surgery for Victims of War*. Geneva: International Committee of the Red Cross, 1988.

Duguid, Colonel A. Fortescue. *Official History of the Canadian Forces in the Great War 1914-1919 – General Series Vol. I* Ottawa: King's Printer, 1938.

Duplacey, James, Romain, Joseph. *Toronto Maple Leafs – Images of Glory*. Toronto: McGraw-Hill Ryerson, 1990.

Eaton, Lady Flora (McCrea). *Memory's Wall*. Toronto: Clarke, Irwin, 1956.

Eayrs, James. *In Defence of Canada – From the Great War to the Great Depression*. Toronto: University of Toronto Press, 1964.

Edmonds, James E. *Military Operations, France and Belgium, 1916, July 2 to End of Somme Battles*. London: HMSO, 1938.

Ellis, Frank H. *Canada's Flying Heritage*. Toronto: University of Toronto Press, 1954, 1980.

English, John. *Shadow of Heaven – The Life of Lester Pearson, Volume One: 1897-1948*. London: Vintage UK, 1990.

Fitzgerald, F. Scott. *The Great Gatsby*. New York: Collier Books, Macmillan Publishing Company, 1925, 1980.

Fussell, Paul. *The Great War and Modern Memory*. London: Oxford University Press, 1975.

General Staff, War Office. *Yeomanry & Mounted Rifle Training, Parts I & II*. London: War Office, 1912.

Graham, Don. *No Name on the Bullet: A Biography of Audie Murphy*. New York: Viking Penguin USA Inc., 1989.

Gray, James H. *The Roar of the Twenties*. Toronto: Macmillan Company of Canada, 1975.

Gray, John, with Peterson, Eric. *Billy Bishop Goes To War*. Vancouver: Talonbooks, 1981.

Greenhous, Brereton, editor. *A Rattle of Pebbles: The First World War Diaries of Two Canadian Airmen*. Ottawa: Directorate of History, DND, 1987.

Grinnell-Milne, Duncan. *Wind in the Wires*. London: Jarrolds Publishers, 1971.

Hawker, Tyrrel M. *Hawker, VC – The Biography of the Late Major Lanoe G. Hawker, VC, DSO, Royal Engineers and Royal Flying Corps*. London: Mitre Press, 1965.

Hallion, Richard P. *Rise of the Fighter Aircraft 1914-1918*. Baltimore: The Nautical & Aviation Publishing Company of America, Inc., 1984.

Harris, Norman John. *Knight of the Air*. Toronto: Macmillan Canada, 1958.

Harrison, Robert. *Aviation Lore in Faulkner*. Amsterdam: John Benjamins Publishing Company, 1985.

Healy, Dr David. *Images of Trauma – From Hysteria to Post-Traumatic Stress Disorder*. London: Faber and Faber, 1993.

Hemingway, Ernest. *A Farewell to Arms*. New York: Collier Books, Macmillan Publishing Company, 1929, 1986.

———. *The Snows of Kilimanjaro and Other Stories*. Charles Scribner's Sons, Macmillan Publishing Company, 1936, 1964.

———. White, William, editor. *Dateline: Toronto – The Complete Toronto Star Dispatches, 1920-1924*. New York: Charles Scribner's Sons, 1985.

Hitchins, Wing Commander Frederick H. *Air Board, Canadian Air Force and Royal Canadian Air Force*. Ottawa: Canadian War Museum, 1972.

———. *The Hitchins List* (so-called). Ottawa: RCAF Air Historical Branch, unpublished combat summaries of Canadian airmen, no date (circa 1940s-50s).

Houston, William. *Inside Maple Leaf Garden – The Rise and Fall of the Toronto Maple Leafs*. Toronto: McGraw-Hill Ryerson, 1989.

Insall, A.J. *Observer – Memoirs of the RFC 1915-1918*. London: William Kimber, 1970.

Jenkins, Alan. *The Twenties*. London: William Heinemann Ltd, 1974.

Jones, H.A. *The War in the Air – Being the Story of the part played in the Great War by the Royal Air Force, Vol. II, III, XI, and Appendices*. Oxford: Clarendon Press, 1928-37.

Jones, James. *Whistle*. New York: Dell Publishing Co., Inc., 1978.

Joubert de la Ferté, Air Chief Marshal Sir Philip. *The Fated Sky*. London: Hutchinson & Co. (Publishers) Ltd., 1952.

Kennett, Lee. *The First Air War 1914-1918*. New York: The Free Press, 1991.

Kilduff, Peter. *Richthofen – Beyond the Legend of the Red Baron*. New York: John Wiley & Sons, Inc., 1994.

King, Peter. *Knights of the Air – The life and times of the extraordinary pioneers who first built British aeroplanes*. London: Constable, 1989.

Klingaman, William A. *1919 – The Year Our World Began*. New York: St. Martin's Press, 1987.

Lee, Arthur Gould. *Open Cockpit – A Pilot of the Royal Flying Corps*. London: Jarrolds Publishers, 1969.

———. *No Parachute – A Fighter Pilot in World War I*. London: Jarrolds Publishers, 1968.

Lewis, Cecil. *Sagittarius Rising*. London: Penguin Books, 1936, 1983.

———. *Farewell to Wings*. London: Temple Press Books, 1964.

Little, Dr Adam S. *Dogtown to Dauphin*. Winnipeg: Watson & Dwyer Publishing, 1988.

Macmillan, Norman. *Offensive Patrol – The story of the RNAS, RFC and RAF in Italy 1917-18*. London: Jarrolds Publishers, 1973.

———. *Sir Sefton Brancker*. London: William Heinemann, 1935.

———. *Into the Blue*. London: Jarrolds Publishers, 1929, 1969.

Marteinson, John, Greenhous, Brereton, Harris, Stephen J., et al. *We Stand on Guard, An Illustrated History of the Canadian Army*. Montreal: Ovale Publications, 1992.

Mathieson, W.D. *Billy Bishop, VC*. Markham: Fitzhenry & Whiteside Limited, 1989.

McCaffery, Dan. *Billy Bishop, Canadian Hero*. Toronto: James Lorimer & Company, Publishers, 1988.

———. *Air Aces – The Lives and Times of Twelve Canadian Fighter Pilots*. Toronto: James Lorimer & Company, Publishers, 1991.

McKenna, Ward, Heard, Lisa, editors. *A History of Tobacco in Canada*. Alymer: The Alymer Express Ltd., 1989.

McWilliams, James L., Steel, R. James. *The Suicide Battalion – 46th Battalion (South Saskatchewan)*. Edmonton: Hurtig Publishers, 1978.

Mead, Peter. *The Eye In The Air – History of Air Observation and Reconnaissance for the Army 1795-1945*. London: HMSO, 1983.

Meek, John F. *Over The Top! The Canadian Infantry in the First World War*. Orangeville: John F. Meek, 1971.

Meyers, Jeffrey. *Hemingway: A Biography*. New York: Harper & Row, Publishers, 1985.

———. *Scott Fitzgerald: A Biography*. New York: Harper-Collins Publishers, 1994.

Milberry, Larry. *Aviation In Canada*. Toronto: McGraw-Hill Ryerson, 1979.

Mitchell, Kent A. *Fairchild Aircraft Since 1926*. Santa Ana: Jonathan Thompson Publishers, 1995.

Mitchell, William. *Winged Defense – The Development and Possibilities of Modern Air Power – Economic and Military*. New York: Dover Publications, Inc., 1925, 1988.

Molson, K.M. *Canada's National Aviation Museum – Its History and Collections*. Ottawa: National Aviation Museum, 1988.

———. *Pioneering in Canadian Air Transport*. Winnipeg: James Richardson & Sons, Limited, 1974.

Morton, Desmond. *Silent Battle – Canadian Prisoners of War in Germany 1914-1919*. Toronto: Lester Publishing Limited, 1992.

———, Granatstein J.L. *Marching to Armageddon – Canadians and the Great War 1914-1919*. Lester & Orpen Dennys Limited, 1989.

Musiciano, Walter A. Lt. Col. *William Barker, Canada's All-Around Ace*. New York: Hobby Helpers Publications, 1973.

Nicholson, Colonel G.W.L. *Canadian Expeditionary Force 1914-1919 – official history of the Canadian Army in the First World War*. Ottawa: Queen's Printer, 1962.

O'Connor, Dr Martin. *Air Aces of the Austro-Hungarian Empire 1914-1918*. Mesa: Champlin Fighter Museum Press, 1986.

Oughton, Frederick, annotator. *The personal diary of Major Edward "Mick" Mannock, VC, DSO (two Bars), MC (one Bar), Royal Flying Corps and Royal Air Force*. London: Spearman, 1966.

Palmer, Henry R. *This Was Air Travel*. New York: Bonanza Books, 1960.

Rawling, Bill. *Surviving Trench Warfare – Technology and the Canadian Corps 1914-1918*. Toronto: University of Toronto Press, 1992.

Regehr, T.D. *The Canadian Northern Railway – Pioneer Road of the Northern Prairies 1895-1918*. Toronto: Macmillan of Canada, 1976.

———. *Remembering Saskatchewan: a history of rural Saskatchewan*. Saskatoon: University of Saskatchewan, 1979.

Robertson, Bruce, editor. *Air Aces of the 1914–1918 War*. Letchworth: Harleyford Publications Limited, 1959.

Roy, Reginald H. *For Most Conspicuous Bravery – A Biography of Major-General George R. Pearkes, VC, through Two World Wars*. Vancouver: University of British Columbia, 1977.

Roy, Reginald H. editor. *The Journal of Private Fraser 1914–1918, Canadian Expeditionary Force*. Victoria: Sono Nis Press 1985.

Russell's Women's Institute. *Banner County – History of Russell & District 1879–1967*. Russell: Russell's Women's Institute with Russell Chamber of Commerce, 1967.

Sheehan, Neil. *A Bright Shining Lie – John Paul Vann and America in Vietnam*. New York: Vintage Books 1989.

Shores, Christopher. *Air Aces*. Greenwich: Bison Books Corp., 1983.

Singh, Darbara. *Ten Eminent Sikhs*. Amritsar: Literature House, 1982.

Smythe, Conn, Young, Scott. *Conn Smythe – If You Can't Beat 'Em in the Alley*. Toronto: McClelland and Stewart, 1981.

Solberg, Carl. *Conquest of the Skies – A History of Commercial Aviation in America*. Boston: Little, Brown and Company, 1979.

Spick, Mike. *The Ace Factor*. New York: Avon Books, 1988.

Springs, Elliott White, editor. *War Birds – Diary of an Unknown Aviator – John MacGavock Grider*. College Station: Texas A&M University Press, 1926, 1988.

Stedman, Air Vice-Marshal Ernest W. *From Boxkite to Jet – The Memoirs of an Aeronautical Engineer*. Ottawa: Canadian War Museum, 1972.

Stegner, Wallace. *Wolf Willow – A History, a Story, and a Memory of the Last Plains Frontier*. Lincoln: University of Nebraska, 1955, 1962.

Stewart, Oliver. *The Story of Air Warfare*. London: Hamish Hamilton, 1958.

Stout, T. Duncan M. *War Surgery and Medicine*. Wellington: War History Branch. Dept. of Internal Affairs, 1954.

Sullivan, Lt. Alan. *Aviation in Canada 1917–1918 – Being a brief account of the work of the Royal Air Force Canada the Aviation Department of the Imperial Munitions Board and the Canadian Aeroplanes Limited*. Toronto: Rous & Mann Limited, 1919.

Sutherland, Alice Gibson. *Canada's Aviation Pioneers – 50 Years of McKee Trophy Winners*. Toronto: McGraw Hill Ryerson Limited, 1978.

Swan, Dr. Kenneth G., Swan, Dr. Roy C. *Gunshot Wounds – Pathophysiology and Management*. Littleton: PSG Publishing Company, Inc., 1980.

Swettenham, John. *McNaughton, Vol. 1 – 1887-1939*. Toronto: The Ryerson Press, 1968.

Tascona, Bruce. *The Militia of Manitoba – A Study of Infantry and Cavalry Regiments since 1883*. Winnipeg: Bruce Tascona, 1979.

Thompson, John Herd. *The Harvests of War – The Prairie West, 1914-1918*. Toronto: McClelland and Stewart, 1978.

Travers, Tim. *The Killing Ground – The British Army, the Western Front and the Emergence of Modern Warfare 1900–1918*. London: Allen & Unwin, 1987.

Tredrey, F.D. *Pioneer Pilot – The Great Smith Barry Who Taught the World to Fly*. London: Peter Davies Limited, 1976.

Trimble, Dr Michael R. *Post-Traumatic Neurosis – From Railway Spine to the Whiplash*. Chichester: John Wiley & Sons, 1981.

Whitehouse, Arch. *Decisive Air Battles of the First World War*. New York: Douell, Sloan and Pearce, 1963.

———. *The Years of the Sky Kings*. New York: Award Books, 1964.

Winter, Denis. *The First of the Few – Fighter Pilots of the First World War*. Harmondsworth: Penguin Books Ltd., 1983.

———. *Haig's Command – A Reassessment*. London: Penguin Books Ltd., 1992.

Wise, S.F. *Canadian Airmen and the First World War – The Official History of the Royal Canadian Air Force, Volume I*. Toronto: University of Toronto and DND, 1980.

Woodman, Harry. *Early Aircraft Armament – The Aeroplane and the Gun up to 1918*. Washington, DC: Smithsonian Institution Press, 1989.

Zeigler, Philip. *King Edward VIII*. New York: Alfred A. Knopf, Inc., 1990.

REFERENCE BOOKS, BOOKLETS & ENCYCLOPAEDIA

Air Historical Section, *RCAF Logbook (Silver Jubilee) – A Chronological Outline of the Origin, Growth and Achievement of the Royal Canadian Air Force*. Ottawa: King's Printer, 1949.

Apostolo G., Bignozzi G. *Color Profiles of World War I Combat Planes*. New York: Crescent Books, 1974.

Bercuson, David J., Granatstein, J.L. *Dictionary of Canadian Military History*. Toronto: Oxford University Press, 1992.

Blatherwick, Surgeon Commander Francis John. *1000 Brave Canadians – The Canadian Gallantry Awards 1854-1989*. Toronto: The Unitrade Press, 1991.

Burke's Peerage, Baronetage and Knightage. London: Burke's Peerage Limited, 1956.

Canada's Air Heritage. Ottawa: Minister of National Defence for Air, 1940.

Canada's Aviation Hall of Fame. Edmonton: Canada's Aviation Hall of Fame, 1973.

Chant, Christopher. *Aircraft*. London: Octopus Books Limited, 1975.

Cooksley, Peter. *Sopwith Fighters in Action – Aircraft Number 110*. Carrollton: Squadron/Signal Publications, Inc., 1991.

———. *BE2 in Action – Aircraft Number 123*. Carrollton: Squadron/Signal Publications, Inc., 1992.

Dupre, Flint O. *US Air Force Biographical Dictionary*. New York: Franklin Watts, Inc., 1965.

Ellis, John R. *The Canadian Civil Aircraft Register, 2 Vols*. Toronto: Canadian Aviation Historical Society, 1965-9, 1972-5.

Filey, Mike. *Mount Pleasant Cemetery – An Illustrated Guide*. Toronto: A Firefly Book, 1990.

Fuller, G.A., Griffin, J.A., Molson, K.M. *125 Years of Canadian Aeronautics – A Chronology 1840-1965*. Toronto: Canadian Aviation Historical Society, 1983.

Greene. B.M., editor. *Who's Who and Why 1921 – An Illustrated Biographical Record of Men and Women of the Time*. Toronto: International Press, Limited, 1921.

———. *Who's Who in Canada*. Toronto: International Press, 1922-29.

Grey, C.G., Bridgman, Leonard, editors. *Jane's All the World's Aircraft 1930*. London: Sampson, Low, Marston Co. Ltd., 1930.

Griffin, John. *Canadian Military Aircraft, Serials and Photographs, 1920-1968*. Ottawa: Canadian War Museum, 1969.

Halliday, H.A. *Chronology of Canadian Military Aviation*. Ottawa: Canadian War Museum, 1975.

Hogg, Ian V., Weeks, John, editors. *Military Small Arms of the Twentieth Century – a comprehensive illustrated encyclopaedia of the world's small calibre firearms*. Northfield: DBI Books, 1985.

Hogg, Ian V., editor. *The Guinness Encyclopaedia of Weaponry – From Stone Spears to Guided Missiles*. Enfield: Guinness Publishers, 1992.

Juptner, Joseph P. *U.S. Civil Aircraft Series, Volume 3 (ATC 201 – ATC 300)*. Blue Ridge Summit: Tab Aero, 1993.

Kostenuk S., Griffin J. *RCAF Squadron Histories and Aircraft 1924-1968*. Ottawa: Canadian War Museum, 1977.

Kludas, Arnold. *Great Passenger Ships of the World*. Cambridge: Patrick Stephens, 1975.

MacDonald, W. James, editor. *A Bibliography of the Victoria Cross*. Baddeck: W. James MacDonald Publishers, 1994.

McGrath, T.M. *History of Canadian Airports*. Ottawa: Transport Canada, 1992.

Molson K., Taylor H. *Canadian Aircraft Since 1909*. Stittsville: Canada's Wings, Inc., 1982.

Parker, Dr C.W., editor. *Who's Who and Why – A Biographical Dictionary of Men and Women of Canada and Newfoundland, Vol. 5, 1914*. Toronto: International Press, Limited, 1914.

Reid, William. *Arms Through the Ages*. New York: Harper & Row, 1976.

Shores, Christopher, Franks, Norman, Guest, Russell. *Above The Trenches – A Complete Record of the Fighter Aces and Units of the British Empire Air Forces 1915-1920*. Stoney Creek: Fortress Publications Inc., 1990.

Sturtivant, Ray, Page, Gordon. *The Camel File*. Tonbridge: Air-Britain (Historians) Ltd., 1993.

Roberts, C.G.D., Tunnell, A.L., editors. *Canadian Who's Who 1936-37, Vol. 11*. Toronto: 1937.

Wallace, W. Stewart, McKay, W.A., editors. *The Macmillan Dictionary of Canadian Biography*. Toronto: Macmillan of Canada, 1978, 1985.

Windrow, Martin C., editor. *Aircraft in Profile, Profile Publications, Vols. 1-9*. New York: Doubleday & Company, 1968-72.

Young, Brigadier Peter, editor-in-chief, et al. *Marshall Cavendish Illustrated Encyclopedia of World War 1. Vol. 9*. New York: Marshall Cavendish, 1986.

ARCHIVES, MUSEUMS, LIBRARIES & RECORDS CENTRES

(Ms.Grp. – *Manuscript Group*)

Library and Archives Canada, Ottawa:
Barker, William George. Papers. Ms.Grp. 30, E195.
Bishop, William Avery. Papers. Ms.Grp. 30, E261.
Brown, Arthur Roy. Papers. Ms.Grp. 30, E378.
Department of Militia and Defence. Record Group 9, Vol. 4946, Folder 464. 1st CMR Regimental War Diary.
Department of National Defence. Record Group 24, Vol. 3192; Reel C5919, File 238.
Eaton, Edward C. Papers. Ms.Grp. 30, E311.
Ferrie, Robert L. Papers. Ms.Grp. 30, E347.
MacLaren, Donald R. Papers. Ms.Grp. 30, E296
McCall, Frederick R.G. Papers. Ms.Grp. 30, E307.
McGill, Frank S. Papers. Ms.Grp. 30, E253.
National Archives, Record Group 37, Vol. 364.

Personnel Records Centre, Ottawa: Barker, William G. Record of military service.

Canada's Aviation Hall of Fame, Wetaskiwin, Alberta: Barker, William George. Papers. Garratt, Philip Clarke. Papers. Williams, Thomas Frederick. Interview.

Champlin Fighter Museum, Mesa, Arizona: Displays. Aircraft.

Canadian War Museum, Ottawa: Snipe 7F.1 fuselage. Medals, Barker. Papers.

The Directorate of History (DHist), Department of National Defence, Ottawa:Barker, William George. Biographical file.
————. Papers. Report by Wing Commander Barker of an aerial attack on HMS *Hood*, and also of his war experiences. 1925.
Report by Wing Commander Barker on visit to Iraq. 1925.
Gordon, James Lindsay. Biographical file.
Hitchins, F.H. W/C. Hitchins list of Canadian flyers in WWI.
McEwen, Clifford McKay. Biographical file.
Scott, James Stanley. Biographical file.
Williams, Thomas Frederick. Biographical file.
DHist File 84/331, Dossier 223. Pariseau, Jean. *Canadian Airmen in the 'Side-Shows' of the First World War, Vol. 11, Italy 1917-1918*. Ottawa.
DHist Permanent Reference File, Canadian Mounted Rifles

Fort Dauphin Museum, Dauphin, Manitoba
Exhibits. Photographs. Papers.

Hagley Museum and Library, Pictorial and AV Dept., Wilmington, Delaware
Dallin, Colonel Victor. Interview, July 1969.

The Library of Congress, Washington DC Manuscript Division:
Fairchild, Sherman. Papers. Boxes 110-113.
Mitchell, William. Papers. Boxes 9-13.

The Provincial Archives of Manitoba, Winnipeg:
Barker, William George. Papers. Ms.Grp. 6, D20.
Ferguson, Eva. Papers. Ms.Grp. Essay No. 55-13.
McLeod, Alan Arnett. Papers. Ms.Grp. P5418.
Official Lists of Casualties to Members of the Canadian Expeditionary Force, Reports 3 to 6, 1 October 1915 – 30 September 1916. Ottawa: Government Printing Bureau, 1916.

Provincial Archives of Ontario, Toronto:
Bishop-Barker Aeroplanes Ltd., Dormant Corporation File # TC2901. RG55, RG55-5, Accession 14180.
Horace Bruce Smith, Estate File, Surrogate Court, York County. RG22, #88125.
Simcoe Jail Register, 1925-1936, RG20, Series F39.

The Ontario Tobacco Museum and Heritage Centre, Delhi: Publications on the history of tobacco growing in Canada.

The Toronto Harbour Commissioner. Archives: RG3/3, BOX 108, folder 14 – Bishop-Barker Aeroplanes, Limited, 1919-20.

Museum of the Regiments. The Lord Strathcona's Horse (Royal Canadians) Archives, Calgary: Yeomanry and Mounted Rifle Training, Parts I & II. General Staff, War Office. 1912.

University of Victoria: Roy, Reginald. Papers. Roy interviews with Pearkes. Special Collections, Social Sciences Research Centre, Accession No. 74.1.

Ministry of Defence. RAF Personnel Management Centre, Innsworth, Gloucester: Barker, William George. Record of military service. Barker, William George. Gallantry awards and citations.

Imperial War Museum, London: Miscellaneous 1695. Ms Aeroplane Log Book for Sopwith Camel B6313.

OTHER GOVERNMENT DOCUMENTS

Court Circulars, Buckingham Palace, The Royal Archives, Windsor Castle

Debates, House of Commons, Ottawa

Reports of the Department of National Defence, 1924-30

DND Canada, List of Officers, Militia Service and Air Service, 1924-30

The Militia Lists, 1919-24

PRIVATE COLLECTIONS AND UNPUBLISHED MANUSCRIPTS

Alguire, Ellen Sainsbury. Sainsbury family collection. White Rock: 1996.

Alguire, William. Alguire family collection. Grandview: 1996.

Barker, Orval. Barker family collection. Ochre Beach: 1996.

Benn, the Right Honourable Anthony. Benn family collection. London, UK: 1995.

Buchannon, Edna Barker. Buchannon family collection. Dauphin: 1996.

Buchannon, Wayne. Buchannon family collection. Winnipeg: 1995.

Birks, Gerald A. Birks family collection. Toronto: 1991.

Creagen, Harry E. Aviation collection. Kingston: 1991.

Dodds, Ronald V. Dodds family collection. Richmond, 1995.

Dunlap, Air Marshal C.R. 'Larry.' Aviation collection. Victoria: 1991.

Fuller, George. Aviation collection. Montreal: 1995.

Hotson, Fred. Aviation collection. Toronto: 1995.

Irvine, Ronald. unpublished ms on Fairchild in Canada. Victoria: 1995.

Mackenzie, David W.G. Mackenzie family collection. Victoria: 1995.

McAskill, Capt M.G. McAskill family collection. Tsawwassen: 1994.

Mitchell, Kent A. Aviation collection. Hagerstown: 1995.

Molson, Kenneth A. Aviation collection. Islington: 1995.

Pasmore, Hubert Martyn. Pasmore family collection. Victoria: 1995.

Pasmore, Godfrey. Pasmore family collection. Montreal: 1995.

Phillips, Stanley H. Aviation collection. Stratford, Conn: 1980.

Richardson, W. Ross. Aviation collection. Montreal: 1995.

Sawyer, Margaret Hilborn. Sawyer family collection. Burnaby: 1996.

Shaw, Susanne. Graphoanalysis of Barker's letters. Port Alice: 1994.

Taylor, Stewart K. Aviation collection. Dutton: 1996.

Williams, Thomas F. Aviation collection. Woodstock: 1981.

HISTORICAL JOURNALS

Journal of the American Aviation Historical Society

Journal of Canadian Studies

Canadian Aviation Historical Society (CAHS) Journal. Toronto.

Canadian Aeronautics and Space Institute (CASI) Journal. Ottawa

Cross & Cockade—Great Britain Journal of the UK Society of World War One Aero Historians

Cross & Cockade. US: Journal of the Society of World War One Aero Historians.

Over the Front. United States: Journal of the League of World War One Aviation Historians.

NEWSPAPERS AND MAGAZINES

Aerial Age Weekly

The Aeroplane, London

Air Classics, Canoga Park, CA

Aviation, Leesburg, VA

Aviation News: the Aero Club, Toronto

Brandon Weekly Sun

Canada

Canadian Aviation, Toronto
Canadian Daily Record, OMFC
Canadian Defence Quarterly
Clickety-Click, 66 Squadron, Italy
The Daily Express, London
The Daily Mail, London
The Daily Sun-Times, Owen Sound
The Daily Telegraph, London
Dauphin Herald
Dauphin Press
The Evening Telegram, Toronto
Esquire Magazine, New York
Flight
Flying
The Gazette, Montreal
The Globe, Toronto
The Herald, Owen Sound
High Flight, Stittsville, ON
Liberty Magazine, New York
MacLean's Magazine, Toronto
The Mail and Empire, Toronto
Manitoba Free Press, Winnipeg
Monitor, United Church magazine
The Montreal Daily Star
The Muskoka Sun
The New York Times
Ottawa Citizen
Ottawa Evening Telegram
The Owen Sound Sun-Times
Popular Flying
RMC Review, Kingston
Roundel, Winnipeg
The Telegram, Montreal
The Times of London
The Times Saturday Review, London
The Toronto Daily Star
The Toronto Star Saturday Magazine
The Toronto Star Weekly
Trail Makers Boys Annual, Toronto
Saturday Night Magazine, Toronto
The Sunday Express, London
The Veteran, Winnipeg
War Birds
Weekend Magazine, Toronto
Wings In Space
The Winnipeg Evening Tribune

NEWSPAPER, MAGAZINE, AND JOURNAL CITATIONS

1911 through 1921

"Auto or Aeroplane," *Manitoba Free Press*, Winnipeg, 14 July 1911
"Winnipeg Fair to Close Today," *Manitoba Free Press*, 22 July 1911
"Mr. and Mrs. J.M. Kilbourn Celebrate Their Golden Wedding," *The Herald*, Owen Sound, 22 July 1911
The Brandon Weekly Sun, 20, 26 May 1915
Dauphin Press, Dec/Jan 1916-17
Clickety Click, Vol. 1, No. 1 & No. 2, June & July 1918, published by authority of Major John W. Whittaker, MC, officer commanding Sixty-Six Squadron, RAF
"The Great Air Fight," *The Times*, London, Nov 1918
"Marvellous Air Fight," *The Daily Telegraph*, Nov 1918
"Canadian Major's Triumph," *The Daily Mail*, Nov 1918
"Death Claims Lieut Alan McLeod, Stonewall's Victoria Cross Hero," *Manitoba Free Press*, Winnipeg, 7 Nov 1918
"Brilliant Fight by British Airman – Attacked by Successive Flights of Enemy Planes – Badly Wounded Makes Escape," *Manitoba Free Press*, Winnipeg, 7 Nov 1918
"Manitoban is Hero of Greatest Air Battle in Annals of War – Major Barker, Who Fought 60 Planes Single-Handed, Is Dauphin Boy," *Manitoba Free Press*, Winnipeg, 16 Nov 1918
Arthur Beverley Baxter, "Great Canadian Airmen – Major William George Barker, VC, DSO, MC, etc," *Canada*, 29 March 1919
"Colonel Bishop Offers 'Ace of Aces' Trophy," *Flying*, April 1919
"Canadian VCs enter Aviation Business – Bishop-Barker Co., Ltd., Will Do Business in England and America," *Manitoba Free Press*, May-June 1919
"Canada's Most Famous Airmen," *Ottawa Evening Telegram*, May-June 1919
"Can Monopolize Aerial Service Col. W.G. Barker Says England and Canada Have Things Own Way," *The Montreal Daily Star*, 5 July 1919
"'Stunt' Flying Thrills Crowds – Spectators at Exhibition Gasp at Feats of Daring Airmen," *The Globe*, Toronto, 25 August 1919
"Barker, Canadian Ace, Has His Arm Frozen, But Continues Race – Makes the Flight Without a Compass – Objects to Doctors Treating His Arm – Meets War Companion Just as He Was Leaving," *The Globe*, Toronto, 27 August 1919
"Big Air Race Is Finished ... Col. Barker's Verdict," *The Globe*, 30 August 1919

"Brilliant VC Hero Returns To The City With Splendid Record," *The Veteran, GWVA Manitoba Command*, No. 27, Nov-Dec 1919

"Colonel Barker Predicts – Barker Says Another War Looming Up – Declares it Will be Fought Altogether by the Air Forces," *Manitoba Free Press*, Winnipeg, November 1919

"P.Q. Great Field For Aviation ... Need for Airdromes," *The Gazette*, Montreal, 25 December 1919

"Will Exhibit Plane," *The Gazette*, Montreal, 3 January 1920

"Motor Show," *The Gazette*, Montreal, 17 January 1920

"Small Fortunes Made in Passenger Carrying and Sale of Aeroplanes," *Flying*, January 1920

Advertisements for Interallied Aircraft, *Flying*, Oct, Nov, 1919; March, May, 1920

"Refused to Fight in Air – Huns Avoided Barker," *The Toronto Evening Telegram*, 17 April 1920

"Told Bishop and Barker how to Fly," *The Globe*, Toronto, 2 July 1920

"Brings Huge Hydroplane For Service To Muskoka – Col. Barker, VC, Arrives With Machine Which Will Be Used To Carry Passengers to Summer Resort," *The Globe*, Toronto, 9 July 1920

"Col. Barker Describes Flight From New York – Is Given Ovation By Rotarians at Their Weekly Luncheon," *The Globe*, Toronto, 14 July 1920

"Many Applying For Certificate – Commercial Flying Will be Success if Business Men Assist," *The Globe*, Toronto, 20 July 1920

"A Wonderful Flight," *The Globe*, Toronto, 28 July 1920

"Chance to See Aerial Circus," *The Globe*, Toronto, 10 September 1920

"The Gin Rickey Lights On A Tree," *The Toronto Daily Star*, 11 September 1920

"Men Cling To Wings As Airplane Crashes – Bishop-Barker Machine Falls Into Tree Tops," *The Globe*, Toronto, 11 September 1920

"Bishop and Barker Contracts Cancelled," *The Montreal Daily Star*, 11 September 1920

"Col. Barker Made Fast Flight, Toronto, Oct. 4," *The Gazette*, Montreal, 5 October 1920

"Government Takes Big Step to Encourage Aviation – Authorizes the Sale of the Famous Navy Coast Patrol HS2 Flying Boats Valued at $18,480 Each for $6,160 per Boat," *The New York Times*, 12 January 1921

"Came by Air Route," *The Gazette*, Montreal, 10 January 1921

"Canada's First Merchandise By Air – New York to Toronto by Col. W.G. Barker," *Aerial Age Weekly*, NYC, Vol. 13, No. 1, 14 March 1921

"June Wedding Bells Begin Merry Peal ... Canadian Ace Weds – Lt. Col. W.G. Barker, VC, DSO, MC, Leads Miss Jean K. Smith to the Altar," *The Toronto Daily Star*, 1 June 1921

Women's Section, *Saturday Night*, Toronto, 2 July 1921

"In Death of Mr. J.M. Kilbourn This City Loses Premier Citizen," *The Owen Sound Sun-Times*, 16 August 1921

"Aviators," *The Toronto Daily Star*, 4 October 1921

"Long Honeymoon Ended By The Police, *The Toronto Daily Star*, 14 October 1921

Lt Colonel W.G. Barker, VC, DSO, MC, "Aircraft in War," in *The Trail Makers Boy's Annual–The All Canadian Annual For Boys*. Vol. II. Toronto: The Musson Book Company Limited, 1921

1922 through 1931

"Editorial – Group Captain James Stanley Scott, MC, AFC, psa, Director, Royal Canadian Air Force," *Canadian Defence Quarterly*, Vol. IV, No. 3, April 1927

Douglas MacKay, "Flights and Forecasts," *MacLean's Magazine*, 15 July 1928

"The Truth About the War – The Reply by Brigadier General Henry J. Reilly – The Rebuttal by Major George A. Drew," *MacLean's Magazine*, 1 November 1928

Aubrey Roberts, "Ottawa-Vancouver in 32 Hours – The stirring story of Canada's first transcontinental air mail flight," *MacLean's Magazine*, 1 December 1928

Major George Drew, "Canada's Fighting Airmen: Five: Barker Wins His First Decoration," *MacLean's Magazine*, 1 May 1929; (through to) Nine: Barker: Hero of Homeric Combat, *MacLean's Magazine*, 1 August 1929

"Colonel W.G. Barker, VC, DSO, appointed vice-president and general manager of Fairchild Aviation Ltd., Montreal," *Canadian Aviation*, February 1930

"Famous War Ace Col. Barker, VC is Visitor to City," unidentified Ottawa newspaper, 12 March 1930

"Taft Borne To Arlington, Receives Soldier's Burial As The Nation Pays Homage – Washington Bows In Rain," *The New York Times*, 12 March 1930

"Crash Kills Canadian Ace – Lt. Col. W.G. Barker, Famous Hero of War, Victim of Accident," *The Winnipeg Evening Tribune*, 12 March 1930

"Inquiry Into Death of Lt. Col. W.G. Barker at Rockcliffe Yesterday to be Resumed Next Wednesday – Funeral to Be Held Tomorrow in Toronto," unidentified Ottawa newspaper, 13 March 1930

Thomas Champion, "Tells How Barker Made Flight With Prince Over German Lines During War," Canadian Press Cable, *Manitoba Free Press*, Winnipeg, 13 March 1930

Thomas Champion, "Shock to Col. Bishop – War-time Comrade Overcome by News of Barker's Death," *The Gazette*, Montreal, 13 March 1930

"Full Air Force Honors for Col. Barker, VC," *The Evening Telegram*, Toronto, 13 March 1930

"Full Military Honors Will Be Paid To Barker – Body of Canada's Flying Ace Taken to Toronto for Burial ... War-Time Leaders and Pilots Unite to Express Their Deep Sorrow," *The Winnipeg Evening Tribune*, 13 March 1930

"Full Military Honors Will Be Paid To Barker," *The Winnipeg Evening Tribune*, 13 March 1930

"Currie Expresses Grief – Barker Was Inspiration to Canadians, He Says," *The Gazette*, Montreal, 13 March 1930

"Fall Kills Barker, Canadian War Ace ... Rickenbacker Praises Flyer," *The New York Times*, 13 March 1930

"Americans Pay Tribute – Daring and Courageous Flier, U.S. Pilot Says," *The Gazette*, Montreal, 13 March 1930

"Barker's Body Lies Here Mourned By An Empire – Comrades Pay Tribute to VC Killed in Crash at Ottawa Yesterday," *The Toronto Daily Star*, 13 March 1930

Obituary, Col. W.G. Barker, *The Daily Telegraph*, London, 15 March 1930

Obituary, Col. W.G. Barker, *The Daily Express*, London, 15 March 1930

"Nation's Leaders Bow At Col. Barker's Bier – Roses Flutter From Soaring Aeroplanes Upon Sacred Earthly Scene – Crusader At Rest – Royal Canadian Air Force Comrades in Escort – Three Volleys Fired," *The Toronto Daily Star*, 15 March 1930

"Canon Scott, in Singing Verse Pays Tribute to Col. Barker," *The Evening Telegram*, Toronto, 15 March 1930

"War Memories Revived by Funeral of Aviator," *Manitoba Free Press*, 16 March 1930

"Nation's Tribute Paid Tribute to Col. Barker, VC," *Manitoba Free Press*, 17 March 1930

Guy Cunliffe, "Funeral of Col. Barker Watched by Thousands Eager to Offer Homage: Child's Presence Pervades Solemnity Like Gleam of Light," *The Mail and Empire*, Toronto, 17 March 1930

K.W. MacTaggart, "Funeral of Col. Barker Watched by Thousands Eager to Offer Homage: Youth Pays Highest Tribute to Hero of Ringing Deeds – Boyhood Remembers," *The Mail and Empire*, Toronto, 17 March 1930

Kim Beattie, "Comrades Pay Honor to Dead Ace from Sky, Drop Petals on Grave," *The Evening Telegram*, Toronto, 17 March 1930

"Toronto Honors Memory of Canadian War Hero," *Manitoba Free Press*, 18 March 1930

"The Late Colonel Barker, VC," *Saturday Night*, Toronto, 22 March 1930

Editorial, *Canadian Defence Quarterly*, Vol. VII, No. 3, April 1930

Michael Delaney, "To Colonel Barker, VC," *Manitoba Free Press*, no date, 1930

R.B. Irvine, "Fairchild Open Air Harbor and New Factory at Montreal," *Canadian Aviation*, October 1930

S.B. Baucutt, "Manitoba's Famous War Ace – Comrade Gives New Account of Exploits of Late Col. Barker, VC, While Squadron Commander on Italian Front," *Winnipeg Free Press*, 22 November 1930

"Canadian Fairchild Grows Steadily in First Year," *Canadian Aviation*, January 1931

"Barker Field Opening is Splendid Function," *Canadian Aviation*, July 1931

Col. W.A. Bishop, "Billy Barker, Deadliest Ace of All," *Liberty Magazine*, 29 August 1931

1932 through 1939

E.C. Cox, "All Quiet on the Italian Front," *Canadian Aviation*, February 1932

Captain J. Mitchell, "Portraits For Posterity – Major W.G. Barker, VC, DSO, M.C.," *Popular Flying*, June 1935

E.A.H. Chegwidden, "Barker's Christmas Party – A True Thriller," *War Birds*, Vol. 31, October 1935

Ernest Hemingway, "The Snows of Kilimanjaro," *Esquire Magazine*, August 1936

"Horace Bruce Smith, Former Owen Sounder, Passes Away Sunday – Noted Barrister and Industrialist Dies at Toronto Home," *The Daily Sun-Times*, Owen Sound, 6 March 1939

1940 to the Present

"Modern Equipment for a Modern Farm – in 1896 ... picture taken at the Barker farm," *The Central Manitoba News and Advertiser*, 19 May 1960.

Cynthia Jones, "Monitor Profile," of AVM Clifford McEwen, *Monitor*, circa 1960s

Air Chief Marshal Sir Philip Joubert, "One Against Sixty ... So He Decided to Ram," *The Sunday Express*, London, 1 April 1962

Air Chief Marshal Sir Phillip Joubert, "How Billy Barker Won His VC, It Was One Against 60 – So He Decided To Ram," *Weekend Magazine*, No. 21, 1963

Hilliard Brooke Bell "The War Experiences of H. Brooke Bell, MC, QC," *The Canadian Aviation Historical Society (CAHS) Journal*, The Canadian Aviation Historical Society, Vol. 1, No. 4, 1963

Ed Cosgrove, "World War I Air Ace 'Black Mike' McEwen, CB, DFC, MC," *Wings In Space*, August/September 1965

Kenneth Molson, "The Made-In-Canada Fairchilds," *Canadian Aeronautics and Space Institute (CASI) Journal*, Vol. 13, No. 2, February 1967

Wayne Braby, "Sketches of No. 28 Squadron RAF," *Cross & Cockade Journal*, The Society of World War I Aero Historians, USA, Vol. 8, No. 3, Autumn 1967

———, "The Way It Was In Italy, An Interview With Captain Thomas Frederick Williams, M.C., Nos. 45 and 28 Squadrons, RFC, RAF," *Cross & Cockade Journal (US)*, Vol. 8, No. 3, Autumn 1967

Douglas H. Robinson, MD, "Aviation Medicine in World War I," *Cross & Cockade (US)*, Vol. 9, No. 1, Spring 1968

Kenneth Molson, "A History of Laurentide Air Service – Canada's First Scheduled Air Service," *CASI Journal*, Vol. 16, No. 7, September 1970

Anthony Brandt, "The First Canadian Fairchild Company, 1922-29," *CAHS Journal*, Vol. 9, No. 2, Summer 1971

Ronald Sykes, "Serving with 201 Squadron RAF," *Cross & Cockade (UK)*, Summer 1971

Kenneth Molson, "The New York – Toronto Air Race," *CAHS Journal*, Fall 1971

Weekend Magazine, 8 September 1973, story and interview with Thomas F. Williams

E. Harlin, N. Franks, F. Bailey, "In Italian Skies – 139 Squadron, RAF," *Cross & Cockade (UK) Journal*, The Society of World War I Aero Historians, Great Britain, Vol. 4, No. 3, Autumn 1973

James Kerr, "Against All Comers – Operations of the K.u.K. Luftfahrtruppen," *Cross & Cockade Journal (US)*, Vol. 15, No. 4, Winter 1974

Frank Bailey, Norman Franks, "66 Squadron in France & Italy," *Cross & Cockade (UK)*, Vol. 6, No. 1, Spring 1975

Somnath Sapru, "Flying Sikh, Hardit Singh Malik," *Cross & Cockade (UK) Journal*, Vol. 6, No. 4, Winter 1975

Rinaldo D'Ami, "The Italian Front Revisited – Expanded Notes," *Cross & Cockade (US)*, Vol. 17, No. 1, Spring 1976

Tony Benn, "A radical in politics," *The Times Saturday Review*, London, 7 May 1977

Kenneth Molson, "Addendum – New York to Toronto Air Race," *CAHS Journal*, Winter 1977

Milton Sheppard, "Camera In The Sky – The Dallin Aerial Surveys Co. 1924-1941," *Journal American Aviation Historical Society*, Spring 1979

"Inaugurated by 'Billy' Bishop and 'Billy' Barker – Canada's first scheduled air service. Toronto to Muskoka," *The Muskoka Sun*, 2 August 1979

Gregory Urwin, "The Sopwith Tiger – The story of Major William George Barker, VC," *Air Classics*, Vol. 15, No. 11, November 1979

Kenneth Molson, "The First 500 Canadian Civil Pilots," *CAHS Journal* reprint, 1980-82

J.R. Ellis, "Early CF Aircraft Register," "Early G-C Aircraft Register," *CAHS Journal* reprint, 1980-82

Ronald Dodds, "Barker, VC – Part I & Part II," *High Flight*, Vol. 1, No. 2 & No. 3, 1980

William J. McAndrew, "The Evolution of Canadian Aviation Policy Following the First World War," *Journal of Canadian Studies*, Vol. 16, Nos. 3&4, Autumn-Fall-Winter 1981

James Kerr, "Caporetto Part III: The Aftermath," *Over the Front*, Journal of the League of World War I Aviation Historians, Vol. 1, No. 4, Winter 1986-87

Obituary of Singh Malik, *Over the Front*, Vol. I, No. 4, Winter 1986-87

Antal Boksay, "Observations Over The Italian Front," compilation of a correspondence by Jon Guttman, *Over The Front*, Vol. 2, No. 1, Spring 1987

Grosz, Haddow, Scheimer, "Some Reflections on Austro-Hungarian Aviation in World War I," *Over the Front*, Vol. 2, No. 2, Summer 1987

Donald Jones, "Historical Toronto – World War I airforce hero who won Victoria Cross," *The Toronto Star Saturday Magazine*, 30 December 1989

William Almon, "The Greatest Fighter Pilot," *Aviation*, March 1993

John Crech, "Harry King Goode, DSO, DFC, AFC," *Cross & Cockade (UK)*, Vol. 24, No. 1, Spring 1993

Major Bill March with Gerald LaGrave, "An Airman's Story," *Roundel*, Vol. 1, No. 11, July 1994

Wayne Ralph, "William Barker, VC, and the Formation of the RCAF," *Airforce*, Vol. 18, No. 3, No. 4, Vol. 19, No. 1, Fall 1994, Winter 94/95, Spring 1995

Ray Whitford, "Fundamentals of Fighter Design, Part 1 – Stability & Control," *AIR International*, Vol. 50, No. 6, June 1996

Barker in B6313 while at 139 Squadron, from his photo album.

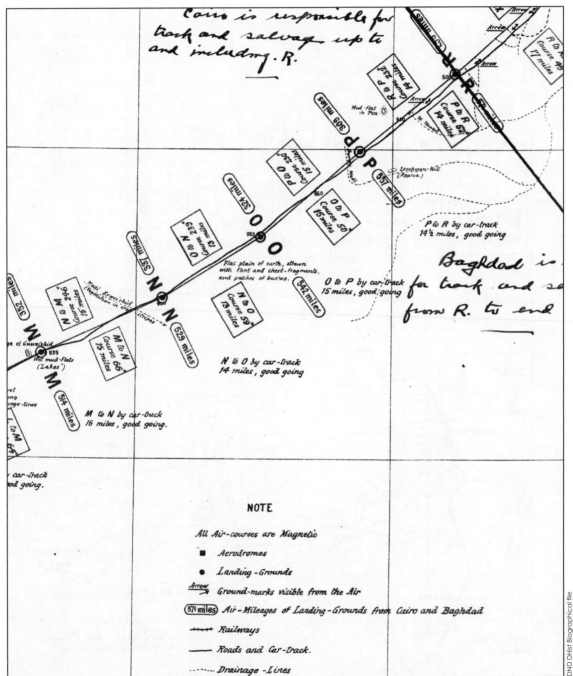

Map of Cairo – Baghdad air route provided by William Barker in the 1925 report.

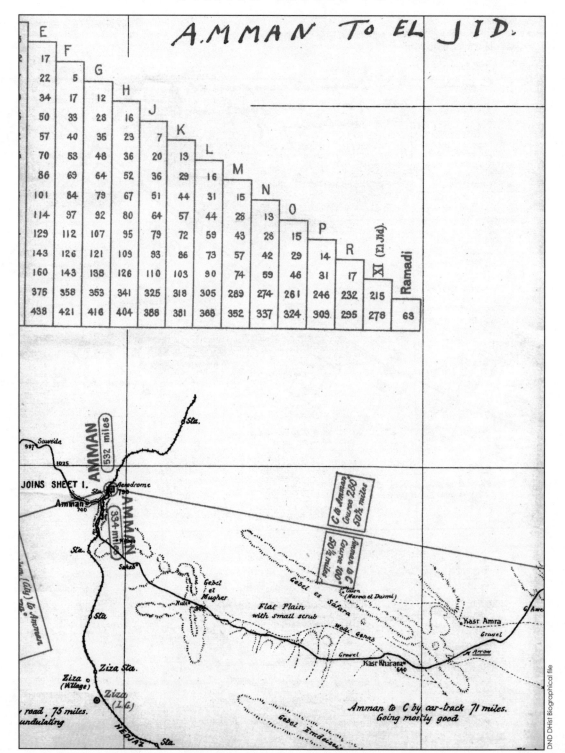

Map of Cairo – Baghdad air route provided by William Barker in the 1925 report.

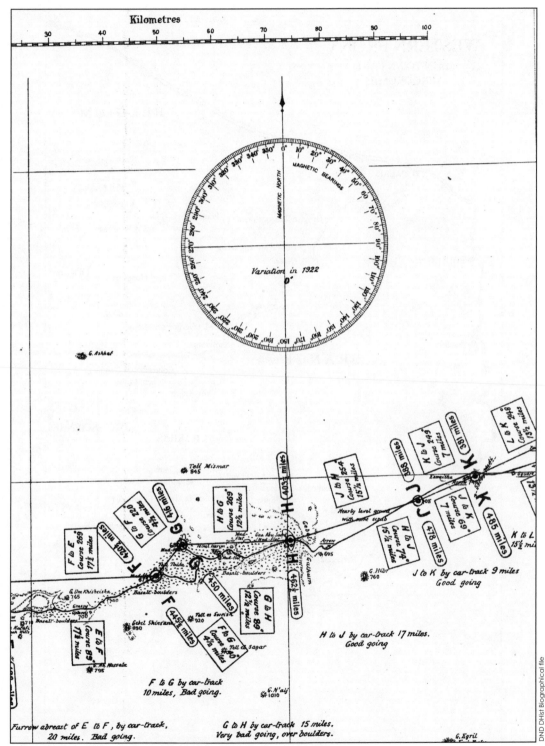

Map of Egypt – Iraq air route provided by William Barker in the 1925 report.

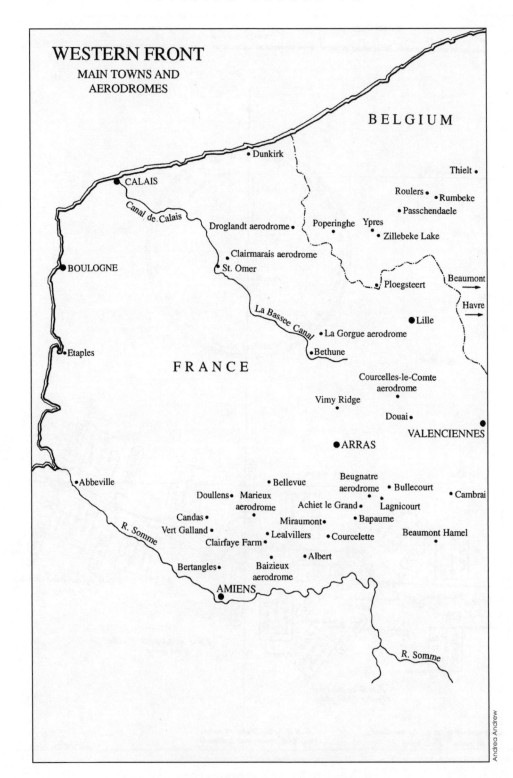

WESTERN FRONT

MAIN TOWNS AND
AERODROMES

BELGIUM

Dunkirk

Thielt

CALAIS

Roulers
Rumbeke

Canal de Calais

Passchendaele

Droglandt aerodrome
Poperinghe
Ypres
Zillebeke Lake

Clairmarais aerodrome

BOULOGNE
St. Omer

Ploegsteert
Beaumont

La Bassée Canal
Havre

Lille

La Gorgue aerodrome

Etaples
Bethune

FRANCE

Courcelles-le-Comte
aerodrome

Vimy Ridge

Douai

VALENCIENNES

ARRAS

Bellevue
Beugnatre
aerodrome

Abbeville
Bullecourt

Doullens
Marieux
aerodrome
Achiet le Grand
Lagnicourt
Cambrai

Candas
Bapaume

Vert Galland
Miraumont

Clairfaye Farm
Lealvillers
Courcelette
Beaumont Hamel

R. Somme
Albert

Bertangles
Baizieux
aerodrome

AMIENS

R. Somme

Andrea Andrew

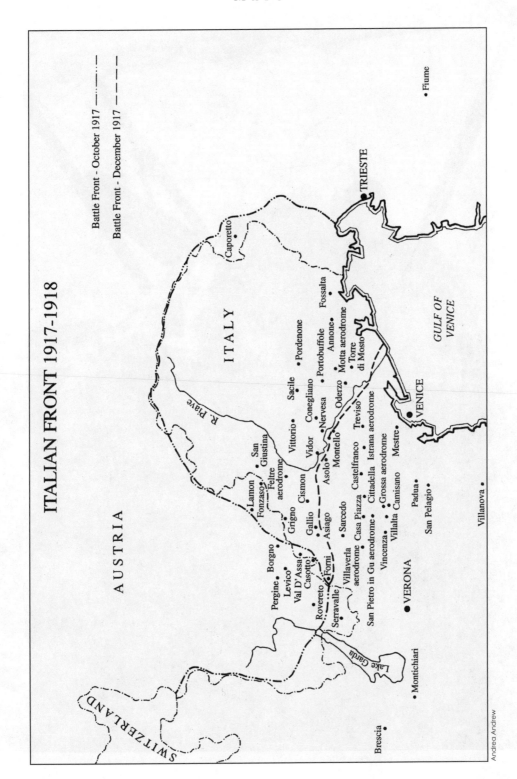

ITALIAN FRONT 1917-1918

Battle Front - October 1917 ——·——
Battle Front - December 1917 — — —

AUSTRIA

ITALY

SWITZERLAND

Lake Garda

R. Piave

GULF OF
VENICE

Fiume

TRIESTE

Caporetto

Fossalta

Portobuffole

Pordenone

Annone

Motta aerodrome

Torre
di Mosto

Sacile

Oderzo

Nervesa

Conegliano

Vidor

Vittorio

Treviso

Istrana aerodrome

Montello

Castelfranco

VENICE

San
Giustina

Asolo

Cittadella

Grossa aerodrome

Mestre

Lamon

Feltre
aerodrome

Cismon

Sarcedo

Casa Piazza

Vincenza

Villalta Camisano

Padua

Fonzaso

Grigno

Gallio

Asiago

Villaverla
aerodrome

San Pietro in Gu aerodrome

San Pelagio

Borgno

Levico

Val D'Assa

Forni

Pergine

Casotto

Rovereto

Serravalle

VERONA

Montichiari

Villanova

Brescia

Andrea Andrew

275

28 Squadron mascot sitting on Barker's Camel, B6313, Italy, 1917.

INDEX